012404192

KU-763-305

The Economics of Europe

3

.L.

1995

1996

For co on

The Economics of Europe

Edward Nevin

Emeritus Professor of Economics
University College of Swansea

MACMILLAN

First published 1990 by
THE MACMILLAN PRESS LTD
Houndmills, Basingstoke, Hampshire RG21 2XS
and London
Companies and representatives
throughout the world

ISBN 0–333–51631–1 (hardcover)
ISBN 0–333–51632–X (paperback)

A catalogue record for this book is available
from the British Library

Printed in Hong Kong

Reprinted 1992

Contents

PART IV   MACROECONOMIC POLICIES

PART V   CONCLUSION

List of Tables and Figures

Tables

Figures

Preface

A commercial advertisement appearing in 1988 described the European Community as 'six republics, five Kingdoms and one Grand Duchy separated by nine languages'. The description was not entirely serious but neither could it be described as entirely meaningless. To the outside observer the Community frequently presents itself as a complex, remote and not entirely credible organisation, inhabited by politicians and bureaucrats but having little bearing on the daily life of the ordinary citizen. Nowhere is this attitude of faint disbelief more widely held than in the United Kingdom. Yet the facts are that for those of us who dwell in Western Europe it is part of our lives and we, in turn, form part of it. Its structure, operation and objectives therefore have become matters deserving of systematic study throughout the educational system and beyond. This book is an attempt to provide a beginner's guide to that process.

In writing such a book there is one insoluble problem: what prior knowledge of what subject can safely be assumed in the reader? It is not a question of answering the question successfully: rather it is one of answering it wrongly to the least possible degree. Since I am primarily concerned with the economic aspects of the European Community, the problem essentially reduces to one of the extent to which the reader can be assumed to be familiar with the basic analytical concepts and constructs of economics. To assume no knowledge whatever would imply a need to indulge in a detailed explanation of almost every basic principle of economics; such a procedure would result in a book whose length would be exceeded only by the tedium it would induce in those to whom the interaction of demand and supply is not entirely a theological mystery. To assume graduate standing in economics, on the other hand, would lead to a work which would be totally unintelligible to the great majority of its potential readers. Compromising, then, I have assumed, roughly speaking, a prior knowledge of economics broadly comparable with that of a first-year university course or perhaps a good Advanced Level grade in the subject. Those better equipped in economics must exercise charity and bear with what will frequently seem an unduly simplified and elementary treatment of some quite sophisticated theoretical problems; those less well equipped may have to take some of the theoretical propositioins on trust and may, indeed, skip Part II altogether.

The book is written with an eye rather firmly fixed on the reader resident in, and concerned with, the United Kingdom. I hope nevertheless that it has not as a result become so introspective as to lose sight of the essentially supranational character of the Community. Residents of Northern Ireland will forgive me, I hope, for having frequently used the terms 'Britain' and 'British' as synonymous with the terms 'United Kingdom of Great Britain and Northern Ireland' and 'citizen of . . .' in order to avoid both undue verbosity and the monotony of repetition. I have also tended to use the term 'European Community' in preference to the awkward but none the less legally correct expression 'European Communities'. Less defensibly, again in the interests of brevity and the avoidance of repetition, I have frequently used the word 'Europe' to refer to the Community where the context does not allow of misunderstanding; I have even used the term 'Mediterranean' to include Portugal. I trust these lapses in geographical accuracy will not irritate overmuch.

Finally, a word should be said about the frequent (and unavoidable) references to monetary magnitudes throughout the book. Since the magnitudes concerned normally involve more than one country they are usually expressed in terms of the European Currency Unit (ECU), despite the undoubted fact that no such currency unit existed prior to 1979. For years prior to 1979 national currency units have been converted into ECUs at their prevailing exchange rates and using the weights given to each currency in 1979 when the ECU was first created. Furthermore, to use contemporary monetary values for events stretching over thirty years would clearly result in figures of little comparative meaning. Unless stated otherwise, therefore, all monetary values have been converted into their equivalents at 1986 prices in order that a sum quoted for, say, 1960 can be compared meaningfully with the corresponding sum for 1980. (This has the convenient result that the sums quoted in ECUs may be taken as equivalent to the same sum in US dollars, a currency unit which still has more meaning than the ECU for most of us; the average rate of exchange of ECUs for dollars in 1986 was almost exactly one.) For similar reasons the national income figures used throughout are those based on the Commission's estimates of the comparative purchasing-powers of various currencies, rather than those based on current exchange rates. There are good arguments for using each of these bases of comparison, but for the purposes of this book I feel that exchange rate instability – especially that of the 1970s – renders national income comparisons based on current exchange rates seriously misleading. The Statistical Appendix contains the data necessary to convert values into current prices in dollars, based on prevailing exchange rates, should any reader feel a compulsive preference for such valuations.

Swansea   EDWARD NEVIN

List of Abbreviations

CEECs   Central & Eastern European Countries

AASM	Associated African States and Malagasy
ACP	African, Caribbean and Pacific States
BENELUX	Belgium–Netherlands–Luxembourg Economic Union
BN.	Billion (10^6)
BRITE	Basic research in industrial technologies for Europe
CAP	Common agricultural policy
CFP	Common fisheries policy
COREPER	Committee of Permanent Representatives
DG	Directorate-General
DM	Deutschemark
EC	European Communities
ECSC	European Coal and Steel Community
ECU	European Currency Unit
EDF	European Development Fund
EEC	European Economic Community
EEIG	European Economic Interest Grouping
EEZ	Exclusive Economic Zone
EFTA	European Free Trade Association
EIB	European Investment Bank
EMS	European Monetary System
ERDF	European Regional Development Fund
ESF	European Social Fund
ESPRIT	European strategic programme for research and development in information technology
EURATOM	European Atomic Energy Community
FECOM	European Monetary Co-operation Fund
FEOGA	European Agricultural Guidance and Guarantee Fund
FR	Franc
GATT	General Agreement on Tariffs and Trade
GDP	Gross domestic product
GNP	Gross national product

GSP	Generalised system of preferences
GWh	Gigawatt hour (10^6 kilowatt hours)
IEA	International Energy Agency
IMF	International Monetary Fund
IMP	Integrated Mediterranean Programmes
JET	Joint European Torus
MCA	Monetary Compensatory Amount
MFA	Multifibre Arrangement
NATO	North Atlantic Treaty Organisation
NTB	Non-tariff barrier
OECD	Organisation for Economic Co-operation and Development
OEEC	Organisation for European Economic Co-operation
OPEC	Organisation of Petroleum Exporting Countries
RACE	Research and development in advanced communication technologies for Europe
STABEX	System for the stabilisation of export earnings
SYSMIN	System for financing mining products
TAC	Total allowable catch
UK	United Kingdom of Great Britain and Northern Ireland
UN	United Nations
UNCTAD	United Nations Conference on Trade and Development
US	United States of America
VAT	Value added tax
VER	Voluntary export restraint

Part I

The Framework

In the Beginning 1

1.1 Postwar Europe

The overwhelming majority of the soldiers of the Allied armies making their weary and dangerous way across Northern Europe in 1944–5 had never before set foot in continental Europe. Even so, many must have reflected on the fact that the towns and villages along their path frequently had names with which they were vaguely familiar, having heard them as children from fathers or uncles; in fact, only a single generation separated them from a similar army engaged in similar battles over the same terrain. Indeed, they might well have pondered on the fact that their generals and field marshals had been field commanders in that earlier war also. There was, in other words, an ominous air of repetition about the whole business.

The second inescapable reality concerning the Europe they encountered was the catastrophic results of this human folly. Literally millions of people wandered through these countries, homeless, cold and very hungry. Other millions, less fortunate, had not survived even to that wretched condition. Europe's physical capital stock, like its human capital, was devastated to a degree echoed only by the biblical lament that not a stone should remain upon stone. When some sort of peace eventually descended, food production was vastly below the level required to meet the most elementary human needs; in the six countries of Western Europe from which the European Economic Community was to emerge, the production of iron and steel was less than a third of the level of 1939 while the production of coal was even less. Economically, Western Europe had literally been laid waste.

For once, the instincts of some at least of the political leaders of the time corresponded to the perceptions of the ordinary citizen. The origins of this calamity which had descended upon Europe scarcely twenty years after its predecessor were, and remain, many and complex; beyond question, however, the rivalry and antagonism of nationalistic governments, pursuing national

3

interests (as they perceived them) at the expense of those of their neighbours – and equally reacting to the same behaviour in those neighbours – had played a major part. One essential step therefore seemed to be a reversal of the division of Europe into an increasing number of compulsively hostile nation-states and a movement towards integration and co-operation between them.

The idea was scarcely new. In the eighteenth century the thirteen separate, and fiercely independent, colonies of North America had eliminated the barriers between one another and formed a customs union – an arrangement whereby no tariffs or other restrictions should be imposed on trade between them – and eventually merged into a single federal republic. The historians record that in the ten years following the end of the Napoleonic wars no less than 16 such customs unions had been established in Europe. Chief among these was Bismarck's Zollverein, a customs union beginning in 1816–17 which abolished tariffs between the separate states of Prussia and established a common, single system of tariffs on their trade with the rest of the world; this too was to steadily expand to form the powerful state of Germany by the turn of the century. A proposal to create a 'Common Market' amongst the countries of Europe had been advanced before the League of Nations by Aristide Briand in 1929 but at that time the lesson had not been learned – or, more precisely, not been sufficiently brutally taught – and the initiative rapidly came to nothing. Under the harrowing pressure of the occupation of their countries, the refugee governments of Belgium, Luxembourg and the Netherlands had agreed in London in 1943 on the formation of a customs union at the end of the war and in fact that union, Benelux, came into being in 1948.

Integration between relatively small and generally friendly states is one thing; a comparable move amongst large, traditionally hostile countries such as France and Germany was manifestly quite another. In themselves economic considerations or even internal political vision, however strong, might well have proved insufficient. There was, however, a second powerful factor at work. The Second World War had not merely devastated the landscape of the countries of Western Europe; it had left them patently and cruelly exposed in the role of buffer between two superpowers, the United States and the Soviet Union, which rapidly adopted an attitude of such deep mutual hostility that the outbreak of World War Three became a frighteningly real prospect. The interface between the two superpowers, unhappily, ran through Europe itself – ran, indeed, through what had been the single country of Germany. But Western Europe, sandwiched between the superpowers, seemed patently incapable of matching either in independent military power. By 1950 the countries of Western Europe found themselves contemplating the unpleasant fact that while the vast forces of one friendly superpower, the United States, were for the most part some 4000 miles across the sea, on their own borders was another, much less obviously friendly state which could match each army division at their disposal with twelve of its own.

These two dominating problems of post-war Europe – the problem of defence and the ingredients needed for economic recovery and growth – were each to contribute to the momentum towards integration amongst the individual countries of the western half of the continent. The political unification implied by the former was to prove unattainable; the way forward to the latter proved, on the other hand, to be steep but, in the end, quite passable.

1.2 The Problem of Defence

By a treaty signed in Brussels in 1948, Britain joined with its wartime allies, France and the three Benelux countries, in a permanent mutual security arrangement by which each country undertook to assist any other of the signatories which suffered attack from outside. In the following year the Soviet occupation of Czechoslovakia made it obvious that the problem of Western defence was not a solely European one and led to the creation of the North Atlantic Treaty Organisation (NATO) in April 1949. By this treaty the concept of mutual defence assistance was extended to include the United States and Canada as well as the five countries of the Brussels Treaty, together with certain other European countries – Norway, Denmark, Iceland and Portugal. (Greece and Turkey were to join in 1952.)

This military alliance amongst Western European countries indicated the need for some corresponding political arrangements, and in May of 1949 it was agreed amongst them that there should be a consultative Parliamentary assembly known as the Council of Europe. The first deliberations of this Council were held in August 1949 in Strasbourg – a city chosen, it is said, by the current British Foreign Secretary, Ernest Bevin, on the grounds that it was difficult to get to. Whatever the reason, Strasbourg thus became the first of the three cities associated with the European Community. Amongst the parliamentarians gathering for this first meeting there were doubtless many who regarded its nominal dedication to the achievement of 'closer union' amongst the member countries as implying that the Council was to be the foundation of a closer political union in Europe, leading ultimately to a single federal state. If so, their optimism proved to be unfounded; the national politicians were almost unanimously opposed to the sacrifice of any of their powers, least of all in the delicate area of defence, and the members of the assembly were given no power of their own – except to make speeches to one another.

The creation of NATO left much of the problem of Western European defence unsolved. Despite a formidable American military presence in Europe, the overwhelming military superiority of the Soviet Union was manifest. The two big European powers, Britain and France, were deeply committed with their associated countries (words such as 'empire' or 'colonies' were rapidly becoming unfashionable) across the globe. Both Germany and Italy, defeated and distrusted, were without any military capability. Yet the border between what was now Western and Eastern Europe ran through Germany itself. The concept of security without the participation of Germany, Europe's major military power, was clearly unrealistic. Yet, with memories of the Second World War still fresh in European (most especially French) minds, the prospect of a rearmed Germany was even less appealing than the proximity of the Soviet army.

The name of Jean Monnet occurs at every stage of the story of European integration during the thirty years following the end of the war. Born in 1888 into a prosperous family of wine-merchants in Cognac, he had become a highly successful businessman in the United States during the inter-war years; he had then taken an important part in the Allied supply machine during the war and had returned to France to head the formidable economic planning administration of France after the war's end. It was his initiative which led to the creation of the European Coal and Steel Community to be described in the following section and was indeed the first President of its High Authority. He was a man of immense ability and great influence. It was largely due to that influence that in August 1950 the Council of Europe passed a resolution calling for the problem of European defence to be solved in much the same way as it was being proposed that the problem of the European steel industry should be solved – namely, by the amalgamation of separate national entities into a single common European organisation. It was certainly due to Monnet's influence that this concept of a European Defence Community (EDC) was taken up with enthusiasm by the Prime Minister of France, M. René Pleven, at a meeting of the NATO Council of Ministers in October 1950; it was a concept which was to become the centre of political discussion in Western Europe for the next four years. The dilemma posed by the need for German rearmament, on the one hand, and the fears generated by it, on the other, was to be resolved by German participation in a defence organisation under European, rather than German, control.

For reasons which will be discussed in the following chapter, the government of the United Kingdom, while looking benignly on this revolutionary proposal, made it very clear from the outset that it had no intention of participating fully in it. It is ironic, however, that the initiative was finally killed off by the National Assembly of France, the country from which it had originated, when the Treaty establishing the EDC came before it for ratification in August 1954. Two months later the only possible alternative was adopted: both Germany and Italy became members of NATO and their relatively modest rearmament proceeded under the umbrella of the NATO agreement. The failure of the EDC initiative had vividly illustrated two hard facts of life. First, the idea of the abandonment of national powers over so delicate an area as defence by a proud and powerful country was well before its time. Secondly, in democratic countries proposals pursued with energy and enthusiasm by political leaders and their officials can be brought to nothing if their legislatures at home do not share that enthusiasm, for any one of many reasons. Both facts of life were to reveal themselves again in the story of the European Community; doubtless they will make their presence felt many times again. But the failure of the EDC ended any hope for the unification of Europe through a direct onslaught on the existing political powers of independent sovereign states.

1.3 The Problem of Steel

The economy of Western Europe in the years immediately after the ending of the Second World War was marked by acute shortages of practically all goods and services; there was, consequently, a huge latent demand for imports to meet at least part of the unsatisfied home needs. Two results followed. First, each individual country sought to preserve its scarce foreign reserves – the only means by which the desired imports could be financed – by imposing severe restrictions on what its citizens were permitted to purchase from foreign countries – including other countries within Europe. This was achieved through the imposition of licensing systems restricting the volume and type of imports and through a close control over the ability of citizens to exchange domestic currency for the foreign currencies required to pay for such imports. The second result was that the United States, by far and away the biggest potential source of so many of the goods in short supply, came under immense pressure to assist the stricken countries of Europe by making more of those goods available than could possibly have been financed from the proceeds of exports from Europe itself.

The response came in 1947 when the US Secretary of State, General Marshall, announced that the United States was in fact prepared to provide aid on a vast scale to assist the reconstruction of Western Europe; officially described as the European Recovery Program, this policy initiative became universally known as the Marshall Plan. A major condition was attached. It was evident that many of the European countries were seeking US aid in order to obtain goods which were actually or potentially available within Europe itself but were unavailable because of the tight restrictions which the European countries were imposing on trade with one another as well as with the rest of the world. Europe was therefore required to put its own house in order by ensuring that Marshall Aid was used only to obtain goods which were physically unavailable within Europe.

The result was the Organisation for European Economic Co-operation established in Paris in 1948; the title was changed to the Organisation for Economic Co-operation and Development in 1961 when the membership of the organisation was expanded to include the United States, Canada and, later, Japan as well as the original 16 OEEC countries. As the title implied (and at British insistence) the organisation involved co-operation only between sovereign states and operated on the rule of unanimity; in no sense was it a supranational body with independent powers. It embarked on what proved to be a highly successful programme of mutually-negotiated reductions of quantitative restrictions on trade between the member countries and on the creation of a European Payments System through which restraints on the exchange of the currencies of the member countries were steadily eased. By common consent it proved an important and effective means of reducing internal trade barriers within Western Europe and encouraging a rapid recovery in the European economy.

In one particular economic sector, however, as in the area of defence, the situation of Germany posed a difficult problem. From 1948 the German economy began a resurgence which was to be named the *Wirtschaftwunder* – the economic miracle. From its state of almost total devastation at the end of the war, German industry (then under the nominal control of an Allied Military Government) was expanding at a phenomenal rate; the operators of its steel industry therefore sought the approval of their military and political masters for a substantial expansion in productive capacity. The analogy with the problem of Germany rearmament was exact: Europe desperately needed the output of what had been its biggest steel industry but, on the other hand, recoiled from the prospect of the re-emergence of a powerful German steel industry, given the political and military connotations which that had in the European (and especially French) mind.

By common consent, the solution advanced by the French Foreign Minister, M. Robert Schuman, in May 1950 was the brainchild of the founding father of the European Community, Jean Monnet. The proposed solution was, quite simply, that all Western European countries – or at least those of them which wished to participate – should place their coal and steel industries (the two are technically almost inseparable) under the control of a single supranational organisation; the much-needed German steel could then be made available to all without the threat of a restored Krupps dynasty. Once again, the idea was not exactly new; it had in fact been advanced by Konrad Adenauer, then the German Chancellor, while he had been Mayor of Cologne in 1923. (This fact naturally did nothing to damage the prospects of the proposal in Germany at least.) M. Schuman himself clearly realised the possible implications of the proposal; it would, he said, 'build the first concrete foundation of a European federation which is indispensable to the preservation of peace'.

The proposal involved little of the threat to the fundamental political powers of national governments implicit in the idea of the EDC. Although for reasons to be discussed later the United Kingdom declined more or less from the outset to become involved in the project, as M. Schuman toured the capitals of Western Europe in 1950 he found considerable enthusiasm for the idea in five other countries – the three Benelux countries, ever enthusiastic for an initiative which held out hope of relieving them of their historic role as the cockpit of their belligerent neighbours, Italy and of course Germany itself, to which almost anything was preferable to Allied Military control. Within less than a year, in

April 1951, these six countries signed the Treaty of Paris which brought into being, with effect from mid-1952, the European Coal and Steel Community. The German steel problem had been solved; in reality the foundations of the European Community had been laid.

The Treaty placed the direction and control of the entire coal and steel industries of the six participating countries (although not their ownership) in the hands of a High Authority, the first President of which was to be, very properly, M. Jean Monnet. The Authority had extensive powers to regulate the production, pricing and marketing activities of all the enterprises under its control although the approval of a Council of Ministers – comprised of one Minister from each member country – was necessary for major policy decisions. Its activities were to be financed by means of a levy payable on each ton of coal or steel produced, and in an apparently casual fashion it was agreed that the headquarters of the Authority should be located in Luxembourg. This was in fact a highly suitable choice of location. Luxembourg, small though it is, was then a substantial producer of steel; it borders physically on three of the five other members; most important, the very fact of its smallness meant that none of the other members felt slighted or threatened by its choice. Luxembourg thus joined Strasbourg and became the second of the three cities in the European story.

1.4 On to Messina

By the mid-1950s, then, two major achievements had been recorded in Western European. First, through the work of the OEEC quantitative and currency restrictions on intra-European trade had been substantially reduced. Tariff barriers, however, remained and those countries with relatively low tariffs were reluctant to dismantle their remaining quantitative restrictions without some corresponding concessions from other countries which were able to protect their domestic industries through a high tariff barrier. Here a new obstacle was encountered. All the OEEC countries were members of the wider, international organisation, the General Agreement on Tariffs and Trade (GATT) established in 1947. Under the rules of GATT, no member country can reduce the rate of tariff levied on its imports from another member country without simultaneously extending that concession to every other GATT member. Hence tariff reductions could be agreed within Europe as a quid pro quo for reductions in quantitative limitations on trade only if those tariff reductions were extended to every other GATT member – which meant virtually the whole of the industrialised Western world. Not many countries in Europe felt themselves able to expose their internal economies to world competition in this way, so that the process of trade liberalisation in Europe began to slow markedly. There is, however, one very important exception to this general GATT rule. Tariff reductions *can* be extended to particular GATT members and not to others if they constitute a movement towards the *total* abolition of tariffs against those members – i.e. the creation of a free trade area or a customs union.

The second major achievement was the ECSC. Contrary to the sceptical predictions of some non-members (the United Kingdom in particular) the ECSC was manifestly successful. (Over the decade 1948–58, in fact, output of coal in the ECSC countries rose by 37 per cent compared with 3 per cent in Britain; output of crude steel rose by 154 per cent compared with 32 per cent.) In 1954, his term as President having come to an end, Jean Monnet announced his retirement in order to push the great cause of European integration even further. He sought to extend the coverage of the ECSC to include the new but crucial sector of nuclear energy (an idea on which France was very keen, as Monnet well knew); the Benelux countries took up the idea and suggested extending the ECSC, in effect, to the whole economy by establishing a customs union between the six members. This had one enormous advantage; the GATT rule concerning the universal extension of any tariff concessions would not apply since the proposed arrangements would lead to the removal of *all* tariffs – i.e. they would constitute a movement towards a completely free trade area.

The outcome of these discussions in the ECSC Ministerial Council was a conference of the Foreign Ministers of the six ECSC member countries at Messina, in Sicily, in June 1955 to investigate the possibilities of further integration. The conference, in turn, established a high-powered committee to prepare detailed proposals under the chairmanship of the Foreign Minister of Belgium, M. Paul-Henri Spaak, who proved to be a proponent of further integration of quite exceptional energy and enthusiasm. The United Kingdom was invited to participate in the work of his committee but it was made clear at the outset that there was room only for delegates prepared to commit themselves to the principle of a customs union – i.e. some degree of sacrifice of sovereignty to a supranational body – at which the United Kingdom delegates promptly departed. The work of the committee continued apace for two years in Brussels, thus establishing the place of that city as the third and last in the story of the Community.

1.5 The Treaty of Rome

By the end of 1956 agreement had been reached that two new Communities should be established along lines roughly similar to those of the ECSC – one to cover the economy generally and establishing a customs union, the European Economic Community (EEC), and the other to be concerned with the development and exploitation of nuclear power, the European Atomic Energy Authority (Euratom). That these two initiatives proceeded in tandem was no coincidence. As already noted, France was especially anxious to acquire nuclear capability and, not unnaturally, was anxious to share the enormous costs of such a development with others; it was very much less enthusiastic about the idea of a full customs union. In a sense its commitment to the second aim was the price it was willing to pay in order to achieve the first. In the end, only the six members of the ECSC became signatories. For reasons explored in the next chapter, the United Kingdom opted out and this virtually eliminated other countries, such as Ireland and the Scandinavian countries, for which at that time the United Kingdom was a much more important trading partner than were the Six. Others, like Austria, Sweden and Switzerland, regarded the proposals as having political, and especially military, overtones incompatible with their tradition of political neutrality, Others again, like Spain and Portugal, were not regarded as having democratic governments and were therefore unacceptable.

The two Treaties were signed simultaneously in Rome on 25 March 1957 and came into force on 1 January 1958. The aim of the Treaty establishing the EEC was stated to be that of establishing 'the foundations of an ever-closer union among the European peoples' by, in particular, establishing a Common market and progresively approximating the economic policies of member states. The aim of Euratom was to promote and co-ordinate nuclear research for peaceful purposes in member states, through a Community programme of research and training and by facilitating the capital investment necessary for the development of nuclear energy in the Community. The precise methods by which it was hoped these laudable aims would be achieved – by the EEC in particular – form the subject-matter of the pages which follow. In April 1965 a Merger Treaty was signed by the Six; this provided that from July 1967 a single Council of Ministers became the supreme decision-making body for the three previously separate communities – the ECSC, the EEC and Euratom. At the same time the separate Commissions serving the three communities were merged into a single body. Although it is legally correct to speak of 'the European Communities', therefore, from this point on it will be convenient, and perhaps more appropriate, to use the expression 'the Community'.

Further Reading

European Commission, *European Unification: the Origins and Growth of the European Community*, 2nd edn (Luxembourg, 1987).
Haas, E. B., *The Unity of Europe* (London: Stevens & Sons, (1968).
Linberg, L. N., *The Political Dynamics of European Economic Integration* (Stanford: Stanford University Press, 1963).
Lipgens, W., *A History of European Integration*, Vol. 1 (Oxford: Clarendon Press, 1982).
Mayne, R., *The Community of Europe* (London: Gollancz, 1962).
Mayne, R., *The Recovery of Europe* (London: Weidenfeld & Nicolson, 1970).
Monnet, J., *Memoirs* (London: Collins, 1978).
Palmer, M. and Lambert, J., *European Unity* (London: Allen & Unwin, 1968).
Pryce, R., *The Politics of the European Community* (London: Butterworth, 1973).

Britain and Europe 2

2.1 With Them, Not of Them

The previous chapter has recorded how the United Kingdom was invited to participate in the three great initiatives towards European integration in the postwar years – the talks early in 1950 leading to the formation of the ECSC, the abortive efforts beginning later the same year to create the European Defence Community and the conference in Messina in 1957 which was to result in the EEC itself – but in each case declined. Some have construed this as reflecting an innate hostility on the part of the United Kingdom to the concept of a unified Europe itself, but this is an over-simplification of the reality. Indeed, the movement towards European integration had been given a very considerable degree of impetus in 1946 by no less a citizen of the United Kingdom than Sir Winston Churchill when he spoke in Zurich of the vision of 'a kind of United States of Europe' with the United Kingdom, the British Commonwealth and the United States as 'friends and sponsors of the New Europe'.

Even so, there can be no doubt but that throughout the 1950s British governments of different colours were clearly and consistently distancing themselves from what was happening in mainland Europe. Equally there is no doubt but that after 1961 the position of the United Kingdom changed fundamentally and dramatically. Successive governments, again of different political hues, became supplicants at the European table, asking to share in initiatives from which they had only a few years previously carefully stood aside, only to find, for the best part of a decade, that France, which had previously extended invitations, now emphatically barred the way. Two questions obviously arise. First, why did the governments of early postwar Britain seem to isolate themselves from Europe in this way? Why was Churchill to say of the Six, only seven years after his Zurich speech, that 'We are with them but not of them'? Second, what caused the dramatic change of stance in the 1960s?

The answers to each, as often in the real world, involve a mixture of politics and economics.

2.2 The Politics of Dissent

Many political analysts have argued that the fundamental philosophy of British foreign policy has been, for centuries rather than years, basically opposed to the idea of unity, and favourably inclined towards dissension, amongst the nations of continental Europe. It is not an implausible proposition. By the close of the Second World War the United Kingdom had been an essentially maritime nation for over two centuries, its political strength being founded on a Royal Navy more powerful than any other – until 1918, indeed, any two other – naval forces in the world. Equally, its economic strength had owed much to territories scattered across the world to which the channel of communication was the sea. In a famous phrase, Churchill was to declare that if Britain had to choose between the European continent and the open sea it would always have to opt for the latter; that, he declared, was where her Empire and her trade lay; that was the highway to her allies, and especially the United States.

Given this fact, it could be argued that disunity in Europe rather than unity was logically to long-term British advantage. Disunity – hostility and friction, indeed – in continental Europe meant that the European nations would dissipate their strength on land armies confronting one another rather than in naval strength which could threaten the rule of Britannia over the waves. Britain could then deploy its diplomacy to hold the balance of power between European nations in perpetually warring camps.

It has to be conceded that in the early postwar days there seemed considerable justification for this historic political philosophy. Of the six countries participating in the ECSC adventure, after all, two – Germany and Italy – had until recently been enemies and had been brought to crushing military disaster. The remaining four had experienced ignominious defeat and occupation. Britain, on the other hand, had emerged victorious and in the privileged role of special friend and ally of the United States. How could it conceivably throw in its lot with this collection of militarily and (so it was privately believed) politically feeble governments? Rather it should remain, to use Churchill's phraseology again, as an influential country at the centre of three powerful political blocs rather than one – Europe, the Commonwealth and the United States with which it had its very special relationship.

To this more or less rational (but not necessarily well-founded) argument some commentators would add a less rational factor – the ancient and deep-rooted hostility between France and the United Kingdom. It is a fact that the two countries had regarded one another as political enemies during most of the years since 1066, this enmity being forgotten from time to time only in the face of an even greater perceived threat from a mutual enemy – typically Germany. (Although Colonel Nasser was to be the last to fill this unenviable role at the time of the ill-fated Suez adventure in 1956.) It did not escape the notice of British politicians and officials that the initiatives towards integration in Europe had an unmistakable French accent; so many of the names quoted in the previous chapter – Briand, Monnet, Schuman, Pleven – were indeed French.

The sentiment, it has to be said, was mutual. In the early postwar years, integration was undoubtedly perceived by French politicians as essentially a means to establish the political supremacy of France in Europe, especially if a Franco-German alliance could be established. The association of the United Kingdom in the process would have seriously compromised that aim. When the ECSC talks were opened in London in 1950, M. Schuman laid down that the acceptance of a supranational authority, which he knew to be totally unacceptable to the British, was an essential precondition of the talks. Significantly, when asked by journalists how many member countries would be needed for the ECSC proposal to work he answered 'If necessary, we shall go ahead with only two'. No one was in any doubt as to which two countries he had in mind.

Yet the truth of the matter was (and to a large degree remains) that the reluctance of the United Kingdom to associate itself with these early moves towards integration in Europe sprang not so much from a positive hostility to the doctrine of European unity in itself (even if expounded in a French accent) but from a fundamental reluctance to contemplate any sacrifice of sovereignty to any other body whatever for any purpose whatever. The concept of sovereignty – the absolute power of Parliament to enact laws and the supremacy of British courts in administering those laws – is a very deeply-rooted one in British political philosophy. The central governments of many countries have limitations placed upon their powers by other powers vested, with equal validity, in lower tiers of government. Equally, many governments are constrained by a written Constitution or a Supreme Court so that laws may be struck down as unconstitutional. No such constraints apply to the Parliament of the United Kingdom. Nor, furthermore, has Britain experienced, as have many nations in continental Europe, the loss of its sovereignty through military occupation.

These considerations were peculiarly relevant at the time of the ECSC initiative, coming as it did when a Labour government had attained office in Britain; after a long struggle for political power its members had embarked on a policy to extend control, and indeed public ownership, over critical sectors of the economy, not least coal and steel. It was hardly surprising that its Prime Minister, Clement Attlee, should say of the Schuman proposals in the House of Commons in 1950 that the United Kingdom could not possibly commit itself in advance to be bound by future decisions of the High Authority – precisely what M. Schuman was demanding as a precondition for further discussions. Not that the sentiment was felt less deeply by members of the opposition Conservative party. Addressing the Council of Europe in Strasbourg later the same year,

Harold Macmillan, later to be Prime Minister and himself an enthusiast for European unity, said bluntly: 'One thing is certain and we may as well face it. Our people will not hand over to any supranational authority the right to close down our pits and our steelworks.' Years later, when the issue of entry into the EEC was being debated, the leader of one of the great political parties in Britain told his party conference in 1962 that to sacrifice sovereignty to this new-fangled entity 'would mean the end of Britain as an independent European state . . . the end of a thousand years of history'. The sentiments and expression were Churchillian; the speaker was in fact Hugh Gaitskell, leader of the Labour Party.

2.3 The Economics of Dissent

Lofty principles held by politicians, however high-flown their expression, seldom withstand the forces of hard economics. In this case, however, economics seemed to reinforce political philosophy. The United Kingdom was, and remains, highly dependent on international trade. A fundamental characteristic of that trade for decades was the special arrangements existing between Britain and the countries of the British Commonwealth; there existed in fact an Imperial Preference system, meaning that Commonwealth imports into Britain entered mostly duty-free or, at worst, over a tariff wall significantly lower than that applied to imports from the rest of the world, while British exports received correspondingly favourable treatment from its Commonwealth partners. As will be seen from Table 2.1 this arrangement naturally had a profound effect on the structure of British trade; in 1950 the Commonwealth accounted for about

Table 2.1
Merchandise trade of the United Kingdom, 1935–88

Region (1)	Average 1935–8 (2)	Percentage distribution					
		1950 (3)	1958 (4)	1968 (5)	1973 (6)	1983 (7)	1988 (8)
Commonwealth	38.4	44.8	43.6	24.4	17.7	10.7	7.8
EEC 6	12.9	12.0	13.6	19.9	25.9	38.0	42.6
Rest of Western Europe	14.4	15.8	13.6	20.8	24.4	19.3	20.2
United States	9.5	6.8	8.9	13.8	11.1	12.6	11.4
Rest of World	24.7	20.7	20.3	21.1	21.0	19.5	18.0
Total	100	100	100	100	100	100	100

SOURCE *Annual Abstract of Statistics* (HMSO, sundry issues). Merchandise trade refers to the total of imports and exports of tangible goods.

45 per cent of the total compared with a mere 12 per cent for the six countries forming the ECSC.

The implications of this for the appraisal of a proposed customs union with the Six will be obvious. A customs union would imply that Britain would have to give preferential access to imports from the Six but positively discriminate against its major supplier, the Commonwealth. The Commonwealth countries, in turn, would naturally withdraw the preferential access previously enjoyed by British exports, with the result that serious damage would inevitably be inflicted on British exporters in what was by far and away the major part of their market. The thing made no economic sense.

There was a corresponding domestic problem. Given its Commonwealth ties, the United Kingdom had been for many decades a country in which the bulk of its supplies of primary products – foodstuffs and raw materials – had been imported, duty-free, from some of the world's most efficient producers. This policy of cheap food and raw materials was advantageous in holding down the costs of its manufacturing base, both directly and indirectly through a relatively low cost of living and hence wage-level. The result had been the reduction of its domestic agriculture to a very small part of the economy, although one of a fairly high degree of efficiency given the need to compete with Commonwealth food suppliers. In 1958, agriculture accounted for under 5 per cent of both Britain's gross domestic product (GDP) and its working population. In the ECSC countries, on the other hand, the opposite situation applied. In 1958 about 22 per cent of the total workforce was engaged in farming, producing about 10 per cent of GDP; the contrast between those two latter figures indicates the relatively very low level of output and income characteristic of their agricultural sector. The interest of the UK therefore lay in low food prices and free international trade in agriculture; the interests of the Six, by contrast, lay in a policy of high food prices and restricted imports in order to advance the interests of their large, and poor, farming population.

In 1950, therefore, when the first major movement towards integration was made, and even more in 1957 when a full-blown customs union was proposed, the economic realities of British society appeared to strongly reinforce the traditional instincts of its political leaders. This was a formidable combination; that both ingredients were to prove to be based on false assumptions about the continuance of the past into the future is irrelevant except to those claiming the gift of prophecy. Despite their tendency to lay claim to this gift, few politicians (or, for that matter, economists) possess it; certainly there was insufficient around in the 1950s to determine the course of events.

The strategy of the British government was therefore not merely to stand aside from the proposed customs union but to outflank it by proposing an alternative. In the counsels of the OEEC the United Kingdom proposed a Free Trade Area in industrial products covering virtually the whole of Western Europe. This would avoid the discrimination against British exports implied by the duty-free access enjoyed by the Six in each other's markets and would indeed give British industry free access to those markets; on the other hand, since separate tariff systems could be applied by members to their trade with the outside world, Britain would be able to maintain its policy of importing food from the cheapest sources available. There was singularly little prospect of this being acceptable to France, a major agricultural country with an industrial base in general very vulnerable to foreign competition. In any event, as has already been noted, the French government was distinctly unenthusiastic about British participation on any terms. A European Free Trade Area in industrial products (EFTA) was in fact established in 1960 by seven countries – Austria, Denmark, Norway, Portugal, Sweden, Switzerland and the United Kingdom (later joined by Finland and Iceland) – which for a variety of economic or political reasons felt unable to join with the Six in the EEC. While having a modest degree of success judged by its own terms of reference, EFTA had little inherent coherence or rationality; in 1959 EFTA countries accounted for only 18 per cent of each other's merchandise trade, whereas the EEC Six accounted for 26 per cent of their trade. The effect was merely that Western Europe was literally at sixes and sevens.

2.4 The 1960s – Coming to Terms

A mere four years after the United Kingdom had emphatically refused an invitation to join the ECSC Six in their venture into a customs union, the policy of the British government underwent a complete transformation. In November 1961, Mr Harold Macmillan – he of the 'Our people will not hand over to any supranational authority' but now Prime Minister – opened negotiations with the EEC with a view to British entry. During the following year difficult negotiations, principally concerning Commonwealth imports, made a good deal of progress. A French delegate, when asked how things were going, was said to have remarked 'Terrible, terrible – the English are agreeing to everything'. This last remark reveals, however, a change in the political scene in the EEC which was to have profound consequences – the accession of General de Gaulle to the Presidency of France in 1958. Had de Gaulle become President shortly before rather than shortly after the signing of the Treaty of Rome it is almost certain that the Treaty would not have been signed at all. As events were to show on many occasions, he was profoundly out of sympathy with the whole concept of supranationality and was to impede its development throughout the 1960s. Given the existence of the EEC, however, he was also profoundly opposed to British membership of it, principally because he regarded it, with some reason, as essentially an enterprise in which France could be the dominant partner, a dominance he had no intention of sharing with the British. Entry into the EEC required the consent of all member governments, and when it appeared that the negotiations might be succeeding President de Gaulle, at a press conference and without consulting his fellow-members, announced that he was exercising his veto. The British, he declared, were not yet ready to be true Europeans.

Six years later, in July 1967, another Prime Minister, Mr Harold Wilson, repeated the attempt but the negotiations were very short-lived. By this time the British were reconciled to the agricultural arrangements now established in the EEC and agreement could have been reached fairly quickly. Hence President de Gaulle took less than six months to exercise his veto in December 1967. Various additional objections to British entry were now advanced, including the admitted weakness of the UK balance of payments situation, but the obvious fact was that there was no prospect of British entry until General de Gaulle departed from the political scene.

This in fact occurred with his resignation from office in 1969. The event was followed by a general election in Britain and a new Prime Minister, Mr Edward Heath, took office on 18 June 1970 – the anniversary, some percipient observers noted, of the Battle of Waterloo in 1815. Within two weeks yet another set of negotiations for entry were opened, Denmark, Ireland and Norway being associated with them. Agreement was reached with comparative rapidity on the terms of entry – substantially concerned with the transitional arrangements for agriculture and budgetary contributions rather than matters of fundamental principle – and the final Treaty of Accession was signed in Brussels and ratified by Parliament in March 1972. On 1 January 1973 the United Kingdom, along with Denmark and Ireland – the Norwegian Parliament declining to approve its country's membership in the end – became a full member of the European Economic Community.

How can this complete reversal of British policy towards the EEC be explained? The answer is that so many of the factors which seemed permanent facts of British life in the early 1950s were in reality about to go into reverse. On the political side, two of the famous three spheres of power were about to decline sharply, if not disappear. The British Empire, with the United Kingdom as the undoubted head and leader, was transforming itself into the Commonwealth; what is more, as colonies became independent states the nature of the organisation, and of the position of the United Kingdom in it, changed fundamentally. The word of the mother country was manifestly becoming further removed from law; the political attitudes of the newer members, especially in Africa, no longer mirrored those of Britain and the older Dominions; the expulsion in 1961 of the Republic of South Africa on political grounds – and much against British wishes – showed that membership of the Commonwealth was no longer merely a matter of past association with the Crown and certainly not within the gift of the United Kingdom. As an operational political grouping the Commonwealth was losing its coherence and the British had certainly lost their dominance.

Nor did the second sphere of influence – the famous special relationship with the United States – retain in 1961 the credibility it had in 1951. As the years of the great wartime alliance receded, so did British influence with the newer and younger leaders of the United States. That country had in fact revealed in 1956 its willingness to turn its back on its ancient ally in insisting on an ignominious withdrawal by British forces from the Suez Canal, allegedly occupied to neutralise an Egypt-Israeli war. If any illusions concerning Britain as an independent, major world power existed in 1956 they had vanished by 1957. It was no coincidence that the first British application for entry into the EEC occurred in the same year as the inauguration of John Kennedy as President of the United States; he was to become the first President for twenty years who declined to defer respectfully to the views of the Prime Minister of Great Britain.

The economic factors had also gone into reverse. As Table 2.1 shows, in 1958 the value of British trade with the Commonwealth was 60 per cent greater than that with the EEC countries and the rest of Western Europe; by 1968 it was 40 per cent less. The Commonwealth countries were increasingly producing for themselves the goods which had previously been imported from Britain; the economies of Western Europe, expecially those of the Six, were on the other hand growing at a rate well above world level (and certainly well above that of the UK) so both providing more rapidly expanding markets for UK exports and increasingly penetrating the UK market with their own. Even the problem of expensive EEC food versus cheap Commonwealth food imports was becoming a relatively small problem: in 1958 over 26 per cent of British consumer expenditure was devoted to food, but by 1968 the proportion was below 21 per cent and still falling.

2.5 The Reluctant European

The conclusion is plain. The reversal of Britain's aloofness to the European adventure was not one born out of philosophic conviction but rather one forced upon it by the logic of reality. The EEC, despite the (often rather condescending) cynicism of British politicians and senior civil servants was in existence, was manifestly surviving and its industries were achieving a rate of economic growth precisely twice the UK average. The spheres of influence open to Britain outside Europe, on the other hand, were shrinking visibly and its leaders were being forced to face the prospect of presiding over an increasingly isolated country, relatively weak economically and impotent politically. The remark of Jean Monnet was to prove, as ever, prophetic: 'There is one thing you British will never understand: an idea. And there is one thing you are supremely good at grasping: a hard fact. We will have to build Europe without you: but then you will come in and join us.'

The price paid for this late, reluctant reversal of policy was not a small one. In negotiation, an adversary's knowledge that at the end of the day you have no real alternative but to accept an offer gives him an enormous advantage. In the end, Britain had to enter on take-it-or-leave-it terms and the perpetual arguments which were to follow over farm spending and budget contributions bear eloquent testimony to the penalty paid. Perhaps more important in the long run, Britain tends to see itself (and is certainly seen by its partners) as having become a member of the Community in, so to speak, a fit of despair rather than as the result of conviction and enthusiasm. That is not a foundation conducive to a fruitful and profitable partnership.

Further Reading

Barker, E., *Britain in a Divided Europe* (London: Weidenfeld & Nicolson, 1971).

Camps, M., *Britain and the European Community, 1955–63* (London: Oxford University Press, 1964).

Evans, D., *While Britain Slept: the Selling of the Common Market* (London: Gollancz, 1975).

Jenkins, R. (ed.), *Britain and the EEC* (London: Macmillan, 1982).

Kitzinger, U., *Diplomacy and Persuasion: How Britain Joined the Common Market* (London: Thames & Hudson, 1973).

Moon, J., *European Integration in British Politics, 1950–1963* (Aldershot: Gower Press, 1985).

Nicholson, F. and East, R., *From the Six to the Twelve* (London: Longman Group, 1987).

Young, J. W., *Britain, France, and the unity of Europe, 1945–51* (Leicester: Leicester University Press, 1984).

Young, J. W. (ed.), *The foreign policy of Churchill's peacetime administration, 1951–55* (Leicester: Leicester University Press, 1988).

The Evolving Community 3

3.1 Introduction

Politicians engaged on matters of state frequently give the impression that their every act and decision is inscribed on tablets of stone, to remain immutable for the rest of time. In fact they realise that virtually nothing can be fixed for eternity: to be unchanged for even a decade is indeed something of an achievement in the world of government. Judged by these standards the Treaty of Rome establishing the EEC has enjoyed a remarkable longevity, being to a large degree unchanged over a period of 30 years. True, from time to time after 1957 it was amended in some matters of detail, especially as regards provisions governing the Community budget, and these changes will be described in the appropriate places in the chapters which follow. Two far-reaching and rather fundamental developments are best described at this stage, however, before proceeding to examine the detail of the Community as it now stands.

The first of these concerns the membership of the Community. At the time of the signing of the Treaties in 1957 it seemed improbable that any countries other than the six signatories would seek membership; they had had an opportunity to do so after the Messina conference, after all, and for various reasons had declined to grasp it. Nevertheless, the possibility of some future change of heart was foreseen, and Article 237 of the Treaty provided that any *European* state could apply to become a member of the EEC. (The question of what qualified a country to describe itself as 'European' was left open; in practice it did not arise until the membership application by Turkey in 1987.) Any such applicant is required to address the request to the Council of Ministers, which is then charged with seeking an informed opinion from the Commission concerning the implications of the application. Having done this, the Council is required to decide on the matter by means of a unanimous vote. This obviously gives to

21

each existing member government the power to veto the admission of any new member, a power which, as has been seen, President de Gaulle had no hesitation in using in 1961 and 1967.

The second major change after 1957 had not been foreseen by the founding members, and in some cases was not particularly welcomed by them. As will be described below, discontent amongst the first directly-elected members of the European Parliament led to a major revision of the entire Treaty in the form of the Single European Act adopted by the Council of Ministers in February 1986 and ratified by the legislatures of all the member countries in 1986–7. Each of these rather fundamental developments will be summarised in turn.

3.2   The First Enlargement, 1973

Much of the background to the negotiations leading to the accession of Denmark, Ireland and the United Kingdom has been described in the previous chapter. Throughout these negotiations Norway had participated in full, and both its official negotiators and the government itself were reasonably happy with the terms finally agreed for Norwegian accession. As was remarked at an earlier point, however, in democratic countries politicians may propose but the ordinary citizen has an awkward habit of disposing. The Norwegian Parliament was unhappy about some of the conditions agreed, most especially those concerning the fishing industry which are the subject of a later chapter. The matter was thus put to a referendum of the electorate in 1972 and the proposal to join the Community was rejected by a majority of 53 per cent to 47 per cent. (The persuasive power of fish was also demonstrated in Greenland, which acceded to the EEC in 1973 as part of the territory of Denmark, voted solidly against membership of the Community in the ensuing referendum in that country and finally opted for unilateral exit from the EEC in 1984, enjoying instead the status of an Overseas Country or Territory. The Community survived this defection.) *See Swann. p 24*

As already noted, the negotiations for British entry were concerned with detail, and especially transitional matters, rather than principle; since the EEC had been established for more than ten years before negotiations commenced it would have been singularly unrealistic to suppose that any fundamental changes could have been secured. The major problems so far as Britain was concerned revolved around the possible impact of accession on its traditional Commonwealth suppliers who feared the loss of what had been their major export market. (Not without good reason; in the five years succeeding the UK accession Australia's share in UK imports fell by 60 per cent.) The most difficult problems were solved by an agreement that there should continue to be duty-free quotas for imports of cheese and lamb from New Zealand and of sugar from the Caribbean. The possible threat to Britain's EFTA suppliers, which might have faced an abrupt transition from duty-free entry to the UK to the barrier of the common EEC tariff proved to be short-lived. Two of those trading partners, Denmark and Ireland, joined the EEC at the same time, while the remaining EFTA countries negotiated free-trade agreements with the EEC on their own behalf. The final major problem – that of the magnitude of the British contribution to the EEC budget – proved far more intractable. To some degree it was alleviated by the agreement on the part of the Community to establish a new European Regional Development Fund (ERDF) from which Britain was expected to be a substantial beneficiary. As later events were to show, however, the problem remained one to sour relations between the UK and its fellow-members for well over a decade to follow.

Even so, the referendum – a thoroughly unfamiliar and mistrusted device in British constitutional practice – held in June 1975 to decide upon the country's continued membership of the Community did not prove the disaster which it had for the hapless Norwegian government: the vote in favour was 67 per cent to 33 per cent against (the Shetland Islands being the only constituency with a majority against – the power of fish again.) The other two countries involved, Denmark and Ireland, had no such doubts; given the fact that with the UK as a member the EEC would account for more than 40 per cent of the exports of the former and nearly 80 per cent of the exports of the latter, doubts over membership could scarcely arise. (Both countries, in fact – with considerable justice – regarded EEC membership as likely to present them with a very considerable economic bonus.) The three countries agreed on a transitional period of five years in which to align their tariffs and their agricultural support system with that of the Community and in the event this proved more or less trouble-free. Indeed, it can be said that the accession of these three countries was widely regarded as natural, desirable and inevitable. It was only the formidable personality of President de Gaulle which could have delayed it so long.

3.3 The Second Enlargement, 1981

This was a good deal more than could be said for the accession of Greece which finally occurred in 1981. Article 238 of the Treaty provides that the Community may conclude agreements embodying reciprocal rights and obligations with any non-member country, and such an agreement had been concluded between the Community and Greece in November 1962. This provided for a gradual movement to a full customs unions (i.e. abolition of all tariffs on trade between the parties and the adoption of common tariffs with the rest of the world) over a period of 12 years and, eventually, for the admission of Greece as a full member of the Community. In 1967, however, the civil government of Greece (not one of notable stability) was overthrown by an army uprising and thereafter a military quasi-dictatorship was in power.

A new situation was now considered to exist. The Preamble to the Treaty of Rome had 'called upon the other peoples of Europe *who share their ideal* to join in their efforts' and this rather grandiose phrase was construed by the Council of Ministers to mean that membership of the Community, or formal association with it, was confined to countries enjoying democratic government, which Greece no longer was. The Treaty of Association between Greece and the Community was therefore treated as being, so to speak, in cold storage.

In July 1974, after a somewhat bewildering succession of plots and counter-plots, the military rulers of Greece announced that the time had come for the government to be returned to civil hands and a new government was duly elected in November 1974. Six months later the government applied not for the re-activation of the Treaty of Association but rather for full membership under Article 237. This rather surprising development was not greeted entirely with enthusiasm by many of the member countries, given both the dubious stability of the new government and the undeniable poverty of the applicant country. (In 1975, income per head in Greece was estimated to be about 55 per cent of the EEC average.) It was difficult to see, however, on what grounds the application could reasonably be refused; Greece could scarcely be held not to be part of Europe unless the foundation of much European culture was itself to be repudiated, nor could it be alleged to be undemocratic. In any event, being a relatively small country with a population of less than 10 million, it was hardly a problem of unbearable magnitude. The main concern was the possible threat it posed to the existing producers of Mediterranean products within the Community, being a considerable (and cheap) producer of fruit, wine and vegetables.

Negotiations were rather protracted, running from 1975 to 1980, but agreement was finally reached whereby Greece became a full member of the Community with effect from 1 January 1981. In general, a period of five years was allowed for the transition to the full requirements of membership, although provision was made for this to be extended to seven for some products; a fairly generous grant-in-aid was conceded to ease this transitional process. In the event Greece could not fully meet this timetable.

3.4   The Third Enlargement, 1986

The path followed by Spain and Portugal to full membership in 1986 was somewhat similar to that of Greece. Both had obtained favourable trade agreements with the Community – Spain in 1970 and Portugal in 1973. No question arose at the outset, however, of their full membership. Since 1932 Portugal had been governed by a dictatorship, as had Spain since 1939. Both regimes came to an end at about the same time. The regime of personal rule ended in Portugal in 1974 and was followed by two years of considerable political instability, with six different governments following one another at short intervals. A general election in 1976 finally established a relatively stable government. In Spain, Prince Juan Carlos had been named by General Franco to be his successor, but on Franco's death in December 1975 the King (as he was by then) announced the restoration of parliamentary government and such a government was established after elections in 1977. The new government immediately applied for membership of the Community under Article 237 and, not surprisingly, the government of Portugal promptly followed suit.

It has to be recorded that these applications were received with even less enthusiasm than that of Greece. Both prospective entrants were relatively poor, with per capita incomes well below the EC average; this had been true of Greece, but these two countries would add nearly 50 million to the Community's total population, compared with 10 million in the case of Greece. The implication was that they were liable to contribute rather less than average to the Community's budgetary resources but impose on them claims which were distinctly above average. Furthermore, both countries, like Greece, are important producers of 'Mediterranean' products (although Portugal cannot accurately be described as a 'Mediterranean' country). This could generate serious problems for the producers of similar products in France and Italy, to say nothing of the neighbouring countries around the Mediterranean to which the Community had already extended preferential trade treatment with respect to such products. Both had manufacturing industries which in general seemed very vulnerable to free competition from the rest of the Community, raising the possibility of the need for some degree of protection for them within the customs union itself. They also (like Greece) have large potential migrant populations which presumably would be entitled to free access to all other member countries. Nevertheless, as with Greece, it was not obvious that any valid grounds could be advanced for refusing entry to two unquestionably European and (perhaps a little less certainly) democratic countries.

The negotiations leading to the Treaties of Accession in 1985 were therefore difficult and protracted. The two countries became full members of the Community with effect from 1 January 1986, a transitional period of seven years being agreed for the full alignment of their tariff barriers to those of the Community, and one of up to ten years for the integration of their agriculture and fishing industries into the Community system. The result, as may be seen from Table 3.1, was to bring the total population of the Community in 1986 to 323 million – a third bigger than that of the United States. In terms of gross domestic product the Community is still somewhat smaller than the United States but is more than twice as large as Japan. In the context of world trade its significance is even greater, the Community being more than twice as important as the United States and four times as important as Japan. It accounts, in fact, for more than a third of all world trade – clearly an economic unit of critical importance to the whole world economy.

Table 3.1
The Community of Twelve, 1986

Country	Total population		Total GDP at P.P. parities*		Merchandise trade*		GDP Per head
	Millions	% of EC	ECUbn	% of EC	ECUbn	% of EC	EC = 100
(1)	(2)	(3)	(4)	(5)	(6)	(7)	(8)
Belgium	9.8	3.0	136.9	3.1	140.6	8.8	102.6
Denmark	5.1	1.6	82.1	1.9	45.8	2.9	118.2
France	55.4	17.2	833.2	19.0	251.9	15.7	110.5
Germany	61.1	18.9	958.9	21.8	441.9	27.6	115.3
Greece	10.0	3.1	76.4	1.7	17.3	1.1	56.1
Ireland	3.5	1.1	30.2	0.7	24.6	1.5	63.4
Italy	57.2	17.7	803.6	18.3	201.3	12.5	103.2
Luxembourg	0.4	0.1	6.4	0.1	†	†	117.5
Netherlands	14.6	4.5	211.6	4.8	167.1	10.4	106.4
Portugal	10.2	3.2	69.9	1.6	16.9	1.0	50.3
Spain	38.7	12.0	382.5	8.7	60.3	3.8	72.6
United Kingdom	56.8	17.6	803.7	18.3	235.2	14.7	103.9
EC 12	322.8	100.0	4395.4	100.0	1602.9	100.0	100.0
United States	241.6	74.8	5148.2	117.1	597.0	37.2	156.5
Japan	121.7	37.7	1841.1	41.9	344.1	21.5	111.1

* At 1986 prices.
† Totals for Luxembourg included with Belgium.

Further accessions seem improbable before 1992 but are likely in the longer run. Both Norway and Austria are obvious and logical candidates for membership, and the latter formally applied for admission in July 1989; only Austria's formal commitment to 'permanent neutrality' presents a legal, but certainly not an insuperable, obstacle to membership. In 1963 the Community entered into an association agreement with Turkey under which the full membership of that country was expected to be the ultimate outcome. Political difficulties have prevented much progress in that direction but Turkey nevertheless made a formal application for membership in 1987. Given the membership of Greece since 1981, and its acquisition thereby of the right of veto on new members, however, the possibility of Turkish membership before the end of the century seems remote. Similarly, an agreement with Cyprus in 1987 provides for a full customs union between that country and the Community early in the next century, but full membership for Cyprus, as for Turkey, is likely to be postponed until the political differences between Greece and Turkey are finally resolved. An application for membership by Malta is also likely at some time in the future.

3.5 The Parliament Stirs

This substantial expansion in its membership was the first fundamental change in the nature of the Community after the signing of the Treaty in 1957. In 1986, however, there occurred a far-reaching revision of the Treaty itself. For reasons explained in a later chapter, the role of the European Parliament had been a very minor one in the early years of the Community. The first direct elections to the Parliament in 1979, however, brought to its deliberations a collection of politicians who, having the authority of being elected representatives rather than mere nominees, were dissatisfied with both the apparent lack of progress towards a genuine economic and political union in Europe – as opposed to the simple creation of a customs union – and with the role which appeared to have been assigned to the Parliament in that process. Largely at the inspiration of a long-standing and dedicated proponent of political integration in Europe, Altiero Spinelli, the Parliament in July 1981 passed a resolution calling for a drastic revision of both the aims of the Community and its method of operation.

So far as the stated aims of the 1957 Treaty were concerned, there was serious discontent with the apparently very slow progress towards agreement on many of the policies which were specifically or implicitly required by the Treaty; this was attributed largely to the practice which had grown up (also explained in a later chapter) whereby decisions were in the hands of a Council of Ministers which operated on rule of unanimity – meaning that the pace of progress was determined by the least enthusiastic Minister present.

It was also felt that a situation in which the elected representatives of the people in Parliament had virtually no influence on major policy decisions was undemocratic and indefensible. So far as the basic aims of the Treaty were concerned, the view of the majority in Parliament was that it was too narrowly confined to purely economic matters and did not contain sufficient ingredients to create a genuine political union; it had effectively established an organisation within which the separate member countries collaborated but remained as independent sovereign states rather than moving towards a genuine federal government for Western Europe as a whole. Hence the Parliament wished to see the Treaty extended to include political matters impinging on national sovereignty – including even defence – as fundamental aims to which the member countries were committed. A draft Treaty establishing a European Union embodying all these proposals was therefore drawn up, approved by an overwhelming majority of the Parliament in February 1984 and duly passed to the Council of Ministers.

As might be expected, a rather mixed reception was given to this document by the political leaders of the member countries when they met to consider it at the next summit conference at Fontainebleau in June 1984. It was in fact a good deal less than enthusiastic in several cases. Members of national governments do not instinctively look kindly on proposals to have power and resources taken out of their hands. Nevertheless, largely due to the strong backing given to the proposals (somewhat unexpectedly) by the French President, M Mitterrand, then holding the presidency of the Council of Ministers, it was agreed by a majority decision (the United Kingdom dissenting) that a special intergovernmental conference should be held to consider them with a view to their embodiment in a new Treaty. Much debate occurred on the question of whether these two broad sets of proposals – one concerned with improving the decision-making processes of the Community, the other with the extension of the Treaty to totally new policy objectives – should be dealt with by two separate documents or brought together in one. Separating them, it was thought, would make it easier for member countries to accept reforms under the first heading which might be rejected if they formed part of a package involving the more far-reaching proposals under the second. It was for precisely this reason – i.e. that the first set might get through and the second be defeated – that the proponents of political integration argued (successfully) that the package had to be dealt with in one document only. Hence the final recommendations of the conference, which were adopted by the Council of Ministers at the end of 1985, were embodied in a draft new Treaty and given the rather curious title of 'The *Single* European Act'. This was signed by all members of the Council of Ministers in February 1986 and ratified by the legislatures of all member countries during that year. The date on which it was to become effective had originally been 1 January 1987, but because formal ratification by Ireland was delayed by a constitutional wrangle in that country it did not come into effect until July of that year.

3.6   The Single European Act, 1986

The Act was a long and very complex document touching upon almost every aspect of the Community's work. A simple list, or even a summary, of its various provisions would be almost meaningless in isolation and for that reason the changes introduced by it are best indicated when specific policies or institutions are discussed in the chapters which follow.

Broadly speaking its first aim of improving the decision-making processes of the Community was achieved to a substantially higher degree than its second aim of extending the Community's authority and declared aims much further into the realm of political union. The major achievement under the first heading was the formal acceptance of the use of majority voting by the Council of Ministers and its agencies – as opposed to the rule of unanimity – in a wide range of matters concerning the Community's internal market. It formally embodied a commitment to abolish all restrictions on transactions within that market by the end of 1992, a commitment which the Council of Ministers had in fact independently accepted earlier in 1985. To some degree the powers of the Commission to take positive steps to achieve this end were strengthened, as were the powers of the Parliament to amend proposals emanating from the Council. All these matters will be discussed in succeeding chapters.

The achievements under the second heading were much more modest; certainly they fell far short of the aspirations of the enthusiasts for closer political union in Western Europe. Certain policy areas which had already emerged as important but had not been specified in the 1957 Treaty – regional policy and monetary integration, for example – were added to the list of the Community's formal objectives. The desirability of closer political co-operation between member countries was also stated in formal terms, although the mechanism for achieving it was not built in to the Community's normal processes of operation. The attempts of the integrationists to have certain other matters placed within the competence of the Community, as opposed to that of national governments, however – development policy, energy and education, for example – failed completely. So did the attempt to extend majority voting to policy areas involving national sovereignty to a significant degree, such as the determination of tax levels, the movement of individuals across national borders and monetary policy.

The Act resulted from an initiative on the part of the Parliament, the first thing of its kind in the history of the Community. Whatever its limitations, it did at least establish that the Parliament could be something more than an impotent talking-shop and that it could pressurise the Council of Ministers into actions which it would have been unlikely to undertake otherwise. But it failed to achieve the fundamental changes which many of the parliamentarians – probably the majority – had hoped to see. This was almost inevitable; amendments to the 1957 Treaty require unanimous approval by the Council of Ministers so that there needed to be only one member government (in fact there were several) whose politicians – or, for that matter, senior officials – were reluctant to concede part of their sovereign power to the Community collectively for any such change to be blocked. It is only realistic to concede that this is likely to remain the case for many years to come. The question of the likely impact of the Act is further discussed in Chapter 27 below.

Further Reading

Nicholson, F. and East, R., *From the Six to the Twelve* (London: Longman Group, 1987).

Pryce, R. (ed.), *The Dynamics of European Union* (London: Croom Helm, 1987).

Seers, D. and Vaitos, C. (eds), *The Second Enlargement of the EEC* (London: Macmillan, 1982).

Tsoukalis, L. (ed.), *The European Community and its Mediterranean Enlargement* (London: Allen & Unwin, 1981).

Yannopoolus, G., *Greece and the EEC* (London: Macmillan, 1986).

Yannopoolus, G., *European integration and the Iberian economies* (London: Macmillan, 1988).

Institutions – Council and Court 4

4.1 The Institutional Framework

The drafters of the Treaty of Rome set out the main objectives of the Community in fairly general terms – the elimination of all obstacles to trade between the member countries, the establishment of a single customs tariff on trade with the rest of the world, the inauguration of common policies on agriculture and transport and so on – but were not foolish enough to attempt to legislate in detail on how these objectives were to be achieved in the inevitably changing world of the years ahead. Rather, they provided for the creation of a network of institutions in and through which detailed policies in these various fields would be formulated and administered. In this and the succeeding chapter the four major such institutions – the Council of Ministers, the Court of Justice, the Commission and the Parliament – will be examined and their roles clarified.

It will be noted that the Treaty made no provision for certain fundamental functions of a sovereign government – most especially external political relations and defence – although some considerable progress has been made in connection with the former of these, outside the framework laid down by the Treaty. It was observed in the preceding chapter that the attempts of enthusiastic European federalists to have these two functions added to the Treaty through the Single European Act were unsuccessful. The entity created by the Treaty therefore lacked two fundamental attributes of a genuinely independent government: the power to enter into political accord with other sovereign states and the means to defend itself in the event of discord with such states. Whether these things can be separated in reality from the purely economic matters with which the Treaty sought to concern itself must be a matter of some doubt. The fact remains that the Treaty established a grouping of independent sovereign states rather than a new federal state. Hence the role of its primary institution, the Council of Ministers representing each of those member states, has inevitably become a dominant one.

This may not have been the original intention of the founding fathers; being democratic people they would have subscribed to the doctrine of the supremacy of an elected legislature and might well have anticipated that the Community equivalent, the European Parliament – actually referred to as the Assembly in the original Treaty – would gradually become the ultimate source of power in the Community. (The Council is in fact listed in the Treaty itself as the *second* of the institutions to be created: the first is the Assembly.) This most emphatically failed to occur; the report of an investigation into the possibilities of increasing the role of the Parliament in Community affairs (the Vedel Report of 1972) concluded that, whatever the original intent, actual experience had increased the dominance of the Council 'to such an extent that the Council . . . has become the sole effective centre of power in the system'. Despite the relatively marginal constraints placed upon the Council's freedom of action by the Single European Act, this remains an accurate summary of the realities of the situation.

4.2   Membership of the Council

The Treaty provided that each government should delegate one person to the Council and referred to those delegates as 'representatives of the Member states'. The Council is in fact the only institution of the Community in which individuals participate (openly) as representatives of their own countries; in all other institutions they are servants of the Community as a whole, whatever their nationality. The series of enlargements of the Community has therefore led to a Council of Ministers consisting of 12 national representatives. The Council is presided over by one of their members acting as President for a period of six months, the selection of President being in no way elective but determined entirely by a rotation of the member governments in strict alphabetical order of their official names as spelt in their own languages. Thus Germany (Deutschland) is succeeded by Greece (Ellas) which is in turn succeeded by Spain (Espana). The Presidency of all the Council's committees is determined in the same way as for the Council itself. The tradition of the Council and its subsidiaries is that meetings adopt the procedure of the *tour de table*, the representative of each country being invited to speak in turn before the discussion moves on to another point. The admirable intention of this is to ensure that no country, however small, is prevented from having its view heard; the result, inevitably, is frequently to make meetings even more tedious than they might have been.

Although the membership of the Council is fixed in number it is highly variable in personality. Since 1972 the heads of the member governments, together with their Foreign Ministers, meet three times a year under the title of the European Council, although the European Council had no official status as a Community institution until it was formalised by the Single European Act of 1986. One of these 'summit' meetings is held in the country contemporaneously occupying the office of President while the third is held in Brussels or Luxembourg. On other occasions membership of the Council is determined on a functional basis; if farming matters are the subject of the meeting, it is comprised of agricultural ministers, if transport is under discussion it is comprised of transport ministers and so on. Typically, around 80 sittings will occur in the course of a year. This specialisation is doubtless understandable but it inevitably leads to the Council becoming mostly a forum in which individual sectional interests are advanced, rather than one which formulates a 'European' view of things. Some countries – notably France – have pursued the logic of the situation and appoint a 'Minister for Europe', but this is unusual.

4.3 On a Show of Hands

In so disparate a body as the Council, in which membership not only varies according to purpose but includes one member (Luxembourg) representing a total population of some 400 000 people while others represent around 60 million people, some systematic voting procedure is clearly necessary. The original Treaty provided that the Community should be brought into being over a period of twelve years, this period being divided into three sub-periods of four years each. In Stage 1, from 1958 to 1961, the Community would be involved in the creation of its institutions and the formulation of broad strategy for the various policy areas. Since these fundamental matters could not conceivably be settled without complete agreement amongst all the members, it was decreed that during this phase the Council should proceed only by unanimous vote; any one country, however small, in other words, would have the right of veto. This led to the quaint Community custom of occasionally defying the passage of time. In December 1961 final agreement had still not been reached on the basis of the Common Agricultural policy, a matter of profound importance to France. In order to postpone the end of Stage 1 on 31 December, after which the formal right of veto was due to disappear, the French persuaded their colleagues to stop the official clocks so that further negotiations could continue. A package was finally agreed on 14 January 1962 but, because of this miraculous mastery over time, the agreement officially came into force on 1 January 1962. (The formal rule of unanimity is retained permanently by the Treaty for certain very fundamental matters such as any revision of the Treaty itself or the admission of new members to the Community.)

With the conclusion of this foundation-building Stage 1, however, the Treaty provided that in Stage 2, from 1962 to 1965, when the Council would be primarily concerned with detailed proposals for the implementation of the (hopefully) agreed broad policy strategies, the decisions of the Council would be based increasingly on a 'qualified' majority. It was envisaged that, from Stage 3 (i.e. 1966) onwards, this would be the normal voting procedure in the Council. To this end, countries were allocated voting powers roughly in accordance with their size but a qualified majority was so defined as to ensure that, on the one hand, a coalition of big powers would be unable to steamroller all the smaller powers and, on the other hand, that a few small countries could not hold up the progress of the Community by sheer perversity or as a form of political blackmail. The distribution of voting powers throughout the life of the Community is shown in Table 4.1.

After the fourth enlargement, the four largest countries were given 10 votes each while Luxembourg, the smallest, has only 2; as col.(6) of the table shows, however, the smaller countries still have voting powers which are considerably greater in relation to their population than the bigger countries. The requirement of 54 for a qualified majority on a proposal coming before the Council from the Commission means, however, that even if the five biggest countries

Table 4.1
Council of Ministers – Voting Allocations

Country				1986 Onwards	
	1958–72	1973–80	1981–5	Total	Per million population, 1989
(1)	(2)	(3)	(4)	(5)	(6)
Belgium	2	5	5	5	0.51
Denmark	–	3	3	3	0.59
France	4	10	10	10	0.18
Germany	4	10	10	10	0.16
Greece	–	–	5	5	0.50
Ireland	–	3	3	3	0.86
Italy	4	10	10	10	0.17
Luxembourg	1	2	2	2	5.41
Netherlands	2	5	5	5	0.34
Portugal	–	–	–	5	0.48
Spain	–	–	–	8	0.21
United Kingdom	–	10	10	10	0.18
Total votes	17	58	63	76	0.23
Qualified majority	12	41	45	54	
Number of countries which must vote in favour*	4	6	6	8	

* For proposals *not* emanating from the Commission.

voted together on a proposal (a somewhat improbable event in itself) they would still need the support of at least two of the smaller countries to get it through. Conversely, the seven smaller member countries could not join forces in order to outvote the five larger ones. Where the proposal is not one originating from the Commission (i.e. may be advancing national rather than Community interests) the requirement is even stricter – the five largest would need the support of at least three of the smaller countries.

Finally, the Treaty provided that when the Council of Ministers was considering proposals submitted by the Commission in execution of decisions which the Council had already made – in other words, making detailed provision for the implementation of agreed policies – then a straight simple majority would carry the day, each member having one vote. The object of this was to ensure that a minority of countries, whatever their size, which might have had second thoughts (inspired perhaps by representations from domestic interests which felt themselves threatened) could not obstruct the implementation of a decision already reached after full discussion.

4.4   Compromise in Luxembourg

All this seemed fair and reasonable, if a shade legalistic. It balanced the rights of small countries against those of more powerful ones and provided for decisions to be made on a Community basis, rather than limiting the organisation to being merely an agreement amongst separate nations to co-operate if, and only if, each individual participant was wholly satisfied. Had General de Gaulle not attained the Presidency of France six months after the Community came into existence it might well have worked well enough. In fact most of the Community's decisions were – and still are – reached without recourse to voting at all, except in matters relating to the Budget. But as already noted, in President de Gaulle the Community had acquired a member – indeed its most dominant member – who was deeply suspicious of the concept of supranationality and consumed with the conviction that the sovereignty and political independence of France had to be preserved at all costs. The supranationality inherent in the concept of majority voting, qualified or otherwise, was bound to come into conflict with this powerful personality sooner or later.

The moment of truth came at the end of June 1965, in the closing days of the French tenure of the Presidency of the Council; the adoption of qualified majority voting as normal procedure was now only six months away. The Commission had proposed that, with the Common Agricultural Policy about to commence operations, the Community should switch to a system of financing itself from its 'own' resources – i.e. revenues accruing directly to it as a matter of right – rather than continuing with the prevailing system whereby it relied on specified contributions by individual member governments roughly in accordance with their national incomes. With this change, the Commission envisaged that a surplus of revenues would be available, even after meeting the costs of agricultural support. It therefore suggested that a proposed disposition of these surpluses should be drawn up annually by the Commission, submitted for comment to the Parliament and then be approved by the Council acting on a majority vote.

In the eyes of President de Gaulle this was emphatically too much; the Commission was getting above itself and trying to turn the Community into an entity independent of, and distinct from, its individual member governments. On his instructions all French delegates were withdrawn from the proceedings of the Community and France's permanent representative at the Community – virtually its Ambassador to it – was recalled from Brussels. In the face of this 'empty chair' policy on the part of its most influential member, the work of the Community virtually came to a standstill.

Six months later – perhaps as a result of a somewhat less than overwhelming victory in the Presidential elections of December 1965 – de Gaulle was persuaded to reconsider his intransigent position and in January 1966 the six member governments reached an agreement known to history as 'the Luxembourg Compromise'. The wording of this agreement was something of a masterpiece of obscurantism, declaring as it did that when 'very important' issues were involved the Council would try within a reasonable time to reach solutions which were acceptable to all but then adding that, in the view of France, under such circumstances discussions would have to continue until unanimous agreement was reached. It then coyly observed that the six delegations noted that there was a divergence of view concerning what should be done in the event of a failure to reach complete agreement.

Whatever the precise meaning, if any, to be attached to this agreement – which had of course no juridical basis whatever in the Treaty of Rome itself – it was widely construed to mean that, in issues deemed to be 'very important' by any member of the Council, that member retained the right of veto over any proposal. The fact that this veto was exercised formally on relatively few occasions is hardly relevant; the fact that it existed meant that it was pointless putting any matter to a vote if a single member was maintaining opposition to it. This was enough to dramatically slow down the decision-making process even when the Council consisted of only six ministers; when the Council was expanded to nine it brought it almost to a total standstill. Its likely effect when the Council was further expanded to twelve required little imagination.

For this reason a restatement of the principle of majority voting, qualified or otherwise, became an essential ingredient of the Single European Act. The attempt to extend majority voting to decisions on every matter was totally unrealistic, but the Act did affirm that it would henceforth apply to all matters concerning the market in goods and services within the Community and to its commercial policy with regard to trade with non-member countries. It is also to be adopted in some areas not mentioned in the original Treaty, such as the allocation of funds from the European Regional Development Fund, and to amendments made by the Parliament at its second reading of Council proposals. It was specifically *not* extended, however, to critical areas such as those of taxation or monetary policy. What is more, the Act made no reference to the Luxembourg Compromise at all – since it was concerned with amendments to the 1957 Treaty it could hardly have done so, the Treaty containing no mention whatever of it. The status, as well as the precise meaning, of that document therefore remains unclear. Mrs Thatcher, for one, stated unambiguously in the House of Commons during a debate on the Act in December 1985 that 'the veto remains intact'.

In reality it could hardly be otherwise where new objectives or radical departures from existing policies are involved. Such developments would inevitably require ratification by national legislatures and this could hardly be sought by a government which was itself opposed to the measure concerned. As was demonstrated by the example of Norway in 1972, such ratification is by no means guaranteed even for measures of which a government actually approves. Since governments are accountable to their legislatures, it is difficult to see how any government could commend at home a decision which it had resisted in Brussels. In the context of the application of agreed policies, however, or relatively modest developments of them – which must, after all, constitute the bulk of the subject-matter of Council discussions – the adoption of majority voting will surely make the decision-making process of the Community distinctly less tortuous and funereal than it proved to be during the 1970s and the greater part of the 1980s.

Much will depend, however, on the degree to which the Ministers are determined to reach agreement. Giving evidence before a House of Lords Committee in 1984, a Commission official of eleven years' experience remarked, with some bitterness, that the Council 'takes far too long to deliberate, even when it says no ... I believe [the Council of Ministers'] preparation focuses very heavily on national departmental viewpoints. I do not think it normally gives much weight to the possible importance of the Commission's proposals to the Community as a whole ...' There are obviously issues here which transcend the mere arithmetic of voting procedures.

4.5 Supporting the Council

One serious problem facing the Council, comprised as it is of Ministers with (presumably) heavy departmental and parliamentary commitments in their own countries, is that the time available to it permits of productive meetings only if the groundwork of its discussions has been thoroughly prepared and their details hammered out well before the Council meets. To some degree this preparatory work is carried out by its own secretariat, which consists of some

2000 officials employed to do nothing else. More importantly, however, most of the preparatory work of negotiation and clarification of the main issues at stake is carried out by a number of subsidiary organisations which act as filters through which all the matters pass before coming before the individual Ministers and then the Council as a whole.

The most important of these are the national delegations of permanent officials which each member country maintains in Brusssels, the headquarters of the Commission. Since 1965 the heads of these delegations, who carry the rank of an Ambassador, have been officially recognised as constituting the Committee of Permanent Representatives (universally referred to by its French acronym COREPER) which meets weekly to prepare Council business and through which pass all matters which are ultimately placed before the Council. The Commission, for example, automatically submits proposals to the COREPER before finalising them for the Council. In this way, most of the disagreements and details are hammered out behind the scenes before reaching Ministers – to such a degree that the approval of the Council frequently becomes a matter of pure formality.

In addition, the Council has created a fair number of specialist committees to which are appointed national representatives of various interest groups – employers, trade unions, the professions and the delicately-named 'representatives of the general interest'.

To these Committees are referred any proposals concerning their particular area for discussion and opinion. The most important of these is the Economic and Social Committee – the only committee for which provision is specifically made in the Treaty – numbering around 200 members and containing subcommittees concerned with specific sectors such as agriculture and transport. The Treaty establishing the European Coal and Steel Community contained provision for a comparable body, the ECSC Consultative Committee which is of course concerned with matters involving the coal and steel industries. There are also specialist advisory committees on monetary, scientific and technical matters and so on. Precisely how useful these committees are is rather arguable. They have of course no powers of decision, as opposed to expression of opinion, and being composed of representatives of special interests with sharply conflicting points of view their discussions frequently result in agreements to disagree or statements of such blandness as to be devoid of real content. Nevertheless, through their specialised knowledge they can and do keep an eye on the detailed implementation of policies in their areas – a fact which the Commission on occasion finds somewhat irritating.

4.6   The Law and the Council

The ultimate authority underlying the decisions of the Council of Ministers is of course the Treaty of Rome itself. Any such decision is required to specify one or more articles of that Treaty as its basis; this ensures that the Council never seeks to act *ultra vires* – that is, beyond the powers properly given to it by the Treaty. Subject to this requirement, it is a fundamental proposition of the Treaty that any decision of the Council automatically has the force of law, becoming part of the law of each member state and, in the event of any conflict between a Council decision and the existing law of a member state, takes precedence over national law. Naturally, any provision of the Treaty requiring a member country to do, or cease doing, something automatically binds each member country to comply with it – for example, Article 12 which requires member states to refrain from introducing any new customs duties or Article 53 which forbids the introduction of any new restrictions on the establishment within member countries of companies from other member countries.

The bulk of Community law, however, has taken the form of decisions reached by the Council of Ministers or the Commission subsequent to the formation of the Community. These may take one of three forms. The most general is a *Regulation* which is in effect an order addressed to whole categories of person (including the legal person known as a company) in the abstract and which binds all such persons in the Community not only to achieve a specified objective but also to achieve it in a particular way. For example, the celebrated Regulation 1463 of 1970 not only required member states to restrict the working hours of the drivers of road freight vehicles within specified limits but also required this to be enforced by the obligatory installation of the measuring instrument known as the tachograph in all relevant vehicles. Such Regulations automatically become law upon their publication in the Community's official journal and do not require separate national legislation to make them effective.

A second form of decision is the *Directive* which obliges member governments to achieve a specified aim but leaves open the method by which each individual government is to achieve it – for example, Directive 56 of 1987 laying down the maximum noise levels permitted in motor-cycles. These will normally involve the introduction or amendment of national legislation, but are not invalidated by the failure of a member government to introduce or amend such legislation. The third form is in fact known as a *Decision* which usually settles a particular matter of dispute and is addressed to a limited number of identifiable governments, persons or companies. Hence they do not normally form part of general Community law.

Needless to say, over the years there has been a formidable accumulation of laws in these various ways; in 1986 alone, for example, the Council adopted 473 Regulations, 74 Directives and 184 Decisions. It should be added, however, that the only juridical authority for all Community law is the Treaty of Rome. Hence such law relates almost exclusively to industrial and commercial activities: as a general rule it does not attempt to encroach on the criminal law affecting the lives of individual citizens in their home countries.

Nevertheless, the accumulation of Community laws, and the perpetual possibility of conflict between Community and national law, clearly requires a body to interpret that law and to adjudicate on its application in particular cases. This, the European Court of Justice, was created by Articles 164–188 of the Treaty and operates in Luxembourg. With the accession of Portugal and Spain, the total number of judges in the Court was raised to 13 – a President elected by the Court for a term of three years and one judge appointed by each of the member countries for a term of six years; the Court operates in six separate Chambers. In practice, one judge is nominated by each government. If this results in an even number of judges – and hence the possibility of the Court being evenly divided – an extra judge is appointed, in practice from one of the four largest countries in turn. (Such a division of opinion could occur, however, only in the private deliberations of the Court – its published judgements are always declared as being unanimous.) There are also six Advocates-General, an office unknown to British law; their function is to carry out preliminary investigations of cases and to submit 'reasoned opinions' for the consideration of the Court with which the Court may agree or (less commonly) disagree. The Court has a supporting staff of some 530 people.

The volume of business carried out by the Court is a formidable one. On average some 300–400 actions are brought to it each year. Roughly a half of these arise from applications from the courts of member countries seeking interpretation of Community law as applied to actions coming before them or testing the validity of actions taken by Community institutions in their countries. (Equally the Commission can challenge the validity of decisions made by national courts.) The Commission itself is a major initiator of actions when it alleges breaches of the Treaty on the part of enterprises or even member governments. On occasion the Parliament has challenged the Council of Ministers in the Court – as in 1985 when it argued, successfully, that the Council was in breach of its Treaty obligations by failing to institute a Common Transport Policy. One member government may bring an action against another for alleged contravention of Treaty obligations; indeed, an action can be brought by any natural or legal person having due interest in a matter falling within the provisions of the Treaty. Until 1989 a great deal of the time of the Court was taken up by dealing with industrial disputes between Community organisations, principally the Commission, and their employees; between its inception and the end of 1986, in fact, 40 per cent of the actions brought before the Court were of this kind.

The immense volume of work undertaken by the Court has undoubtedly been a major cause of one of the chief criticisms levelled at it – the interminable delays (even by the normal standards of the law) associated with proceedings before it. In mid-1989 there were over 600 cases still pending – more than three times as many as it had actually settled in the course of recent years. In 1975 the Court took, on average, nine months to reach a decision on a case submitted to it; by 1988 the average was over 21 months. Hence the Single European Act sought to alleviate the situation with a provision that the number of judges should be doubled and that a new Court of First Instance should be created to deal with all matters submitted by litigants other than the Commission, the Council of Ministers or member governments. The new Court, comprising one judge nominated by each member country, commenced operations in September 1989. Its primary function is to relieve the main Court from serving as the Community's labour tribunal and finding itself bogged down with relatively minor matters; the main Court itself remains, however, as a court of appeal from the new Court of First Instance.

One other Court established by the Treaty is worthy of mention. Article 206 provided for the establishment of a committee of control composed of 'auditors of indisputable independence' whose function is to ascertain that all revenues and expenditures flowing through the Community's budget 'are lawful and proper and that the financial management is sound'. In 1975 this Audit Board was formally reconstituted as the Court of Auditors. It comprises one member nominated by each member government and a staff of around 300 officials. Its function is to ensure that all Community expenditure is not only legal but is also based on 'sound principles'. Despite its complete lack of power to formulate or administer policy measures, given the magnitude and complexity of Community operations in at least thirteen different currencies and throughout and beyond the Community's borders, it is probably the Community's most necessary, and most overworked, institution.

Further Reading

European Commission, *The Court of Justice of the European Community*, 4th edn (Luxembourg, 1986).

Freestone, D. A. C. and Davidson, J. S., *The Institutional Framework of the European Communities* (London: Croom Helm, 1988).

Lodge, J. (ed.), *Institutions and Policies of the European Community* (London: Frances Pinter, 1983).

Nugent, N., *The Government and Politics of the European Community* (London: Macmillan, 1989).

Sasse, C. (ed.), *Decision-making in the European Community* (London: Praeger, 1977).

Wallace, H. (ed.), *Policy-making in the European Community*, 2nd edn (Chichester: Wiley, 1983).

Institutions: Commission and Parliament 5

5.1 The Collegiate Body

If the Council of Ministers is roughly equivalent to the government of a national state the Commission may be likened to its Civil Service, although it has to be said that in neither case is the analogy exact. Strictly, the Commission is a collegiate body comprising (since 1986) 17 individuals nominated by member governments; by convention, two are nominated by each of the five biggest member countries and one by each of the remaining seven member countries. Commissioners are appointed for a term of four years although they may be reappointed by the nominating government at the end of their term. They are in no sense representatives of the nominating countries; indeed, the Treaty requires that they shall be chosen for their general competence and be 'of indisputable independence'. In practice they have almost always tended to be people with an established political record behind them; less frequently, they have a political future still ahead of them in their own countries. The established convention in the United Kingdom is that one of the two Commissioners will be drawn from each of the two major political parties; this political diversification, however, is by no means invariably the practice with other countries having the power to nominate two Commissioners. Until 1989 the Commissioners were exclusively male but this tradition was broken when both France and Greece nominated women Commissioners, the Prime Minister of Greece, Mr Papandreou, nominating Ms Vasso Papandreou. (The two people were not in fact related.)

The degree to which Commissioners can in fact act as people 'of indisputable independence' of their home governments must be open to some doubt in reality. Their selection is exclusively in the gift of the leader of the political party in office in their home country at the time of the vacancy; the nomination of someone totally out of sympathy with the aims of that party is therefore singularly unlikely. Furthermore, their renomination at the end of a term of office is far from automatic, a fact which can scarcely be totally absent from their minds during their term of office. (The salary of around ECU 120 000 is not ungenerous.) There have been many instances of Commissioners failing to secure reappointment on blatantly political grounds – in some instances (one at least involving the United Kingdom) precisely because their commitment to the concept of the Community was deemed to have taken undue priority over the national interests of their home government.

Since 1976, the European Council first appoints the President of the Commission; on taking office, the Commissioners appoint (currently six) Vice-Presidents from amongst their number. The President and Vice-Presidents each hold office for a (renewable) term of two years. The practice is for the Presidency to move round the member countries in turn and for the nationalities of the Vice-Presidents to be different from that of the President. The precise standing of the President has tended to depend on the occupant of the office; some have seen the appointment to be roughly equivalent to that of the Head of the Community Civil Service with little or no independent policy-making role. Others have sought to elevate the position to one of at least equivalence with membership of the Council of Ministers, a tendency which the Council has not surprisingly tended to discourage. (When the first President of the Commission, Walter Hallstein, sought to receive the Permanent Representatives to the Community after the manner of a head of state receiving Ambassadors he was put firmly in his place by President de Gaulle.)

Presidents of the Commission naturally seek to influence the choice of new Commissioners to fill vacancies but have usually found that their preferences are liable to be overridden by the national governments having the power of nomination. (During the discussions leading to the Single European Act an attempt was made by the Netherlands to require that the President of the Commission should first be nominated by the Council, after consultation with the Parliament, and that the remaining Commissioners should be appointed on the proposal of the President, but this proposal was somehow lost because of an alleged lack of time for debate.) In principle the Commission is a single body acting collectively; when a vote proves necessary each Commissioner has equal voting power. In practice each Commissioner is given responsibility for a specified section of the Community's field of action and has a large degree of independence in the appropriate fields. The importance of these responsibilities naturally varies considerably and the periodic reallocation of them amongst the members of the Commission is an exercise of some political delicacy

In common usage the term 'the Commission' is used to mean not only the collegiate body of 17 Commissioners but its secretariat, a formidable assembly of officials located mostly at Berlaymont in Brussels but also in Luxembourg.

The size of this bureaucracy, drawn from all member countries – around 14 000 – naturally gives rise to sometimes sarcastic comment. In the nature of the organisation, however, a great many of these officials are required simply to deal with the colossal work of translating documents from and into one or other of the Community's nine official languages with a total of 72 potential combinations – a process which involved the translation of some 900 000 pages in 1988. Unfavourable comparisons are frequently made in this context between the Community, which requires nine official languages for twelve member countries, and the United Nations, with 159 members, which manages with only six official languages. The comparison is less than fair; unlike the documentation of the United Nations, regulations and directives issued by the Community become part of, or have to be embodied in, national law so that their precise wording in each national language is imperative.

The EEC secretariat is headed by a Secretary-General and organised into 30 Directorates-General and Services, each concerned with a particular area of Community activity – competition, agriculture, transport and so on. The efficiency of this large organisation must necessarily be less than that of a comparable national body, being composed as it is of officials with vastly different backgrounds, traditions and styles of work, quite apart from the difficulties added by a total of nine official languages. On top of this must be placed the inherent complexity of the flow of detailed rules and regulations pouring continuously out of the Commission's offices. A distinguished literary figure has observed that while the Lord's Prayer contains 56 words, the Ten Commandments 297 and the American Declaration of Independence 300, the EEC directive on the export of duck eggs contains 26 911 words.

5.2 The Tasks of the Commission

What is the job of the Commission – using the word from this point to mean the collegiate Commission itself plus its formidable bureaucratic infrastructure? One of its tasks is certainly that of the conventional civil service – to carry out the detailed implementation of decisions reached by its political master, the Council of Ministers: in the words of the Treaty, 'to exercise the competence conferred on it by the Council for the implementation of the rules laid down by the latter'. Typically this can involve the drafting, scrutiny or issue of upwards of 12 000 Regulations, Directives, Decisions and so on in the course of a year, even though the bulk of the administration of policy – revenue collection, agricultural marketing and the rest – is in fact carried out by the administrations of the member countries themselves.

The Commission also has its own powers of decision, however, apart from those exercised directly by the Council. It has, for example, to handle very considerable flows of revenue and expenditure through funds associated with various policies, such as the European Agricultural Guidance and Guarantee Fund (FEOGA), the European Social Fund and the European Regional Development Fund. It also has very considerable independent powers of investigation and punishment under the provisions of the Community's competition policy.

Thirdly, the Commission is charged with the duty to 'formulate recommendations or opinions in matters which are the subject of this Treaty' – that is, to propose to the Council on policy matters as well as to merely dispose of Council decisions. This clearly distinguishes it from a national civil service which exists (theoretically at any rate) only in order to carry out policy decisions handed down to it. The policy-making role of the Commission is obviously implicit in the different rules governing voting in the Council of Ministers referred to in the preceding chapter. Where a matter under discussion has emanated from the Commission – and therefore presumably embodies a Community view after discussions between the Commission, its advisory committees and the national delegations – the voting powers of the smaller countries are in effect enhanced. The Treaty itself frequently emphasises this power of the Commission; Article 149, for example, provides that if the Council seeks to amend a Commission proposal it can do so only by means of a unanimous vote. The Commission's primary role is indeed to initiate the Community's policies; the Council of Ministers has the power of decision, but it can reach a decision only on a proposal emanating from the Commission.

Fourthly, and perhaps in sharpest contrast with the operation of a national civil service, the Treaty instructs the Commission to 'ensure the application of the provisions of this Treaty and of the provisions enacted by the institutions of the Community in pursuance thereof'; it is, in other words, the guardian of the Treaty and charged with responsibility for investigating breaches of it by anyone – including the Council of Ministers – and if necessary bringing the offenders before the Court of Justice for due retribution.

There is no national body or agency granted this spread of notional powers – to not merely obey the instructions of the governing body, the Council, and administer its policy decisions but also to initiate policy itself and, in addition, to act as the policeman of the Treaty and take legal action against national governments or even the Council itself. As a result there has been a tendency for the Commission to take on a life and character of its own and, given the size and complexity of the organisation, for many of its detailed proposals to go through the decision-making process with many Commissioners, not to say Ministers, knowing little or nothing of their content. Like all bureaucracies, it has spawned a formidable collection of advisory committees and quasi-official administrative bodies operating with a large degree of autonomy; it was estimated in the early 1980s that some 250 such 'Euroquangos' had been brought into existence, including such esoteric organisations as the silkworm section of the Advisory Committee on Flax and Hemp.

Yet in practice the power of the Commission to initiate substantial policy proposals and to continuously impel the Council onwards in the integration process has been constricted to a high degree by the reluctance of the Council to share its policy-making powers, to say nothing of its members' instinctive unwillingness to concede national sovereignty to any substantial extent. The failure of the Community to make any serious progress in major policy areas after the mid-1970s can be attributed to a large extent to this emasculation of the Commission's role as the power-house of policy formulation. The drafters of the Single European Act were conscious of this fact and, in particular, of the provision in the Treaty that the Commission was required to exercise 'the competence conferred on it' by the Council; if (as appeared to happen rather often) the Council refrained from explicitly conferring such executive powers in connection with any of its decisions or, more typically, subjected such executive powers to the approval of advisory or supervisory committees composed of national officials, then the hands of the Commission were effectively tied by the least enthusiastic member of the Council.

The Commission, with the support of the Netherlands, was successful in securing a provision in the Single European Act which provides that, when a decision is reached by the Council of Ministers, the Commission will automatically exercise whatever powers are necessary to implement it, unless the Council votes unanimously to reserve such powers to itself. After the date of implementation of the Single European Act, in other words, the presumption concerning the executive powers of the Commission is in effect reversed. Instead of the Commission being unable to act on any Council decision until and unless specifically empowered to do so, it will henceforth be automatically entitled to act unless the Council specifically withholds its authority in specified respects. On the face of it this should significantly strengthen (and expedite) the Commission's arm; whether it will in fact do so remains to be seen.

5.3 Honourable Members

Being robust democrats, the founding fathers of the Community specified as the first of its institutions an Assembly composed initially of 142 delegates nominated from the Parliaments of the member countries; this was to replace, and build on the foundations of, the supervisory Assembly of the ECSC.

The Treaty of Rome further decreed, however, that the Assembly should proceed to draw up proposals whereby its members would be directly elected, rather than nominated as in the case of the ECSC Assembly, according to a uniform procedure in all member states. At its very first sitting the Assembly expressed its desire to be known as a 'Parliament' rather than an Assembly; the title 'Parliament' (despite its derivation from the French *parlement*, literally meaning 'talking') was presumably thought to carry overtones of authority and independence greater than those associated with a mere 'Assembly'. For more than 20 years it consistently referred to itself as a Parliament, a title also used by the Commission, but the Council of Ministers invariably used the Treaty expression 'Assembly'. By the Single European Act, however, the title of Parliament was at last formally conceded in the amended Treaty.

The movement to direct elections rather than nomination was almost as long in implementation. A system of direct elections to the Parliament was finally agreed in 1976, eighteen years after the creation of the Community, but the ideal of a uniform procedure for these elections proved to be impracticable, given the considerable differences in the electoral systems of the member states. The first direct elections to the European Parliament therefore occurred in 1979 and the members are elected for a period of five years by whatever method is used in each member country for the election of its national legislature. It was also found impracticable for the members to be paid in a uniform manner and they are accordingly rewarded at whatever rate is applicable to the members of their national legislature.

Like members of the Commission, persons elected to the European Parliament are expected to act as members of the Community and are not in any respect the representatives of their own countries or its interests. They are grouped in the Parliament, therefore, according to political rather than national affiliations. Thus the main groups are labelled Socialists, the European People's Party (roughly equivalent to the European Christian Democrats), the European Democratic Group (in which reside all of the Conservative members from the United Kingdom), Communist and Allies and the Liberal, Democratic and Reformist Group. As may be seen from Table 5.1, the size of national representation in the Parliament is roughly in accordance with the population of member countries but, as with voting power in the Council of Ministers, the smaller countries are in fact given a disproportionate representation.

The Parliament elects its own President and a total of 13 Vice-Presidents, typically for a (renewable) term of two years; eight of this total of 14 are drawn from the four largest countries. Again by convention the office of President – the official spokesman for the Parliament and therefore a person of some consequence – is taken in turn by MEPs from different member countries. Unlike the Council of Ministers, with its rather arcane rules of voting, the Parliament normally acts by simple absolute majority voting. Much of its work is in fact carried out by one or another of around 20 committees specialising in areas ranging from budgetary control to women's rights; in general, each committee concerns itself with the work of one of the Commission's directorates.

Once a month, however, it meets in plenary session for about a week at a time. The location of this meeting has been a matter of dispute for many years. In 1965 the Council of Ministers resolved that the Secretariat of the Parliament, consisting of around 3000 officials, should remain in Luxembourg but on the insistence of France (which regarded it as only proper that at least one of the Community institutions should be located in French territory) plenary sessions were held in alternate months in the Council of Europe Assembly building in

Table 5.1
The European Parliament, 1958–89

Country	Total number of MEPs					Per million population, 1989
(1)	1958–72 (2)	1973–8 (3)	1979–80 (4)	1981–5 (5)	1986 on (6)	(7)
Belgium	14	14	24	24	24	2.4
Denmark	—	10	16	16	16	3.1
France	36	36	81	81	81	1.4
Germany	36	36	81	81	81	1.3
Greece	—	—	—	24	24	2.4
Ireland	—	10	15	15	15	4.2
Italy	36	36	81	81	81	1.4
Luxembourg	6	6	6	6	6	16.2
Netherlands	14	14	25	25	25	1.7
Portugal	—	—	—	—	24	2.3
Spain	—	—	—	—	60	1.5
United Kingdom	—	36	81	81	81	1.4
Total MEPs	142	198	410	434	518	1.6

Strasbourg rather than in Luxembourg. (This was not merely a matter of national pride; each Parliamentary session is estimated to attract at least 2000 observers, journalists and so on mostly financed by fairly generous expense accounts.) This peripatetic existence was so to some degree simplified when, with the accession of Greece in 1981, the Luxembourg building could no longer contain all the MEPs and the Parliament resolved that its future sessions should be held only in Strasbourg and that its committee meetings (around 400 of them each year) should be conducted in Brussels, the main home of the Commission. The Court of Justice upheld the claim of the Grand Duchy of Luxembourg, however, that the 1965 decision of the Council of Ministers made it unlawful for the permanent home of the Secretariat to be anywhere other than in Luxembourg.

A ludicrous system therefore exists whereby the business of the Parliament is conducted partly in Strasbourg and partly in Brussels with the aid of a secretariat domiciled in Luxembourg. This involves the frequent transportation of some 50 tons of documents, a very considerable bill for travel and accommodation expenses and manifest delay and inefficiency in the work of all concerned. The Parliament's President estimated in the mid-1980s that this three-way split of business was costing the Community's taxpayers something over ECU 60 million every year. An attempt in 1987 to obtain agreement on a new permanent building for the Parliament and its secretariat in Brussels was however blocked by France; the Prime Minister of France, M. Chirac, firmly declared in September of that year that 'Strasbourg is not negotiable. . . . The French government will never back down on the issue'.

5.4 The Powers of Parliament

According to the Treaty of Rome the Parliament 'shall exercise the powers of deliberation and of control which are conferred upon it by this Treaty'. In fact the Treaty endowed the Parliament with a great deal by way of powers of deliberation but precious little by way of powers of control. It has, first, the right under 17 separate Articles of the Treaty to be consulted on most important matters coming before the Council of Ministers. This takes the form of an entitlement to examine any proposals being drawn up by the Commission and to comment on them before they are submitted to the Council and, thereafter, to propose amendments to decisions reached by the Council on them. The Treaty did no more, however, than to require the Council to take these proposed amendments into due consideration; there was no obligation on the Council to accept them. On the other hand, the Court of Justice ruled in 1970 that, where the Treaty required the Council of Ministers to seek the opinion of the Parliament on any decision, that decision could not become valid until Parliament had in fact expressed its opinion, thus giving the Parliament a formidable delaying power.

Secondly, the Treaty empowered the Parliament to address written or oral questions to the Commission or (by grace and favour rather than of right) to the Council of Ministers. This privilege came greatly into favour especially after the appearance of British MEPs in the Parliament; up to 5000 oral or written questions are nowadays tabled every year. How effective a weapon this is must remain a matter of some doubt. Parliamentary Questions in a national legislature are typically a means whereby individual members may gain publicity through unearthing hitherto unknown facts or otherwise embarrassing their political opponents; the limited interest shown by the general public in the proceedings of the European Parliament must seriously reduce the value of its questioning process in this regard.

Thirdly, the Treaty did give Parliament the specific power to pass a motion of censure on the Commission (i.e. the collegiate body) *collectively* – i.e. not on any individual Commissioner. If such a motion is adopted by a two-thirds majority of the total votes cast – provided that this represents a majority of all MEPs – the members of the Commission are then required to resign their office in a body. Since the Parliament has no power whatever to appoint new Commissioners (a power exclusively reserved to the governments of member states) this drastic measure is scarcely of practical value. Indeed, even if it were successfully adopted, the ousted Commission could be immediately reappointed by the

Council of Ministers. Two such motions have in fact been discussed in the Parliament: neither attracted anything approaching the requisite majority. In reality events were to be such as to make the Parliament and Commission allies in their common struggle with the Council of Ministers, rather than opponents threatening one another with dismissal.

Finally, the provisions governing the preparation and approval of the annual Community budget provided that when the Council had completed its draft budget for the following year it should be transmitted to the Parliament which was then entitled to propose amendments to it. If this occurred, however, the Council was then merely required to discuss the matter with the Commission and having done so could proceed to finally adopt the budget by means of a qualified majority vote. The real budgetary powers of Parliament, in other words, were effectively zero. This situation was somewhat modified when the Council agreed in 1969 to move to a system of 'own resources' as opposed to reliance on individual national contributions; this system was formally adopted in a treaty signed in Luxembourg in 1970 which gave the Parliament relatively minor but none the less real power over part of the budget. The details of these arrangements are best left to Chapter 21 which deals with the Community's budget; in essence it was agreed that the expenditures proposed in the budget for any year should be divided into 'compulsory' and 'non-compulsory' items and that the Parliament would have the power to increase the latter by a maximum laid down by a rather complex formula. What it meant in practice was that the Parliament could increase budget expenditures by a total amounting to between 1 per cent and 2 per cent of the whole budget. It was power of a sort but manifestly fell far short of that real financial control on which the authority of national legislatures ultimately rests. A Budgetary Powers Treaty signed in Brussels in 1975, however, extended the powers of Parliament to include the right to reject the Budget in its entirety.

It was hardly surprising that when the first directly-elected Parliament assembled in 1979 there was acute dissatisfaction amongst the members with their apparent lack of real legislative power; a great deal of effort was therefore expended on ensuring that something was done about it in the proposals which ultimately became the Single European Act. The proponents of an increased role for the Parliament sought to secure agreement to a revision of the Treaty providing that Parliament would be given the right to a 'second reading' of any decisions of the Council, in addition to that of a 'first reading' at the proposal stage, and that any amendments suggested by the Parliament – or, indeed, its outright rejection of a decision – would have to stand unless positively rejected by the Council. Such a rejection would require a qualified majority vote in the Council if the Parliamentary amendments were not supported by the Commission but a unanimous vote if they were. In principle this would have raised the profile of the Parliament very considerably; since its proposals are more often than not supported by the Commission – if indeed they do not actually embody Commission proposals – the implication is that Parliamentary amendments would have to be accepted unless every single member of the Council of Ministers was opposed to them, a somewhat improbable state of affairs.

Not surprisingly this proposed extension of the powers of Parliament was unacceptable to some member governments – most conspicuously those of Denmark and the United Kingdom – and in the final version of the Single European Act the revised 'co-operation procedure' (as it was discreetly labelled) was adopted only for decisions taken by the Council by a qualified majority on matters related to the Community's internal market, social policy, economic and social cohesion (a characteristically vague expression) and the Community's research programme. It was however strengthened by the provision that Parliamentary amendments (or rejection) would have to stand unless modified by the Council of Ministers within three months of the second reading; this covered the possibility that the Council might dispose of Parliamentary amendments by simply ignoring them indefinitely. The Parliament was also given a real 'constitutional' power in that the Council of Ministers may now adopt a decision under Articles 237 and 238 – providing for the admission of new members to the Community and for agreements with non-member countries respectively – only with the approval of the Parliament and not (as in the 1957 Treaty) after merely consulting it.

How far the Single European Act increased the real, as opposed to the theoretical, power of the Parliament is open to some debate. Certainly in alliance with the Commission and at least one member government the Parliament can now force the Council to accept amendments or abandon a proposal altogether, but given the adoption of qualified majority voting this end could have been achieved in any event at the first reading stage. The power to reject a Council proposal outright is probably more apparent than real; the usual situation is that Council proposals do not go far enough for the Parliament's liking, rather than going too far, and to reject a proposal altogether on this ground would be somewhat quixotic. The power to veto new members or association agreements with non-members is real enough but these are not matters which recur frequently. And, of course, behind all the scaffolding of Parliamentary consultation remains the undefined but threatening position of the Luxembourg Compromise.

Whatever may be written into however many Treaties, two inescapable facts of reality restrict the real power of the Parliament to the barest minimum. The first is that it has no revenue-raising powers and throughout political history the authority of any legislature has been a direct function of its powers of taxation. In the end the people who hold the moneybags hold the power of decision; and there is no possibility in the foreseeable future that the European Parliament will find itself given powers to levy its own taxes on the Community. The second is that any increase in the power given to the European Parliament, fiscal or otherwise, is necessarily a reduction in the corresponding power currently enjoyed by national legislatures; an inescapable conflict of interest therefore arises between national and European Parliaments. Since the approval of the former is necessary for any amendment to the Treaty, the possibility of this conflict being resolved is not great. The governments of both France and the United Kingdom, for this very reason, agreed to accept direct elections to the European Parliament only on the understanding that the powers of the European Parliament remained substantially unchanged.

The problem is inherent in the present standing of the Community. In its structure it is considerably more than a mere machine for facilitating inter-governmental co-operation but it is even more considerably short of a genuine Federation with sovereign power resting in the hands of a central Federal government. Lincoln remarked that a nation could not stand half-slave, half-free; for how long the Community can remain half-unitary, half-Federal is the great question which remains unanswered.

Further Reading

European Commission, *The European Commission and the administration of the Community* (Luxembourg: Commission of the European Communities, 1989).

Fitzmaurice, J., *The European Parliament* (London: Saxon House, 1978).

Freestone, D. A. C. and Davidson, J. S., *The Institutional Framework of the European Communities* (London: Croom Helm, 1988).

Herman, V. and Lodge, J., *The European Parliament and the European Community* (London: Macmillan, 1978).

Lodge, J. (ed.), *Institutions and Policies of the European Community* (London: Frances Pinter, 1983).

Palmer, J., *Trading Places* (London: Century Hutchinson, 1988).

Palmer, M., *The European Parliament* (London: Pergamon Press, 1981).

Pryce, R. (ed.), *The Dynamics of European Union* (London: Croom Helm, 1987).

Scaling, P., *The European Parliament* (London: Aldwych Press, 1980).

Part II

The Theory of Economic Integration

The Economics of Integration 6

6.1 What is Economic Integration?

The subsection of economic analysis known as the theory of international economic integration is a relatively new one; according to one authority there is no trace of the use of the expression prior to 1942. It is now widely understood as being concerned with the effects of agreed arrangements between two or more sovereign states as a result of which economic transactions between them are conducted on a basis more favourable to the other participants than that applicable to countries outside the agreement. Agreements of this kind can be one of five broad types involving an ascending order of degrees of integration between the participants.

The lowest level of integration is that of a *preferential tariff* in which the participating countries – referred to for simplicity from this point as the 'members' – agree to levy a lower rate of tax on imports from each other than that levied on similar imports emanating from non-member countries; the degree of preference so extended may vary from one product, or one product-group, to another. Such an arrangement is typical of countries having some special political relationship with each other. An example was the Imperial Preference system applicable throughout the British Commonwealth from 1932 until UK accession to the Community in 1973; under this arrangement, exports from Commonwealth countries enjoyed favourable tariff treatment in the UK (often amounting to exemption from tariffs altogether) while UK exports enjoyed similarly favourable treatment in Commonwealth countries.

A second, and higher, form of integration represents a limiting case of the preferential tariff in that *all* imports from member countries enter at a zero tariff while comparable imports from non-member countries are subject to a tariff barrier; this is the *free trade area*. The agreement may extend only over a

55

specified range of goods, as was the case with the European Free Trade Area (EFTA) mentioned in an earlier chapter; this related only to trade in industrial products. While free trade treatment is extended to the other member countries, each participant remains free to adopt whatever tariff policy it chooses towards non-member countries so that no loss of sovereign power is involved. It follows that quite complicated arrangements may have to be set up to ensure that national tariff barriers are not evaded through artificial trade switching – the problem of origin. Suppose that country A has a general tariff of 20 per cent on a certain category of imports from the rest of the world, C, while country B operates a tariff of only 10 per cent. If A and B now enter into a free trade agreement there is a danger that C will switch its exports from A to agents in B, thus encountering the low tariff barrier; the agents then re-export them to A under the free trade arrangements. The power of A to operate an independent tariff regime with C would therefore be lost. Hence it is usual for such arrangements to incorporate provisions whereby only products genuinely originating in the partner country are allowed duty-free access; unfortunately, the administration of these provisions may seriously compromise the attainment of genuine free trade between the member countries.

The next higher level of integration, however, does involve the genuine sacrifice of some degree of control over their own affairs on the part of the member coutries; this is the *customs union*. A customs union involves not only completely free trade in all products between the members but also the application of a commonly-agreed tariff on all imports of a specified product from the rest of the world. In principle, such a system disposes of the problem of origin; imports from the rest of the world, C, will experience the same tariff treatment whichever member country they enter so that artificial diversion of exports from A to B would serve no purpose whatever. The member countries, A and B, have however necessarily lost some of their sovereign power in two important respects. In the first place, since a *common* external tariff now exists for trade with C, neither A nor B is any longer able to decide its tariff policy with regard to C independently. The member countries must set up some supranational organisation between them to exercise this power jointly. Secondly, since goods imported into A may be exported freely to B without passing through any tariff barriers, the tariff revenues collected by A may in fact be arising from goods which are destined to be sold eventually in B, so that it is the citizens of B who will in fact be the final payers of the tax. Similar considerations apply to tariff revenues collected in B on goods ultimately sold in A. The only solution is that all tariff revenues have to become common property, accruing to some joint organisation and being used or shared out according to some agreed set of rules.

The fourth level of integration carriers this logic one step further and leads to the creation of a *common market*. This goes further than a customs union in two fundamental respects. First, free trade between the member countries is ensured not only by the abolition of tariffs on trade between them but also by the removal of all other obstacles – non-tariff barriers (NTBs) – to the free exchange of goods and services; these can take the form of licences, quotas, foreign exchange controls, customs procedures, regulations concerned with safety, health or the environment and indirect taxes other than tariffs. Secondly, a common market implies the complete integration of what had previously been separate markets in factors of production as well as those in goods and services; this implies the complete freedom of movement of labour between member countries, the right of enterprises domiciled in A to establish themselves in B, and the abolition of all restrictions on the transfer of capital from one member country to another.

The fifth, and ultimate, level of economic integration is achieved by a full *economic union*. (Many would argue, plausibly, that the achievement of the fourth level must automatically and necessarily lead to the fifth.) An economic union implies a high degree of integration amongst the member countries of policies other than those involving markets in goods and factors of production, particularly monetary and fiscal policies which affect the entire macroeconomic scene in the countries concerned. When this is achieved the member countries have in fact ceased to be independent economic units at all and it is almost inconceivable that they could remain separate political entities either. The United States is a collection of separate states having a considerable degree of independence in many respects but the States share a single monetary system and are subservient to a federal government which has an overwhelming dominance over public revenues and expenditure. There is no way, therefore, in which an individual state can determine its own rate of inflation, foreign exchange rate or rate of economic growth. The several states form a single economic union.

The theory of international economic integration therefore has a very broad scope; it is concerned with any process by which hitherto separate economies are combined into a single, larger region. Such a process may involve *negative* measures of integration – i.e. measures which involve the removal of obstacles to economic exchanges between countries – or *positive* measures which require the creation of new institutions, or the modification of existing institutions, and the appropriation of resources in 'order to achieve specified ends. Since the Community is still far removed from the stage of being a full economic union it will be sufficient for most of the purposes of this book to confine the discussion to the case of a customs union, although at a later stage the wider implications of monetary union must necessarily be investigated.

6.2 The Ideal World of Free Trade

Given its assumptions, the logic of orthodox microeconomic analysis leads inescapably to the conclusion that any outside interference in the free play of market forces must in itself reduce economic welfare. The conclusion is a very familiar one but it may be as well to summarise the standard argument. Let the line AD in Figure 6.1 represent the demand schedule for a particular product; the assumption is that the height of this line at any point reflects the valuation placed on each unit (its marginal utility) by the consumer concerned. Again, given all the standard assumptions of a world of perfect competition the line SS', the supply curve, reflects the average (and marginal) cost of producing each unit of the product. Given a free market, with no monopoly, no restrictions on entry into the industry, no artificial distortions through advertising and so on, market price will settle at $0S$ ($= BQ_1$) at which the cost of the last unit sold just equals the price the consumer is willing to pay for it. At this point, the total satisfaction derived by consumers from this product is given by the area $A0Q_1B$ while the total satisfaction sacrificed by buying it (i.e. the total amount spent on it by consumers) is given by $OSBQ_1$. The difference between this gain and loss – the triangle ASB – measures total *consumers' surplus*, the net gain in welfare arising from the fact that all but the final unit is available to consumers at a price less than that which they would in fact have been willing to pay for it.

Let a tax SS_1 – any tax, including (but not necessarily only) an import duty – be imposed on the product so that the price rises to $0S_1$ and the quantity

---

FIGURE 6.1
The Deadweight Loss of Tax

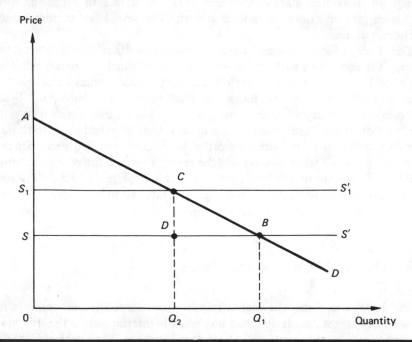

purchased falls to $0Q_2$. The triangle measuring consumers' surplus thus falls to AS_1C and consumers' welfare has thus fallen by an amount represented by the area SS_1CB. Of this, the rectangle SS_1CD is offset by the increase in the government's tax revenue – a tax of SS_1 on the quantity $0Q_2$ – so that the government can compensate consumers for their loss by some appropriate policy measure. The remaining area, triangle CDB, however, is a loss by consumers which is not offset by a gain elsewhere in the economy. It is the deadweight loss of welfare caused by the intervention of the taxing authorities in the market for this product. (It will be realised, of course, that there will be distributional changes in the system if the government spends the tax proceeds on a group of citizens other than those who pay the taxes; as a result nothing can be said about the overall effects on welfare generally. But this is another, much more complicated story.)

If the imposition of indirect taxes, including import duties, necessarily reduces economic welfare in the country concerned, it therefore follows logically that completely free international trade would achieve the maximum possible welfare; it also appears to follow logically that if import duties are in existence in the first place, any abolition of them – even if only on imports from *some* countries rather than all – must necessarily increase welfare. A customs union does precisely that; it does not create a situation of completely free international trade but it is a move towards it. Any move *towards* an ideal which maximises welfare must surely in itself increase welfare.

This rather comfortable conclusion was destroyed in 1950 in a book entitled *The Customs Union Issue* by a distinguished American economist, Jacob Viner; the book was to form the foundation for a more general set of propositions known as 'theory of the second best'. The latter demonstrates that, while a certain situation may be ideal from an economic point of view, a policy measure which moves a system only *partly* towards that ideal situation, and not wholly to it, may reduce welfare rather than increase it. In the particular case of a customs union, Viner was able to show that while entry into a customs union may raise a country's economic welfare it may also reduce it. The reasoning behind this result will be investigated in the next chapter. Before proceeding to this, however, it is necessary to understand some of the reservations which have to be borne in mind concerning the power of microeconomic theory in the context of any customs union.

6.3 The Boundaries of Economic Analysis

As will be seen in due course, the Vinerian argument is most conveniently conducted through partial equilibrium analysis – that is to say, the effects of entry into a customs union are examined in the context of a market for one particular product, as in the example of Figure 6.1 above. Conclusions concerning this single market are then assumed to hold for all markets and are thus generalised to the whole economy. A critical requirement of such analysis is the assumption that the market under investigation is sufficiently small in relation to the rest of the economy for it to be reasonable to neglect the repercussions of changes in it on the markets for other products. The analysis proceeds on the assumption, in other words, that the prices of all other products remain the same; this is implicit in the use of a demand schedule which relates the quantity purchased of a product solely to the price of that product and nothing else.

Now in the real world this is obviously not the case. If the price of fuel oil is raised for any reason, for example, some demand for oil-fired heating systems will be switched to electricity-based systems – the demand for electricity, in other words, is dependent on the price of oil as well as the price of electricity itself. The loss of consumers' surplus in the market for oil may therefore be offset partly or wholly by an increase in the consumers' surplus in the market for electricity, so that conclusions based only on an examination of the market for fuel oil may prove to be invalid. The situation of a customs union is complicated even further by the fact that tariff changes will be occurring for a whole range of products, to different degrees and even in different directions, and not merely for one product in isolation. These problems can in fact be overcome by the techniques of general equilibrium analysis, in which the repercussions in all markets are considered simultaneously; unfortunately such analysis involves the use of algebra or geometry of such a high degree of complexity that its use in this book would almost certainly be less than helpful. It will simply have to be stated baldly, therefore, that it can be shown that the conclusions arrived at with the aid of simple partial equilibrium analysis are in general validated by the much more rigorous tools of general equilibrium analysis.

The Viner arguments concerning customs unions must be treated with caution, however, for much more compelling reasons. First, as will be seen, like all microeconomic analysis it is concerned with the impact of a policy change – in this case, tariff changes – on the allocation of resources between different products and different markets. It addresses itself solely to the criterion of economic efficiency. Subsequent reflection has established, however, that a customs union may, and almost certainly will, have effects in areas of economic policy other than that of efficient resource allocation; it may influence the overall level of output and employment, the rate of economic growth and the distribution of income both within and between member countries, all of which are largely pushed to one side or totally ignored by the assumptions underlying the perfectly-competitive world of the textbooks. The problem is not so much that gains or losses under the heading of resource allocation may be offset or augmented by gains and losses in these other areas of economic policy. It is rather that an evaluation of the trade-offs between them is beyond the scope and competence of economics; whether a measured gain in the efficiency of resource allocation is or is not more than offset by an accompanying change in the distribution of income, for example, is simply not an economic question: it is a political or ethical matter on which economists have (or at least should have) nothing to say.

Secondly, even within the narrowly-defined area of resource allocation the truth of the matter is that the measurement of the effects of a customs union is an exceedingly difficult – some would say an impossible – task. Such effects are traditionally classified as either static or dynamic. By static effects are meant those which do not involve any changes in the underlying conditions of production and demand and have a once-and-for-all impact. By dynamic effects are meant precisely such changes induced by the impact of increased competition, technological advance and so on; of their nature they persist through time, rather than affecting the economy on one occasion only. As will be seen in a later chapter, several researchers have made valiant attempts to measure the static changes induced by the EEC with varying degrees of plausibility; the measurement of its dynamic effects, however, has proved nearly impossible. Any predictions of economic theory which cannot be tested empirically must therefore be treated as having strictly limited usefulness.

Finally, it has to be remembered that a customs union can never be treated as a purely economic matter; indeed, Viner himself concluded that such an arrangement was inherently a political matter and could never be justified on strictly economic grounds. (As will be seen in due course, subsequent analysis has shown that this conclusion was not entirely well-founded.) Even a nodding acquaintance with the background to the European Community is sufficient to establish the fact that the primary motivation behind its formation was political rather than economic and in the view of many this remains the case today. The opening words of the Treaty of Rome declare that its intention is 'to establish the foundations of an ever closer union among the European peoples'; only *after* this does there occur a reference to 'economic and social progress'. A judgement on the value or otherwise of membership of a customs union is therefore in the final resort totally beyond the competence of economics; nothing in the subject even begins to answer the question of whether a small diminution in the likelihood of war is or is not worth a large contribution to the Community budget. This by no means renders economics irrelevant or useless. Its function is to predict (and ideally quantify) consequences which can then form the basis for what will hopefully be better-informed judgements on the part of those people charged with the responsibility of making them.

6.4 Settling for Second-best

There is one final problem in the strictly economic field. The Viner verdict referred to above – that a customs union could only be an essentially political arrangement – rested on the fact that, given its assumptions, orthodox microeconomic analysis leads inescapably to the conclusion that completely free international trade is always the optimum situation. Any benefit which a country derives from membership of a customs union will always be smaller than the benefits which it would enjoy by going for the complete abolition of all tariff and non-tariff barriers to imports rather than by eliminating those against a limited number of countries. Why then should any country choose to opt for the second-best solution of a customs union rather than the first-best solution of completely free trade?

The answer may of course lie in political considerations, as mentioned above. Even apart from these, however, there may be practical reasons why the first-best solution (in this case completely free trade) is simply not feasible so that countries have to settle for the second-best. These practical considerations may themselves have a political basis; for example, trade with certain countries may be banned, as with embargoes placed against the exports of countries whose political regimes meet with disapproval. Trade in certain products may be discouraged on grounds of defence (i.e. an unwillingness to strengthen the armoury of potential or actual enemies) or for social reasons, as in the case of drugs.

From a strictly economic point of view, the first-best solution may be ruled out quite simply on the grounds that its establishment would involve costs in excess of the admitted benefits. Ideally, for example, the taxation imposed on any citizen should be calculated according to the precise circumstances of each individual in particular, rather than according to broad rules applying to large groups of individuals. The costs of creating a separate tax regime for every individual citizen, however, would almost certainly far exceed any foreseeable gains from moving away from a rough-and-ready-justice system. In the context of international trade, the costs in question are those of the adjustment process generated by tariff reductions. In the world of the classical textbooks such costs are simply assumed away; all factors of production, including labour, are completely informed and completely mobile; full employment exists continually; calculation and economic rationality rule everywhere. The world of reality is rather different. To abolish a tariff is to invite the contraction, or even destruction, of less efficient domestic enterprises; only in the textbooks will this be attained without the infliction of painful adjustment burdens somewhere. To consider such an action when a corresponding concession is being offered by a customs union partner is one thing; to undertake it unilaterally by adopting a policy of completely free trade is quite another. It is possible to cope with the adjustments implied by removing barriers to imports from a small number of countries of roughly equal competitiveness; the consequences of doing the same for every country in the world could well be too great for reasonable people to contemplate.

Ideal solutions, in other words, belong to ideal worlds. In the world of reality it is frequently sensible – sometimes totally unavoidable – to settle for something which is short of the ideal but an improvement on what currently exists. The object of the chapters which follow is to examine the circumstances under which membership of a customs union would constitute such an improvement from a strictly economic point of view.

Further Reading

El-Agraa, A. M. and Jones, A. J., *The Theory of Customs Unions* (Deddington: Philip Allan, 1980).

Robson, P., *The Economics of International Integration*, 2nd edn (London: Allen & Unwin, 1984).

factors of production (handwritten annotation in left margin)

Trade Creation and Trade Diversion 7

7.1 Definitions and Assumptions

Let it be supposed that country A is contemplating membership of a customs union with another group of countries represented, for the sake of simplicity, as Country B. The consequences of membership would be, first, that all tariffs will be removed on trade between A and B; secondly, A and B will adopt a common external tariff on imports from the rest of the world, the latter, again for the sake of simplicity, being denoted as Country C; finally, any revenues arising from the application of that tariff will become the common property of A and B together, the ultimate disposal of those revenues being a matter to be agreed between them. (It is assumed that membership will involve some change, somewhere, in the level and pattern of the previous internal or external tariff levels; if no such change occurs then there will be no effects on international trade.) The object of the analysis is to examine the implications of membership of such a customs union for the economic welfare of the members of the union – both individually and collectively – and for that of the rest of the world. For the time being it will be concerned only with static effects – that is, no changes are assumed in the underlying conditions of demand or supply.

In all economic analysis certain simplifying assumptions must be made at the outset; the world of reality is far too complex for any alternative procedure to be feasible. In the analysis which follows, for example, it is assumed that the costs of transporting goods and services between the countries concerned are small enough to be neglected; it is also assumed that the only impediment to international trade takes the form of import taxes, tariffs, of a fixed value per unit. Neither of these assumptions is particularly realistic but in fact their removal would add considerably to the complications of exposition without significantly affecting the major conclusions.

64

Two other assumptions underlying the traditional microeconomic analysis of customs unions are however of quite crucial importance. These are, first, that perfect competition prevails within the member countries and in international trade and, second, that the factors of production, labour and capital, are completely mobile within each member country but not between them.

These two assumptions are of far-reaching significance. The first implies that every price in every market, including that for labour, is precisely equal to the marginal cost of the last unit bought or sold. Hence the cost of production of any product is taken to be equal to its opportunity cost – that is, the value of output which could have been produced in some alternative activity had the resources in question not been absorbed in whatever is their current use. The second, that of complete mobility, implies a constant state of full employment of labour and capital. This follows necessarily from the assumption that the current price paid to factors of production – the wage in the case of labour – is equal to what that factor could be earning elsewhere. If it is released from the production of one commodity, therefore, each factor will immediately proceed to its alternative occupation and earn precisely as much as before. In this imaginary frictionless, timeless but completely rational world, no productive resources can be consigned to idleness because alternative, and equally rewarding, occupations always exist. That both assumptions are of questionable validity (except perhaps in the famous long run of orthodox theory) hardly requires stress.

One further assumption will be made about the proposed customs union for the time being. This is that the assumption of perfect competition – the world of a very large number of separate sellers and an equally large number of separate buyers – extends to its position in world international trade. That is to say, the customs union, regarded as a single buyer in world markets, is a sufficiently small element in those markets to prevent any changes in its demand for imports from affecting their world prices. In other words, the supply curve of imports from the rest of the world, C, can be treated as a horizontal line, the world price remaining unchanged whatever quantities are imported by A and B together. The consequences of removing this assumption will be explored at a later stage.

The core of Viner's analysis involves the three concepts of *trade creation, trade diversion* and *trade suppression*, the word 'trade' in this context being a shorthand expression for international trade. By trade creation is meant a process through which the total volume of trade in a given product, or products in aggregate, is increased through the establishment of a customs union. Such a development could be the result of either of two separate causes or from both of them operating simultaneously. The first is known as the *consumption effect* – that is, an increase in the total consumption of a product as a result of a fall in its domestic market price; consumers are stimulated by the price reduction to substitute the product concerned for other products which have now become relatively expensive. The second is known as the *production effect* – the displacement of high-cost domestic production by cheaper imports from abroad. Such displacement, it will be recalled, merely means that the resources in question are diverted to production of equal value elsewhere in the economy.

By trade diversion, secondly, is meant the process whereby entry into a customs union results in a displacement of a given volume of Country A's imports which previously came from the rest of the world, C, by imports from the partner country, B. Like trade creation, this can have effects on both domestic consumption and domestic production. If the imports from the partner country B are sold in A at a higher price than the previous imports from C, consumption in A will be switched to other substitutes which were not previously preferred. Equally, the increase in the domestic price will stimulate an increase in higher-cost production within A. Opposite effects would obviously follow if the diversion of imports results in a lower domestic price than before. Finally, trade suppression refers to the possibility that as the result of entry into a customs union the total volume of trade is smaller than before, once again leading to both consumption and production effects within the members of the customs union.

The range of the possible situations in which a customs union may be formed is literally infinite. Three possible types of case will therefore be examined in what follows; between them they illustrate more or less all the types of consequence which may be experienced. The first refers to a situation in which before the formation of the union no international trade whatever existed in the (specimen) product concerned. The second involves a situation in which trade was taking place but leaves the home country, A, with a lower external tariff on imports from C than before. The third involves the opposite situation in which the union results in A having a higher tariff on imports from C than before entry into the union.

7.2 The No-trade Case

Let the initial situation of the market for some product in the two prospective union partners, A and B, be that represented in Figure 7.1. Both have domestic industries capable of manufacturing the product at the costs shown in the supply curves S_a and S_b respectively. The product can be imported from the rest of the world, C, at the constant price denoted by S_c; quite obviously neither domestic industry could survive if imports were allowed in freely from C. The governments of A and B, determined to keep their domestic industries in business, therefore impose a tariff on all imports of such a height as to ensure that domestic demand is met entirely from domestic production. In A this involves a tariff of SP_{0a} so that the domestic price, P_{0a} is sufficient to permit the domestic industry to meet internal demand fully. After having the tariff imposed on them, exporters in C cannot undercut A's producers; obviously potential exporters in B are even less competitive when the tariff is imposed on their

FIGURE 7.1
A No-trade Pre-entry Customs Union

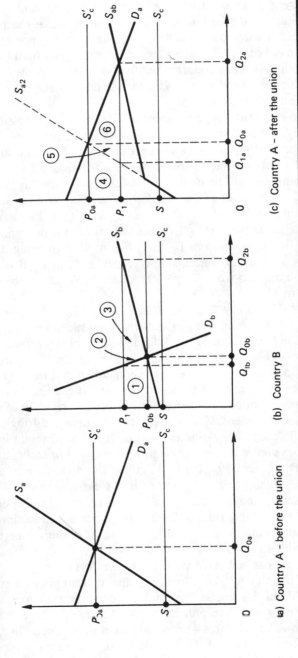

(a) Country A – before the union

(b) Country B

(c) Country A – after the union

products. There would be no point in country A trying to raise the domestic price above this level through a higher tariff; the demand at a higher price would be insufficient to absorb the domestic output which would be forthcoming at that price and the excess supply would simply force the price down again. Similarly, in country B a tariff SP_{0b} is applied to all imports; this is lower than the tariff in A because B, while a less efficient supplier than C, is somewhat less inefficient than A. Each country therefore satisfies its domestic demand entirely through domestic production and no trade takes place either between them or with the rest of the world, C.

Suppose now that the government of B, perceiving a possible export market in A if only A's tariff wall could be demolished, approaches the government of A with a proposal that the two countries should form a customs union. They agree that tariffs on trade between them will be abolished and that both will adopt a common tariff on imports from C of such a level as to ensure that C will continue to be shut out of their markets. The effective domestic supply curve of the product in A is now that shown as S_{ab} in Figure 7.1(c); once the domestic price in A rises above that in B, domestic output in A is augmented by what are now duty-free imports from B. The price needed to bring demand in A into equality with this augmented supply curve is P_1; a tariff of SP_1 is therefore imposed on imports from C by both A and B. What are the consequences for each country?

The case of country B is shown in Figure 7.1(b). The rise in the tariff has permitted producers in B to raise their domestic price to P_1; as a result the consumers in B are robbed of the consumers' surplus represented by areas 1 and 2. Their loss is however much more than offset by the gains enjoyed by the producers in B. The area 1 is a loss to consumers but represents a higher profit to producers since each item they are now selling domestically, $0Q_{1b}$, is being sold at a higher price than before. It is a simple transfer of income within B which the government, if it wished, could correct through appropriate tax measures. The area 2 is a different matter; it is a deadweight loss of consumers' surplus. However, duty-free access to A at the new price P_1 allows producers in B to export a quantity $Q_{1b}Q_{2b}$ to A, giving them excess profits denoted by the area above the cost line, S_b. Country B has clearly profited from the arrangement; consumers may have lost area 2 – the (negative) consumption effect – but producers have gained areas $2+3$, the positive production effect whereby resources are being used to produce output of higher value than would have been available to them elsewhere. The producers could compensate consumers fully for their loss and still have extra profits left over.

What of country A? The reduction of the internal price from P_{0a} to P_1 has led to a considerable increase in domestic consumption and a corresponding increase in consumers' surplus shown by the area $4+5+6$. Not all of this is a net gain, however. The area 4 previously went to producers in A as excess profit, being revenues in excess of the costs denoted by the supply curve S_a; once again it is a simple redistribution of income which could be reversed if the government so chose. Areas 5 and 6, on the other hand, are clear gains to country A. Area 5 is the production effect; domestic production has been reduced by the fall in price from Q_{0a} to Q_{1a}, but the goods to which that output corresponded, are now being imported at a cost to A of only P_1 each; previously they were produced by domestic resources which, according to the supply curve S_a, can now be switched to alternative production having a value higher than this amounting to the area 5. The area 6, the consumption effect, is equally a clear gain. Because of the fall in the domestic price, consumers are able to purchase an extra $Q_{0a}Q_{2a}$ units at the price P_1 which yields them a net gain of area 6 in satisfaction.

This, then, is a pure trade-creating customs union. No trade previously took place in the product; now imports amounting to $Q_{1a}Q_{2a}$ are flowing from B to A. There is no trade diversion because previously there was no trade at all. Hence it is clear that a customs union which is trade-creating must necessarily raise economic welfare, on the assumption that the welfare effects of the changes in the distribution of income involved in all such policy changes may be regarded as neutral. In fact, welfare is raised not only for the union collectively but for each of the individual members A and B. True, as Viner insisted, their welfare would have been raised even more if, instead of retaining the tariff on imports from C, both countries had adopted completely free trade. But if the union is a second-best policy at least it is one which is an improvement on the previous situation. Furthermore, it brings a welfare gain which country B could not have attained unilaterally: the agreement of A was an essential requirement.

7.3 A Low-tariff Union

A situation in which no trade whatever existed prior to the customs union is one which is hardly likely to exist in reality. The second case to be considered is more probable: one in which some trade is occurring with the world at large but tariffs are also being used to protect domestic industry. Such a case is shown in Figure 7.2. Here the situation in the partner country, B, is the same as before: a tariff SP_{0b} is being levied on all imports so as to ensure that the domestic market is satisfied entirely from domestic output. In country A, on the other hand, the tariff SP_{0a} is such as to allow some domestic output, $0Q_{0a}$, to survive at the initial price P_{0a} but also to allow the penetration of some imports, $Q_{0a}Q_{1a}$, from C even after the imposition of the tariff. Country B, however, being less efficient than C, would be unable to compete with C in A's market.

The two countries A and B now agree to form a customs union, the common external tariff once more being designed to exclude imports from C. The new common tariff therefore becomes SP_1 and A's imports are switched entirely to the products of country B, which being free of duty are able to undercut the tariff-carrying imports from C. So far as country B is concerned, the result is the same as in the previous case; the new tariff against C causes the domestic price in

FIGURE 7.2
A Low-tariff Union

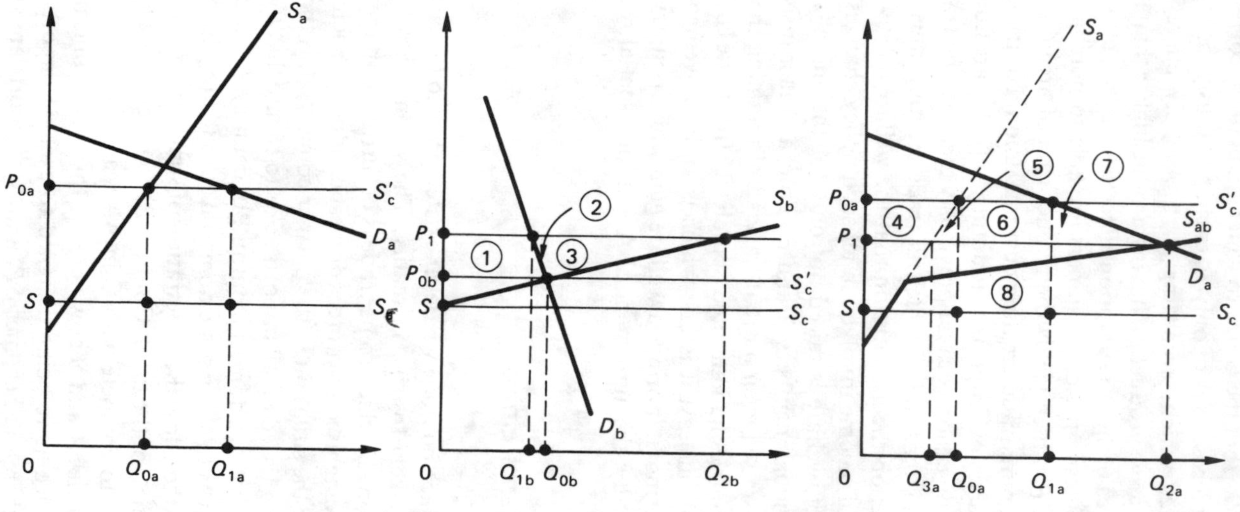

(a) Country A – before the union

(b) Country B

(c) Country A – after the union

B to rise from P_{0b} to P_1, causing a fall in domestic consumption but a rise in domestic output as exports of $Q_{1b}Q_{2b}$ to A become possible. Area 1 in country B represents a redistribution of income away from consumers and in favour of producers in the form of higher profits. Area 2 is the consumer loss in B which is more than offset by the additional profits amounting to areas $2 + 3$ on the sale of exports at a price in excess of costs. Country B is, as before, unambiguously better off.

The position in country A is, however, a little more complex. As before, because the domestic price falls to P_1 as a result of the greatly increased inflow of imports – $Q_{2a}Q_{3a}$ from country B compared with the previous level of $Q_{0a}Q_{1a}$ from C – consumers' surplus expands by an amount denoted by the sum of areas $4 + 5 + 6 + 7$. Some of this gain, however, is a mere transfer to A's consumers from other people in country A rather than a net gain for A as a whole. Area 4, for example, consists of excess profits previously in the hands of A's domestic producers which are now transferred to consumers through the mechanism of smaller domestic production (a fall from $0Q_{0a}$ to $0Q_{3a}$) and a lower price (P_1 rather than P_{0a}). Similarly, area 6 is not a net gain for A as a whole. Before the formation of the customs union the tax revenues accruing to the government of country A on imports from C amounted to the sum of areas $6 + 8$ – a duty of SP_{0a} on imports of $Q_{0a}Q_{1a}$. All imports into A are now coming from B and are free of duty. Area 6 may therefore be a gain to the consumers of the product but it is equally a loss to the citizens who previously enjoyed the benefits of the tax revenues accruing from imports; it is a transfer within A and not a net gain.

The net gain to country A therefore consists of the sum of areas 5 and 7. The former is the production effect – resources previously producing goods now available at P_1 each have been switched to alternative production with a gain in value-added of area 5; the latter is the consumption effect as increased consumption of the product whose price has now fallen to P_1 displaces less attractive substitutes. But this is not the end of the story. The government of A has lost the entire tax revenue from the product, $6 + 8$; consumers have gained the area 6 but the area 8 is a loss of tax revenue not compensated by a gain elsewhere in A. This would remain true even if some imports continued from C under the new tariff regime because the tax revenues on these would be the common property of the union and would no longer accrue solely to country A. The gains to consumers of areas 5 and 7 constitute the gains to A from the trade creation effects of the union; area 8 represents the loss to A from its trade diversion effects – the switch of imports from the relatively low-cost supplier C to the relatively high-cost partner country B.

The overall effect on welfare is thus decidedly ambiguous. Country B is clearly better off as a result of membership of the union. Country A, however, is gaining from the trade creation effects but losing from the trade diversion effects. The former may or may not be greater than the latter: this must depend on the height of the original tariff (and thus the size of the initial tariff revenues), the relative production costs in B and C (and thus the extent of the price fall in A when duty-free imports from B displace imports from C) and the elasticity of demand for the product (and thus the magnitude of the increase in consumption when the domestic price falls.) It is perfectly conceivable that A will find itself worse off after entry into the union than it was before.

If this proves to be so, why on earth should country A contemplate entry into the customs union? This is a question to which the discussion will return later but one thing which can be said at this point is that the customs union is trade-creating on balance – that is to say, the volume of trade created exceeds the volume of trade diverted. This must be so since the price of the product in A has been reduced and its consumption has increased, despite a fall in domestic production. It must necessarily be importing more after the event than before it, so that the trade created with B must be greater than the trade diverted from C. Since B imported nothing in the first place, the union as a whole must have increased its trade and overall welfare must therefore have risen. People would not be importing more than before unless they preferred to do so. Even if country A is on balance worse off, therefore, the welfare gains to B must be at least large enough to enable it to compensate A; the trade diversion loss to A is, after all, only part of the trade creation gain to B. The analysis thus establishes two important propositions of which the founders of any customs union (including the EEC) would be well advised to take note. First, that a customs union which benefits the member countries as a collective group may neverthe-less injure one or more members individually. Second, that because of this fact a highly desirable feature of any such arrangement is the existence of some systematic mechanism whereby the gains obtained by the winners may be partly used to compensate any losers: a customs union with permanently uncompen-sated losing members is unlikely to survive very long.

7.4   A High-tariff Union

The third and final specimen case to be considered is that in which the external tariff agreed on after the establishment of the customs union is in fact higher than that generally applied before it. (Of course, the external tariff may fall for some countries and increase for others: the test is whether the average tariff, weighted by the levels of consumption of the product in the different countries, has increased or decreased.) This case is illustrated in Figure 7.3.

The situation of B is assumed to be the same as before; it clearly gains from the capture of A's market and the expansion of exports which yield excess profits to its producers well in excess of the small loss in the surplus enjoyed by its consumers. The situation in A is very different. Prior to the customs union (Figure 7.3a) it had applied a low tariff (S_{p0}) and imported most of its supplies from C at a price P_{0a}; as the result of adopting the higher tariff necessary to keep

FIGURE 7.3
A High-tariff Union

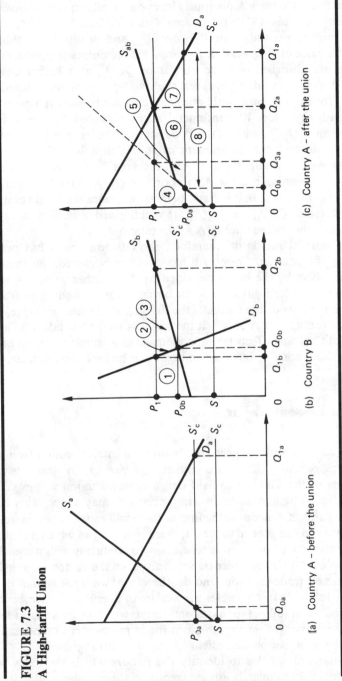

(a) Country A – before the union

(b) Country B

(c) Country A – after the union

out imports from C (SP_1) duty-free imports come in from B and the domestic price rises to P_1. Country A obviously loses out in all respects. Consumers suffer a total loss of areas $4+5+6+7$; area 4 is transferred to producers in A as domestic output expands from $0Q_{0a}$ to $0Q_{3a}$ and products sell this expanded output at a price of P_1 instead of P_{0a}; area 5 is the domestic production effect as resources are absorbed into the output of $Q_{0a}Q_{3a}$ at a higher cost than the previous import price of P_{0a}; area 6 is the trade-diversion loss caused by paying a price P_1 for imports previously obtainable by consumers at a price P_{0a}; area 7 is the deadweight loss of consumers' surplus caused by the switch of the consumption of $Q_{1a}Q_{2a}$ units of this product to some less-preferred substitute. In addition to all this, the government of A has now lost all the tax revenues previously levied on imports from C – the area 8. The customs union is not merely trade-diverting because A's imports of $Q_{2a}Q_{3a}$ have been switched from low-cost C to high-cost B; it is *trade-suppressing*, since the total volume of trade has fallen from $Q_{0a}Q_{1a}$ to $Q_{2a}Q_{3a}$, the combined effect of a fall in total consumption and an increase in A's domestic output.

By any normal standards, therefore, the customs union has proved to be something of a disaster. Country B has admittedly gained, but these gains are more than offset by the losses sustained by A; in other words, A would have done better to make a gift to B of the amount corresponding to B's gains and then remained outside the union. If the union goes ahead, therefore, there must be some advantages to A of which the analysis so far has taken no account; on the basis of the trade effects taken in themselves it would be an act of folly. The nature of these possible other advantages will be investigated later.

7.5   The Lessons so Far

The three cases considered here are obviously a small selection from an infinite range of possibilities. They are sufficient, however, to illustrate the major conclusions of the Viner analysis. First, a customs union will in general have both trade-creating and trade-diverting effects; it may conceivably have trade-suppressing effects. Since only the first of these will raise economic welfare while the other two will in general reduce it, there is no way in which a customs union can be described a priori as either increasing or reducing welfare; each case has to be considered on its own merits. Secondly, even if a customs union leads, as a whole, to net trade-creation and is therefore welfare-raising, it does not necessarily follow that it increases the welfare of every single member country; a similar conclusion follows for a customs union which is, overall, trade-diverting or trade-suppressing. Some mechanism for intra-country compensation would therefore be an advisable ingredient in any such arrangement.

The analysis also helps to identify the factors which are likely to make a customs union economically advantageous to the member countries. It shows quite clearly that a customs union is likely to be trade-creating if the common external tariff adopted after the union is in general lower than before; conversely, a move to a higher external tariff is likely to lead to both trade diversion and trade suppression effects. Beneficial consumption effects are more likely the higher the initial external tariff, and thus the greater the potential price reduction as duty-free imports come in from partner countries; they are also likely to be greater if the products in question face a high price-elasticity of demand. Beneficial production effects are more likely the higher the initial tariff and the greater the domestic elasticity of supply of the product. Adverse trade diversion effects are reduced as the number of countries participating in the union increase, since trade will be diverted to the least (relatively) inefficient producers in the union. They are also reduced the more similar are the economic structures of the countries participating; if both A and B are manufacturing countries, no large trade-diversion effects are likely to occur in the agricultural sector, whereas if A is largely agricultural and B largely industrial trade-diversion (to high-cost partners) can occur on a large scale in both sectors.

Whatever the particular situation, however, the general Viner conclusion appears to stand: any gains arising from entry into a customs union will be smaller than those obtainable by a move to completely free international trade. It would appear, as Viner argued, that in the last resort a customs union must be an essentially political arrangement. Later work was to show, however, that this conclusion is not necessarily valid. Some of the considerations which Viner's basic analysis neglected will be explored in the chapters which follow.

Further Reading

Balassa, B. A. (ed.), *European Economic Integration* (Amsterdam: North-Holland, 1975).

El-Agraa, A. M. and Jones, A. J., *The Theory of Customs Unions* (Deddington: Philip Allan, 1980).

Robson, P., *The Economics of International Integration*, 2nd edn (London: Allen & Unwin, 1984).

Scale and Externalities 8

8.1 Why Economies of Scale?

The Viner analysis rested on the assumption that all the economies concerned operated under conditions of perfect competition. On the supply side this implies that the number of producers in any market is so large that no single producer can affect market price through changes in output, and also that each of them supplies products identical in every respect to those of the others. On the demand side it implies that consumers (equally large in number) have no preference for the output of one producer rather than another, and that they are completely informed of market prices everywhere. Transport costs are assumed non-existent and completely free entry into the market is possible for all. For many purposes these obviously unrealistic assumptions greatly facilitate exposition without significantly affecting the outcome of the analysis. In the particular case of the customs union issue, however, the predictions of the analysis can be seriously affected by them.

The possibility of the existence of unexploited economies of scale is one of the considerations opened up when the perfect competition assumption is dropped. So long as that assumption holds, it follows logically that for every producer the level of operation adopted is that at which average costs are at a minimum and any increase in output will necessarily raise the average cost of the product. If average cost could be reduced by increasing output, the argument runs, at least one of these highly competitive producers would seize the opportunity thus offered, undercut all the rest and expand until competition gave way to a single monopoly. The possibility of unused economies of scale – i.e. a reduction in average cost of production through the expansion of the scale of output – is excluded once perfect competition is assumed.

In the world of reality economies of scale are not merely a possibility but an observed fact, certainly over a wide range of production activities. Were a condition of completely free international trade to exist it could be assumed (although not always realistically) that the search for profit would stimulate

76

producers to expand to that level of output at which those economies had been completely exploited, average costs thus being minimised and profits maximised. If their domestic markets were too small to absorb the large outputs thus generated, the producers concerned could expand into the markets of other countries by exporting; their scope for increasing output would be limited only by the size of the entire world market – and it seems improbable that any economies of scale would require markets larger than that to be attainable. But restrictions on international trade, whether in the form of tariffs or non-tariff barriers, may well stand in the way of this process. Domestic markets may be served by industries protected from outside competition, with the result that every country will be operating industries at an output below the level necessary to take advantage of the available technology.

Theoretically, completely free international trade is the remedy. If this is unattainable, however, a customs union may well be a second-best solution; by creating a single market between them, the partner countries may make it possible for industries to adopt levels of output which were not feasible as long as their sales were restricted to their individual domestic markets. Consumers may therefore gain in two related but distinguishable ways. On the one hand, an increase in the scale of the enterprises serving the market may lead to a fall in the cost of the product and thus, hopefully, in its price. On the other hand, since the unrealistic assumption that each market consists of a single, homogeneous product regardless of supplier can now be dropped, the possibility exists that imports may provide consumers with a choice of varieties of the product which individual domestic producers were unwilling to provide because of their pursuit of economies of scale through concentration on a limited range (or even a single version) of the product. That such possibilities could well exist in the context of the European Community seems far from improbable. Even the largest member countries, such as Germany and the United Kingdom, presented domestic markets which were only around a quarter of the size of the United States in terms of population and considerably less in terms of purchasing power.

As usual, an infinite number of situations could be postulated but once again three types of case will be sufficient to illustrate the main predictions – one in which no trade previously took place between the partner countries and the rest of the world, one in which the customs union leads to some trade diversion but overall trade creation and one in which trade suppression occurs. The last is of particular interest since it reveals the possibility of an overall gain in economic welfare by the partner countries even though the reverse of trade creation occurs, a possibility which the Viner analysis specifically denied. For simplicity it is assumed that the governments of the partner countries so adjust tariffs as to ensure that products are sold in their markets at average cost (including normal profit); in reality some of these potential gains to consumers may be absorbed by excess profits enjoyed by producers but this affects the distribution of the gains rather than their magnitude and the essential conclusions are not affected.

8.2   The Gains from a Customs Union

The first, and simplest, case is shown in Figure 8.1. The costs of producing the product in question are shown by the supply schedules S_a and S_b; since the assumption of perfect competition has now been dropped these schedules will represent the average cost of the product and not the marginal cost.

In both countries the schedules are downward-sloping – that is, unexploited economies of scale still exist at the point of production. The cost of purchasing the product from the rest of the world, C, is given in each case by S_c. Clearly neither A nor B would be able to compete with C if free international trade existed. In the initial situation, however, both countries are applying an external tariff of such a height that domestic demand can be met entirely from domestic output; A imposes a tariff SP_{0a} resulting in a domestic price P_{0a}, while B imposes a tariff SP_{0b} resulting in a domestic price P_{0b}.

Country B perceives that it has a competitive advantage over A and therefore proposes that the two countries enter into a customs union, applying a common tariff against C such that C remains excluded from the two markets. Figure 8.1(c) shows that the combined demand in the two countries, D_{ab}, obtained by summing D_a and D_b at each price, intersects B's supply curve, S_b, at the price P_1; a common tariff of SP_1 is therefore imposed on imports from C, effectively confining the market to supplies from B. Both A and B are clearly better off as a result. In A, consumers' surplus is increased by areas 1 and 2; area 1 is a beneficial production effect, high-cost output from A being replaced by lower-cost imports from B, while area 2 is a beneficial consumption effect, since the fall in domestic price allows consumers to substitute additional units $Q_{0a}Q_{1a}$ of the product for less-preferred substitutes. In B, consumers' surplus is increased by areas 3 and 4; area 3 is the production gain arising from the fall in the average

FIGURE 8.1
Pure Trade Creation

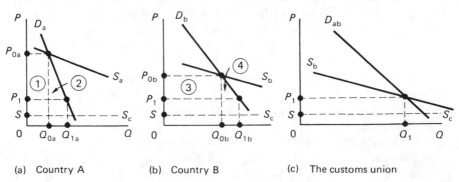

(a)   Country A   (b)   Country B   (c)   The customs union

cost of the initial output Q_{0b} from P_{0b} to P_1, while area 4 is the consumption gain arising from the increase of $Q_{0b}Q_{1b}$ in total consumption. No trade diversion occurs because no trade existed previously. Consumers gain not merely from the increase in trade as such but also because the amalgamation of the two markets enables producers in B to enjoy economies of scale which were unexploited at their previous level of output.

The second case is illustrated in Figure 8.2. This differs from the previous case only in that country A, reluctant to enforce a domestic price high enough to fully protect its own industry, initially imposed a somewhat smaller tariff, SP_{0A}, and as a result imported all its supplies, Q_{0a}, from C, collecting tariff revenues equal to areas $1+5$ in the process. As before, a customs union is agreed and a common tariff SP_1 is imposed on imports from C. Country B is in precisely the same position as before, gaining welfare corresponding to areas $3+4$. Country A, however, is in a slightly different position. Area 1 is no longer a net gain; previously it accrued to the government in the form of tax revenue and now accrues to the consumers of the product. It is therefore a transfer of income within A. Area 2 remains a net gain to consumers, the consumption effect. The area 5 is a loss of tariff revenue, however – the trade-diversion effect – since the initial imports Q_{0a} are now drawn from B, with a zero tariff, at a cost of P_1 rather than from C at a cost of S but with tariff revenues represented by Areas $1+5$. Thus country A may or may not be better off. Since the customs union as a whole is trade-creating, however – total consumption having risen – gains to B must be great enough to compensate A for any losses and still leave B better off. As before, the customs union benefits its members not merely through increased trade but through lower costs of production.

The third case, illustrated in Figure 8.3, involves the possibility that production costs in country A are higher than those in B at the original levels of output

FIGURE 8.2
Trade Creation and Trade Diversion

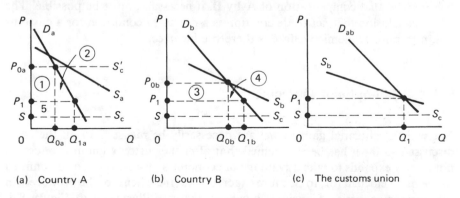

(a) Country A   (b) Country B   (c) The customs union

FIGURE 8.3
Trade Suppression

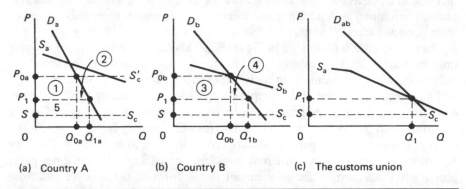

(a) Country A   (b) Country B   (c) The customs union

but fall below those of B if the industry expands to the size required to satisfy markets in both A and B simultaneously. Figure 8.3(c) indicates that the combined demand curve, D_{ab}, will intersect A's supply curve before that of B. The creation of a customs union, giving A duty-free access to B, will therefore cause A's industry to expand and capture the whole market, the new tariff on C being sufficient to eliminate C's exports to A.

The result is therefore that total trade in the product after the formation of the customs union is in fact smaller than before; imports into B (Q_{1b}, entirely from country A) will have increased, since previously B imported nothing, but imports into A (previously Q_{0a}, entirely from C) were much bigger and have now been totally replaced by domestic production in A. Once again there is a net trade-diversion effect in A, area 5, to offset the consumption gain, area 2, so that A may or may not be a net gainer. Since price has fallen and consumption has risen in both countries, however, economic welfare in the union as a whole has risen so that compensation of A by B, if necessary, must be possible. The Viner conclusion that net trade creation is a necessary condition for a customs union to raise economic welfare is therefore incorrect.

8.3   A Sub-optimal Outcome

But will the potential gain in welfare necessarily be realised? In all the cases discussed so far it has been assumed that after the customs union production not merely expands to take advantage of economies of scale but is also confined to the more efficient (or, to be more exact, the less inefficient) of the producers in the partner countries. Consider, however, the case illustrated in Figure 8.4.

FIGURE 8.4
A Sub-optimal Outcome

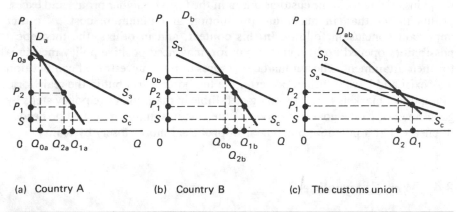

(a) Country A (b) Country B (c) The customs union

Prior to the customs union both A and B were imposing tariffs of sufficient height to exclude all imports. As a result, the domestic prices were initially P_{0a} in A and P_{0b} in B, the latter price being lower than the former. Now this is a little odd, because, as Figure 8.4(c) shows, average costs in A are *lower* than those in B at every level of output. The explanation, of course, is that the demand for the product is lower in A than in B at any given price; the result is that while neither country is fully exploiting the potential economies of scale, country B's larger market has enabled its industry to proceed further along the output path than has so far been possible for A.

The position which would theoretically exist after the customs union is shown in Figure 8.4(c); the industry in country A would immediately expand its output to Q_1, at which its price, P_1, would be such as to put B's industry out of business altogether. But in the world of reality such adjustments of production can never be instantaneous, and the fact is that at the commencement of the union B's price is lower than that in A. It would therefore hardly be surprising if, in the initial stages, consumers in A switch to imports from B, which are cheaper. This will push B's output further down the path of economies of scale and increase its cost advantage; producers in A, on the other hand, will find demand for their product actually falling and output may be cut back, increasing their cost disadvantage. If this sequence continues the ultimate result could easily be that it is the industry in A which finds itself out of business and the market will settle down at the price P_2 with production concentrated on B rather than A. As a result, the gain in welfare in both countries will be well below the level possible.

Of course, this non-optimal result would be avoided if producers in A had perfect foresight of what could happen and instantaneously adjusted their prices to the ultimate equilibrium value, P_1. Such foresight is seldom possessed in the real world. What is more, if the industry was in the hands of monopolists, or near-monopolists, in both countries it is by no means beyond the realm of possibility that they will collude to share markets between themselves, acquiring the gains arising from the customs union in the form of higher profits and excess profits rather than in maximum production and minimum cost. A rather important conclusion follows. In this context, and in others, the theoretical possibilities opened up by a customs union may need positive policy measures for their attainment. The automatic pressures of pure, unrestricted competition may exist and have sufficient power in the textbook world but in the real world of imperfect markets (to say nothing of fallible humanity) active policy steps by governments, or the governing body of the customs union, may well be needed to ensure that a potential outcome is approached more closely by reality.

8.4   Why Externalities?

The relaxation of the assumption of perfect competition has a second consequence for the analysis of the effects of the formation of a customs union. In the textbook world of perfect competition the market prices of all products are necessarily equal to the consumers' valuation of the benefit derived from consuming them. Similarly, the prices of factors of production are necessarily equal to the valuation of the output they could have produced in their best alternative use; market price is therefore an accurate measure of the loss suffered by society in using resources in their current employment. In the real world neither of these propositions may be valid.

The use of resources in a particular way may confer benefits or impose losses on persons other than those paying for them, so that the price paid by the user of those resources neglects the effects on others within the society. There are, in other words, *externalities of production or consumption*. Put alternatively again, there may exist *public goods* as well as private goods – certain types of resource use may confer benefits or impose burdens on people who cannot be directly charged for those benefits or compensated for the burdens. Market price therefore fails to reflect true costs of production or gains from consumption.

Instances of such external effects are really quite common. In the realm of consumption, it is well known that enjoyment derived by one person may necessarily impose the reverse experience on others. Loud music may give much pleasure to one person but cause considerable annoyance to his neighbour; each new car purchased adds to congestion and thus reduces the utility of a car to all existing owners; a new house to one is a loss of view to another, and so on. Benefits may also be unintentionally, or even unknowingly, conferred on others; the transformation of a front yard into a beautiful garden will not only give its owner pleasure but may improve the value of houses on either side; each new telephone installed increases the potential usefulness of all existing telephones.

In the present context, however, externalities of production are much more relevant. The money costs incurred by the manufacturer of a particular product may take no account of costs which fall on others – the pollution generated by a factory chimney, the lost sleep resulting from the noise of an airport, the congestion imposed on existing road users by increased factory traffic, and so on. In such cases the apparent costs which determine production decisions are less than the true costs imposed on society as a whole; as a result, market-determined output will be too high. On the other hand, output may confer benefits on society which are not reflected in the costs of its inputs – the creation of (say) transport and communication facilities of benefit to persons other than the producer, the development of skills in a workforce which will increase its value to other employers, the growth of marketing facilities which will benefit other producers etc.

These external effects are most obvious in developing countries in which industrialisation as such will ultimately encourage the emergence of a skilled and disciplined labour force of benefit to the economy at large; the value of this may greatly supplement the market value of the output initially produced by a particular employer. They are by no means negligible in the developed world, however. The United States space programme, it is said, has led to technological spin-offs in areas far removed from the original military area; countries such as those of the Community clearly perceive social and political advantages in maintaining their family farms, quite apart from the market value of their output; imported computers or nuclear reactors may well be cheaper than corresponding domestic products, but the total reliance on imports may leave a country bereft of technological skills in those areas at a high ultimate cost nationally; it would appear that even the maintenance of a national airline confers some political or psychological gain sufficient to justify what would otherwise be a wholly uneconomic existence. These external social benefits may or may not be real in some sense; if they are perceived to exist, however, governments may rationally seek to ensure that the astigmatism of unalloyed market forces does not prevent their enjoyment.

8.5 First-best and Second-best Again

The logic of economic analysis leaves no doubt as to the optimum policy to be pursued in these cases where market prices fail to reflect accurately the social as well as individual costs and benefits arising from economic activities: it is to use taxes and subsidies to bring market prices into alignment with the true costs or benefits involved. Consider the example shown in Figure 8.5(a). Here country A has a domestic industry capable of producing a certain product with a marginal cost curve Sa; the product can be imported from the rest of the world at a fixed price P_0. In the absence of any government intervention the domestic industry would produce an output Q_0 and import the rest of its consumption, Q_0Q_1, from country C. Suppose, however, that in country A some social benefits are deemed to arise from the production of this product (perhaps the avoidance of unemployment benefits which would otherwise have to be paid) valued at an amount BC per unit. The true marginal cost per unit of domestic production is thus given by the marginal cost curve S'_a and the optimum level of domestic output is therefore Q_2 rather than Q_0, this being the output at which the marginal cost of the last unit produced is just equal to the import cost. To produce a greater domestic output would involve domestic costs in excess of the opportunity cost of imports; to produce a smaller output would mean that the product would be imported at a cost which was greater than its true domestic cost.

The solution is therefore to pay the domestic producers a subsidy of the amount BC for every unit produced. The effective cost curve would thus move down to S'_a, the domestic price would be unchanged at P_0 and imports would contract from Q_0Q_1 to Q_2Q_1. Since both price and total consumption would remain unchanged, consumers are neither better nor worse off. The areas $2 + 5$ would however accrue to country A as an additional benefit – a value BC on each unit of the additional output Q_0Q_2. True, the subsidies to the producers would need to be financed by additional taxation within the country, but this would be a simple matter of a redistribution of income from taxpayers to producers and would presumably cancel out for the country as a whole. (In the opposite case in which social costs exceed money costs of production, of course, the reverse would apply – a tax corresponding to the difference would be applied to every unit produced, thus reducing domestic output to the required optimum level.)

In a textbook world this would be the end of the matter but in the world of reality the first-best solution may not be costless or even feasible. Paying a subsidy per unit to producers week by week or month by month sounds a simple enough business but in practice will require a fairly sophisticated system of tax-collection, accounting and subsidy-payment to ensure that the payments come from and go to the right people. If the producers happen to be a large number of small producers dispersed over the country, lacking detailed accounts and records (but not necessarily cunning) – say, an agricultural sector – the costs of effective administration may be very considerable indeed. Conversely, if the producers as a group are relatively rich while taxpayers as a group are relatively poor the process may present formidable political difficulties internally; if the expanded output is partly exported the subsidies would indeed be illegal under the rules of GATT.

The first-best solution being unduly expensive or politically impossible, the government of A may turn to the second-best solution: a tariff on imports of P_0P_1; the effects of this are shown in Figure 8.5(b). So far as the consequences for the domestic industry are concerned, they are the same as in the subsidy case: the internal price rises to P_1 and domestic output rises to the desired

FIGURE 8.5

(a) The Subsidy System.   **(b) The Tariff System**

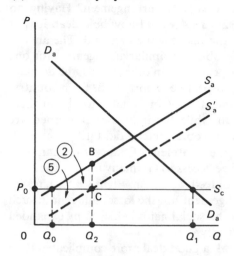   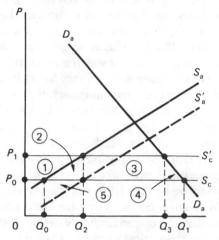

optimum level Q_2. The consequences for the consumers in A, however, are very different. The rise in the internal price causes the loss of consumers' surplus represented by the area $1+2+3+4$; consumers are emphatically worse off. True, area 1 may be disregarded, being a mere transfer within the country from consumers to producers, to whom the area represents an addition to profits over and above their costs. Area 2 also is offset by the social benefits arising from the increased domestic output. Similarly, area 3 may be disregarded since this passes to the government in the form of an import duty P_0P_1 on imports Q_2Q_3. Area 4, however, is an uncompensated consumption loss arising from the replacement of Q_1Q_3 units of this product by less-preferred substitutes in response to its increased domestic price. For the country as a whole the true gain is thus only area 5 minus area 4. If the latter exceeds the former the whole policy is in fact a mistake and should be abandoned; even if 4 is smaller than 5, however, the net gain to country A must be smaller than under the subsidy/tax regime.

So far the question of a customs union does not arise. But suppose the supply curve S_a referred to the industry of a prospective partner country B? Without some preferential treatment B can manage to export only Q_0 to A in view of the superiority of its rival producer C. If it can induce A to form a customs union with it, however, adopting the external tariff P_0P_1 against C, all the gains represented by areas $1+2+5$ will now accrue to B as a result of its duty-free access to A; not only will it obtain the advantage of a higher price for its exports to A but will also glean the social benefits represented by areas 2 and 5.

But why would A conceivably agree to such an arrangement? Having no domestic production the entire area $1+2+3+4$ would now be a dead loss; it would not even have the consolation of the tax revenue in area 3. The answer must be that by mutual bargaining it can obtain a similar arrangement for one of its own industries which is in a similar position – in other words, the demand curve in Figure 8.5(b) is that facing its prospective exports to B. Each country, in other words, has industries offering social gains but unable to obtain them because its domestic market is too small while the industries concerned are unable to compete internationally without some preferential tariff treatment. France, in other words, concedes duty-free treatment of imports of manufactures from Germany in return for duty-free access to Germany for its exports of agricultural products. The result may indeed be, as in Figure 8.5, a trade-diverting or even trade-suppressing arrangement but the losses inherent in such an arrangement are more than offset by the social gains achieved by expanded production of certain industries domestically.

The theoretical predictions begin to look a good deal more complicated than those of the orthodox Viner analysis. Trade creation may indeed justify a presumption that a customs union will raise welfare amongst its participants, but it is clearly not a *necessary* condition for that end to be secured. A customs union may raise welfare even if it results in a reduction of the total volume of trade amongst the participants if, as a result of the union, one or more members secure hitherto unexploited economies of scale or attain externalities of production (or indeed consumption) which their separate domestic markets were too small to achieve. Even this is not the end of the story.

Further Reading

Balassa, B. A. (ed.), *European Economic Integration* (Amsterdam: North-Holland, 1975).

El-Agraa, A. M. and Jones, A. J., *The Theory of Customs Unions* (Deddington: Philip Allan, 1980).

Owen, N., *Economies of Scale, Competitiveness and Trade Patterns within the European Community* (London: Oxford University Press, 1983) Ch.1.

Robson, P., *The Economics of International Economic Integration*, 2nd edn (London: Allen & Unwin, 1984).

Terms of Trade and Dynamic Effects 9

9.1 The Optimum Tariff

[handwritten annotation: Prey. assumed C.U. small, ∴ no effect on world price.]

In the analysis of Chapter 7 the assumption of perfect competition was extended to the world market and not merely to domestic markets. In particular it was assumed that the countries forming a customs union represented so small a share in the total world trade in a product, even collectively, that the world market price of that product was unaffected by changes in the union's demand for imports of it. Hence the rest-of-the-world supply curves used in earlier diagrams were shown as horizontal lines, implying that the world price was fixed regardless of the union's demand for the product. The customs union, in other words, was 'small' in relation to the total world market. The assumption is not always realistic. As noted in Chapter 3, in 1988 the European Community of twelve countries accounted for more than a third of total world imports; even excluding intra-community trade it accounted for around 22 per cent of world imports. This is not small by any standards; the consequences of removing the assumption of a 'small' customs union therefore need to be investigated.

Even if all the other assumptions of the perfectly-competitive world are regarded as valid, it is *not* the case in reality that completely free trade will necessarily maximise a country's economic welfare if the world supply curve of a product to it is upward-sloping – that is, if the price charged by exporters rises as the demand for imports grow because production is being carried out under conditions of decreasing returns. Consider country A portrayed in Figure 9.1. Its demand curve for a certain product, which it does not itself manufacture, is shown by D_a, while the supply schedule of imports from country C is given by S_c. Left to completely free market forces, the price of the product in A would settle at P_0 and the quantity imported at Q_0. Percipient observers in the government of A notice, however, that the price it is paying for each unit

FIGURE 9.1
The Optimum Tariff

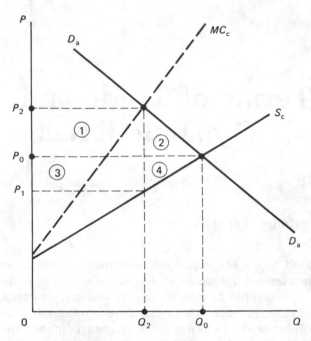

imported does not accurately reflect its additional *cost* to the country as a whole. With every additional unit imported a higher price has to be paid to cover the higher cost of production; this increased price has to be paid, however, not merely on the last unit imported but on all the other units imported, since only a single price can prevail in the market at any time. The additional cost of each import is thus greater than its market price because the cost of the previous level of imports is also being raised each time. The observers in A therefore calculate the *marginal cost* of each unit – its own supply price plus the addition to the previous price it involves for all other existing imports; this is shown by the curve MC_c in Figure 9.1.

It will be immediately apparent that under free trade conditions country A is importing too much of this product for its own good. Each unit in excess of the quantity Q_2 gives less welfare, as reflected in the demand curve D_a, than it is costing, as reflected in the marginal cost curve MC_c. Each such additional import is therefore *reducing* economic welfare. Maximum welfare is obtained when the import volume is Q_2, no more and no less. To attain this desired state of affairs, a tariff of P_1P_2 is levied on each unit. The domestic price thus rises until, at the price P_2, demand is brought down to the desired level Q_2. Consumer surplus is admittedly reduced by areas 1 + 2, but of this area 1 accrues to the government in tax revenue, while the government also collects the tax revenue in area 3. Consumers can therefore be compensated for the deadweight loss embodied in area 2 and still leave the government with additional revenues to finance all kinds of welfare-raising activities. The 'optimum' rate of tariff is therefore one which maximises the net gain – area 3 minus area 2 – and it can be shown that this optimum rate will be zero (i.e. welfare is maximised by completely free trade) if and only if the elasticity of supply of imports is infinite, giving the horizontal supply curve of the previous diagrams. (The formal proof of this involves some rather unprepossessing algebra and is therefore relegated to the appendix to this chapter.)

The gain represented by area 3 has not appeared from nowhere, of course. It is in fact an extraction of excess profits previously enjoyed by producers in country C on their exports at the price P_0; on their remaining exports, $0Q_2$, the net price they are now receiving has been reduced by the amount P_0P_1. Area 3 is thus a transfer from country C to country A. But it will not have escaped notice that there is also a fourth area in Figure 9.1 – the triangle marked 4. This is the obverse of the deadweight welfare loss, area 2, suffered by country A; it is a deadweight welfare loss inflicted on the supplier C. C has found its exports reduced by the quantity Q_0Q_2, for which it previously received a price of P_0 per unit. This price exceeded its production costs, as shown in the supply curve, by the area of the triangle 4; C has therefore lost that much producers' surplus, but, unlike the welfare embodied in area 3, it is not one which is simply transferred to A. The gain secured by country A, in other words, arises not only from extracting some excess profits from C but also from inflicting an additional deadweight loss on C. This immediately suggests that the optimum tariff game is a dangerous one at which two can play. If country C is small and relatively weak it may not be in a position to do much about the situation; if it is a fairly powerful economy, however, it may well threaten to retaliate against A with an optimum tariff policy of its own, with the result that A may find itself in the end worse off rather than better off. (Hence the expression 'beggar-my-neighbour' for trade policies by which countries, through competitive tariff wars, may achieve the intelligent result of leaving *everyone* worse off than when they started.) At the very least, C may demand compensation from A which will moderate A's initial gain; the rules of GATT, indeed, make specific provision for a member country injured by tariff changes introduced by another to obtain compensation for any injury they may cause.

It will be clear why the adoption of such a tariff is described as benefiting the country concerned through changes in its *terms of trade*. This expression refers to the prices obtained by a country for its exports relative to those paid for its imports. Any improvement in the terms of trade raises the welfare of a country because it means that a smaller volume of its exports is required to purchase a given volume of imports – the real unit cost of its imports has been reduced. In the example of Figure 9.1 country A has succeeded in forcing down the unit price paid to C from P_0 to P_1. If the price of A's exports remain unchanged, its terms of trade have clearly improved. The possibility of retaliation by C, of course, means that the assumption of unchanged export prices may be a questionable one in practice.

9.2   Customs Unions and the Terms of Trade

It is not difficult to see why the formation of a customs union between member countries, giving them a combined bargaining power greater than that of any single participating member, can be used to apply an optimum tariff policy for the union as a whole and thereby extract terms of trade gains from the rest of the world. A simple example is given in Figure 9.2 in which, for ease of exposition, it is assumed that neither of the two member countries A and B have a domestic supply of the product in question. In practice this is rather unlikely to be the case and there could well be the standard trade-creation and trade-diversion effects in addition. The simplifying assumption, however, allows the analysis to concentrate on the terms-of-trade effects without these additional complications. The example is also a numerical one in the interests of clarity.

The initial position of country A is shown in Figure 9.2(a); at this stage it is assumed that country B has not entered the market for the product concerned at all. Without an optimum tariff the demand and foreign supply conditions are such that imports of 7 units would be purchased by country A at a price of $8.

FIGURE 9.2
A Customs Union and the Terms of Trade

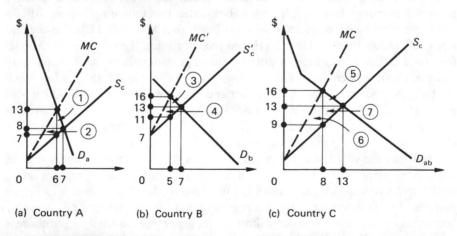

(a) Country A   (b) Country B   (c) Country C

The marginal cost curve for imports indicates that the optimum level of imports would in fact be 6 units; a tariff of $6 is thus imposed, raising the domestic price to $13 and reducing demand to 6. The net gain to A is given by area 2 minus area 1. In this case, area 2 consists of a $1 tax on 6 units of imports (the remaining $5 of tax being paid by consumers in the form of the higher price), a total of $6. The deadweight consumption loss is given by triangle 1, equal to one-half of the reduction in imports of 1 unit multiplied by the increase of $5 in domestic price, a total of $2.5. Country A has therefore increased its welfare by $3.5 as a result of the tariff.

Suppose that country B now enters the market for this product; its position is represented by Figure 9.2(b). Since country A is already absorbing 6 units of world supply, the supply curve to B starts at the minimum cost of $7 corresponding to a supply of 6 to A and zero to B; with a completely free market, domestic price in B would thus settle at $13 and imports would amount to 7 units. Like A, country B determines the optimum level for its imports in the light of their marginal cost; this is 5 units, and a tariff of $5, bringing the domestic price to $16, is necessary to secure this end. In country B, then, the terms-of-trade gain in area 4 is $2 × 5 while the consumer loss in triangle 3 is 0.5 ($3 × 2), a net total of $7. Between them, therefore, A and B are able to secure a total gain of $10.5 through independent tariff action.

Let A and B now form a customs union, constituting one single market and establishing a single tariff on imports from C; this is shown in Figure 9.2(c). With a zero tariff market price in the union would be established at $13 and total imports would amount to 13 units. Calculating the marginal cost of imports as before, the union collectively establishes a tariff of $7 per unit, raising the internal price to $16 and reducing imports to the optimum level of 8 units. The union as a whole has obtained the terms-of-trade gain represented by area 6 – $4 × 8 – and suffered the consumer loss of triangle 5 – 0.5 ($3 × 5) – a net total of $24.5. The formation of the customs union has increased their collective net terms-of-trade gain from $10.5 to $24.5.

There remains, of course, area 7, the terms-of-trade loss inflicted on C, amounting to 0.5 ($4 × 5) = $10. As noted earlier, country C may not be disposed to accept this loss, which is considerably greater than would have been experienced if A and B had acted independently. Some of the union's gains may therefore be removed through retaliation by C or by an agreed compensation. This will depend on the relative economic and political bargaining powers of the two groups; as usual with this type of activity it is advisable for the customs union to deploy its power against small countries rather than large ones. There is also the problem that the individual tariff revenues previously accruing to each member independently now form a common pool (slightly smaller than before because of the fall in total imports from 11 to 8) which will have to be shared out between them in some way. As the experience of the European Community demonstrates, this is not necessarily a painless or costless exercise.

9.3   Dynamic Effects

The effects of the formation of a customs union so far discussed have been essentially static in nature; they involve no fundamental change in underlying conditions of demand or supply and are of a once-for-all nature. That is to say, the effects work themselves out and induce no further changes in welfare thereafter. This is not to say that they cease to apply at all but merely that the improvement secured in resource allocation can be achieved only once. Dynamic effects, on the other hand, by their nature continue into the future, adding to output not merely over a single period but continuously over time. This is because they involve shifts primarily on the supply side of the economy, causing an addition to output which persists permanently.

Two such effects are associated with the destruction of tariff barriers and therefore with the formation of a customs union. The first is the stimulus to greater efficiency induced in domestic entrepreneurs by the threat or reality of increased competition from foreign producers against whose products they previously received some degree of protection through tariffs or other trade restrictions. In the textbook world of perfect competition such a stimulus would be totally unnecessary in order to ensure that entrepreneurs constantly and immediately operated at the frontier of the prevailing technology; an all-consuming desire to maximise profit is sufficient to ensure that costs are everywhere minimised. The evidence of reality does not conform with this textbook image. As long ago as 1969 an American economist, Harvey Lieben-stein, demonstrated empirically that wide differences of productive efficiency existed within any given industry, a finding incompatible with the assertion that all entrepreneurs invariably operated so as to ensure that they secured the maximum potential level of profit.

Many explanations may be advanced for this but one which is supported by common experience is that the so-called psychic costs of attaining this theoretical maximum exceed the monetary benefits thereby achieved. The process of ensuring that every element, and particularly every person – not least the entrepreneur himself – is operating at the highest possible level, with the greatest possible efficiency and at every moment of the working day, is not one which is conducive to a comfortable existence. The attainment of a *satisfactory* profit may therefore be preferable to the ulcers or lost games of golf involved in attaining the *maximum* profit. Intense competition from foreign producers, however, may remove this option from the entrepreneur and force him closer to the potential production frontier, if not all the way to it. The process may be somewhat less than pleasant for the entrepreneur (and his employees) but is of undoubted benefit to the consumer, who is now being supplied with products at lower cost.

The second, and related, dynamic effect of a customs union is the stimulus given to the rate of investment. The opening up of new markets, and the expansion of output this implies for some, necessarily involves additional investment in productive capacity. (This is not offset by negative investment on the part of the enterprises losing out in this process; investment in such enterprises may fall to zero but gross investment can never be negative.) Such an increase in the rate of investment may raise the rate of growth in the economy in two ways, one microeconomic and the other macroeconomic. On the microeconomic side, new investment never merely raises total output; it invariably embodies a later, and therefore presumably superior, technology than that embodied in existing plant and equipment. The result is a rise not merely in total output but in overall productivity – output per unit of input. A high-investment economy is almost synonymous with an economy characterised by rapidly-growing productivity. Secondly, the rate of investment is a crucial component in the level of aggregate demand. Through the multiplier process an increase of one unit of expenditure in investment will generate an increase of two or three units in overall demand in the economy, and a steadily rising level of aggregate demand (in real terms) is an essential ingredient in a high and sustained rate of economic growth. From both the supply and demand sides, therefore, the investment generated by membership of a customs union is likely to induce a higher rate of real economic growth.

The fact that these dynamic effects of a customs union can be described briefly, and only in rather general terms, should not be allowed to convey the impression that they are therefore less important than the static effects which have been examined at considerably more length in the foregoing pages. Of their nature it is difficult to analyse the impact of these effects in precise terms but,

Table 9.1
The Impact of Dynamic Gains

Year	Before the customs union		After the customs union			
	Efficiency ratio 0.85 Growth rate 0.04		Efficiency ratio 0.9		Growth rate 0.05	
	Potential GNP	Actual GNP	Actual GNP	Gain % (4–3)	Actual GNP	Gain % (6–3)
(1)	(2)	(3)	(4)	(5)	(6)	(7)
0	100.0	85.0				
1	104.0	88.4	93.6	5.2	94.5	6.1
2	108.2	92.0	97.4	5.4	99.3	7.3
3	112.5	95.6	101.3	5.7	104.2	8.6
4	117.0	99.5	105.3	5.8	109.4	9.9
5	121.7	103.4	109.5	6.1	114.8	11.4
6	126.5	107.5	113.9	6.4	120.6	13.1
7	131.6	111.9	118.4	6.5	126.6	14.7
8	136.9	116.4	123.2	6.8	132.9	16.5
9	142.3	121.0	128.1	7.1	139.6	18.6
10	148.0	125.8	133.2	7.4	146.6	20.8

also of their nature, over a period of years they are likely to be of much greater importance. The simple numerical example of Table 9.1 will illustrate this. In columns (2) and (3) of the table it is assumed that in the absence of membership of a customs union a country commencing with a gross national product of 100 and operating at 85 per cent of its maximum potential efficiency is on a steady path of growth amounting to 4 per cent per annum. After a period of ten years its national income will have risen from 85.0 to 125.8, an increase of 48 per cent. Suppose now that entry into a customs union stimulates its entrepreneurs into achieving 90 per cent rather than 85 per cent of their potential efficiency. The results are seen in columns (4) and (5); after ten years the country's national income will have risen 57 per cent rather than 48 per cent – a very substantial improvement. The results of an increase in the overall growth rate from 4 per cent to 5 per cent, shown in the final two columns, are even more dramatic; after the lapse of ten years the two effects together – efficiency and growth – will have raised national income by 72 per cent. These are changes far in excess of any which could possibly be attained by once-for-all static effects.

9.4   To Conclude

The predictions of economic theory about the effects of entry into a customs union are now a great deal more complex than the original Viner analysis. The general results of that analysis are by no means invalidated but they must certainly be qualified and augmented. It remains true to conclude, as did Viner, that a customs union will raise the overall economic welfare of its members if its trade-creating effects exceed its trade-diverting or trade-suppressing effects. It also remains true to conclude that such an overall increase in economic welfare is perfectly consistent with a loss of welfare on the part of one or more members of the union, so that some form of compensation mechanism is almost certain to be required for the union's survival in the long run. It is no longer safe to conclude, however, that such net trade creation is either a necessary or a sufficient condition for the increase of economic welfare as a result of the formation of a customs union.

It is not a necessary condition because, as has been seen, members of a customs union may gain through the exploitation of economies of scale, through the achievement of social as opposed to private benefits or through an improvement in their terms of trade, even if the union is on balance trade-diverting or even trade-suppressing. It is not sufficient precisely because losses experienced under any of these headings may outweigh the gains achieved through trade creation. Above all, the dynamic effects arising from membership of a customs union may easily outweigh substantial losses incurred through its static trade effects – a theoretical possibility transformed into hope, if not assertion, by the United Kingdom in the early 1970s, as will be noted in the discussion of the attempts to quantify these various effects which now follows.

Further Reading

Balassa, B. A. (ed.), *European Economic Integration* (Amsterdam: North Holland, 1975).
El-Agraa, A. M. and Jones, A. J., *The Theory of Customs Unions* (Deddington: Philip Allan, 1980).
Robson, P., *The Economics of International Economic Integration*, 2nd edn (London: Allen & Unwin, 1984).

Appendix

The incidence of an expenditure tax

Suppose that, in Figure 9.3, a quantity Q of a product is initially sold at the price P. A fixed tax, $T (= AB + BC)$ is now imposed on each unit sold; market price rises to P' and sales fall to Q'. The absolute magnitude (modulus) of the elasticity of demand for the product, e_d, is given by $e_d = dQ/Q \div dP/P = dQ/dP . P/Q$, where dQ and dP are the changes in quantity demanded and price respectively. In Figure 9.3, therefore,

$$e_d = BR/AB . P/Q$$

so that the rise in the price to consumers, $dP (= AB)$ is given by

$$AB = BR/e_d . P/Q \tag{1}$$

Similarly, the elasticity of supply for a product, e_s, is given by

$$e_s = dQ/dP . P/Q$$

and, in Figure 9.3, the fall in the price received by producers, $dP (= BC)$ is given by

$$BC = BR/e_s . P/Q \tag{2}$$

The ratio of the shares of the tax borne by consumers and producers respectively is therefore given by (1) divided by (2), i.e.

$$AB/BC = BR/e_d . P/Q \div BR/e_s . P/Q = e_s/e_d$$

so that the share borne by consumers, $AB, = BC.e_s/e_d$ and the share borne by producers, $BC, = AB.e_d/e_s$. The share of the total tax $(AB + BC)$ passed on to the consumer is therefore:

$$AB/(AB + BC) = BC . e_s/e_d \div BC . e_s/e_d + BC$$
$$= e_s / (e_s + e_d)$$

while that absorbed by the producer is:

$$BC/(AB + BC) = AB . e_d/e_s \div AB + AB . e_d/e_s$$
$$= e_d / (e_s + e_d)$$

FIGURE 9.3
Incidence of a Tax

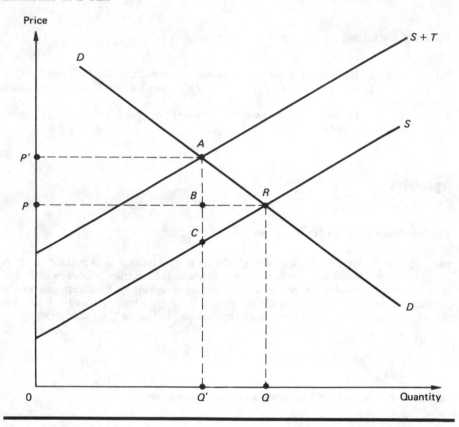

Writing E for $(e_s + e_d)$, therefore, the shares of the tax borne by consumers and producers respectively become e_s/E and e_d/E.

The optimum tariff

Let the increase in price to the consumer in Figure 9.1 (P_0P_2) be denoted by dP_1, the fall in the price received by the producer in country C (P_0P_1) by dP_2, the initial quantity imported by Q and the fall in imports (Q_0Q_2) by dQ. The net increase in country A's welfare, W', is then given by area 3 minus area 2, i.e.

$$W' = (Q\text{-}dQ).dP_2 - 0.5(dQ.dP_1) \tag{3}$$

With the imposition of the tariff, t, the price changes to the consumer and producer respectively become

$$dP_1 = t.e_s/E \quad \text{and} \quad dP_2 = t.e_d/E \tag{4}$$

The price-elasticity of demand can therefore be written:

$$e_d = dQ.P/t.(e_s/E).Q$$

from which

$$dQ = (t/E).(Q/P).e_s.e_d \tag{5}$$

Substituting (4) and (5) for dP_1, dP_2 and dQ into the welfare expression at (1),

$$W' = Q.(t/E).e_d - (t/E).(Q/P).e_s.e_d. \ (t/E).e_d - 0.5(t/E).(Q/P).e_s.e_d.(t/E).e_s$$

$$= Q.(t/E).e_d \{1 - t/EP.e_s.e_d - 0.5(t/EP).e_s^2\} \tag{6}$$

Welfare will be maximised by differentiating (6) and setting the first derivative to zero, i.e.

$$dW'/dt = (Q/E).e_d - 2t.(Q/E^2.P).e_s.e_d^2 - t.(Q/E^2.P).e_d.e_s^2 = 0$$

so that

$$-t\{2(Q/E^2.P).e_s.e_d^2 + (Q/E^2.P).e_d.e_s^2\} = -(Q/E).e_d \tag{7}$$

The second-order condition for a maximum is obviously satisfied since $d^2W'/dt^2 < 0$.

Dividing both sides of (7) by $-(Q/E).e_d$,

$$t\{2.(e_s.e_d/EP) + (e_s^2/EP)\} = 1$$

so that

$$t = EP/(2.e_s.e_d + e_s^2) \tag{8}$$

Substituting $e_s + e_d$ for E in (8) and dividing both the numerator and the denominator of the RHS by e_s gives

$$t = P.(1 + e_d/e_s) / (2.e_d + e_s)$$

Hence, finally,

$$t/P = \frac{1 + e_d/e_s}{2.e_d + e_s}$$

Obviously the optimum tariff rate, t/P, can be zero if and only if e_s is infinity.

Testing the Theory 10

10.1   Some General Considerations

The purpose of economic theory is twofold. First, its objective is to identify those assumptions to which the predicted results are critically sensitive. This enables the user to judge the relevance of the analysis to a situation in which those assumptions are to some degree invalid. Second, the aim is to produce predictions concerning the results which may be expected to follow from specified changes in the situation. The predictions will hopefully be useful in formulating judgements as to whether the postulated changes are or are not in some sense advantageous; testing such predictions against observed reality also enables an assessment to be made of the validity of the underlying theory. In the case of customs union theory such testing is of particular relevance, since the analysis which has now been explored at some length indicates that the outcome of entry into a customs union is a distinctly ambiguous entity: the result may be a gain in some circumstances and a loss in others.

There now exists a small library of publications containing the results of research into the impact of the formation of the EEC. The overwhelming bulk of these studies consists of attempts to measure the static trade effects of the union, not so much because such effects are likely to be more important than others – indeed, it has already been argued that the reverse is almost certain to be the case – but because, quite frankly, the difficulties surrounding the measurement of trade effects are somewhat less formidable than those raised by the measurement of others.

The various estimates of the trade effects of the formation of the EEC rest essentially on the Vinerian proposition that the overall impact of the union is measured by the extent of net trade creation, i.e. the excess of gross trade creation over gross trade diversion or suppression. This is a measure of the combined production and consumption effects, since the net increase in trade results from both (a) an increase in total consumption as the result of lower domestic prices within the union and (b) a decrease in domestic production now displaced by cheaper imports from partner countries. Such an increased trade flow is not in itself a measure of increased welfare; this is estimated by the areas of the two triangles corresponding to the production and consumption effects. If it can be assumed that domestic prices fall by the full amount of the external tariff (since partner-country imports now enter tariff-free) then the total welfare gain will be given by one half of the net trade creation multiplied by the external tariff. It will be noted that already one crucial assumption has been made – namely that domestic prices fall by the full amount of the external tariff. This is almost certainly too strong; evidence indicates that exporters tend to set prices so as to be competitive with the corresponding local products, so that some of the tariff may be absorbed by the exporter rather than passed on to domestic consumers. If this is the case, the removal of the tariff will obviously not be fully reflected in import prices.

This is merely the beginning of the problems. A greater difficulty is to determine the magnitude of the trade creation attributable to the formation of the union; two main types of approach have been adopted in attempting to overcome it. On the one hand, analytical methods of varying degrees of sophistication have been used in order to predict *ex ante* the consequences of the known changes in tariff levels. If the elasticities of demand and supply for the products in question are known, then the corresponding welfare gain can be calculated. The main weakness of such methods (apart from the assumption, common to all estimates, that prices change by the full amount of the tariff) is that the estimates both of changes in trade flows and of their welfare consequences are crucially dependent on the validity of the underlying estimates of the elasticities of supply and demand. This is difficult in itself and made even more hazardous by the probability, established on both theoretical and empirical grounds, that such elasticities are substantially higher in the long run than in the short run, for fairly obvious reasons. The results of the estimates will therefore vary widely according to the time period over which they are made.

Most estimates have therefore been made on an *ex post* rather than an *ex ante* basis – that is to say, the pattern of trade at some point after the formation of the union has been compared with what that pattern would have been in the absence of the union, any differences thus observed being attributed to the effects of the customs union. Unfortunately this involves three very formidable difficulties. First, the hypothetical pattern of trade which would have existed in the absence of the customs union has to be estimated; as will be seen, different researchers have adopted different approaches to this tricky problem. Secondly, to attribute any observed differences in trade patterns exclusively to the effects of the customs union implies that the formation of the union was the *only* substantial factor operating over the period in question. This is clearly implausible. When the EEC was brought into existence so also was EFTA, and it is by no means easy to disentangle the effects of the one from the effects of the other. Again, the period of the 1960s, when the EEC came into operation, was one in which other obstacles to international trade – tariffs as well as restrictions on the exchange of domestic for foreign currencies – were being reduced on a worldwide scale. Indeed, two global rounds of general tariff reductions were conducted through GATT in that decade.

Finally, and perhaps most important, it is exceedingly difficult to separate the two conceptually separate types of effect generated by the formation of a customs union. On the one hand there are the static trade effects induced by integration; on the other hand there are its dynamic effects on the rate of economic growth. The two are obviously interconnected but, as was shown earlier, the dynamic effects, even if initially small, are likely to dominate as time passes. To escape this difficulty it is tempting to use only a relatively short period of time for the analysis in order to establish the trade effects; unfortunately this means that even some of the static effects may not have worked themselves out fully within the period considered.

Given all these very formidable problems, some observers have been tempted to conclude that no estimates of the effects of the formation of the EEC are worth the computer paper on which they are printed. This may perhaps be unduly pessimistic; certainly a collection of totally worthless estimates do not add up to a single meaningful one, but the estimates which have been made are imperfect rather than worthless. If they tend to convey and confirm broad orders of magnitude – indeed, if they show a consensus only on the *sign* of their results – they form some improvement on the vague generalities of predictions which inform us that something will happen subject to the proviso that, on the other hand, something quite different may occur.

10.2   Predicting Trade Patterns

Perhaps the most detailed investigation into the impact of the EEC on trade in manufactured goods was that published by Truman in 1975. This was based on changes in the pattern of trade in EEC and EFTA countries between 1960 and 1968, allowance being made for the effects in those two years of differences in the general level of economic prosperity. (It is almost universally the case that imports tend to accelerate when an economy is at a high level of activity and to decelerate when recessionary influences are in operation.) Using the simplifying device of denoting the countries entering into a customs union as A and B and denoting the rest of the world as C, in essence the analysis proceeded by examining the share of the total consumption of different product-groups in A accounted for by (i) production in A, (ii) imports from B and (iii) imports from C, all in the two years 1960 and 1968. The logic of the argument is that if the ratio (i) had decreased the union had been trade-creating – and to a measurable amount reflected in the size of that decrease. If ratio (ii) had increased and ratio (iii) decreased, the union would have been trade-diverting, and so on. An obvious objection to this would have been that it assumed that the various ratios would have been unchanged in the absence of the formation of the EEC. Clearly, ratio (i) might have been falling and (ii) and (iii) increasing in any event, simply because of the general easing of restrictions on world trade. A second set of estimates was therefore made on the assumption that the hypothetical shares in 1968 were *not* the same as those in 1960 but were at the level they would have reached by 1968 if the trend observed in them during the 1950s had continued through the 1960s.

The central figures derived from these two sets of estimates are shown in line 6 of Table 10.1. They suggested that the EEC had been quite definitely trade-creating; the estimated volume of trade creation exceeded the estimated trade diverted and suppressed by roughly 200 per cent. They also indicated that EFTA had been trade-creating on balance as well, but by a much smaller margin – around 40 per cent. Having said that, the estimates indicated that the magnitude of this net trade creation was relatively small, amounting to perhaps 4–5 per cent of the growth in potential demand over the period concerned. They

Table 10.1
The Static Trade Effects of the EEC (Equivalent in 1986 ECU bn)

Author of study	Methodology of study	Year to which estimate relates	ECU bn		
			Trade creation	Trade diversion	Net trade creation
(1)	(2)	(3)	(4)	(5)	(6)
A. All trade					
1. Balassa	Growth-adjusted imports	1970	46.5	1.2	45.3
2. Prewo	Input–output analysis	1970	81.5	− 10.3	91.8
3. Aitken	Normalised cross-section	1967	45.5	3.0	42.5
Average			57.8	− 2.0	59.8
B. Trade in manufactures					
4. Balassa	Growth-adjusted imports	1970	46.9	0.4	46.5
5. Prewo	Input–output analysis	1970	74.1	− 12.8	86.9
6. Truman	Adjusted import shares	1968	44.2	− 4.8	49.0
7. Kreinin	US normalised	1969/70	29.9	7.6	22.3
8. Williamson-Bottrill	Normalised on rest of world	1969	51.6	—	51.6
9. Verdoorn-Schwartz	Normalised on world trade	1968	48.5	5.3	53.8
Average			49.2	− 0.7	49.9

SOURCE   Based on data given in B. Balassa, 'Trade creation and trade diversion in the European Common Market: an appraisal of the evidence', in B. Balassa (ed.), *European Economic Integration* (Amsterdam: North-Holland, 1975), Ch. 3, Table 3.5.

also indicated that the trade-diversion effects of the EEC were concentrated almost entirely on EFTA and the United States; there appeared to have been substantial (external) trade creation with the rest of the world. The fact that roughly a half of this external trade creation occurred with Japan, however, emphasises the danger of assuming that these trade changes occurred solely as the result of the creation of the EEC; between 1960 and 1970 the share of Japan in total world exports increased from 3.6 per cent to 6.9 per cent, a phenomenon scarcely attributable to the Treaty of Rome.

A second major investigation, the results of which were published at about the same time, that of Balassa, adopted a different approach to this crucial issue of the hypothetical pattern of trade against which the actual post-EEC pattern was to be compared. The study examined the changes in trade patterns between 1959 and 1970, covering trade in agricultural products as well as in manufactures. Instead of hypothesising that in the absence of the EEC the pattern of trade would have been the same as that prior to its formation, or adjusted by a rather arbitrary trend in it, the analysis was based on estimates of the import income-elasticity of demand and so took account of the significant rise in real incomes amongst the EEC countries during the 1960s. Put formally, if M_b represents total imports by country A from country B, M_c its imports from country C, Y its national income and dM_b, dM_c and dY the changes in each of these totals over a given period (1953–9 in this case) then the import income-elasticities, E_b and E_c respectively, are given by

$$E_b = (dM_b/dY)/(Y/M_b) \quad \text{and} \quad E_c = (dM_c/dY)/(Y/M_c).$$

If the change in income over the period concerned (1959 to 1970) is known, the expected values for the changes in imports from B and C can be calculated. As with the Truman study, comparison of the actual changes with these expected changes can be used to measure the trade creation and trade diversion effects.

It will be clear that this method is an improvement on the Truman approach in that it takes specific account of changes which could have been expected to occur solely as a result of rising real income, quite apart from those induced by integration. Nevertheless it rests on the assumption that the elasticities calculated from the experience of 1953–9 remained unchanged during 1959–70. This is questionable because such elasticities may themselves be affected by increases in the level of income; income increases may be trade-biased (i.e. people may prefer French wine to British cider as they become richer) or anti-trade-biased (i.e. people may spend more of each addition to their income on domestic leisure pursuits rather than on imported manufactures). Furthermore, such elasticities are liable to vary with changes in the relative prices of domestic and imported products, including those induced by movements in the rate of exchange. There is also the familiar problem that trade patterns were being influenced during this period by relaxations in foreign exchange controls and worldwide tariff negotiations.

The conclusions drawn from this study were in fact quite similar to those of the Truman study. So far as trade in manufactures was concerned, trade diversion was estimated to be virtually nil while net trade creation was estimated to be somewhat greater than in the Truman calculations. Not surprisingly, given the establishment of the Common Agricultural Policy in the mid-1960s, the Balassa study indicated considerable trade diversion in agricultural products, food imports into the EEC in 1970 being roughly 20 per cent smaller than would have been expected from the 1953–9 income elasticities. Even so, the EEC appeared to have been trade-creating overall to a considerable degree.

A number of other studies have adopted a totally different approach to the problem of estimating the trade pattern which would have existed in the absence of the EEC. This is the so-called 'normalisation' method by which it is assumed that had the EEC not come into existence the level and pattern of the trade of the member countries would have developed in the same way as that observed over the same period in some comparable country or group of countries outside the EEC which is assumed to exhibit the 'normal' development. The difference between this 'normalised' trade structure and the one actually observed is, as before, attributed to the effects of integration. The main difficulty here, of course, is to decide which country or group of countries can be regarded as normal. One study (Aitken) assumed that the normal development of trade patterns would be that exhibited within Western Europe as a whole; another (Krcinen) took the United States as the standard of comparison; a third (Williamson and Bottrill) took the rest of the world outside the EEC as the standard; a fourth (Verdoorn and Schwartz) took world trade as a whole as the standard. Despite these differences in the basis of comparison, the resulting estimates were really quite similar; in every case they indicated that the trade creation effects of the EEC had been positive and very much larger than its trade diversion effects.

Finally, mention should be made of one *ex ante* study – that is, an attempt to predict the effects of the formation of the EEC on the basis of data available at the time of its inception rather than by comparing the actual outcome, after the event, with some hypothesised alternative. This is an analysis by Prewo based on an input–output model – that is, a numerical representation of the network of trade relationships between the 6 and the rest of the world. The model enables estimates to be made of the trade consequences of the known rate of growth, using as its basis the relationship between the output of individual industries and the various kinds of inputs necessary to produce those outputs. This type of analysis has been shown to have immense powers of prediction over short periods of time but its application over a period of more than a year or two is suspect, precisely because it rests on the implicit assumption of constancy in the technology of each industry – the level and pattern of inputs required for its output. Such an assumption over a decade like the 1960s, featured by rapid technological change, is very questionable. The results indicated a degree of trade creation of much greater magnitude than that suggested by other studies and, more surprisingly, negative trade diversion even in the agricultural sector.

This implies that the EEC actually caused imports from the rest of the world to be higher than would otherwise be the case.

The main results of all these studies are summarised in Table 10.1. At first sight they give an impression of bewildering disagreement, confirming the suspicion that estimates involving so many heroic assumptions concerning so many variables could scarcely attain credibility. Yet there exists a broad consensus. Without exception they indicate trade creation effects of far greater magnitude than trade diversion effects. Of the seven different studies included, five yield estimates of gross trade creation in the range of ECU 44–52 bn and of gross trade diversion in the range of − ECU 5 bn to + ECU 5 bn. To say that the EEC resulted in net trade creation of around ECU 50–60 bn by the end of the 1960s would therefore be a not unreasonable guess. If this is accepted, it has to be concluded that the *welfare* gains from the trade effects of integration must have been very small indeed. Net trade creation of even ECU 60 bn, given an internal tariff reduction of around 12 per cent, would imply a welfare gain of only around ECU 3.6 bn – about 0.18 per cent of the Community's national income in 1970.

10.3   Scale and the Terms of Trade

If there are forbidding difficulties in estimating the static trade effects of the creation of the EEC, those surrounding estimates of its other static effects take on Olympian proportions. The measurement of economies of scale has long been a matter of (generally amicable) dispute amongst econometricians. One well-known study by Walters in 1963 was based on the experience of the United States in the first half of the twentieth century and concluded that an increase of 100 per cent in the inputs to US industry over that period had resulted in an increase of 130 per cent in total output. If it can be assumed (and the 'if' is a large one) that this economy of inputs was due solely to economies of scale, it follows that the reduction in the unit cost of the additional output (a saving of 30 per cent of inputs on 130 per cent additional output) amounted to about 23 per cent. Again assuming that the guestimated maximum net trade creation of some ECU 60 bn represented additional output resulting from the formation of the EEC, the gains from economies of scale would amount to around ECU 14 bn – about 0.7 per cent of national income compared with the 0.18 per cent attributable to the trade effects.

A more recent study (by Dr N. Owen in 1983) has suggested that the gains from economies of scale may have been considerably greater than this. In the first place it is argued, not unreasonably, that the full effects of integration on the scale and location of output would have taken a fair amount of time and if the trade expansion of the 1960s had continued through the 1970s the increased trade generated by integration would have doubled by 1980 to around

ECU 100 bn. This would have two effects. First, roughly a quarter of the additional trade would have benefited consumers purely through the greater variety of choice it gave them rather than through inceased output as such, a benefit estimated at 20 per cent of price or about ECU 5 bn. The remaining 75 per cent of the additional trade, representing an increase in total output, would have secured resource-saving benefits which are estimated at upwards of 50 per cent of total costs. The direct gains from economies of scale in traded goods in 1980 would thus be at least ECU 40 bn and conceivably much more. Further, US experience indicates that productivity gains in manufacturing industry lead to gains of about a third of their magnitude in the non-manufacturing sectors, so that the scale effects in the economy as a whole could amount to anything between 3 per cent and 6 per cent of the national income.

The fragile nature of so much of the estimation in these studies will be too obvious to require stress. They do appear to suggest, however, that the welfare gains identified by the standard trade-creation, trade-diversion analysis are likely to have been of quite minor importance in comparison with those generated by the exploitation of economies of scale in the larger, integrated market of a customs union. The inherent difficulty of their measurement in no way implies their unimportance.

The appraisal of the impact of integration on the terms of trade of the members of a customs union raises such enormous problems that very few researchers have attempted it. The exercise required here is a comparison of the relative prices of the exports and imports of member countries after the formation of the union with what those relative prices would have been had the union not been formed. Given the inability of skilled professionals to predict the world prices of goods – primary products especially – even one year ahead in the world as it exists, the attempt to do the same for some notional world which would have existed in the absence of events which did in fact occur is not one which most people would be anxious to undertake. One purely theoretical investigation (by Petith in 1977) attempted to reach some conclusions on the basis of postulated elasticities of demand and supply; the results indicated that terms-of-trade gains through the formation of the EEC could have amounted to between 0.3 per cent and 0.9 per cent of national income. To treat this as a positive estimate would however be unfair to the study itself; at most it can be interpreted as raising the possibility that such gains, like those from the exploitation of economies of scale, may well be considerably greater in magnitude than the direct trade-creation gains of the standard Viner analysis.

10.4 Dynamic effects

The estimation problems involved with the dynamic effects of a customs union are even greater than those generated by the estimation of static effects. The difficulty lies not so much with the measurement of changes in the rate of growth between two periods but with the attribution of their causes. The process of economic growth is not one which is well understood; there is common agreement, however, that the factors contributing to it are many and various, ranging from the rate of investment to the educational level of the workforce. By definition, dynamic effects can make themselves felt only over a substantial period of time and the longer the time period involved in any analysis the more likely is it that a multiplicity of factors will be interacting with each other, rendering the separation of contributory causes immensely difficult. In such circumstances there is a strong temptation for researchers to try to eliminate factors which *can* be measured (such as additions to the capital stock or to the working population) and to then attribute the unexplained residual to some favoured explanation. The results of such an analysis therefore depend crucially on which factors are chosen for elimination and which are left as residuals.

Because of the almost insurmountable statistical problems involved there have been very few attempts at systematic estimation of the impact of the formation of the EEC on the rate of growth – that is, on the one hand, of the improvements in efficiency generated by the increased competition following upon the elimination of tariffs and, on the other hand, of the increase in investment generated by the expansion of markets. One exception is the investigation by Marques Mendes (1986) the results of which are summarised in Table 10.2. These results are, in many respects, surprising and place something of a strain on credulity; even so, the investigation deserves respect (recalling Dr Johnson on the subject of female preachers) not so much because it yielded surprising results but because it was carried out at all.

The first illuminating feature is that an attempt was made to isolate the *dynamic* effects of changes in the terms of trade during the two periods 1961–72 and 1974–81 rather than the static effects discussed earlier. Such effects arise from the fact that exports, by generating incomes within an economy, add to the growth of aggregate demand within it whereas imports, which generate incomes outside the economy, reduce it. A rise in the total expenditure on imports relative to the total value of exports will therefore reduce the internal rate of growth; such a rise could of course be the result of a rise in the prices of imports relative to those of exports as well as in their volume. This investigation suggests that during 1961–72 such a change (i.e. in the terms of trade) actually reduced the overall growth rate in the EEC countries by 0.34 per cent per annum. During 1974–81, on the other hand, this effect was reversed. It need hardly be added that to say that a decline *occurred* in the terms of trade of the EEC during the 1960s is quite a different matter from saying that the decline was *caused* by the establishment of the EEC.

The estimates of the internal dynamic effects are perhaps of more interest. For the earlier period they are put at an additional growth rate of 0.20 per cent; the figure may seem small but, being equivalent in 1971 to over ECU 4 bn, it

Table 10.2
The Dynamic Effects of European Integration

| Country | 1961–1972 | | | | 1974–1981 | | | |
| | Effect on growth rate (%) | | Value in 1986 (ECU bn) | | Effect on growth rate (%) | | Value in 1986 (ECU bn) | |
(1)	Terms of trade (2)	Other dynamic effects (3)	Terms of trade (4)	Other dynamic effects (5)	Terms of trade (6)	Other dynamic effects (7)	Terms of trade (8)	Other dynamic effects (9)
Belgium/Luxembourg	+ 0.17	+ 2.28	+ 0.19	+ 2.58	+ 0.22	+ 0.49	+ 0.30	+ 0.67
France	− 0.57	− 2.14*	− 3.44	− 12.92	+ 0.39	+ 1.18	+ 2.93	+ 8.85
Germany	− 0.02	—	− 0.15	—	+ 0.01	+ 0.90	+ 0.09	+ 7.95
Italy	− 0.94	+ 1.98	− 4.71	+ 9.92	− 0.05	+ 0.47	− 0.32	+ 2.97
Nethe-lands	− 0.19	+ 3.13	− 0.28	+ 4.68	− 0.07	+ 0.60	− 0.13	+ 1.12
Total, EC 6	− 0.34	+ 0.20	− 7.22	+ 4.26	+ 0.11	+ 0.83	+ 2.87	+21.56
Denmark					+ 1.51	− 0.87	+ 1.06	− 0.61
Ireland					− 0.32	+ 0.63	− 0.09	+ 0.19
United Kingdom					+ 0.31	+ 0.06	+ 2.04	+ 0.39
Total, EC 9	− 0.34	+ 0.20	− 7.22	+ 4.26	+ 0.18	+ 0.64	+ 5.88	+21.53

* Principally attributed to a deterioration in the balance of payments; this estimate is however subject to a particularly large residual error.

SOURCE Based on data given in A. J. Marques Mendes, 'The contribution of the European Community to economic growth', *Journal of Common Market Studies*, Vol. XXIV, No. 4, June 1986, Tables 1 and 2.

implies an increase of welfare greater than that estimated for the static trade effects. What is more, it is a continuing gain and not simply a once-for-all-matter. That the overall figure is so low is due entirely to the fact that for Germany the dynamic effects were estimated at zero while for France they were estimated to be substantially negative. The former result, while surprising, is perhaps explicable on the basis that for Germany entry into the EEC resulted in an external tariff which was in general higher rather than lower than before. While French industry was relatively very vulnerable to competition from abroad, and especially from Germany, the suggestion of a rather large negative dynamic effect of entry into the EEC is a little difficult to believe.

The extension of the analysis to the period after the first enlargement of the Community yields results which are in general much more credible – although this fact neither increases nor reduces their inherent reliability. What is notable about them is the very large magnitude of the estimated internal dynamic effects attributed to union. If the 1981 value of around ECU 22 bn (more than 1 per cent of the 1970 national income *per annum*) is anywhere near the truth, these effects, continuing year by year would be far greater than any conceivable gains arising from the static effects of the union.

Given the enormous conceptual and statistical problems inherent in this sort of exercise, this conclusion is perhaps the only one to be drawn from it with any degree of confidence. An additional 1 per cent of national income every year (as in the cases of France and Germany) is a very considerable benefit, especially in relation to a total rate of growth which had fallen (in the original Six) from a little over 5 per cent a year during the 1960s to less than 2.5 per cent in the 1970s. If even the broad order of magnitude of these results are accepted, Viner's conclusion that a customs union brings essentially political, rather than economic, advantage is clearly in need of substantial revision.

Further Reading

Balassa, B. A. (ed.), *European Economic Integration* (Amsterdam: North-Holland, 1975).

Marques Mendes, A. J., 'The contribution of the European Community to economic growth', *Journal of Common Market Studies*, Vol. xxiv, No. 4, June 1986.

Marques Mendes, A. J., *Economic integration and growth in Europe* (London: Croom Helm, 1986).

Mayes, D. G., 'The effects of economic integration on trade', *Journal of Common Market Studies*, Vol. xvii, No. 1, September 1978.

Owen, N., *Economies of Scale ... within the European Community* (London: Oxford University Press, 1983).

Robson, P., *The Economics of International Integration*, 2nd edn (London: Allen & Unwin, 1964).

The Impact on Britain 11

11.1 Small Expectations

In the early months of 1970, when the departure of President de Gaulle had once more revived the possibility of British membership of the Community, a Labour government was in office and under its direction a White Paper, *Britain and the European Communities: an Economic Assessment* (Cmd 4289), was published setting out the official estimates of the likely consequences of membership. The main features of these are shown in Table 11.1. The view was taken that, so far as trade in manufactures was concerned, both imports from and exports to the Community would be increased by much the same extent so that gains from net trade creation in manufactured goods were not expected to be of any significant amount. This was not entirely unreasonable; the average

Table 11.1
UK Static Gains and Losses from EC Membership, 1980 (ECU bn at 1986 prices)

Estimate	Trade creation	Trade diversion	Terms of trade	Budget	Total
(1)	(2)	(3)	(4)	(5)	(6)
1970 White Paper (inelastic)	—	− 3.72	+ 1.61	− 6.06	− 8.17
1970 White Paper (elastic)	—	− 2.26	+ 0.73	− 3.91	− 5.44
1971 White Paper	—	− 1.83	+ 0.36	− 2.83	− 4.30
Miller and Spencer (1977)	+ 0.43	− 1.58	+ 0.91	− 4.80	− 5.04
Josling and Williamson (1977)	+ 0.58	− 1.01	+ 0.38	− 4.43	− 3.48

SOURCE Based on data given by P. Robson, *The Economics of International Integration* (London: Allen & Unwin, 1980).

109

UK tariff was now only around 6 per cent and its abolition on intra-Community trade could be expected to have only relatively small effects. That there would be substantial trade diversion in agricultural products was however a certainty, given the need for Britain to participate in the Common Agricultural Policy and thus switch imports from the traditional low-cost producers – the British Commonwealth and the United States – to relatively high-cost producers in Europe. The magnitude of this would depend on the elasticity of demand for food, and thus the effects of price increases on consumption, and on the elasticity of supply from domestic agriculture and the output responses to those same price increases. On an optimistic view the net loss by 1980, when the transitional period would have been completed, would be the equivalent of about ECU 2.3 bn; on a more pessimistic view it was put at about ECU 3.7 bn.

Somewhat surprisingly, however, substantial gains were anticipated from an improvement in the terms of trade on remaining imports from the rest of the world as a result of the reduced volume of imports of agricultural products, a gain offset to a small degree from an anticipated worsening of the UK terms of trade on manufactures as British exporters were forced to reduce prices to meet fiercer competition from continental producers. On an optimistic assessment this net gain was estimated at around ECU 1.6 bn; a more pessimistic assessment placed it at only around ECU 0.7 bn. Finally, on top of all this had to be added the 'transfer' cost of British membership – that is, the net contribution which Britain was expected to have to make to the community budget. This also depended heavily on the extent to which UK agriculture could increase output; on the one hand, this would reduce the levies on non-Community agricultural imports paid over to Brussels and, on the other hand, bring benefits from the Community budget's dominant item, payments under the common agricultural policy. The overall loss was put at anything between ECU 4 bn and ECU 6 bn.

The overall prediction was therefore a distinctly pessimistic one; it was not a question of whether membership would be economically disadvantageous but rather one of the size of the burden. At best, by 1980 it would amount to around ECU 5.5 bn a year; at worst, it would be over ECU 8 bn. Some rather vague references were made to the possibility of substantial dynamic effects to offset this loss, but the tone of the references did not carry a great deal of conviction.

The accession of a Conservative government in the second half of 1970 and the ensuing negotiations in Brussels led to a second White Paper in 1971 – *The United Kingdom and the European Communities* (Cmd 4715). This displayed a remarkable increase in both the precision and the optimism of the official forecasts of the impact by 1980. The assumption that gains from net trade creation in manufactures would be insignificant was retained. The estimate of the loss from trade diversion in agricultural products was however sharply reduced, as Table 11.1 shows, to one which was well below the most optimistic figure in the 1970 White Paper; the corresponding gain from improved terms of trade with the rest of the world in agricultural products had correspondingly to fall well below the previous estimates. Similarly, the estimated net contribution to the Community budget was also sharply reduced to a figure well below those of 1971. The result was that the estimated overall net cost of membership was now considered to be some 20 per cent below the optimistic end of the 1970 range and only a little more than a half of the pessimistic end. This net cost would represent a mere 0.6 per cent of what proved to be the country's national income in 1980, compared with something between 0.8 per cent and 1.2 per cent. What is more, much greater emphasis was now placed on the likely dynamic effect of membership on the overall rate of growth of the British economy; even a very small contribution from this direction, it was argued with some force, would rapidly more than offset this rather small once-for-all loss from the static effects.

Subsequent private estimates, as will be seen from Table 11.1 tended to confirm the comparative optimism of the 1971 White Paper rather than its predecessor. Somewhat more importance was attached to the possible gains from net trade creation in manufactures; in the light of experience, however, the budgetary burden involved was being revised upwards. But the general impression was similar; membership of the Community was to be a rather costly luxury so far as its static effects were concerned.

11.2 The Trade Effects

The period following its accession to the Community was undoubtedly one of overall trade expansion for the United Kingdom. Merchandise trade accounted for 36 per cent of its GDP in 1973 but 44 per cent by 1980. What is more, the expansion of trade with the Community was much more marked than its overseas trade in general; between those years exports to the Community rose from 32 per cent of the total to 43 per cent, while imports from the Community rose from just under 33 per cent to nearly 39 per cent. As had been foreseen, a substantial outflow of foreign exchange occurred because of the contribution Britain was required to make to the Community budget, although the increase of some ECU 1.2 bn was considerably less than had been feared. As Table 11.2 shows, Britain's balance of trade with the EEC countries improved dramatically from a deficit in 1973 to a surplus in 1980.

Two qualifications must immediately be made to this comforting picture. First, the period of the late 1970s saw a very rapid upsurge of oil exports from the UK and this was the major factor behind the improvement of Britain's trade balance with the world as a whole from a deficit of ECU 13.5 bn in 1973 to a surplus of ECU 3.3 bn in 1980; entry into the EEC obviously played no part in that. Secondly, as Table 11.2 shows, 1980 was something of a freak year; within three years the UK balance of trade with the Community was back into substantial deficit.

Table 11.2
UK Balance of Payments with the EC 1973–87 (ECU bn at 1986 prices)

(1)	1973 (2)	1980 (3)	1987 (4)
Exports	32.22	51.63	53.19
Imports	43.34	49.80	65.46
Balance of trade	− 11.12	+ 1.83	− 12.27
Government transfers (net)	− 1.12	− 2.10	− 2.63
Other invisibles (net)	+ 1.92	+ 0.60	− 3.03
Balance of payments on current account	− 10.32	+ 0.33	− 17.93

SOURCE   Based on data in *Balance of Payments of the United Kingdom* (London: HMSO, 1984 and 1988).

When attention is focused on Britain's trade in manufactures, the picture begins to look rather different. In 1973 there had been a deficit of around ECU 2.3 bn on UK trade in manufactured goods with the EEC; by 1980 this had risen to about ECU 3.2 bn; by 1983 the deficit was over ECU 14 bn. Once again it would be quite erroneous to attribute this deterioration to membership of the EEC. It was in fact a mirror image of Britain's declining competitiveness with the world as a whole and, conversely, with the emergence of Japan as the world's most formidable exporter of industrial products. The rate of growth of the deficit in manufacturing trade with the EEC countries over this period was in fact almost identical to that with the rest of the world. Leaving aside for a moment the effects of this growing deficit on the internal rate of growth of the economy, most researchers in this area have concluded that there was on balance a small net trade creation effect in manufactured products as the result of UK entry. Estimates of its size vary widely but a recent extensive study (Winters, 1987) puts the total for manufactures in 1979 at the equivalent of around ECU 23.6 bn. Assuming a price reduction of 6 per cent as the result of the abolition of the tariff, this would imply a net welfare gain of about ECU 0.7 bn – very much in line with the two earlier private estimates shown in col.(2) of Table 11.1.

So far as agricultural trade is concerned the picture is of course totally different. Domestic agricultural output rose by some 20 per cent between 1972 and 1980 – a rate of growth not in fact markedly different from that of the previous decade or so – leading to some trade suppression. Much more important, there was a massive trade diversion effect, UK imports of food, drink and tobacco from the EEC rising from less than 12 per cent of the total in 1972 to more than 22 per cent in 1978. Since the prices being paid for European produce were well above the general world level, the welfare effect was clearly negative. One detailed investigation (Harvey and Thomson, 1985) has estimated that the gains to UK producers as a result of accession to the EEC, through both higher output and higher prices, amounted in 1984 to around ECU 6.7 bn; the loss to consumers through higher prices (apart from their losses as taxpayers to the EEC budget) amounted to around ECU 8.7 bn, making a net welfare loss for the UK of ECU 2 bn – a distinctly higher figure than that advanced in either of the earlier private estimates.

The task of estimating UK gains or losses through changes in its terms of trade deriving from accession to the EEC is of course immensely difficult, especially as the period concerned witnessed both the emergence of the UK as a major oil producer and a doubling of the world price of oil in 1978–9. The task is so forbidding, in fact, that very few researchers have been prepared to undertake it. It will be recalled that in the previous chapter (Table 10.2) one estimate suggested that in 1981 the improvement in the UK terms of trade resulting from accession could have been worth the equivalent of some ECU 2.0 bn; it is an estimate which must be treated with a great deal of caution. The final element in the cost of entry, however, is known with a high degree of accuracy. As Table 11.2 shows, net payments to the Community budget by UK taxpayers in 1980 amounted to ECU 2.3 bn.

11.3 Other Effects

Widespread disagreement inevitably exists over what benefits, if any, were experienced by Britain as the result of economies of scale arising from additional output generated by accession to the EEC. Winters (1987) has estimated that additional exports to the EEC countries as a consequence of accession amounted in 1979 to the equivalent of ECU 13.1 bn, whereas exports diverted from the rest of the world amounted to ECU 4.9 bn, giving net export creation of some ECU 8.2 bn. If, following Walters, it is assumed that the cost reduction achieved by this additional output averaged 23 per cent, the gain in resource use would be valued at ECU 1.9 bn. If, on the other hand, the Owen approach described in the previous chapter is adopted, the gain would have amounted to around ECU 3.5 bn.

It has to be said that other writers have expressed considerable scepticism concerning the additional economies of scale likely to be obtained as a result of entry into the EEC. The evidence suggests that the size of the UK market was already large enough to enable producers to operate at the minimum efficient scale and it is also known that at the time of UK entry the size of manufacturing plants in the UK was in general much larger than was typical in the Six. What is more, a great many of the multinational corporations producing for world, rather than domestic, markets were already established in the UK before entry; hence the abolition of a relatively small tariff on exports to the Community would have been unlikely to induce any very marked expansion of their scale of operation.

The discussion of the possible dynamic effects of entry has evoked equal disagreement and the evidence is necessarily thin. One approach has been to compare the comparative growth rates of the UK and the Six during the periods immediately before and immediately after 1973 and to attribute the difference to the dynamic impact of accession. If this were to be accepted (and the heroic assumption being adopted is plain) then it would be argued that the increase in the *comparative* growth rate of the UK between 1963–72 and 1973–80, from 64 per cent to 71 per cent of that of the Six, would imply a rise in the UK growth rate of 0.16 per cent per annum, equivalent in 1980 to about ECU 1.1 bn. On the other hand, the estimates summarised in Table 10.2 suggest that (terms of trade effects apart) accession had raised the UK growth rate by somewhat less – 0.06 per cent per annum – equivalent in 1980 to only some ECU 0.4 bn.

Even this has been questioned, doubts being expressed as to whether a relatively small reduction in tariffs would be likely to have any significant impact on European (and especially British) entrepreneurs distinguished by their inclination to avoid risk rather than to maximise profit, and by their preference for market-sharing rather than market-capturing. (The continuous pursuit and prosecution by the Commission of the operators of market-sharing arrangements throughout the life of the Community, described in the next chapter, tends to confirm that the latter is especially prevalent.) But the admittedly fragmentary evidence does give modest support to a belief in the likely existence of some dynamic impact. The share of US and Japanese overseas investment coming to the United Kingdom steadily increased after Britain's accession and it seems not implausible to conclude that this owed something to the advantage now enjoyed by the UK as a base for duty-free access to the Community.

11.4   To Conclude

The evidence is obviously too flimsy and incomplete to permit of categoric conclusions. It is perhaps unfortunate that it is strongest (in relative terms) on the traditional static effects and weakest on dynamic effects – which in the long run are bound to be of greater importance. In 1980 it would appear that the trade diversion costs associated with agricultural products (around ECU 2 bn) heavily outweighed any possible gains from trade creation in manufactures (say ECU 0.7 bn) and the transfer costs of the EEC budget certainly imposed a cost of around ECU 2.3 billion. This total, representing a net loss of about ECU 3.6 bn a year is really remarkably close to that estimated by the 1971 White Paper. Whether this can be substantially offset by gains accruing from changes in the UK's terms of trade or from additional economies of scale must remain a matter of some dispute; estimates suggest that it might be more than offset, but their statistical basis has to be conceded to be very uncertain indeed.

The question thus reduces to one of whether this probable annual loss of the order of ECU 3–4 bn made accession something of a disaster from a purely economic point of view. The answer must depend in the last resort on the view taken of the change, if any, induced in the trend of the growth rate of the British economy. An annual loss of even ECU 4 bn a year in 1980 amounted, after all, to only 0.6 per cent of the UK national income. Even the lower of the two estimates of the dynamic impact, equivalent to 0.06 per cent of national income, would imply that 70 per cent of that loss had already been recouped through higher growth by 1980 and that by the tenth anniversary of UK accession the true annual cost would be zero. From that point on the gains might be small but they would be positive.

The fact is that, unlike the original Six, Britain entered into this far-reaching experiment at a time when the economy of the industrialised world was entering a phase of quite severe recession so that most governments, and most entrepreneurs, were concerned with damage-limitation rather than a dash for expansion. The evidence certainly indicates that the opportunities presented by the enlargement of the Community were seized more effectively by the older Continental partners than by the newcomers but it is not unreasonable to conclude that, trade diversion losses or no, the 1980s would have been distinctly bleaker for the United Kingdom if it had been outside rather than inside the Community. That is far from being an established fact but it is reasonable to conclude that the balance of probabilities lies on that side.

Further Reading

Davenport, M., 'The economic impact of the EEC', in A. Boltho (ed.), *The European Economy* (London: Oxford University Press, 1982).

El-Agraa, A. M. (ed.), *Britain within the European Community* (London: Macmillan, 1983).

Harvey, D., and Thomson, K. J., 'Costs, benefits and the future of the Common Agricultural Policy', *Journal of Common Market Studies*, Vol. xxiv, No. 1, September 1985.

Jenkins, R. (ed.), *Britain and the EEC* (London: Macmillan, 1982).

Mayes, D. G., 'The effects of economic integration on trade', *Journal of Common Market Studies*, Vol. xxvii, No. 1, September 1978.

Wallace, W. (ed.), *Britain in Europe* (London: Heinemann, 1980).

Winters, L., 'Britain in Europe: a Survey of quantitative studies', *Journal of Common Market Studies*, Vol. xxv, No. 4, June 1987.

Part III

Microeconomic policies

Competition Policy 12

12.1 Why a Policy?

The most obvious manifestation of the formation of a customs union is that the partner countries agree to abolish all tariff duties on trade with each other. Hence Article 13 of the Treaty of Rome required the member countries to abolish all customs duties on trade with one another, in a series of steps of 10 per cent of the initial tariff level, between 1 January 1959 and 31 December 1969. For once the declared intentions of politicians bore a close resemblance to what subsequently occurred; indeed, by July 1968, eighteen months ahead of schedule, the final tariff reduction was applied. From that date onwards all duties on trade between member countries were abolished and a common external tariff on trade with non-member countries was established. (The only, rather sad, exception to this generalisation is that the common tariff is not applied to trade between East and West Germany; the latter, declining to accept the partition of Germany as a legal reality, to this day has officially no *imports* from East Germany. Goods passing from East to West Germany and then subsequently travelling elsewhere in the Community, however, are then subjected to the common external tariff.)

As the theoretical discussion of Part II emphasised, however, the consequences of such tariff reductions predicted for a perfectly competitive world may fail to materialise in the real world in which markets are far from perfect. The founding fathers of the Community were not so ingenuous as to be unaware of this fact and Part Three of the Treaty therefore provided for, amongst other things, common rules governing competition – what would be more generally described as a competition policy.

The term 'competition policy' is a rather vague and elusive one. It refers in general to laws and other executive actions by a government – or, in this case, the Community as a whole acting through the Commission – designed to eliminate, or at least discourage, restrictive business practices such as cartels, monopolies or other non-tariff barriers which have as their effect, in the words of the Treaty, 'the prevention, restriction or distortion of competition'. Competition policy, in other words, is concerned with market behaviour; it is aimed at ensuring that business enterprises conduct their affairs in a manner as close as possible to that postulated by the textbook world of perfect competition. It may therefore concern itself with a very wide range of practices. These may include (a) agreements or arrangements whereby collusion is established between nominally independent competing enterprises, (b) market control exercised through monopolistic power possessed by single enterprises or (c) distortions of the market engendered by governments through subsidies, administrative or legal devices or purchasing policies.

The whole economic philosophy of the Treaty of Rome is in fact shot through with the concept of the superiority and supremacy of the operation of fully and freely competitive markets. The essential core of the competition policy embodied in the Treaty is however contained in three particular articles. Article 85 is concerned with arrangements arrived at between nominally independent enterprises. Article 86 is concerned with the behaviour of individual enterprises having a dominant position in their industries. Finally, Article 92 is concerned with actions by governments which have the effect of interfering with the natural outcome of the free play of market forces. Before considering the provisions of these articles, however, it is necessary to examine the powers with which the drafters of the Treaty endowed the Commission in order that the latter should effectively seek to realise their aims.

12.2 Power to the Commission's Elbow

Article 87 of the Treaty of Rome provided that within three years of its entry into force the Council of Ministers would lay down any regulations necessary to ensure that the principles embodied in Articles 85 and 86 were applied in practice. To do this effectively, the Commission clearly needed powers of discovery, since businessmen making arrangements to qualify the free operation of market forces do not normally do so in the broad light of day; it also needed power to acquire the information necessary to establish that such arrangements had the effect of preventing or distorting competition; finally it needed powers to ensure that such arrangements, once their existence had been established, were suitably modified or abandoned.

The satisfaction of the requirements of Article 87 fell a little behind the timetable specified, but in 1962 the Council agreed on Regulation 17/62 which gave the Commission very far-reaching powers which it could exercise on its own initiative and without seeking further Ministerial approval. Broadly, it was authorised to receive and investigate complaints submitted to it by anyone having a legitimate interest in the matters involved but also to initiate its own enquiries and investigations. To these ends it was also given powers of search and seizure – the right to obtain entry into any business premises and to demand any books or records contained in them which the Commission considered relevant to its enquiries. Finally, having conducted such investigations it was empowered to produce a 'reasoned decision' embodying its findings; if these were that a breach of the Treaty had been committed, then it could require the appropriate member government to take measures to remedy the situation or could itself impose a penalty on the offending parties of anything up to 10 per cent of their annual turnover. The alleged offenders would of course have the right to appeal to the Court of Justice and seek to have the decision overturned.

These extensive powers became the subject of considerable concern in more than one member country; they seem to breach the fundamental principles of jurisprudence in that the Commission was able to exercise the threefold power of investigator, prosecutor and judge, functions which are normally discharged separately by the police, the legal profession and the judiciary. The rights of the accused – in this case, the firms under investigation – seemed, on the other hand, to be very limited. (In one celebrated case, that of Hoffman-la-Roche in 1976, the rights of informants to strict confidentiality were also treated in a rather casual manner with consequences for the principal informant in that case, a British businessman, which proved to be not only catastrophic but tragic.)

Under pressure, therefore, the powers of the Commission were modified in 1982. Firms under investigation were given the right, which they had not previously possessed, to see the Commssion's files on their case, although this did not extend to documents which contained confidential matters relating to other firms nor documents which identified complainants. The Commission was required to allocate the task of preparing the 'reasoned opinion' to a Hearings Officer who had not been involved in the preliminary investigations, thus to some degree separating its prosecution and judicial functions. The Commission's previous power to carry out 'dawn raids' on firms – that is to say, to appear at a firm's premises without notice and to demand more or less unlimited access to all its records – was somewhat modified; notice of such visits have now to be given to the appropriate legal authorities in the country concerned and, in general, to the firm concerned. The inspectors from Brussels are also required to specify more or less precisely the kind of information they are seeking. Even so, the Commission retains very considerable powers of investigation and decision. In 1987 the German chemical giant, Hoechst, contested the Commission's right to enter and search its Frankfurt headquarters without possessing the Court warrant which would have been required by the Bundeskartellamt, the branch of the German government responsible for competition law. In 1989, however, the Court effectively ruled in favour of the Commission, demonstrating that member states have no alternative but to defer to Community law in competition matters.

In common with most national governments which operate some kind of control over restrictive business practices, the Commission operates a notification system under which firms operating business agreements with each other can submit details of them to the Commission for its scrutiny. Having examined such an agreement the Commission may conclude that it is not in contravention of the Treaty and the parties to it are therefore safe from the Commission's pursuit. A great deal of the work of the Competition Directorate is in fact devoted to this scrutiny of notified agreements; at the end of 1986 there were well over 3000 such notifications awaiting a decision. Quite frequently matters are settled out of court, so to speak, without the preparation of a formal opinion; agreements are modified so as to remove offending features or the parties concerned bow to the Commission's disapproval and agree to terminate the arrangement concerned. (Some 300 agreements were disposed of in this way in the course of 1986.) There is some incentive for firms to march into the lion's den in this fashion; as will be seen, firms can approach the Court for exemption from the rules on various grounds but only if they had previously notified the agreement concerned to the Commission. In the Quinine Case of 1969 a group of firms operating a 'gentlemen's agreement' with regard to their pricing policy wished to seek exemption from the Commission's ruling that they were in breach of the Treaty; because they had been advised to notify the Commission of the arrangement and had chosen not to do so, however, the Court refused to consider their plea for exemption.

12.3   Article 85

The first of the three major prongs in the Community's competition policy is provided by Article 85 which is concerned with agreements between firms or other concerted practices which are likely to affect trade between the member countries and have as their object or result the prevention, distortion or restriction of competition. It was established very early on that the agreements covered by Article 85 need not be embodied in a formal written document. In the Aniline Dyestuffs case of 1972 it was established that nominally independent suppliers of aniline dyes systematically increased their selling prices in different member countries in almost exactly equal proportions and within a few days of one another. There was no written agreement between the firms requiring them to act in this manner, but the Court was satisfied that they were in effect informing each other of their proposed price changes in such a way as to encourage their (nominal) competitors to take similar action. Such similarity of pricing policies could not in itself establish conclusively that collusion was occurring, since it would occur in the perfectly competitive market of the textbooks. But it was enough to create a presumption which, together with other evidence, led the Court to find that a breach of the Treaty had in fact occurred.

This same case illustrates another feature of Article 85. It refers to practices which 'are likely to affect trade between the member states' and this has been held to mean that it is not necessary that the offending firms should themselves be resident within the Community; all that is necessary is that Community trade should be affected by their actions. The Aniline Dyestuffs case in fact involved firms in Switzerland and the UK (ICI) neither of which was at the time a member country, although the latter firm did in fact have subsidiaries located within the EEC. In the Genuine Vegetable Parchment Case of 1978, however, a fine was imposed on a Finnish company which belonged to a trade organisation located in Sweden; the Court held that the cartel arrangements operated by the association *affected* the Community's internal trade, which was sufficient to bring them within the jurisdiction of the Commission. From time to time the legality of the doctrine that the Commission's writ can run beyond the Community's borders has been called into question. In 1988, however, in the Ahlstrom Osakeyhtio case, the Court ruled very specifically that it is the impact on trade between member countries which is the crucial factor, not the location or nationality of the participants in an agreement. In that case a group of US, Canadian and Finnish producers of wood pulp had been fined by the Commission in 1984 for operating a price-fixing agreement with respect to their exports to the Community. The firms appealed against the fines on the grounds that the Commission had no authority to interfere with companies operating outside the Community. The Court firmly rejected this submission; the decisive factor, it held, was not the place where an agreement was established or administered but the place in which its effect was felt.

Article 85 identifies five specific types of arrangements between firms which would constitute a breach of the Treaty (although it does not exclude the possibility that other types might be placed in this category). The first is one which fixes prices or any other trading conditions, whether directly or indirectly. As has been noted, the existence of a written agreement is not a necessary condition. Nor is the prohibition avoided if the arrangement nominally has a purpose other than price-fixing. On several occasions the Commission has argued (and the Court has agreed) that what purported to be merely information-sharing arrangements in fact had the effect of preventing genuine competition. In the Paper-Machine Wire Case of 1978, for example, members of an international trade association provided a central secretariat with details of their prices and other trading conditions and in return obtained similar information from their competitors. The object, it was asserted, was to prevent their members from being given false information by prospective customers concerning the terms they had been offered by other suppliers. The Commission was not convinced, especially as it was conceded that this mutual exchange of information was not extended to potential buyers; the arrangement was therefore dismantled.

The second outlawed practice is any arrangement aimed at limiting or controlling production, markets or technical development; such cartels have been widespread in the past, especially in international trade, as producers seek to prevent potential competitors from entering their established markets. This has been extended by the Commission to include situations in which information has merely been *withheld* with that intention or effect. In the IBM case of 1984, for example, after ten years of energetic pressure from the Commission, the world leader in the production of computers finally agreed to abandon its practice of making a close secret of technical developments in its forthcoming products; this had had the result that competition in computer peripherals and software, as opposed to the machines themselves, was effectively prevented. The firm was finally persuaded to give reasonable notice in advance of such developments in the future. Both this and the preceding case illustrate how the Commission enforces its policy by persuasion (admittedly with a potential threat in the background) as well as by the imposition of penalties.

The third practice specified in Article 85 is one of the most widely-used devices to moderate international competition – arrangements whereby supplies or, more commonly, markets are shared out by agreement between independent producers who prefer a comfortable, secured market to the full rigours of genuine competition. There have been very many instances of such arrangements and of their successful prosecution by the Commission. A notable example occurred in 1986 when a group of fifteen companies, mostly multinational corporations, was held to have been in breach of the Treaty since 1977 by operating a market-sharing and price-fixing cartel in the polypropylene markets in member countries. The Commission's displeasure at both the extent of the arrangements and the reluctance of the participants to come quietly, so to speak, was reflected in the record fine imposed on them – some ECU 58 million.

The evidence suggests that the fourth practice listed is also extremely common in practice – the application of different terms and conditions to different purchasers of the same product, enforced in the context of international trade by attempts to prevent 'parallel imports'. In a leading case, Pioneer Electronics of 1979, the official distributors of the (Japanese) company's hi-fi products complained that other importers of the products were selling them at prices lower than their own and persuaded the parent company to withhold supplies from such unofficial importers. The outcome was a fine equivalent to ECU 8 m, the highest awarded until that year. A similar case of interest to the United Kingdom was that of the Distillers Company in 1980. In this it was established that the company had been supplying one of its leading products, Johnny Walker Red Label whisky, at a price of ECU 21 within the UK and to its own distributors in the Community but was charging a price of ECU 34 to other prospective customers in the Community. The company pleaded that this discrimination was necessary to cover the costs of promotion and stockholding which its distributors were required to bear but which other purchasers did not. The Commission was once more unimpressed and required the company to either sell the product at the same price in both the UK and the remainder of the Community or to cease selling the product at all in one or other market. The Company opted for the latter.

Another example of the control of parallel imports of interest in the UK was the case of the two leading car manufacturers, British Leyland (as it then was) and Ford in 1984. Identical models were being sold by these companies at a much lower price in the competitive EC market – in Belgium in particular – than in the UK. When this fact became known, a significant trade developed in which UK dealers purchased cars in Belgium and imported them into the UK. To discourage this irritating habit, BL and Ford had used their power to issue (or withhold) the official 'type approval' certificates necessary for imported cars in such a way as to make such imports of their own products virtually impossible. Again the Commission disapproved and prevailed on the companies to abandon their objections to parallel imports, provided that prices being charged in the UK and in other EC markets did not differ by more than 12 per cent. Subsequent efforts to make deliveries of right-hand drive vehicles in Belgium either impossible or achievable only after long delay were also declared illegal by the Commission.

Article 85 finally prohibits any arrangement whereby a prospective purchaser of a product is required to purchase other, unconnected products as a condition of sale. This refers to the long-established practice of 'full-line forcing' used by producers having a monopoly, or at least market dominance, in one particular product-line to push other products in which their competitive position is much weaker. Tenants of British public houses benefited under this provision in 1987 when the Commission ruled as a contravention of the Treaty the prevailing practice whereby the tenants of 'tied' public houses were required to purchase their supplies, other than those of beer, through the brewery company owning the establishment.

The scope of the Commission's remit is therefore extremely wide so far as restrictive trade agreements are concerned. But there are escape clauses. Adopting the legal maxim of *de minimis non curat lex*, the Commission does not trouble itself with agreements which are technically in breach of Article 85 but are deemed to be of 'minor importance'; this is nowadays construed to mean agreements between firms whose share of the market does not exceed 5 per cent and whose combined annual turnover does not exceed ECU 200 m. More importantly, exemptions from the provision of Article 85 may be sought if the firms concerned can demonstrate that the arrangements contribute to improvements in either the production or the distribution of goods, or to the promotion of technical progress. It has to be established, however, that consumers obtain an 'equitable' share in the benefits so obtained and that competition is not eliminated for a substantial part of the market concerned. The Commission has in fact set up a system of block exemptions, a set of rules which, if satisfied, enables the parties to an agreement to go ahead without formally notifying Brussels. Such exemptions are common but by no means automatic; an attempt on the part of Peugeot-Talbot to secure exemption for distribution arrangements which involved restrictions, or price-supplements, on the supply of right-hand drive cars to its Benelux agents in 1986 was firmly squashed.

12.4   Article 86

The restriction or distortion of competition is frequently achieved by collusive agreements between independent firms: that is the business of Artice 85. Equally it may be achieved by a single enterprise using its monopoly or quasi-monopoly position to restrict competition through its own market power rather than through agreements with other firms. This is the business of Article 86, which uses terms almost identical to those of Article 85 to prohibit restrictive practices which result when firms seek 'to take improper advantage of a dominant position within the Common Market or within a substantial part of it'. The practices condemned are identical to those specified in Article 85 with the obvious omission of market-sharing arrangements; since the Article is aimed at restrictions operated by dominant firms the question of 'sharing' arrangements does not arise.

It will be noted that the wording of Article 86 involves two concepts not found in Article 85. First, it applies to firms which have a 'dominant position' in the market, and the definition of the meaning of those two words has naturally given the legal profession a considerable number of field days. It could hardly be denied that a firm which is the sole supplier of an identifiably separate product would have a dominant position but this state of affairs seldom exists. In any event, a 100 per cent share of the market is by no means essential for a position of dominance, any more than 100 per cent ownership of a company by an individual is necessary for that individual to exercise effective control of it. Dominance is therefore a matter to be settled in the light of the facts of particular instances and over the years the Commission and Court have built up a considerable body of case law on the matter. Thus in the Hoffmann-la-Roche case of 1976 the Court held that the company, which accounted for 47 per cent of the sales of drugs in the Vitamin A group, had such a technical lead in the market – in which a considerable degree of over-capacity also existed – that potential competitiors would be deterred from attempting entry, thus making Hoffman-la-Roche a dominant firm. Similarly, in the same year it was held in the United Brands case that while the firm accounted for only 40 per cent of the market for bananas its competitors were much smaller in an industry in which economies of scale (including those of advertisement) were very important; hence a share of 40 per cent was quite sufficient to establish dominance.

Even if the existence of a dominant position is established, however, considerable difficulty can arise over the meaning of the words 'to take improper advantage' of it. A firm may have achieved a dominant position, after all, simply by being more efficient than its competitors; it would be strange if this fact in itself were to be regarded as a breach of the Treaty. If a firm exploits its market power by adopting *abnormal business methods*, however, with the sole and specific intention of preserving its dominance, there can be little doubt but that this would be taking improper advantage of it. Thus, in the Akzo Chemie case of 1985, a company which resorted to practices of a kind specified in Article 86 for the purpose of forcing a small competitor out of business was clearly using its market power improperly.

In a celebrated case, Continental Can Company of 1972, however, the Commission sought to extend the definition of 'improper advantage' very much further and the Court appeared to give its support to it. In this instance the company was seeking to take over a Dutch firm which was in fact one of its few competitors in the market for meat tins. The Commission intervened and argued that such a merger would increase the power of Continental Can to act unilaterally in the market without needing to take account of competitors or, for that matter, its customers. In the end the Commission lost its case in the Court on the grounds that, while Continental Can had few competitors in the market for meat tins, there was plenty of potential competition from manufacturers of glass or plastic containers or from those of other types of metal container. The Commission, in other words, had sought to define the product, and therefore the 'market', too narrowly. But nevertheless the Court did appear to uphold the principle of the Commission's submission that a firm which enjoyed a dominant position automatically took improper advantage of it by seeking to strengthen that position even further by a merger.

The problem of defining a product, and therefore a market, was illustrated even more clearly a few years later in the case of GKN and Sachs AG in 1976. In this case the two firms concerned – one British and the other German – were proposing to merge together, a matter requiring the approval of the Commission. (In fact the Commission was acting in this instance under Article 66 of the 1951 Treaty creating the ECSC; this requires the approval of the High Authority for any concentration in the steel industry in order to ensure that such a merger would not compromise effective competition). The Commission duly approved the merger on the grounds that it would not significantly affect competition in the *steel* industry. The office of the West Germany government concerned with monopoly, the Bundeskartellamt, took a different view, however; it objected to the merger on the grounds that it would restrict competition in the German market for *clutches*. It was a classic case of conflict between Community law and national law and theoretically the former should automatically have prevailed. At that time the Commission was exceedingly reluctant to enter into a dispute with a member government, least of all that of Germany, and the Commission ultimately concluded that there was no real conflict because the two decisions related to two different markets, as elegant a ducking of the issue as could be conceived. The Hoechst case of 1987, however, indicated that the Commission has since shed this inclination to defer to the governments of even the larger member countries.

The GKN case illustrates two fundamental difficulties which have arisen with Article 86 and have not in general arisen with Article 85. First, national policies with regard to mergers can and do differ between countries and therefore from that of the Community to an extent not in general encountered with restrictive business agreements between companies. When conflicts occur with national governments the Commission must perforce walk somewhat more warily than than when it is dealing merely with private companies, whatever their nationality. Second, there may well be a conflict between the requirements of competition policy, in which there exists an inherent presumption against mergers between existing firms, and that of *industrial* policy, in which such mergers may be deemed to be essential. The problem is best left until the discussion of industrial policy in the next chapter.

12.5   Article 92

The reference to the reluctance of the Commission to engage in open conflict with governments, as opposed to private companies, leads naturally to the third prong of Community competition policy contained in Article 92 – provisions concerning aids of various forms given to enterprises by their own national governments. This provides flatly that state aids, given in any manner whatsoever, which distort competition by favouring certain enterprises shall be deemed to be incompatible with the Common Market. If the Commission finds that such aid is being given by a member government it is empowered to require the government concerned to abolish or modify the aid measure and, if the government fails to comply, to refer the matter to the Court of Justice for an appropriate ruling.

The drafters of the Treaty were clearly aware that they were here walking on very thin ice. Hence, notwithstanding its overall condemnation of state aids which distort competition, Article 92 immediately proceeds to exempt certain types of aid which *are* deemed to be compatible with the Treaty and others which *may* be deemed to be compatible. Among the former are aids given to individual consumers on social grounds, provided that they do not discriminate between products with different national origins, aids to remedy damage caused by natural calamities 'or other extraordinary events' and aids granted to certain regions of Germany to compensate for difficulties arising from the separation of East and West Germany – obviously the situation of Berlin was very much in their minds. Among the latter are aids intended to promote the economies of disadvantaged regions or to 'facilitate the development of certain activities' or those to 'remedy a serious disturbance of the economy of a Member State'.

Even if this had not provided a sufficient number of loopholes, governments of the member countries have shown such enthusiasm and energy in discovering others that it is probably fair to say that, despite Article 92, competition within the Community has been restricted far more by governmental intervention than by the private cartels and monopolies against which the guns of Articles 85 and 86 were so heavily directed. In its 'First inventory of State aids' published in 1988, the Commission estimated that the governments of the four largest member countries were pouring an average of ECU 85 bn a year into subsidies for their domestic industries – the equivalent of 2.5 per cent of their national incomes. And subsidies are only one of many forms of state aid to industry. As will be seen in a later chapter, the cause of disadvantaged regions (a term which in some of the smaller member states covers the entire country) has frequently been pleaded when the true objective was the support of ailing industries rather than ailing regions.

Nor, as just noted, need a 'state aid' to an industry necessarily take the form of the direct expenditure of taxpayers' money on it. The requirements of public health or consumer protection have been cited as justification for attempts to prevent the importation of beer into Germany (the provisions of a law passed in 1516 being cited as authority), vinegar made from malt or pasta made from soft wheat into Italy, lamb into France, and milk into the United Kingdom. The Commission scored a very important victory of principle in this context, however, in the celebrated case of *Cassis de Dijon* in 1978. In this case a German merchant had wished to import a French liqueur, Cassis, but had been prevented from doing so by the German authorities (with much urging from domestic interests) on the grounds that under German law the prospective import did not contain sufficient alcohol to be classified as a liqueur. As a result of the Commission's challenge, the Court ruled that this action was not compatible with the Treaty; the government of a member country could not prohibit a product whose sale was permitted in another member country unless it could be positively established that the imports concerned would be injurious on grounds of health, fair trading or consumer protection. In the Cassis case the German government could not establish that any such injuries were likely to follow, nor had it even attempted to.

Despite determined efforts by the Commission to apply this general principle to all internal trade, restraints imposed by governments have impeded internal trade to a steadily increasing degree. As will be described in Chapter 27, although purchases of any significant size offered by government agencies are in theory open to tender by enterprises anywhere within the Community without discrimination, in reality very few such orders go to enterprises outside the country concerned. Trading standards have been called in aid to demand that imports of furniture into Ireland shall carry inscriptions in Gaelic; a law on labelling dangerous goods has been cited to insist that all hammers imported into Germany should carry their manufacturers' name; French customs authorities insisted at one stage that all snails imported into France should pass through a small number of remote offices equipped with snail-testing machines, thus ensuring that the majority were long dead on arrival; defence considerations, which require that all 'essential' cargoes shall be carried in national ships, have ensured that imports of British barley by the Spanish state brewing monopoly are carried by Spanish ships at a cost some 30 per cent above the going rate; and so on. The list is virtually endless.

12.6   A Summary

The essential philosophy of the Treaty is (with the conspicuous exception of agriculture) clearly that of the free competitive market. Its provisions concerning competition policy nevertheless recognise the fact that, left to themselves, markets cannot be assumed to operate freely and without restraint as a matter of course; hence the Commission is given very far-reaching powers to identify and remedy any such market imperfection. There can be no doubt that it has sought to exercise those powers with considerable energy and persistence. At the end of 1986 it had more than 3500 cases under investigation, more than 80 per cent of them being licensing or distribution agreements, and in the course of that year it had brought 27 actions concerning breaches of the rules of competition before the Court.

Yet the evidence persists that the Community is still far from being a genuine Common Market in the sense that a single price exists for any given product throughout all member states. Some of this is due to differences in tax treatment, a matter which will be discussed at length later. Some is due to the inevitable costs of transporting goods from one market to another; the experience of the United States suggests, for example, that price differences of up to 5 per cent can persist between one adjoining state and another before trade seeking to exploit such differences becomes worthwhile. The bulk, however, is due to the failure of the Community, after 30 years existence, to eliminate market imperfections which succeed in maintaining national boundaries in what is theoretically a single market. Doubtless these imperfections are smaller than they would have been in the absence of the continuous campaign by the Commission to eliminate them. That is not a proposition of fact, since no method has yet been devised of measuring the quantitative impact of the Commission's activities; nevertheless it is not an unreasonable hypothesis. Even so it is inescapably the case that those activities have achieved something a good deal less than complete success.

Some of the responsibility for this has been placed on the manner in which the Commission has applied its competition policy. It has, according to some, long German procedures but only a small French staff to apply them. Certainly its investigations are notoriously slow and long-winded, on occasion being so late in their findings as to make them irrelevant by the time of their publication. (A relatively minor case in 1988 was reported to have involved the parties in hearings lasting 15 days and the employment of some 50 lawyers.) The fines imposed have tended to be relatively small in relation to the gains achieved through restrictive practices in the meantime, although in recent years substantial increases in their level have been witnessed – particularly, it must be added, those imposed on firms whose parent companies are resident outside the Community. (Even so, the record fine of ECU 58 m mentioned earlier represented well below 1 per cent of the annual turnover of the companies involved.)

Further, the Commission has been noticeably diplomatic in the pursuit of member governments whose activities have become a major source of market distortion. Even when such activities have been condemned by the Court it is impossible to force sovereign governments to abandon or modify them if the government concerned declines to do so. The Italian government is notoriously delinquent in this respect; in January 1988 the number of Court directions to governments which remained unfulfilled amounted to two for the United Kingdom, five for France, nine for West Germany – and 28 for Italy.

During the later 1970s and 1980s, however, it became increasingly apparent that the problem involved matters of much deeper significance than the administrative competence of the Commission. Largely as a result of the pressures imposed by the economic slow-down of that period, the Community had become riddled with non-tariff barriers of all sorts, ranging from administrative delays and complex procedures at borders to national regulations governing technical or professional standards. Chapter 27 below describes how this worsening condition of 'Eurosclerosis' led to, amongst other things, a determined programme to establish a genuine single market in the Community by the end of 1992. This programme includes proposals which extend over an area which is very much wider than that of competition policy as defined by Articles 85, 86 and 92; different constituents of the programme will be referred to in the appropriate contexts in the chapters which follow. So far as competition policy itself is concerned, however, the important point was that the principle of the *Cassis de Dijon* case – that of 'mutual recognition' – was formally enshrined in the Single European Act of 1986. This means that it was firmly established that, from 1987 onwards, products legally on sale in one member country may not be declared illegal in another without good and explicit reason. The general prospects for the attainment of a genuine single market by the end of 1992 will be further discussed in Chapter 27; the experience of competition policy so far, however, is clearly that the responsibility for any qualifications to its success must be attributed primarily to individual member governments rather than to inadequate provisions in the Treaty or to an imperfect enforcement of them by the Commission.

Further Reading

Allen, D., 'Managing the Common Market: the Community's competition policy', in H. Wallace (ed.), *Policy-making in the European Community*, 2nd edn (Chichester: John Wiley, 1983).

European Commission, *Europe without Frontiers: Completing the Internal Market* (Luxembourg, 1987).

European Commission, *EEC Competition Policy in the Single Market*, 2nd edn (Luxembourg, 1989).

Swann, D., *Competition and Industrial Policy in the European Community* (London: Methuen, 1983).

Industrial Policy 13

13.1 What Is It?

If the concept of competition policy is a little vague, the precise meaning of the term 'industrial policy' is almost invisible; one writer has indeed described it as 'more a state of mind than a self-explanatory prescription for action'. Yet, like the elephant, while difficult to define it is unmistakable when encountered; in fact almost all governments have some form of industrial policy – even if it consists of no more than letting industry decide its own destiny. Without attempting any sophisticated semantics, the expression will be used here to refer to any measures adopted by governments with a view to promoting the efficient development of its industries. In particular, such measures may be directed at either the structure of individual firms, regardless of their industrial classification, or the restructuring of specified industries. The former usually apply to situations in which potential gains from economies of scale or more rapid technological development require changes in the size or structure of a firm, changes which for one reason or another unaided market forces fail to bring about. They might also apply, however, where it is desired to encourage the establishment or growth of *small* firms for social or technological reasons. The restructuring of industries, rather than individual firms, is involved when growth potential is inadequately exploited by unassisted market forces or, alternatively, when the process of industrial decline involves human or physical losses which cannot reasonably be left uncompensated.

Industrial policy, in other words, rests on the proposition that unrestricted market forces do not necessarily secure optimum social results, or at least do not attain them as rapidly or as fully as might otherwise be the case. Consequently it is hardly surprising that there is no mention whatever of a 'Common industrial policy' in the Treaty of Rome. Any attempt to define one, in even the vaguest of terms, would immediately have exposed fundamental differences of economic philosophy between the two dominant member countries at the time, France

132

and Germany. At the time of the drafting of the Treaty (and indeed since) the government of France was inclined towards the concept of *l'economie concertée* – the need for government to guide and influence the development of industry, if not to centrally plan it in a socialist sense. Germany, on the other hand, was and remains philosophically wedded to the virtues of *laissez-faire* and reliance on unrestricted market forces. Not even the founding fathers of the Community would have sought to square this circle.

So far as concerns the second element in industrial policy – the need for governments, or the Community, to become involved in the restructuring of entire industries – virtually nothing was attempted at a Community level until the hands of the politicians were forced by the harsh realities of the onset of recession in the mid-1970s. As always, the instinct for survival then overcame the luxury of philosophical disputation. Industrial restructuring has a habit of being a matter of either ministration to lame ducks or enticement to front-runners. The decade beginning in the mid-1970s belonged emphatically to the former. This part of the story will be left to one side for the moment.

The experience of the 1960s had already shown, however, that the absence of a coherent Community industrial strategy was a serious weakness in the context of the first element in industrial policy – measures designed to influence the size and structure of individual enterprises. On the one hand, as the previous chapter has indicated, the Commission's DG IV, the directorate concerned with competition, was concluding that its powers were inadequate. Article 86 gave it the ability to intervene when firms *had acquired* a dominant position and sought to abuse it, but in a sense this was closing the stable door after the horse had departed. The Commission could intervene after a firm had acquired dominance but was powerless to prevent that dominance emerging in the first place. As was noted in connection with the case of Continental Can, the Commission appeared to be arguing that any merger between a dominant firm and another was in itself an abuse of dominance, although this assertion rested on a highly questionable interpretation of the law; even then the fact of dominance was a prior condition. What was more, any attempt by the Commission to intervene in a merger between firms was liable to run foul of national legislation on such matters, as in the GKN–Sachs case. This was not a satisfactory state of affairs.

There was clearly a second, and more fundamental problem. Conflict existed not only between the Commission and member governments on the correct policy to be adopted towards mergers but also between two aspects of the Community's own policy. On the one hand, competition policy rested on the proposition that mergers, being likely to reduce competition, must be presumed to be undesirable, even though the presumption might be a rebuttable one. On the other hand, the need to secure the maximum economies of scale made possible by the opening of a single internal market, and to attain rapid growth in newer industries being established in it, implied that fewer, larger firms operating in the market as a whole were needed to replace the larger number of smaller firms designed to serve separate national markets.

The evidence suggested that the latter was not happening. Indeed, as late as 1988 the Commission estimated that achieving the potential economies of scale still remaining unexploited because of the fragmentation of the Community's market could increase Community output by 4.5 per cent and reduce costs by 6 per cent. What was worse, such economies of scale as were being achieved seemed to be being reaped by foreign as much as by Community firms. Of 1057 international mergers involving member country firms during the 1960s, the Commission estimated that nearly 80 per cent involved firms from non-member countries, notably the United States, while only 20 per cent were mergers within the Community. (The situation has changed little since; in 1984 the Chairman of Olivetti was lamenting that of 200 joint-venture agreements by European electronics firms in the previous year, 50 per cent involved American partners and 30 per cent Japanese partners.) DG III, the Community directorate concerned with industrial and technological affairs – significantly enough, created only at the time of the merger of the communities in 1967 – therefore looked on the industrial scene from a standpoint precisely the reverse of that of DG IV. Rationalisation of industry was necessary to reap the potential gains of the expanded market but the mergers thus implied were not happening; what then were the obstacles to such mergers and how could they be removed?

13.2   The Emergence of Eurocompanies

In March 1970, the Commissioner responsible for DG IV, Guido Colonna, presented the Council of Ministers with a 'Memorandum on industrial policy in the Communities'; as is the custom, the document became known thereafter as the Colonna Report. It began by stressing the need for positive measures to ensure the creation of a single market and a single industrial base in the Community, the need for harmonisation of technical standards, the elimination of non-tariff obstacles to trade between member countries and so on – all startlingly similar to the sentiments to be expressed 15 years later in the Delors/ Cockfield report and the Single European Act. A large number of specific proposals were advanced, by no means all of them being entirely welcome to the Ministers. Primary stress was laid, however, on the need to create a single industrial system by making it possible for enterprises to operate on a community-wide basis, by abolishing existing restrictions on the movement of capital from one member country to another and by enabling a commercial patent taken out by any enterprise to have effect throughout the Community.

In an action programme on industrial and technical policy prepared by the Commission in 1973 it was noted that, despite the general approval given to the Colonna Report, very little progress had in fact been made. Two possible lines of approach were suggested. In the first place greater urgency could be shown in the matter of harmonising national company law in the separate member states so as to make it increasingly possible for an enterprise incorporated in one member country to operate freely in any other. The second possible approach was to create a separate Community company law which would allow an enterprise incorporated under it to operate in any member country.

The latter – the creation of a Eurocompany – was an approach long favoured by the Commission; this was hardly surprising since it obviously had a distinctly Community rather than a national character. It had in fact produced its own European Company statute and submitted it for approval by the Council – and, hopefully, incorporation in a Regulation – in June 1970. The proposal languished in the shadow of acute disagreement for nearly twenty years, and in mid-1989 the Commission was submitting yet another draft Company Statute for the approval of Ministers.

Trying the alternative approach, the provisions governing the proposed Eurocompany were closely reflected in a draft Fifth Directive drawn up by the Commission in 1972, the nominal objective of which was the harmonisation of the separate national laws governing companies. This also met with considerable resistance and has also remained a draft ever since. The problem is essentially that no member government is anxious to abandon any provision concerning the ownership or operation of companies within its boundaries which, for good reason or otherwise, it deems necessary in its national interest. Any common Eurocompany law, or harmonised system of national laws, would therefore have to contain any restrictions currently operated by any member government, so as to prevent the evasion of such restrictions by companies choosing to incorporate under the Eurocompany law for precisely that purpose. A major example of such a difficulty was provided by the provision of German law that all companies of any significant size should operate under a supervisory board of directors some of which should be elected by the employees of the company. Had the Eurocompany proposal not embodied this feature (which in fact it did) German firms would have been able to evade the requirement by simply reconstituting themselves as Eurocompanies, a development on which the German government would not look kindly. If it did embody such a feature, however, all member countries would thereby be committed to a system of industrial relations of which some at least did not approve. It is the old problem of politicians (and officials) fiercely resisting any encroachment on their power to determine how the affairs of their own country are to be run. (The worker-participation issue itself is discussed briefly in Chapter 19 below.)

It follows that progress along the lines of the second approach – the gradual harmonisation of what remain essentially national laws governing the operation of companies – has also been slow. It is not only that each country seeks to preserve what it regards as essential safeguards, such as the participation of workers in management (or its absence), or the ability of foreigners to acquire ownership in domestic enterprises. Companies are an important source of tax revenue and whenever they operate in more than one country there is necessarily more than one group of tax-collectors diligently guarding its interests in both the profits and the assets of the companies concerned – interests which inevitably come into conflict.

This is not to say that over twenty years no progress whatever has been made in the harmonisation of Community company law. By 1988, seven Directives had been adopted governing matters such as the disclosure of information required from companies, the form of the annual accounts and reports by public companies, the protection of the interests of creditors and employees when companies are merged, the manner in which the accounts of parent and subsidiary companies are to be consolidated and the qualifications required for persons to act as company auditors. In 1985 the Council of Ministers also approved a regulation governing the establishment from 1989 onwards of European Economic Interest Groupings (EEIG); this characteristically inelegant title describes an arrangement whereby firms in different member countries may enter into agreements governing the sharing of technology, research and development within the protective framework of Community law. (Such a proposal was advanced in the Colonna Report, so that it took almost exactly 20 years to come into effect.) Even so, it remains true to say that a company seeking to operate in more than one member country faces legal and fiscal complexities far greater than those experienced if it is resident solely in one.

13.3   Controlling the Mergers

The Commissions's 1973 memorandum exhorting the Community to take positive steps to create a single industrial base necessarily stressed the desirability of cross-border co-operation and mergers. The drafters in DG III, however, were not allowed a totally free run by their colleagues in DG IV, the competition directorate. While extolling the merits of cross-border mergers, the document hastily went on to emphasise the equal importance of keeping a careful watch on them to ensure that they did not compromise genuine competition. This was only to be expected; the document was appearing less than a year after DG IV had sought to argue, in the Continental Can case, that a dominant firm necessarily abused its position by seeking a merger with another firm.

The Commission went one step further by submitting, in the same year, a draft directive on merger control which represented a notable shift of emphasis away from reliance on the *attained* dominant position and towards the prevention of the acquisition of such power in the first place. It proposed that the list of actions deemed to be contrary to the Treaty should be extended to include any transaction which had the effect of bringing about a concentration between undertakings 'whereby they acquire or enhance the power to hinder effective competition in the Common Market or in a substantial part thereof'.

As with Article 85, the Commission was prepared to consider exemptions for mergers which had such effects but were considered 'indispensable to the attainment of an objective which is given priority treatment in the common interest of the Community'. The scope for argument given by this last phrase must have been such as to bring tears of pleasure to many legal eyes.

If the Commission had hoped that the proposed extension of its powers would be happily accepted by the Council of Ministers it must have been sorely disappointed. Most Ministers would have looked with deep suspicion on the proposition that the Commission could now reach into their countries to prohibit mergers which they themselves would have approved. Britain and France, in particular, questioned the competence of the Commission to rule on mergers involving highly complex technical issues; doubts also existed as to whether it could be sufficiently independent of the interests involved (very possibly in different countries) to reach a wholly non-political judgement. What is more, the experience of the time taken by the Commission to rule on much simpler matters – generally involving observed facts rather than expectations concerning future events – hardly suggested that effective merger negotiations would be facilitated.

The Commission is nothing if not persistent. Over a period of no less than sixteen years a succession of proposals were put to the Council, a combination of reasoned argument and (more importantly) an adjustment of its perceptions of the politically possible leading the Commission to advocate steadily less ambitious arrangements. Finally, at the end of 1989, agreement was reached in the Council that the vetting of proposed mergers in any member country should be carried out by the Commission provided that the mergers concerned satisfied each of three separate criteria. First, the combined annual (worldwide) turnover of the proposed merger must exceed ECU 5 billion. This represented a substantial retreat from the Commission's earlier proposals that the threshold size above which its approval had to be obtained would have been as low as ECU 1 billion – although even this lower threshold, it was estimated at the time, would have left about two-thirds of the mergers then occurring in the Community outside the Commission's power of scrutiny. Secondly, whatever the worldwide turnover of the proposed merger, the Commission's approval is necessary for it only if the annual turnover of the merged enterprise within the Community itself exceeds ECU 250 million. This ensures that activities of multinational companies located within member countries fall under Commission scrutiny only if they have a substantial impact within the Community itself. Thirdly, and finally, the Commission would have no power to intervene in a merger proposal if more than two-thirds of the turnover of any participating enterprise occurred within a single member country. Once again the effect is to confine the Commission's attention to mergers likely to have a significant impact on intra-Community trade rather than within a single country which could be assumed to be capable of looking after its own affairs. As a concession to the misgivings concerning the tendency of the Commission to bog itself down in its own tortuous procedures, its verdict on any proposed merger must be given within six months of its notification.

These much modified proposals received general approval: it is estimated that it would bring no more than 34–45 mergers under Commission scrutiny each year. Some governments, notably that of Germany, are anxious to retain some rights of national veto over merger proposals on grounds of national interest, but it is likely that the definition of 'national interest' will be closely circumscribed (e.g. matters of national defence) and will not be allowed to justify mere interference with genuine competition. Despite the long record of disagreement in this area, it is only logical that some such system must be established sooner or later. If in fact a single market is to be created by 1992 – and all member governments are legally committed to the aim – it is absurd that member governments should retain separate laws governing mergers relating to national markets. The concept of a national market will indeed cease to have validity. Harmonisation of national laws, assuming this could be achieved, is scarcely an adequate substitute; if threats to competition are to be assessed in the context of the Community market as a whole it is scarcely sensible to have such threats assessed by twelve separate jurisdictions whose consistency could be ensured only by some miraculous divine intervention. In the view of the Commission, the issue is not one of *whether* there should be a common merger policy but rather one of what the nature of that policy should be. In the view of some member governments, on the other hand (and most especially the British), a common policy in this area will be acceptable only if it does not boil down to the lowest common denominator of existing national regulations, leading to greater bureaucratic restriction in what were previously open and flexible capital markets.

The debate over mergers involves one end of the spectrum of policy regarding the size and structure of firms – the large firm end. Policy under this heading may equally relate to the other end of the market – small, and particularly new, enterprises. Although most governments adopt measures of some sort to encourage the growth of small enterprises, the matter has received relatively little attention at Community level. This is scarcely surprising; the Community is concerned with industrial matters only in so far as trade within the Community is affected to a significant degree, and almost by definition small firms are unlikely to have such effects. In 1985, however, the Council emphasised the need to promote small businesses as part of a general strategy to promote growth and employment in the Community. In the following year it approved a Commission action programme to encourage and co-ordinate national measures in this field – training for small businesses, easier access to capital, help in developing export markets and so on. It is not the type of activity likely to merit headlines in financial journals; it is, however, one element in the mass of detailed, day-to-day activities conducted by the Commission in the pooling of information and experience, a process which hopefully encourages the transformation of twelve separate markets into one.

13.4 Helping Lame Ducks

The Colonna Report had laid a good deal of stress on the importance of the second element of industrial policy – the improvement and adaptation of whole industries to take account of changing technology. By the misfortune of its timing, however, the translation of its generalities into policy became concentrated not on the positive stimulus to the emerging high-technology industries, which it had primarily had in mind, but rather on the negative task of coming to the rescue of old-established industries faced with the need to retract in the face of falling markets. It is sometimes argued that it was the onset of recession after the explosion of world oil prices in 1973–4 which originated the problem. That the recession did greatly magnify and accelerate the problems of Europe's older industries is undoubtedly true; it could hardly be otherwise in an economic environment which saw unemployment in the Community rise from less than 2 per cent of the working population in 1970 to nearly 6 per cent by 1980. But the fact is that the recession accentuated the problem rather than caused it. Throughout the 1960s the competitiveness of the older industries of Western Europe was steadily falling behind that of the same industries in the newly-industrialised countries, especially those of the Near and Far East. Nowhere was the impact greater that in the traditional industries of shipbuilding, textiles and steel.

13.4.1 Shipbuilding

Chronologically, shipbuilding was the industry in which the problem first manifested itself. Even during the 1960s it had been apparent that sales of European ships on the world market were feasible only with the aid of considerable state subsidy – to offset, it was claimed, even greater subsidies being poured into the industry by Europe's competitors, especially Japan. Article 92 or not, therefore, there was no way in which such subsidies could be eliminated; the most that the Commission could achieve was a Directive in 1969 which sought to harmonise the aid being given to the industry by member governments in such as way as to minimise any consequential distortion of competition between member states. The declared aim was indeed to eliminate all such state aids eventually, but that was a hope for the future.

The oil crisis of 1973/4, and the resulting sharp contraction of world trade, dramatically altered the situation; a fall in world freight rates led to a sharp fall in the demand for new ships and within three years the tonnage of ships completed in Community yards had fallen by more than 40 per cent. In all highly capitalistic industries a fall in demand, and the ensuing emergence of expensive idle capacity, generates a strong temptation to resort to drastic price-cutting in the belief that any sales which make some contribution to the fixed overheads are better than none. For one producer in isolation the trick may work; if a group of producers indulge in it on a competitive basis, however, the result is almost certain disaster. The policy of the Commission had therefore to be one of damage-limitation – an attempt to establish a collective response to the situation rather than a descent into mutual destruction.

The aim of eliminating all state aids to the industry was clearly unattainable and in 1978 a Directive postponed this desirable objective indefinitely. It sought, instead, to insist that all such aids must be submitted to two tests. First, they must be aimed at positively increasing the efficiency of shipyards, rather than merely allowing them to continue operating at a loss; second, they must seek to merely maintain (or better still reduce) capacity rather than to increase it and thereby compound the problem. An attempt in 1979 to persuade Ministers to adopt a policy of building one ton of new ships and scrapping two tons of old – thus simultaneously generating employment and reducing total capacity – was singularly unsuccessful. Externally, the Commission also did what it could to bring overseas competitors into line – trying 'to persuade the leading Far Eastern shipbuilders', as one report delicately put it, 'to adopt a stance more in keeping with the market'.

The policy was continued until the mid-1980s, by which time the industry appeared to have bottomed-out at a level of about one-third of its output a decade earlier; the emphasis of a new Directive in 1986 was therefore placed on modernising the industry with the aim, as always, of phasing out state aids altogether. How far the costs and hardships endured by the industry as a result of its traumatic adjustment had been reduced by the intervention of the Commission is impossible to say. It seems not unreasonable to suppose, however, that the consequences of a totally unrestrained and unco-ordinated battle for survival amongst the Community shipbuilders would have been even more unpleasant than they were in the event.

13.4.2   Textiles

The story of the textile industry is very similar. The steady penetration of the market by imports from the Near and Far East led the Commission in 1971 to prepare a policy document on the rules for national aids to the textile industry. Once again, having little hope of outlawing such aids altogether the Commission sought to make them conform to the same rules as for shipbuilding. In other words, state aids should not merely subsidise inefficiency but should be aimed at improving competitiveness and eliminating outdated capacity. In the years which followed it showed some vigilance in ensuring observance of these rules, the industry (consisting of a much larger number of small-scale enterprises) being much difficult to police than shipbuilding. During the later 1970s and early 1980s the Commission found itself in frequent conflict with member governments, especially that of Italy, which discovered many ingenious ways of subsidising their domestic producers without nominally doing anything of the kind.

So far as imports were concerned, the Commission adopted a progressively more protectionist stance in its renegotiations of the Multi-Fibre Arrangement, a system whereby market quotas in textile products were nominally guaranteed for developing countries. (The system is discussed in more detail in Chapter 26.) An attempt by DG III in 1982 to establish domestic production quotas in the industry with a view to eliminating excess capacity, however, was successfully resisted by DG IV on the grounds that such arrangements conflicted with Article 85: the old schizophrenia. By the mid-1980s the downward trend in the industry appeared to have come to an end and, as with shipbuilding, the emphasis shifted from the regulation of state aids to their progressive elimination through modernisation and innovation in the industry.

13.4.3 Steel

The policies adopted in the third sector, steel, were considerably more drastic; whatever protests may have been heard from DG IV, they also conflicted openly and flagrantly with the provisions of Article 85. This was made possible partly because the Commission was operating under the provisions of the 1951 Treaty establishing the ECSC; this gave the Commission, in its capacity as the High Authority for the industry, much wider powers of independent action. The recession first hit the industry in 1975; by 1977 output had fallen by some 20 per cent and the industry was operating at only 60 per cent of its capacity. For so capital-intensive an industry this was a catastrophic position; it was estimated that in 1977 the industry in the Community as a whole was operating at a loss equivalent to more than ECU 6.5 billion. A system of voluntary production quotas was introduced; this was followed by the establishment of minimum prices and the imposition of anti-dumping duties on steel imports. (These are permitted by the rules of GATT if it can be shown that imports are entering at less than their true cost of production.)

The decline continued. A state of manifest crisis was declared in 1980; the production quotas were made mandatory and under the so-called Davignon plan (Count Davignon being the Commissioner for DG III) a programme of compulsory reductions in capacity was embarked on. Internal consumption of steel was now running at not much over 100 m tonnes a year while the industry had a capacity to produce 200 m tonnes a year. The quotas continued to be enforced through the early 1980s, the Commission regularly issuing 20 to 30 adverse decisions every year in respect of enterprises failing to comply with them. The pressure on imports was maintained, with the Commission entering into 'voluntary' export restraint agreements with 15 foreign countries accounting for 75 per cent of the Community's imports. By 1985 the end of the tunnel appeared to be in sight; domestic consumption had stabilised at around 110 m tonnes a year and output at around 120 m; allowing for net exports, however, the industry still appeared to have a capacity some 20–25 m tonnes in excess of its likely needs in 1990. Nevertheless it was believed that the crisis situation was passing and it was therefore agreed that the production quota and minimum price system should be phased out by 1988, which indeed it was.

Once again it is impossible to quantify the benefits derived from the drastic control over the industry exercised by the Commission during this period. Complaints of inequitable treatment were frequent and universal; the degree of compliance with the Commission's Directives varied considerably from one country to another; doubtless much of the reduction in capacity which was achieved would have occurred anyway, without the Commission's intervention. Yet the fact remains that it was able to reduce very substantially the extent to which European steel producers damaged one another in their fight to survive, a process which would undoubtedly have made the adjustment far more costly and wasteful than proved to be the case in reality. Furthermore, the exercise of collective bargaining-power through the Commission unquestionably had greater effect on the prices and policies of overseas competitors than the member countries could have exercised individually.

The main virtues of a Community industrial policy in all these cases is clear. First, by striving to prevent the emergence of beggar-my-neighbour tactics against fellow member-states (which could only worsen the situation for all concerned) the Commission was able to bring some degree of orderliness into an inevitably painful adjustment. Second, by acting collectively the Community was able to protect Community interests against foreign competitors to a far greater degree than would have been possible had the member countries acted individually. Third, the Commission was able to take a somewhat more objective view of the degree to which essentially short-run panic measures had ceased to be necessary. The terms in which it expressed the need to revert to normality in the steel industry were revealing: the Community, it said 'cannot permanently maintain the steel production quota system protecting ageing structures and loss-making firms ... market forces must dictate the changes needed.' Individual governments, faced with the pressure-groups always vociferous amongst protected industries, would have found it difficult to say that, however much they might have known it to be true. There is always a good deal to be said for having someone to blame (preferably a bureaucrat in a foreign city) when apparently being forced to do the unpopular thing – especially when it happens to be something which everyone knows has to be done anyway.

13.5 Backing the Winners

The Colonna report envisaged a Community industrial policy as being concerned with the creation or expansion of the newer, high-technology industries rather than with preserving the relics of the old; it was sheer economic bad luck that in the decade which followed its appearance events were to dictate otherwise. The need for Community action in advancing technological frontiers nevertheless remained. In the reorganisation of the Commission in 1967 a new directorate, DG XII, had been given responsibility for research, science and education and in 1971 it issued a memorandum on the subject of Community action in the field of research and development in science and technology. Its major conclusion was that there was an increasing proliferation of agencies concerned with R & D activities within the Community and that some co-ordination was needed as a matter of urgency.

It is obvious that in the creation and expansion of new industries the Community as such can play only a limited and indirect role. It does not have the financial resources, nor does the Commission have the technical competence, to positively enter into business and establish industrial undertakings of its own; the likely consequences of commercial activity by so highly political an organisation would in any event be terrifying. But in the area of the research and development which forms the essential precondition of such industrial innovation its potential role is considerable. Research and development is an extremely high-risk, high-cost business; national industries, looking primarily to national markets, may well prefer to leave such things to the giant multinationals, especially foreign ones. Where such R & D does take place in the separate member countries, on the other hand, there is likely to be considerable duplication and overlapping unless some central co-ordination can be effectively developed.

Such was the view of DG XII in 1971. Its intention of bringing some coherence into Community R & D was unfortunately far from realised in the decade which followed. In fact, the 1970s and early 1980s witnessed a proliferation throughout the Community of organisations and groups adopting a bewildering array of acronyms and rendering the R & D scene more confusing every year. In 1986 the Single European Act called a halt; it required the Community to strengthen the scientific and technological basis of European industry and, in particular, to adopt a multi-annual framework setting out all its activities in the R & D field, defining the objectives, the priorities and the amounts required.

This obligation was honoured by the Commission in 1986 in the shape of a framework programme of Community activities in the R & D field for the five years 1987–91. This provides for eight areas of activity with a total budget estimated at ECU 7.7 bn, the main areas being information technology, telecommunications, energy, biotechnology and the exploitation of marine resources. Most of these represent a continuation of the work of various programmes established in the 1970s or early 1980s and previously working in a somewhat random manner; they rejoice in such exotic titles as BRITE (Basic research for industrial technology in Europe), ESPRIT (European strategic programme for research and development in information technology), JET (Joint European Torus) and RACE (Research and development in advanced communication technology for Europe). Although some of the work is performed in a Joint Research Centre under the control of DG XII – the 'Centre' is in fact a network of four research institutes employing some 2000 people in Belgium, Denmark, Italy and the Netherlands – the bulk is carried out in national research centres with the Community typically meeting 50 per cent of the cost. It should perhaps be noted that during the 1970s and 1980s by far the largest proportion of the Community's research budget has gone into the exceedingly expensive field of nuclear energy, a matter discussed further in Chapter 18.

To quantify the impact of all this activity on the development of the high-technology industries in the Community is of course quite impossible. The fact that the Community's research expenditure is relatively small – around 4 per cent of the Community budget – is not in itself particularly revealing, since much of the expenditure is used to meet only part of the cost of research work which is being simultaneously funded by national governments. Further, community-sponsored R & D is itself only part, probably a very small part of the total research effort funded by both governments and private enterprises in the Community. The potential benefits of collaboration and exchange in this area are clearly very large; it can only be hoped that the Community's programme will enable them to be secured to a greater degree than seems to have occurred in the past.

All the R & D in the world will avail little, however, if the fragmentation of the Community's market by differing technical standards, patent requirements and nationalistic public purchasing programmes persists. In 1988 there were seven different digital switching systems being installed in the EEC, while the United States managed with three; the Community boasted ten manufacturers of turbo-generators while the United States had two; it had 12 manufacturers of large industrial boilers compared with the American six. The shape of the Community's industrial base in the year 2000 will doubtless owe much to the work of the scientists in their laboratories: the outcome of their labours will however owe a great deal more to the creation of a genuine single market.

Further Reading

Curzon-Price, V., *Industrial Policies in the European Community* (London: Macmillan, 1981).

European Commission, *The European Community's Research Policy*, 2nd edn (Luxembourg, 1985).

Hall, G. (ed.), *European industrial policy* (London: Croom Helm, 1986).

Hodges, M., 'Industrial policy: hard times or great expectations?', in H. Wallace (ed.), *Policy-making in the European Community*, 2nd edn (Chichester: John Wiley, 1983).

Swann, D., *Competition and Industrial Policy in the European Community* (London: Methuen, 1983).

The Birth of the Common Agricultural Policy

14

14.1 The Problematic Farmer

The Treaty of Rome made reference to only two particular sectors of the economy: transport and agriculture. In the event policy with regard to the latter has proved easily the most expensive, the most troublesome and (some would argue) the most indefensible in the history of the Community. The first question which arises is therefore: why should the founding fathers have made such special provisions in the Treaty for this particular sector of the economy?

One rather obvious answer is that it was necessary in order to ensure that France became a signatory. The commitment to abolish tariffs on imports of manufactures from the other member countries, most especially those from Germany, certainly represented a formidable risk for French industry in the early 1960s; a quid pro quo through some form of privileged access for its agricultural exports (in which France had some comparative advantage) was therefore an essential element in the deal. Not for nothing did the French President, M Giscard d'Estaing, describe the Common Agricultural Policy as 'France's green oil'. Similarly, it was a French Prime Minister, M Raymond Barre, who responded to charges that the Common Agricultural Policy was an absurdity with the somewhat cryptic remark (which he attributed to Lord Balfour) that it was 'better to do an absurd thing which has always been done than a wise thing which has never been done'.

This rather obscure phrase hints at an important truth. If something has been done for many years it is as well to begin with the presumption that there may well be some good reason why it has been done, however foolish the action may appear at first sight. Now the fact is that in modern times virtually every

146

developed country, of whatever political character, has treated its agriculture as a special case meriting special policy measures. This was certainly true of the original Six. In 1958, nearly 20 per cent of their working population was engaged in agriculture, typically on very small family holdings; the low efficiency of the sector was revealed by the fact that this 20 per cent of the workforce produced only 10 per cent of total national income, implying that average income in this sector was little more than 40 per cent of the average elsewhere in the economy. The farming population was therefore both large and poor, a combination to be neglected by elected politicians only at their peril. Yet this still leaves open the question: why a special *policy* for the *industry*, rather than general measures to assist needful *individuals*?

The answer lies in two problems afflicting agriculture to a much higher degree than any other sector in the economy. There is first the *short-term* problem of price instability. This arises from three universal characteristics of the agricultural sector. First, its output is subject to random shocks due to natural forces quite outside the control of producers – climatic changes, plant and animal diseases and so on. Second, there is a rather long and inescapable lag between output decisions, when crops are planted or animals bred, and the flow of the corresponding output to the market. Third, the demand for most foodstuffs (like that for virtually all necessities) has a low price-elasticity. The combination of these gives rise to the famous 'cobweb' model of economic theory.

Suppose that *DD* and *SS* in Figure 14.1 represent the demand and supply schedules for a particular agricultural product. Initially the market is in equilibrium with output at Q_0 and price at P_0. The weather now turns unexpectedly bad and the crop falls to Q_1. In a manufacturing industry any such shortfall could probably be made good by drawing on stocks or working overtime; this is not possible for the farmers. The reduced supply therefore forces market price to P_1. When the planting season comes round farmers, assuming the new price P_1 will continue, plan a crop of Q_2, the output they would normally produce in response to this higher price. When this higher output reaches the market in the following year, demand being relatively inelastic, price falls to P_2. In the light of this fall in price, farmers cut back their projected crop to Q_3, which causes price to rise in the following year to P_3. And so the oscillation of price and output continues. The picture is obviously an over-simplified one, but the principle is clear.

In manufacturing industry such instability would be unlikely and even if it occurred producers could react by switching capital and labour to or from alternative products or, if necessary, by moving out into some other industry altogether. The small family farm, however, has both human and physical resources of a highly specialised kind and can scarcely move from one industry to another; furthermore it is unlikely to possess sufficient reserves to ride out bad times philosophically until good times return. The politician with a large farming constituency can scarcely stand by indifferent.

That is the short-run problem. There is a long-term problem as well. The

FIGURE 14.1
The Cobweb Phenomenon

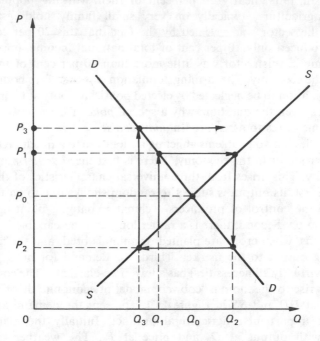

demand for foodstuffs is relatively inelastic not only with respect to changes in price; the evidence demonstrates that it is inelastic with respect to changes in income as well. That is to say, as incomes rise the demand for foodstuffs is unlikely to rise as rapidly, if for no other reason than that the capacity of the human stomach is limited. (It has been estimated, for example, that in the UK the income-elasticity of demand for food is about 0.45 compared with one of around 1.8 for services; this implies that a 10 per cent increase in income will lead to a rise of 18 per cent in the demand for services but an increase of only 4.5 per cent for food). The implications for the agricultural sector are very far-reaching. Unlike other industries, it cannot raise its income year by year by simply increasing output in parallel with the rest of the economy; given the low income-elasticity of demand, the result would merely be to force down prices. Incomes in the agricultural sector can therefore keep pace with those in the rest of the economy only through a rise in output *per head* rather than through a rise in *total* output.

These considerations explain why such prominence was given in the Treaty of Rome to 'the establishment of a common agricultural policy among the Member States'. They also indicate, however, that an effective policy needed a long-term dimension as well as a short-term price support and stability dimension. To concentrate only on the short-term problem, maintaining output from a constant farming population, would merely have the effect of worsening the long-term problem. Unfortunately the solution to the long-term problem was to prove much less popular in political terms than the remedy for the short-term problem; the consequences were predictable enough.

14.2   What Sort of Policy?

Both commonsense and economic theory – the two frequently coincide – indicate that if it is desired to give some sort of assistance to disadvantaged members of society it is done most effectively by tailoring aid measures to the particular needs and circumstances of each individual, attaching to such assistance whatever conditions and requirements as may seem desirable. In the context of European agriculture this was scarcely feasible; individual assessments would have to be made of literally millions of people scattered throughout the land – people, furthermore, whose inability to provide accurate details of their circumstances would be exceeded only by their unwillingness to do anything of the sort. Hence policy necessarily had to proceed on the basis of measures for the industry as a whole, accepting the almost inevitable consequence that aid would thereby be given indiscriminately to both those in real need and those who could survive perfectly well on their own resources.

It was shown in Chapter 8 that where it is desired to maintain a stable and acceptable level of income for a particular group of producers the most efficient policy is one in which those producers are given a subsidy on each unit produced; they are then left to sell their output at whatever price the market determines for it. In this way the amount of aid being given is precisely calculable – and adjustable in the light of circumstances – while any loss in consumers' surplus due to artificially high prices is avoided. This system – known as a 'deficiency payments' system – was the one in use in the United Kingdom prior to its entry into the Community. To avoid abuse of public funds, it implies the existence of an efficient administrative system, so that the operating costs of the policy do not exceed such benefits as the policy is believed to achieve. Given the relatively small size of the farming sector in Britain, this condition was satisfied. Since the number of consumers far exceeded the number of farmers, the avoidance of the loss of consumers' surplus was of much greater value than the administrative costs involved. The fact that, an agreed subsidy apart, output had to be disposed of at the prevailing market price ensured that production responded to market forces to a substantial degree.

The situation in the Six was very different. Here, the agricultural sector involved, in 1960, about 15 million people operating on holdings averaging about 11 hectares (around 26 acres) in size – about a third of the size of the average agricultural holding in the United Kingdom. What is more, few of the countries concerned had an administrative machine able to handle transactions involving such vast numbers of individuals with reasonable efficiency. An alternative, second-best policy may therefore be unavoidable in such a situation; this is to attempt to support farm incomes through high prices, maintaining those prices by imposing tariffs to keep out potentially cheaper imports or by restricting the quantity of such imports in some other way. The supplementation of farm income then ceases to require complex administrative machinery; in effect, consumers do the job for the government by simply paying more for their daily food than would otherwise have been necessary.

That such a system is inherently inefficient is obvious. Any gain to farmers is offset to some degree by the loss to consumers as a result of higher prices, although where farmers form a substantial proportion of the consuming population – as in the case of the Six in the early 1960s – the two largely cancel out. There is also the problem of reconciling the quantities which farmers will seek to produce at these high prices with the quantities which consumers will be willing to buy at those prices. If, as emphatically proved to be the case in the EEC, the former consistently exceed the latter, some intervention agency must stand ready to absorb the surplus and dispose of it in some way which does not undermine the high domestic price level. Furthermore, it so happens that roughly 40 per cent of the costs incurred by farmers originate in purchases of the output of other farmers. Hence, as events were also to demonstrate, the system tends to be self-defeating in the long run as the higher prices secured from sales come to be reflected in the higher costs of farm inputs. Between 1973 and 1986, for example, while the prices received by Community farmers for their output increased by around 93 per cent, the prices they paid for their agricultural inputs rose by over 130 per cent. One farmer's higher prices are another farmer's higher costs.

So much for the short-term policy aim of income support from one year to the next. The long-term policy aim must be to simultaneously raise farm productivity and reduce total agricultural manpower; to achieve the former without the latter would merely raise total output more rapidly than demand is likely to increase and thus exert a constant downward pressure on prices. The former can be achieved in many ways: credit facilities to encourage the application of greater capital per head, agricultural extension programmes to improve crop and animal husbandry and general farm management, research and publicity on disease eradication, and so on. The latter is infinitely more difficult since farmers display a robust disinclination to be pushed off the land – a prior condition if holdings are to be amalgamated and raised to a viable size. (Even in 1970 the average farm in France, even though well under a half of the average size in Britain, was divided into 18 separate parcels). All that a democratic government can do is to provide inducements for older farmers, or those on the smallest holdings, to retire voluntarily, to encourage the amalgamation of holdings or to provide alternative occupations in rural areas for young people. To provide water for the horse to drink, however, is one thing; persuading the horse to imbibe is quite another.

14.3 Enter The CAP

Part Two of the Treaty of Rome set out the 'bases' of the EEC and its second section ('Title II') was devoted exclusively to agriculture. Here no less than five separate objectives of the proposed Common Agricultural Policy (CAP) were set out in detail. First, it was to increase agricultural productivity. Second, 'to ensure thereby' a 'fair' standard of living for the agricultural population. (It has been remarked that the word 'thereby' used here is probably the most neglected word in the whole of the Treaty of Rome). Third, it was to stabilise markets. Fourth, it was to guarantee regular supplies of farm products. Finally, it was to ensure 'reasonable' prices to consumers. Wisely, the drafters of the Treaty did not attempt to specify precisely how these admirable (but not obviously compatible) objectives were to be achieved; they merely placed an obligation on the Commission to convene a conference of member states and thereafter, within two years of the commencement of the Community, to submit proposals for an agricultural policy and the ways in which it should be put into effect.

The Commission accordingly convened a conference on agriculture at Stresa in July 1958, the chairman being the first Commissioner responsible for agriculture, Dr Sicco Mansholt of the Netherlands. This drew up an agreed list of objectives spelling out in a little more detail those specified in the Treaty but rather ominously adding the objective 'to preserve the family structure of farming'. At this stage three possible variants of such a policy could have been adopted. First, the Community could have settled for common rules governing agricultural trade, and perhaps the common objectives of the policy, and then left individual member governments to pursue them in whatever way they thought best. Second, a common marketing system could be established for the Community as a whole with national governments being responsible for its financing within their own countries. Third, a single system could be operated for the Community as a whole with its financing also being a common, rather than a national, responsibility.

The Stresa conference opted for the third option. It laid down three fundamental characteristics which the CAP would possess. First, there was to be a single market in agricultural products throughout the Community, with free movement of products and common prices in all member countries. Second, it was to establish Community preference for such products with a single, common barrier against imports from the rest of the world. Thirdly, there was to be joint financial responsibility so that the costs of the policy would be met not by the country in which output was created but through a common fund. This was subsequently known as the FEOGA, the acronym of its French name, Fonds Européen d'Orientation et de Garantie Agricole.

Armed with this mandate, towards the end of 1960 the Commission presented its proposals to the Council of Ministers for a system based essentially upon variable levies to be imposed on food imports from outside the Community so as to protect and preserve guaranteed prices established annually. These proposals were agreed easily enough in general principle, but the details of their application not surprisingly caused a great deal of argument. Since the Treaty provided that policy proposals had to be established within the first three years of its entry into force – i.e. by 31 December 1961 – discussions continued throughout that year. As mentioned in Chapter 4, on 18 December, complete agreement not having been reached, the Council resorted to the ingenious device of deeming Community clocks to have stopped while a marathon session of negotiations continued. Final agreement on the mechanisms of the policy – but not at that stage on the actual level of prices for any product – was eventually reached in the early hours of 14 January 1962 when, with its fine disregard for reality, the Council resolved that the new common agricultural policy should come into effect at midnight on 31 December 1961.

14.4   The Short-run – Guaranteed Prices

Conceding that the agricultural problem had both short-run and long-run dimensions, the CAP (like the fund from which it was to be financed) made provision for both Guarantees – i.e. measures concerned with annual arrangements for the support of prices and farm incomes – and Guidance (Orientation) or long-term structural changes. For something over 90 per cent of Community farm products there was to be established a minimum level below which market price would not be allowed to fall. The jargon used for this minimum price varies from product to product – it can be an intervention price, a guaranteed price, a basic price or a norm price – but the purpose is the same in every market. (In 1985 a consumers' guide to Community jargon, describing itself as 'one of the most cataclysmically boring' books in recent memory, hoped to be of assistance to those who thought that Norm Price was a Brussels official.) For a few specialised crops, such as durum wheat or tobacco (or silkworms!), where the Community cannot hope to be self-sufficient, a system of direct grants to producers related to output or farm areas is operated; in total, however, these account for no more than 3 per cent of Community farm output and the details need not be discussed here.

The exact manner in which the guaranteed prices are established each year varies in detail from product to product, although the general principles underlying the system are virtually the same for all. It is customary, and convenient, to use the market in soft wheat as the exemplar of the whole price-support system, not least because it was the first price to be agreed in December 1964 to come into effect for the 1967/68 crop year. This was more than mere chance; the cereal price is in fact the linchpin of the entire agricultural price system. Since grains are a major input into the rearing of poultry and pigs, the guaranteed price of pigmeat can hardly be established until cereal prices are known; similarly, since pigmeat and beef are fairly close substitutes, the price of beef cannot be fixed until pigmeat prices are known; the price of milk, in turn, is closely linked with the price of beef.

In or about April of each year the Council of Ministers meets to determine the guaranteed prices for the approaching crop season. The first objective is to set the *target* price for the year – that is, the theoretical price towards which the market price will hopefully tend. It is defined as the wholesale price (for wheat) prevailing in the city of Duisburg, in the Ruhr. (This city was chosen on the grounds that it is the place in which local supplies are likely to be smallest in relation to local demand; the price there is therefore likely to be higher than in any other area of the Community.) In Figure 14.2 this is shown as P_0. From this target price is calculated the effective guarantee or *intervention* price, shown as P_2 in Figure 14.2; this is typically between 12 per cent and 20 per cent below the target price. If market prices settle above this level, no action need be taken by

FIGURE 14.2
The CAP Price-support System

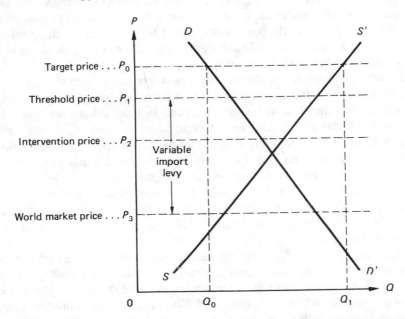

the authorities, although farmers may therefore find themselves receiving somewhat less than the theoretical target price. If market price falls to or below the intervention level, however, the CAP intervention agencies in the countries concerned will be required to purchase any wheat offered to it at the intervention price, paying for it with funds drawn from the FEOGA. (Each country has such an agency – typically a semi-official producers' organisation – for each major product.) It will be responsible for paying for the storage of any product purchased – 'taken into intervention' – or disposing of it in some other way. It has been a source of much discontent amongst producers of 'Mediterranean' products, particularly fruit and vegetables, that their intervention prices are typically set much lower in relation to the target price than those of the 'northern' products; the former can indeed be less than a half of the latter. The reason for this is that such products are exceedingly expensive to keep in storage; hence the intervention agencies are naturally disinclined to find themselves presiding over mountains of rotting tomatoes. Nevertheless the grievance remains.

This deals with the marketing problems of domestic producers. If the target price is higher than the prevailing world price for the product, however – and, as will be seen, this is typically the case – the problem arises of preventing domestic prices being forced down by low-cost imports from abroad. The solution is simple. From the target price is subtracted the estimated transport and handling costs involved in delivering imported wheat from Europe's major port, Rotterdam, to the market in Duisburg; the result is known as the *threshold* price and is shown as P_1 in Figure 14.2. If on any day the lowest-cost imported wheat can be delivered to Rotterdam at the price P_3, a variable levy (i.e. tax) amounting to P_1P_3 is imposed on it by the port authorities. The result is that, after paying the levy and the transport costs to Duisburg, no importer of wheat would be able to sell it profitably at less than the target price.

The basic philosophy of the price-support system is therefore clear. The demand for a product in any area is met first from local suppliers; the transport and other costs involved in bringing supplies in from other areas gives local farmers a natural cost advantage. Any unsatisfied demand is then met by supplies from other Community sources. Imports from the rest of the world will be able to compete if and only if Community demand so outstrips Community supply as to force market price above the target price. The target price is of course set at such a level as to make this an extremely improbable event. Typically the reverse situation prevails: the intervention price is such that local supply tends to outstrip local demand, with results to be considered in the following chapter.

Although the price-support system summarised here is broadly typical of all the major products of Community agriculture, a mention should perhaps be made of the special case of sugar. It is an important case because it is the only significant crop in which the product of Community agriculture (beet sugar) competes directly with a major crop of the developing world (cane sugar). In order to make beet production profitable in certain areas, mainly Italy and some French overseas territories, a relatively high intervention price was considered necessary. At this price, however, it was feared (with good reason) that the resulting expansion of output throughout the Community – beet being a rather easy crop to grow on almost any land – would result in intolerable surpluses. From the outset, therefore, in contrast to the rest of the CAP system, production quotas were imposed on each member country and the guaranteed intervention price was paid only up to the limit of those quotas. In contrast with other products, a levy is imposed on any surpluses which have to be exported and sold at the price they can fetch in the open world market. As will be seen at a later stage, this has not prevented the emergence of a conflict between the interests of the Community and those of many developing countries.

14.5 The Long-run – Seeking Guidance

In principle, the CAP (like its financial manifestation the FEOGA) had two equally important elements: the guarantee section relating to short-term policy and the guidance section concerned with long-term structural reform. Hence the reference in the Treaty to the rational development of agricultural production so as 'to ensure thereby' a fair standard of living for the farmers. In practice the structural side of the policy rapidly took a back seat. It was only after the long years of wrangling over the details of the price support system that the first serious proposals concerning long-term agricultural policy were aired. These were contained in a document submitted to the Council of Ministers in December 1968 by the agricultural Commissioner, Dr Sicco Mansholt, the crucial part of which was entitled *Memorandum on the Reform of Agriculture* and forthwith became known as the Mansholt Plan. It set out proposals for structural changes in the Community's agriculture during the decade of the 1970s.

The basic premise of the plan was that the system of price-support now painfully established was not in itself sufficient to achieve the declared aim of steadily rising living standards in the agricultural sector; price support, indeed, could well be counterproductive in that long-term context. If guaranteed prices had the effect of simply maintaining the existence of the large number of existing holdings – many of which, the memorandum suggested, because of their size and generally low technology, could never be truly viable – the object of significantly raising per capita productivity could not be achieved. Hence it was proposed that over the coming decade the migration of labour out of agriculture should be positively encouraged. The plan envisaged a relatively small reduction of around 7 per cent in the area under cultivation but a very large reduction in the number of people employed on it – one of 5 million people or about a half of the existing workforce.

A number of measures was proposed to achieve this dramatic change. National retirement schemes for farmers over the age of 55 were to be partly financed from Community funds. Marginal farms were to be given priority in the allocation of land becoming available as a result of such retirements. Farms which were manifestly non-viable and likely to remain so were to be phased out through relatively low price guarantees. Farming technology was to be improved through Community-subsidised training programmes, loans for farm mechanisation, provision of consultants and so on.

Although the logic of these proposals was clear enough their political implications were such that the report was greeted with outrage. Dr Mansholt was accused of seeking to destroy the family farm which the Stresa conference had regarded as the very foundation of European agriculture; he was labelled the 'peasant killer' and one German newspaper published his photograph over the caption 'This man should be killed'. The Council of Ministers, knowing a stick of political dynamite when they met one, declined to give the document even the benefit of a formal discussion.

The impact of the Mansholt Plan was not entirely nil. In 1972 three directives were adopted which were later described as 'a pale reflection' of some of its proposals. Directive 72/159 permitted member countries to assist their farmers in modernisation through grants or subsidised interest rates provided that the farms concerned had a prospect of generating a level of income comparable to that of other occupations locally. Directive 72/160 allowed member countries to give lump-sum payments or annuities to farm workers in the 55–65 age-group to help persuade them to leave the industry, while Directive 72/161 provided that countries would be encouraged to create 'socio-economic guidance services' aimed at the retraining and relocation of farm workers. For all such measures funds could be allocated from the FEOGA to meet up to 25 per cent of their total cost – indeed, up to 65 per cent for Ireland and Italy. But it will be noted that all three directives were permissive rather than mandatory. It was left to national governments to adopt such measures, or none, as they pleased.

The evidence does not suggest that an over-enthusiastic response was forthcoming. Over their lifetime, the decade 1975–84, annual grants by the FEOGA under the three Regulations taken together averaged a little less than ECU 100 m (at 1986 prices) – not a large sum in relation to the total of nearly 4 million farms of less than 10 hectares in area at the beginning of that period. In 1985 the Regulations were replaced by a new ten-year structural plan. This reflected two conclusions following inescapably from the experience of the 1970s – first, that the problem of surpluses made it unrealistic to look for a solution to the small-farm problem through increased output and, secondly, that the deceleration in economic growth made the task of finding alternative occupations in rural areas more difficult than ever. The emphasis in the new programme was thus placed on cost reduction and quality improvement rather than on a search for fundamental changes in farm structure. The requirement of ultimately producing incomes comparable with non-agricultural occupations was simply abandoned as unattainable. The objective is no longer to transform small farms into larger ones generating high incomes but rather to enable small farms to survive with a reasonable quality of living. An annual average of ECU 420 m was earmarked for this purpose during 1985–94, with a further ECU 270 m a year hopefully being made availabe for schemes to improve agricultural marketing and processing. Whether this plan will prove more successful than its predecessors remains to be seen.

The plan did not abandon entirely the aim of structural reform. Proposals were advanced under which the Community would meet 50 per cent of the cost of national 'set-aside' schemes – payments to farmers who agreed to withdraw land from agricultural production altogether. Once again, the results proved only marginal. In the first year of the scheme's operation, 1988–9, the area set aside was less than a half of the 1 m hectare target; cereal production, running at over 160 m tonnes, fell by less than 2 m tonnes.

The truth is that despite the introduction from time to time of relatively modest initiatives in particular areas – most especially the 'Integrated Mediterranean Programmes' designed to mollify the southern farmers in France and Italy and, especially, Greece – it is difficult to argue that there exists any coherent Community policy for the long-term structural reform of the agricultural sector. Since the price-support system was brought into operation the resources of the FEOGA have been largely swallowed up by it. In 1963–4, before price guarantees came into operation, the guidance element of the CAP absorbed a respectable 15 per cent of the total FEOGA budget, but four years later, in 1968–9, only about 5.5 per cent of FEOGA expenditure was devoted to the guidance section. In 1973 the share still stood at 5.3 per cent but by 1986 it had fallen even further to 3.8 per cent. Individual member countries pursue such structural measures as they judge best with little reference to the Community, and indeed frequently adopt measures in direct contravention of the Treaty. In 1980 the Commission was able to list 51 different aids to agriculture operated by national governments which appeared to contravene the Treaty, 39 of them in France. In fact, the Commission has compiled an inventory of state aids to agriculture in member countries which is believed to occupy nine volumes. Because of the acute political sensitivity of the subject these volumes are not publicly available. A report prepared for the Commission indicated, however, that annual aids to agriculture by national governments during 1975–80 amounted to about double the total annual expenditure of the FEOGA. In the light of all this the Community would appear to be little nearer a genuine and effective long-term structural policy for agriculture than it was when Dr Mansholt became, for Europe, Public Enemy Number One.

Further Reading

Balassa, B. A. (ed.), *European Economic Integration* (Amsterdam: North-Holland, 1975).

Coffey, P. (ed.), *Economic Policies of the Common Market* (London: Macmillan, 1979).

European Commission, *The Agricultural Policy of the European Community*, 3rd edn (Luxembourg, 1983).

Harris, S. *et al.*, *The Food and Farm Policies of the European Community* (Chichester: John Wiley & Sons, 1983).

Hill, B. E., *The Common Agricultural Policy* (London: Methuen, 1984).

Pearce, J., 'The common agricultural policy: the accumulation of special interests', in Wallace, H. (ed.), *Policy-making in the European Community*, 2nd edn (Chichester: John Wiley & Sons, 1983).

The Life of the Common Agricultural Policy 15

15.1 The Bottomless Purse

The Treaty of Rome made little more than a passing reference to the delicate matter of how the common agricultural policy was to be financed. Article 40 contained the vague provision that 'one or more agricultural orientation and guarantee funds may be established'. (The word 'orientation' is Eurojargon for guidance or structural.) Difficult though it may be to comprehend with the benefit of hindsight, there was a presumption that the CAP would be broadly self-financing. The theory was that the price-stabilisation function would lead to profits and losses which would balance out over a period of years. The intervention agencies would need funds to absorb surpluses when market prices were tending to fall below target prices; these would be recovered, however, as they disposed of those surpluses in due course when market prices were tending to rise above the target. Indeed, by buying at relatively low prices and selling at relatively high prices the intervention agencies should have been profit-making concerns. So far as the long-term structural side of the policy was concerned, sufficient finance would be raised through the proceeds of the variable levies on imports.

It soon became apparent that both propositions were fallacies. True, if an intervention agency seeks to keep market price within a narrow range of a genuine long-term equilibrium level in the long run losses should be more than offset by gains. The key element in this conclusion, however, is the assumption that intervention is related to a price which is in some sense a genuine equilibrium price. Unhappily, the function of maintaining the *stability* of prices is almost always confused in practice with the aim of maintaining, or even increasing, the *level* of prices in an attempt to raise producer incomes. The CAP was to provide a classic example of this confusion of purpose.

Had agricultural prices been reasonably similar throughout the Six, and broadly comparable to prevailing world prices, when target prices for the first crop year, 1967–8, were being determined all might have been well. Neither in fact was true. For the sake of simplicity it will be convenient to talk of the weighted average price of four representative products – wheat, sugarbeet, beef and milk – as representing farm prices in general. On this basis farm prices in the mid-1960s were around 40 per cent higher than those in the UK, where food prices were in general determined by those on the open world market. Further, within the Six farm prices varied significantly, those in Germany and Italy being typically some 20 per cent higher than those in France and the Netherlands. Naturally it was almost axiomatic that no member country could agree to a significant *cut* in the price received by its farmers for any product (peasant-killers having a short life expectancy in Community politics) so that the inevitable result was that the target price for each product approximated fairly closely to the highest price prevailing in any member country.

In the first year of the operation of the CAP, therefore, agricultural prices in the Six (as represented by the average of the four products quoted) were nearly three times the prevailing world level and approached nearly four times world level in 1969–70 before falling back slightly in 1970–71. The results were predictable; internal production began to expand while imports were checked by the high variable levies needed to protect the high targets; while the demand for foodstuffs, as noted earlier, is relatively inelastic with regard to price it is hardly *totally* unaffected by it, so that consumption was certainly discouraged. As may be seen from Table 15.1, the value of net imports of agricultural products from the rest of the world fell sharply, from nearly ECU 26 bn in 1966 to a little over ECU 19 bn in 1973. At the beginning of the 1960s the Six had produced about 4 per cent less than their consumption of the four products quoted earlier but by 1973 they were producing 6 per cent more than their total consumption.

The problem building up was to some degree obscured by the fact that during the years 1971–6 food prices in world markets rose rather sharply, so that the discrepancy between them and the target prices being maintained by the Community fell substantially. Indeed, for some products it became necessary to impose levies on *exports* in order to prevent an outflow to world markets and an unacceptable increase in domestic prices. In the second half of the decade, however, world prices fell back and the glaring discrepancy returned, with Community prices returning to around three times world prices. By 1981 net imports of food into the Community were approaching zero and its self-sufficiency ratio of 1.06 in 1973 had risen to 1.13. As Figure 14.2 illustrates, if an attempt is made to consistently maintain an intervention price significantly higher than the genuine equilibrium price, the inevitable result is an excess supply which has to be both financed and disposed of.

Table 15.1
Agriculture in the European Community, 1958–86*

(1)	Units (2)	Europe 6			Europe 9		Europe 10	
		1958 (3)	1966 (4)	1973 (5)	1973 (6)	1981 (7)	1981 (8)	1986 (9)
1. Total area in use	Million hectares	63.4	64.2	59.1	88.0	85.2	88.7	87.7
2. Total workforce	Million	11.5	8.2	4.9	6.0	5.3	5.7	5.2
3. Value of crop output	ECU bn at 1986 prices	21.7	26.4	34.8	40.0	54.7	59.2	73.5
4. Value of animal output		27.8	36.1	41.8	53.5	76.4	78.6	86.2
5. Total final output		49.5	62.5	76.6	93.5	131.1	137.8	159.7
6. Intermediate inputs		12.5	22.7	29.8	38.4	57.4	57.5	68.8
7. Gross value added		37.0	39.8	46.8	55.1	73.7	80.3	90.9
8. Gross value added:								
(a) Per hectare	000 ECU at 1986 prices	0.58	0.62	0.79	0.63	0.87	0.91	1.04
(b) Per person employed		3.22	4.85	9.55	9.18	13.91	14.09	17.48
9. Per capita value added as % of whole economy†	%	46.1	43.2	43.5	46.7	50.8	47.9	51.6
10. Total trade in food, beverages and tobacco	ECU bn at 1986 prices							
Imports		37.3	52.1	70.7	95.2	90.8	92.0	89.8
Exports		16.9	26.4	51.4	66.2	83.9	85.3	79.4
Net imports		20.4	25.7	19.3	29.0	6.9	6.7	10.4

* Rows 1–8 refer to holdings of 1 hectare or more.
† Calculated from national income statistics.

The financial consequences were of course horrendous. In 1968, the first year in which guaranteed prices were fully applied, expenditure on agricultural policy had amounted (in 1986 prices) to around ECU 6 bn. Ten years later this had risen to ECU 19 bn, of which 96 per cent was being spent on the price intervention system; so much for the self-financing nature of the system. By 1986, FEOGA expenditure had risen to ECU 23 bn – 70 per cent of the entire Community budget – with more than 96 per cent still going into the guarantee section. Of this huge total, 36 per cent was devoted to export refunds – that is, to subsidies paid to dealers to compensate them for disposing of surpluses on world markets and at world prices. Another 19 per cent was being spent on the costs of maintaining stocks of the surpluses still not disposed of, including allowance for the fact that much of those stocks was rotting into unsaleability.

The administrative consequences, and the ensuing scope for inefficiency, wastage and, indeed, downright fraud have been equally monumental. In 1988 there were 80 different classifications of beef products and 11 different rates of export refunds for such products. The resulting 800-odd different combinations of product and refund rate are (to put it mildly) a formidable administrative tangle. Products taken into intervention storage constitute a similar administrative nightmare. By the end of 1987 it was estimated that the surplus stocks of butter held in storage throughout the Community would make a slab twice as high as Nelson's Column, while the wheat held in storage could make a wall of loaves of bread 75 feet high and stretching from Land's End to John o' Groats.

Nor were the expectations of revenues accruing from import levies any more soundly based. Given the fact that the price system was specifically aimed at replacing imported with domestic supplies, it was hardly likely that levies on imports could keep pace with domestic expenditure on agriculture. In 1971 revenues from the import levies and those on sugar exports had amounted to nearly 40 per cent of total FEOGA spending; by 1986 the proportion had fallen to less than 10 per cent. (It is worth noting that the position would have been even worse had it not been for the relative growth in the revenue from levies on the Community's *exports* of sugar, which accounted for about 18 per cent of total agricultural revenues in 1974 but nearly 50 per cent in 1986.) In a word, the CAP may be said to be many things but even its most devoted supporters could hardly describe it as self-financing.

15.2   Using Green Money

The financial problems of the CAP have not been confined to its apparently infinite capacity to absorb taxpayers' money. The system rests on the assumption that a target price, once defined, can be translated into each of the currencies of the member countries – which is the only meaningful unit for the farmers concerned – and still ensure that there is a genuinely common market in farm products, in the sense that (neglecting transport costs) the final price received by a farmer for a given product will be the same wherever it is sold within the Community. To this end the Six agreed to establish a notional Unit of Account (since replaced by the ECU, of which more later) in which target and intervention prices would be defined. Suppose that the notional unit of account is defined as being equal to $1 (which it was initially); the price of a product in any country could then be defined in terms of any national currency by simply converting the target price in any year into the domestic currency at the prevailing rate of exchange on the foreign exchange market.

Let the market exchange rates in a given year be such that $1 = 6 French francs or 4 Deutschemarks; the Community's unit of account is assumed to be defined as equal to $1. If the target price for wheat is fixed as 50 units of account (UA) per 100 kg then the domestic target price in France will be Frs 300 and in Germany it will be DM 200. For the sake of simplicity it is assumed that market prices are currently at their target level. If a French farmer decides to export his wheat to a German dealer rather than sell it in France, he will receive a price of DM 200 which, when converted through the banking system, will amount to Frs (200/4) × 6 = Frs 300. Transport and financial costs apart, the price is the same wherever the product is sold.

This conclusion rests on the assumption that foreign exchange rates remain stable, as indeed they had been for many years when the CAP system was inaugurated. In August 1969, however, inflation in France caused the government to announce a reduction of something over 11 per cent in the official rate of exchange of the franc. In terms of the simple example just quoted, exchange rates had now become (taking a 10 per cent devaluation to simplify the example) $1 = Frs 6.6 = DM 4. Logically this would have implied that the target price for wheat would now become Frs 330 in France but remain at DM 200 in Germany. The government of France, however, already having an inflation problem on their hands, were understandably reluctant to contemplate a sudden rise of this kind in the price of food, with all its implications for increased pressure for higher wages and salaries. Nor were the other member countries attracted by the prospect of the rise in French output which such a price increase would undoubtedly have stimulated. The French government thus sought, and obtained, permission for the price-adjustment to be phased in over two years and for the franc exchange rate *for the purposes of the CAP*, the so-called Green rate – officially known as 'the representative rate' – to remain at its existing level for the time being. The internal price of wheat in France would thus remain at its previous level of Frs 300.

This immediately created a problem of trade diversion. Suppose our hypothetical farmer had decided to export wheat to Germany, receiving the German price of DM 200. Converting these receipts through the banking system he would now be given the new exchange rate prevailing in the foreign exchange market – i.e. Frs 6.6 = DM 4 and his sale of DM 200 will bring in Frs (200/4) × 6.6 = Frs 330, Frs 30 more than he would have obtained by selling in

France. The result could be predicted – wheat exports to Germany would suddenly increase, rapidly bringing market price there down towards the intervention level. German farmers, on the other hand, would find exports to France exceedingly unprofitable, since selling there at the prevailing price of Frs 300 and converting the proceeds would bring them in only DM (300/6.6) × 4 = DM 182, much less than the internal German price of DM 200. German wheat previously exported to France would now be diverted to the home market, causing further downward pressure on the domestic price level.

German and other farmers in the Six naturally contemplated this possibility with less than wild enthusiasm and the response of the Community was therefore to create a system of Monetary Compensatory Amounts (MCAs) to prevent their exchange-rate concession to France from having these unacceptable effects. In essence the MCA is a tax levied on agricultural exports from a country (France in this example) whose green rate is above its current market rate of exchange and a subsidy paid on imports into that country from its partners in the Community. The object is to offset gains and losses which the discrepancy in exchange rates would otherwise cause. In the example of France, the (negative) MCA would be 10 per cent on all exports; the gross receipt of Frs 330 would thus be reduced to Frs 300, the same as the internal price, and the stimulus to exports would be eliminated. Similarly, German exporters to France would receive a positive MCA – a 10 per cent bonus on their sales, so that the receipts of DM 182 would be brought into line with the domestic price of DM 200.

This rather tortuous method of handling the devaluation of the franc in August 1969 had scarcely been invented when the reverse problem was presented by the decision of the German authorities to raise the official rate of exchange of their currency by a little over 9 per cent in October 1969. The opposite consequences now followed. If the Deutschemark now exchanged for, say, DM 3.63 to $1, the internal target price of wheat (defined as the domestic equivalent of $50) would logically have fallen from DM 200 to DM 181. Political life being what it is, this fall in domestic prices – naturally distinctly unpopular with the farmers – was just as unwelcome to the German government as a sudden rise in food prices would have been to the French government. Germany therefore also applied for a postponement of the evil hour, this time for three years; the hope was that over three years the generally upward rise in prices would allow them to bring their prices into line by merely holding their prices stable, or allowing them to rise more slowly, until inflation in its partner countries had caught up with the appreciation in their currency. The 'green rate' for German agricultural prices was therefore held at the old rate of $1 = DM 4, a (positive) MCA of 9.3 per cent was paid by the FEOGA on German agricultural exports and a negative MCA (i.e. a tax) of 9.3 per cent was levied on agricultural exports to Germany by other member countries. Thus a French farmer selling wheat for DM 200 in Germany would be charged a 9.3 per cent MCA at the German border, leaving him with net proceeds of DM 181.4. Converting this at the new market rate of Frs 6.6 = DM 3.63 would leave him with a total of Frs 330. The previously-established 10 per cent MCA levied on exports at the French border would have taken Frs 30 (10 per cent of the French market value of Frs 300), so that the end result would be that he would be left with the same net selling price as if the wheat had been sold in France in the first place.

All this was complicated enough but at least it was regarded as a strictly temporary arrangement, giving a breathing space of two years to France and three years to Germany to adjust to what was regarded as an exceedingly unusual event – a once-for-all readjustment of exchange rates in response to a particular disequilibrium in the relative inflation rates in the two countries. Within two years, however, this comforting conclusion was shattered. For some 13 years the industrialised world, including the countries of Western Europe, had operated the so-called Bretton Woods international monetary system; essentially this reduced to a system in which each country maintained its currency at a rate of exchange fixed in relation to the US dollar. In 1971, however, for reasons whose explanation lies beyond the scope of this book, the US dollar ceased to be the fixed reference-point against which all other currencies could be measured. The problem was not merely that the dollar itself fell in value in the world foreign exchange markets; what was much worse was that its value changed to varying degrees against different currencies and from one day to the next. The world had moved away from a regime in which exchange rates were held constant for long periods of time to a floating exchange-rate regime in which they varied unpredictably in the open market.

The consequences for the CAP price support system were considerable. All the complications raised by the 'once-for-all' revaluation of two currencies in 1969 were now being raised for five (and after the second enlargement of the Community in 1973, seven) different currencies whose value varied from day to day not merely in relation to the dollar but, necessarily, in relation to one another. The same political objections to varying farm prices were raised, but now they were being experienced by nine separate governments. The result was that Regulation 974 of 1971 introduced the rigmarole of positive and negative MCAs for all member currencies – not as a temporary measure to meet a once-for-all adjustment but as a quasi-permanent feature of the system. Furthermore, the adjustment of a country's representative, or green, rate of exchange for CAP purposes was held to come within the mantle of the Luxembourg Compromise; the decision to retain or amend the green rate was one which rested solely with the government concerned. At a later stage it was even agreed that a currency's green rate could be varied to different degrees for different products if the country concerned saw some advantage to be gained thereby; as a result, by 1988 there were no less than 49 different green rates within the 11 currencies of the member states.

The CAP could never have been described as a system distinguished by its administrative simplicity but its operation now became an administrative nightmare. It was clearly impossible to calculate MCAs on an hourly or even daily basis, given the fluctuations in foreign exchange markets from one hour to another. Hence they were calculated on a weekly basis, the amount payable in any week being based on the average daily rates of exchange over the five working days ending on Tuesday of the preceding week. Since they were payable on the date on which a consignment passed through the customs it was impossible for importers or exporters to know in advance precisely what amount of refund or levy would be involved in a transaction. The risks and uncertainties attached to any international trade transaction took a sudden leap upwards. The scope for graft and corruption was correspondingly widened. Belgian farmers took to walking cattle into Holland at night for slaughtering and reimporting them into Belgium, thereby collecting the sum of Belgian and Dutch MCAs – probably of the order of 10 per cent – in addition to the normal sale price. Irish farmers drove cereals into Northern Ireland, collecting an MCA of up to 25 per cent of their value, and then drove them back (overnight and on unregulated roads) to collect the higher price payable in the Republic.

Perhaps more importantly, the MCA system made a nonsense of the concept of a 'common price' throughout the Community. When the divergences between green rates and actual market rates were at their greatest, in 1978, farm prices in the UK were around 30 per cent below the Community average and German prices were about 10 per cent above it, giving rise to huge variations in the prices paid by consumers for the same products. Farm prices had become substantially a matter for national rather than Community determination, since each government was free to adjust its green rates or not according to its political preferences. Inevitably those countries receiving positive MCAs – i.e. subsidies on their agricultural exports – tended to delay adjustments to their green rate while those receiving negative MCAs – i.e. being in effect taxed on their exports – made adjustments fairly rapidly.

The budgetary consequences of this are not difficult to envisage. The balance of positive and negative MCAs inevitably moved heavily in favour of the former with, as usual, a vast drain on taxpayers' pockets – about ECU 2.2 bn was absorbed by MCAs in 1977, representing more than 11 per cent of the total FEOGA budget. Fortunately, the return of relative stability in foreign exchange markets since 1979, and in particular the creation of the European Monetary System in that year (a matter discussed at length in Chapter 23 below), has much moderated the need for MCAs to accommodate exchange-rate discrepancies within the Community. At the outset of the EMS in March 1979, indeed, the Council of Ministers resolved that no new positive MCAs should be created or existing ones increased: in 1980 it was resolved that they should be phased out altogether. The Community has not been entirely successful in this regard: in 1986 a provision of ECU 144 m was made for MCAs, but since this represented less than 1 per cent of the total budget the matter has ceased to be one of pressing importance. Nevertheless the fact remains that in 1988 the average difference between the green rates for crop products and prevailing market rates was still just over 10 per cent; excluding the Greek drachma, the average difference was a little over 8 per cent. The entire episode illustrates the critical importance of exchange-rate stability for the whole system. This was more or less taken for granted in the early days of the CAP; experience shows the fragile nature of the assumption.

15.3 Appraising the CAP

In 1980, after the CAP had been in full operation for more than a decade, the Commission thought it proper to reach a verdict on its general performance. In its report, *Reflections on the Common Agricultural Policy*, its general conclusion was summarised by its opening statement: 'The Common Agricultural Policy has broadly achieved its main aims.' This comforting statement came as something of a surprise to the majority of outside observers and when tested against the objective evidence does not fare too well. The CAP had five objectives spelt out for it in the Treaty of Rome; twenty years after its inception it is not unreasonable to examine the extent to which these objectives appear to have been attained.

The first objective was to increase the productivity of the Community's agricultural sector. In the twenty years 1965–85 the output of the agricultural sector in the Community (taking out the effect its enlargement from six to nine members over that period) rose by roughly 48 per cent while its workforce fell by about 52 per cent; output per person employed therefore increased by about 210 per cent over the period. A comparable calculation for manufacturing industry suggests a rise of about 106 per cent over the same period. In both absolute and relative terms, therefore, the first objective of the Treaty could be said to have been achieved. To attribute this to the CAP itself, however, is rather questionable. The 1960s and 1970s were decades of very marked technological advance in agriculture. The increase of some 600 per cent in the use of nitrogenous fertilisers since 1950, for example, has been held to account for one third of the doubling in the crop of wheat per hectare over that period; new strains of crops and animals and rapid developments in pesticides have also played a major part in the process. Even so, technological advances were also occurring in other sectors, and the evidence must be held to be consistent with the proposition that the desired increase (of significant proportions) in agricultural productivity in the Community has in fact been achieved.

The second objective, however, was to secure by means of this increased productivity an increase in the real income of the farming population and, specifically, to reduce the gap between agricultural earnings and those in the rest of the economy. Here the record is less impressive. In its 1980 report the Commission made much of the fact that during 1968–76 real incomes in agriculture had risen at a rate equal to that of other branches of the economy. This was doubtless true, but since that period began with the value added per head in farming averaging less than 41 per cent of the average for the whole economy the implication was that the gap between agriculture and the rest had not been substantially narrowed. Between 1965 and 1985, in fact, the relative gap between value-added per head in agriculture and in the remainder of the economy narrowed by a little over 23 per cent, which of course implies that in *absolute terms* the gap in real incomes was wider than ever. In 1965 per capita value added in agriculture fell below the average for the rest of the economy by around ECU 5700 (in 1986 prices); by 1985 the gap had increased to about ECU 7500.

What is more, by common consent the CAP had benefited the large and prosperous farmer rather than the vast bulk of small farmers. The price-support mechanism of the CAP is such that the sums handed out are directly related to the level of farm output; it therefore follows that the biggest beneficiaries are the larger farms with both the land and capital equipment necessary to achieve the undoubted economies of scale attached to modern farming. In 1983 Community farms classified as 'small, very small or minimum' produced a net value added per unit of input equal to 46 per cent of the average for Community farms as a whole; those classified as 'large or very large' produced 167 per cent of the Community average. Hence it was hardly surprising that about 75 per cent of FEOGA expenditure was received by 25 per cent of the total number of farms, almost all in the northern half of Europe, while the other 25 per cent of expenditure was spread over the remaining farms yielding an annual income of around 10 per cent of the large farms. The conclusion is clear: the CAP has done little to raise the relative level of farm incomes in the Community and what it has done has benefited the large (and relatively prosperous) farmer at the expense of the small.

The third objective, that of stabilising markets, has certainly been achieved in the sense that since 1967 the overall level of agricultural prices within the Community has never fallen from one year to the next; in fact it has typically risen rather more slowly than the general level of prices over the lifetime of the CAP. On the other hand, the emergence of persistent surpluses within the Community, many of which have led to widescale dumping at knockdown prices in the outside world, has undoubtedly destabilised markets so far as producers in the rest of the world are concerned. Further, the persistent reluctance of the agricultural ministers to contemplate any reduction in prices, whatever the prevailing balance of supply and demand, has been a mixed blessing; price movements, after all, remain the mechanism whereby changes in the level of surpluses or shortages can be transmitted to producers in order that disequilibria can be corrected.

Equally, the fourth objective, that of guaranteeing regular supplies, has certainly been attained. Before the creation of the CAP the Community had produced about 5 per cent less than its total needs in the 10 products which account for about 70 per cent of its total agricultural output. By 1983 it was producing 18 per cent more than its total needs. The only product in that list of

10 in which a substantial increase did not occur was the humble potato – significantly enough the only product in the list for which no guaranteed intervention system exists. 'Regular supplies' is one thing: a system which consistently over-produces to the tune of 18 per cent is quite another. It could scarcely be described as an unmitigated success.

The final objective, that of ensuring 'reasonable prices' to consumers, could hardly be said to have been achieved unless a very strange meaning is attached to the word 'reasonable'. As has been remarked earlier, the CAP has consistently held prices to Community consumers well above world levels. This might perhaps be regarded as an acceptable burden in return for the well-being of what would otherwise be an impoverished agricultural sector; that food prices, of especial significance for the less well-off members of society, should be anything up to double the world level in order to further increase the profits of a minority of rich farmers, however, is quite a different matter.

The conclusion that the CAP has 'achieved its main aims' is therefore rather lacking in empirical foundation. The fact which had become obvious by the early 1980s was that the CAP was not merely proving inefficient in terms of its own stated objectives but was doing so at enormous cost. The estimates presented in Table 15.2 demonstrate the reality beyond reasonable doubt. In 1984 the farmers of the Community (the bigger ones especially) were gaining some ECU 52 bn as a result of the CAP. Against this, consumers were losing nearly ECU 48 bn through having to pay prices for their food well in excess of the true opportunity cost represented by world prices; in addition, in their capacity as taxpayers they were also losing nearly ECU 20 bn in the form of contributions to the Community budget soaked up by the FEOGA. Costs

Table 15.2
Annual Benefits and Costs of the CAP, 1984 (ECU bn at 1986 prices)

Country (1)	Producers' gain (2)	Consumers loss (3)	Taxpayers loss (4)	Total net benefit (5)	Cost/benefit ratio (6)
Belgium/Luxembourg	1.79	1.57	0.78	− 0.56	1.29
Denmark	1.90	0.90	0.45	0.55	0.66
France	12.20	9.18	3.36	− 0.34	1.03
Germany	12.76	13.21	6.16	− 6.61	1.51
Greece	2.57	2.35	0.45	− 0.23	1.06
Ireland	0.78	0.56	0.22	—	0.95
Italy	9.18	7.72	3.25	− 1.79	1.20
Netherlands	4.03	2.57	1.01	0.45	0.88
United Kingdom	6.72	8.73	4.25	− 6.26	1.94
EC 10	52.05	47.57	19.92	−15.44	1.30

* Based on D. Harvey and K. J. Thomson, 'Costs, benefits and the future of the Common Agricultural Policy', *Journal of Common Market Studies*, Vol. XXIV, No. 1, September 1985.

exceeded benefits by around ECU 15 bn, or 30 per cent. The Germans and British, in particular, were paying out nearly ECU 13 bn more than their farmers were gaining. Corner-stone of the Community the CAP might be, as the French in particular were fond of maintaining; economic commonsense it certainly was not.

15.4   Reforming the CAP

By the beginning of the 1980s harsh realities were at last beginning to intrude. At the end of 1983 surplus stocks of wheat held in public storage accounted for about 12.5 per cent of total annual production; for butter the surplus stocks amounted to 30 per cent of annual output, while for skimmed milk powder the ratio was 39 per cent. The financial consequences were of course frightening. The share of the total Community budget taken by the FEOGA had risen from 64 per cent in 1982 to 68 per cent in 1983 and was still rising – by 1985, in fact, it has reached 73 per cent. At this point the Community had reached virtually the limit of its revenue-raising powers so that unless member governments were willing to increase their contributions (which one or two most emphatically were not) the steadily-growing FEOGA expenditures would soon be enforcing a positive reduction in other expenditures. In addition, the gradual integration of Greece, Portugal and Spain into the CAP clearly threatened a worsening of the situation.

The first medicine which the Council and Commission sought to apply was the extension of the principle of a 'co-responsibility levy' on producers – that is, a tax on the final price, paid in theory by the suppliers, which would hopefully (a) reduce the output of products in excess supply and (b) provide finance for schemes to encourage greater consumption of the product. As was mentioned in the previous chapter, such levies had been established for sugar more or less from the outset of the CAP. They had also been introduced (at a level of 1.5 per cent of the target price) for milk in 1977 and stood at 2 per cent in 1980. The principle of such levies was therefore not a new one.

In 1980 the Commission proposed that the levy on milk should be dramatically increased (to 30 per cent) and that the principle of co-responsibility levies should be extended to cereals, beef, olive oil and fruit and vegetables as well. The proposal was greeted with cries of outrage from the Parliament and the Council of Ministers, not surprisingly, backed away from this piece of political dynamite. The furthest that the Council was able to go was to allow an increase in the milk levy from 2 to 2.5 per cent and to concede that the 'principle' of extending the levy to cereals had some merit. It was not until 1988, however, that such a levy (of 3 per cent) was actually introduced for cereals.

It is hardly surprising that the device had no substantial effect. Political necessity required that the levy be very small indeed. Ministers, in fact, would have been reluctant to see things otherwise (even if it had been feasible) lest the Commission find itself with a new source of revenue beyond national control. The levy failed to distinguish between large producers who could bear a tax of 2 or 3 per cent with ease and small producers who could not, thus worsening the distributive effects of the CAP. Furthermore, since national governments inevitably collected the revenue by means of a levy on all its producers there was no particular incentive for any one producer in isolation to reduce output.

The Commission then turned its attention to the possibility of a second control device – the introduction of physical limits to the quantities which would be eligible for price support through intervention. This again was a principle which had been established early on in connection with sugar. It proved equally unpopular for rather obvious reasons. In 1984 the Council of Ministers agreed to the introduction of national quotas for milk production, dairy products being by far the most expensive category and also the one in which excess production was the most flagrant. The quotas were aimed at bringing total milk production roughly back to its 1981 level – an overall reduction of around 5 per cent. In the following year the principle was extended to processed tomatoes. As mentioned below, in 1988, after long and bitter argument, the principle of 'stabilisers' – i.e. maximum quantities on which the guaranteed prices would be paid – was extended to all major products, but the levels at which these maximum quantities were set were only marginally lower than current production in most cases.

While such quotas are likely to be more effective than the co-responsibility levies, they clearly fall short of an efficient solution to the problem. In the first place their enforcement upon millions of small farmers dispersed throughout the Community represents a formidable and expensive administrative exercise. More important, they fail to distinguish between efficient and inefficient producers, giving the latter in fact a form of concealed protection. This difficulty can to some extent be overcome by allowing individual quotas to be bought and sold on the open market – as is the case with the milk quotas. This may have the consequence, however, that sellers prove to be farmers who would probably not have met their quota in full (why sell otherwise?), and are thus likely to use resources set free by such sales in order to produce something else. The buyers, on the other hand, most certainly will use the additional quota – why buy otherwise? In the end, the reduction in total production may prove to be much smaller than would have seemed likely. The inescapable fact is that any attempt to lay down patterns of output, or patterns of prices, is bound to keep an industry out of touch with changes in the pattern of demand and the development of technology, leading to inefficient production and ultimate failure.

As the Community was ultimately to concede in its annual report on agriculture for 1986, 'It is the price and market policy which will have to play the major role in improving the situation. Prices are of fundamental importance in this connection.' The essential cause of the CAP problem has been the attempt to maintain prices consistently and markedly above world level. From the 1980s onwards the Commission has therefore sought to persuade the Council of Ministers at its annual price review to hold prices down, if not indeed to reduce them. The attempt has invariably encountered fierce resistance from one or more ministers with a nervous eye on the farm vote back home. In 1984, for the first time, the Council agreed on a set of prices which was, on average and in ECU terms, 0.5 per cent lower than in the previous year. By the time various adjustments had been made to green rates and MCAs, however, the agreed prices in terms of national currencies were on average 3.3 per cent higher than in the previous year. Between 1985 and 1989, settlements were formulated in which ECU prices were virtually unchanged (and prices in national currencies raised by less than 2 per cent – less than half the rate of inflation). An attempt to reduce the ECU price of cereals in 1985, however, was described by Germany as injuring its 'major national interest' and the Luxembourg Compromise was invoked to veto it. It was subsequently agreed that the German government would be permitted to make special payments to its farmers to protect them from the effects of the cut in cereal prices. So much for common markets and common prices.

The stresses generated by the relentless increase in spending, combined with the exhaustion of revenue sources, were nevertheless bound to prevail in the end. By the time of the meeting of the European Council in Brussels in February 1988 reality had broken through. The principle of 'stabilisers' – quantitative limits to the application of price guarantees – was accepted for virtually all products, even cereals. (For the latter, a maximum quota of 160 m tonnes was established, a figure roughly equivalent to average production during 1984–6.) In addition, the principle was adopted that if a quota was exceeded in any year the intervention price for the product concerned would be reduced in a systematic manner in subsequent years. For cereals, indeed, a 'provisional' co-responsibility levy of 3 per cent is to be deducted from intervention prices at the beginning of each crop year, in addition to the basic levy; this is to be refunded only if production during the year proves to be less than 3 per cent over the quota. As mentioned in sec. 5 of the preceding chapter, agreement was also reached that the Community should meet up to 50 per cent of any sums paid by governments to their farmers for setting land aside from production.

Most important of all, it was agreed that henceforth the rate of increase of FEOGA spending in any year could be no more than 74 per cent of the increase in the Community's GNP in the preceding year. Miraculously – largely because of anticipated savings in export restitutions as the result of a rise in world food prices in 1988 – the 1989 budget provided for smaller agricultural expenditure than in the preceding year, a unique event. If this provision proves adequate, the share of agricultural spending in the total budget would then fall below 60 per cent.

The long-term impact of all this remains to be seen; similar resolutions have been adopted in the past and then gone the way of many another good intention. By the end of 1988 some progress could apparently be observed. Accumulated surpluses of skimmed milk powder had fallen from over 700 000 tonnes at end-1987 to a mere 13 000 tonnes; those of butter had fallen from over a million tonnes to 183 000; even the stockpile of wheat had fallen from over 5 m tonnes in 1987 to a mere 4 m tonnes. The bulk of this improvement, however, was attributable to large-scale disposal on world markets, rather than reduced domestic output – severe drought in the United States and the application of large subsidies to exports of dairy products to the Soviet Union were the major factors at work.

It is surely clear beyond doubt that the CAP suffers from fundamental weaknesses. For these, relatively marginal measures like co-responsibility levies or production quotas can never be cures; annual wrangles over prices for each coming harvest season are equally unlikely to constitute a satisfactory solution. In the first place there is a division of responsibility between those who determine guaranteed prices (with an eye firmly on their domestic political consequences) and those who have to find the money for them. The division is twofold. On the one hand, the agricultural ministers decide prices in isolation from the finance ministers deciding prospective budgetary revenues; on the other hand, the countries whose farmers generate unwanted surpluses are not necessarily the countries which have to find the revenue to pay for them. An obvious solution, frequently suggested, is that payments to farmers arising from the CAP should be made not from the Community budget in general but from the national exchequers of the countries in which they live. France, in particular, has consistently refused to consider any such solution. The CAP, it argues, is the major policy achievement of the Community and national financing would make agricultural policy a national rather than a common policy, thus destroying 'the corner-stone of the Community'.

The argument is not entirely convincing. Prices of farm products in recent years have varied so markedly in different member countries that the notion of a single, uniform price is theoretical rather than actual. As has been noted earlier, national governments spend far more on their own agricultural sectors than does the FEOGA, so that the notion of a common policy is hardly entirely realistic. Worst of all, both the budgetary demands made by the CAP and the annual political arguments generated by it have unquestionably hindered the development and application of common policies in other sectors of an importance at least equal to that of agriculture. The notion of the CAP as 'the corner-stone' of the Community may therefore be in danger of being the reverse of the truth.

There is, however, a more fundamental question to be raised about the CAP. In the early days of the Community agriculture represented well over 20 per cent of its entire working population; administrative reasons, if no other, therefore dictated that any policy dealing with farmers on an individual basis, rather than collectively, was scarcely feasible. In 1986, even after the accession of Greece, Portugal and Spain, the numbers engaged in agriculture represented only 7 per cent of its working population. The question thus arises as to whether it is any longer defensible to be attempting to raise farm incomes through a system of very high consumer prices and the virtual prohibition of imports – with all the welfare losses associated with such a system – rather than through a system of income supplements related to the needs of individual farmers and not their capacity to produce (inefficiently) outputs far in excess of genuine consumer demand. The logic of economic analysis, and indeed the spirit of the Commission's 1985 structural plan, point unambiguously in the direction of the latter; the political realities, unfortunately, point in other directions for the foreseeable future.

Further Reading

Buckwell, A. (ed.), *The Costs of the Common Agricultural Policy* (London: Croom Helm, 1982).

Demekas, D. *et al.*, 'The effects of the CAP: a survey of the literature', *Journal of Common Market Studies*, Vol xxvii, No. 2, December 1988.

Duchene, F. (ed.), *New Limits on European Agriculture: Politics and the CAP* (London: Croom Helm, 1985).

European Commission, *The Community's Agricultural Policy and its Reform*, 4th edn (Luxembourg, 1987).

Harris, S. *et al.*, *The Food and Farm Policies of the European Community* (Chichester: John Wiley & Sons, 1983).

Harvey, D. and Thomson, K. J., 'Costs, benefits and the future of the common agricultural policy', *Journal of Common Market Studies*, Vol. xxiv, No. 1, September 1985.

Hill, B. E., *The Common Agricultural Policy: Past, Present and Future* (London: Methuen, 1984).

Marsh, J. S. and Swanney, P. J., *Agriculture and the European Community* (London: Allen & Unwin, 1980).

Strasser, D., *The Finances of Europe* (Brussels: European Perspectives Press, 1981).

The Common
Fisheries Policy 16

16.1 The Fishing Background

The second sentence of the section of the Treaty of Rome dealing with the
Common Agricultural Policy declares that 'Agricultural products shall mean
the products of the soil, of stock-breeding and of fisheries.' The inclusion of
fisheries is not entirely illogical, since the industry shares many of the basic
attributes of agriculture. Given the highly specialised nature of its human and
physical capital, its supply tends to be highly inelastic in the short run; the price-
elasticity of demand for its output, on the other hand, like that for agricultural
products, tends to be rather low: the combination is, of course, a recipe for
potential price instability. The income-elasticity of demand for its output is also
low. Like farming, it is subject to random shocks arising from natural causes
over which producers have no control. Like farming, also, the industry is made
up (certainly so far as fishing in coastal waters is concerned) of a large number
of small, self-employed producers of a particularly independent frame of mind.

There is one respect, indeed, in which a *common* policy makes more sense for
fishing than it does for agriculture. Most of the industry's activities are
conducted across and beyond the territorial waters of individual states; its
quarry, the fish, displays a fine disregard for such boundaries. Nearly 90 per
cent of the codfish in the North Sea, for example, spend their first year in waters
off the Danish, Dutch and German coasts, but by the time they are three years
old (and therefore profitable to catch) threequarters have transferred their
residence to the territorial waters of the UK. It follows that activity by the
fishermen of one country can have a direct (and quite possibly damaging) effect
on the livelihood of fishermen in another.

Even so it is somewhat surprising that so small an industry should have
generated discussions and dissensions on the scale to be witnessed in the context

175

of Community fishing during the 1970s. In the early 1980s the total number of people engaged in commercial fishing in the Community amounted to no more than around 140 000 – about 0.1 per cent of the total working population. If the numbers engaged in activities ancillary to fishing – processing, transport, ship maintenance etc. – are added in the total admittedly rises to some 1.2 million, but this still represents only about 1 per cent of the Community's total workforce. Why then should so much attention have been devoted to the industry?

The answer lies in the fact that, like farming, the fishing industry attracts a degree of political attention out of all proportion to its size. Although total numbers are small in national terms, the industry is highly localised in a small number of areas in which it involves whole communities; in addition, the localities involved are typically rather remote so that alternative occupations are not easy to find. Bad times in the industry therefore have a concentrated impact with corresponding political repercussions. Politicians with fishing communities in their constituencies therefore neglect the industry at their peril. To this it has to be added that the industry attracts a disproportionate amount of popular sympathy because it is in fact probably the most dangerous civilian occupation in existence, not excluding coal-mining.

There were two technical features of the industry during the 1970s, however, which would have made some kind of supranational action necessary even if the European Community had never existed. Both were fundamentally undermining the long tradition in the industry that on the open seas vessels were free to look for as much fish as they wished without let or hindrance. The only exception to that tradition was the provision that, within (usually) a twelve-mile limit around the coasts of any country, the right to fish was restricted to the fishermen resident in that country, except for fishermen from other countries who had traditionally fished in those zones and could thus claim historic rights.

The first factor of change was the rapid advance of technology in the industry. As a spin-off from the Second World War in the 1960s vessels were increasingly being equipped with sonar and radar capabilities; as a result, boats were spending far less time merely looking for fish (frequently unsuccessfully) and far more time actually catching them. Synthetic fibres were enabling nets of immensely increased capacity to be operated; larger, factory-like ships were increasingly spending weeks at sea, refrigerating catches as they came, rather than spending most of their days departing from or returning to port. In other industries such technological advance tends to result in higher output – even if, as in the case of farming, much of the addition ends up in public storage. The ultimate output of the fishing industry, however, is drawn from a stock of fish the numbers of which do not increase *pari passu* with the efficiency of their hunters. Steadily rising catch capability combined with a more or less fixed fish population presents an obvious threat of biological disaster – the decline of the fish population below a point at which it is capable of sustaining itself. Between 1965 and 1975 the herring catch in the North Atlantic fell catastrophically from nearly 1.5 million tonnes to around 0.5 million; only a complete ban on herring fishing for a number of years enabled the species to survive in that area at all.

The second dramatic change in the situation of the Community fishing industry resulted from changes in international law and practice concerning the right of fishermen to operate in the territorial waters of other countries. The process began with the unilateral declaration by Iceland in 1971 that in future it would claim, and exercise, exclusive fishing rights in waters within 50 miles of its coast. This was followed two years later by the decision of a United Nations Conference on the Law of the Sea that henceforth any country could establish an Exclusive Economic Zone (EEZ) in waters up to 200 miles from its coastline – subject, of course, to similar rights for other countries whose territorial waters, so defined, also came within the same 200 miles.

This change had profound implications for several members of the Community. Fishermen from the member countries had traditionally operated in waters well within the new 200-mile limit around the coasts of non-EC countries such as Iceland, Norway and Canada; in 1973 more than a quarter of the Community fish harvest in fact came from such waters. Conversely, the monopoly of those three countries in their newly-extended waters significantly increased their catch and thus intensified their competitiveness in the Community market. Barred from the 'big-catch' waters in which the (now very high) energy costs of fishing vessels could be spread over large catches, Community fishermen found their unit costs rising sharply at precisely the time when the competitiveness of their rivals outside the Community had been increased.

Even in the absence of the European Community, then, the countries of Western Europe would have needed to mount some co-operative response to these fundamental challenges to the viability of their fishing industries. But of course the Treaty *did* exist and already provided the juridical foundation not merely for co-operation but for the creation of a common policy.

16.2 A Policy Emerges

During the 1960s, while the CAP was being hammered out by the Six, there was in fact little interest in or enthusiasm for a comparable policy with regard to fisheries except on the part of France. This is hardly surprising given the differences of economic interest amongst them. France, with a large fishing industry had traditionally protected it with tariffs of between 25 per cent and 50 per cent on competing imports; as an inevitable result it had an inefficient industry with high unit costs. The remaining countries, with fishing industries of relatively small capacity in relation to internal demand, had relatively low tariffs on imports with, consequentially, fishing fleets of relatively high efficiency. The gradual move to a common external tariff in the region of 20 per cent, together with the elimination of tariffs on intra-Community trade in fishery products, therefore led to severe competitive pressure on the French fishing industry; fish imports into France rose from 95 000 tonnes in 1957 to 282 000 tonnes in 1966. Not surprisingly, the French were anxious to establish a special regime for fishing; on the other hand, the remaining countries saw no particular reason for adopting anything other than the general policy of a common external tariff combined with free competitive markets within the Community. Some rather tentative proposals for a common fishing policy were in fact put before the Council by the Commission in 1966, but they generated little enthusiasm and were quickly lost to sight.

Within four years a dramatic change of attitude in the matter of fishing had occurred in the Community; in a submission to the Council of Ministers in May 1970 the Commission made no attempt to conceal the reasons for it. With the departure of President de Gaulle a new element had entered the situation – the impending accession of Britain, Denmark, Ireland and (at that time) Norway, all of them countries with extensive territorial waters and rich fishing grounds. Before the negotiations for the entry of these countries opened, the Commission suggested, it would be desirable to have some Community law on fishing rights which could then be extended to cover the new members. In other words, the Commission was urging the Council to fix the rules of the club to its own advantage before the new members arrived.

With remarkable dispatch the basic foundations of a common policy were agreed at the end of June 1970 – by coincidence, on the day before negotiations with the prospective new members were due to begin. The policy was to rest on the fundamental principle of equal access; since all member countries were notionally one single market, all should have an unrestricted right to go fishing in the territorial waters of all other member countries – that is to say, in the area extending 200 miles from the Atlantic and North Sea coasts. At first sight this may seem no more than logical, but the fact is that such a proposition had never been advanced (for obvious reasons) in relation to offshore oil or gas deposits or, for that matter, inland deposits of coal or iron ore. That citizens of each member country have the *right of establishment* in all others is of course built into the Treaty; such establishments would then form part of the industry in the country concerned and be subject to the laws of that country. But this was not the object of the exercise here; the intention was rather to secure unrestricted access to the territorial waters of the incoming members which (excluding Norway) would account for something over 80 per cent of Community territorial waters in the Atlantic and North Sea. (The Italians, whose fleet operates almost exclusively in the Mediterranean and off the coast of Africa, had little interest in the matter.)

Following the precedent of the CAP, the proposed policy had two compo- nents. One, embodied in Regulation 2141 of 1970, represented a long-term structural policy concerned primarily with conservation and broadly compar- able to the guidance section of the CAP. This provided that the Commission would draw up conservation rules to be applied by all members from time to time – minimum mesh size for nets, minimum sizes of fish to be landed, the duration of fishing seasons and so on.

Most important, the Commission, acting on scientific advice, would be authorised to specify annually the maximum quantity of each main species to be caught by the Community fleet as a whole – the Total Allowable Catch (TAC). This total is based on biological rather than economic criteria; in effect it specifies the maximum number of fish which can be caught without reducing the total fish population to a level at which it would be incapable of maintaining itself. It would therefore vary from one year to another according to natural variations in the size of the fish stock. The allocation of this annual TAC between the member countries would then be a matter for periodic discussion and (hopefully) agreement.

The second element in the policy – paralleling the price-guarantee section of the CAP – was embodied in Regulation 2142 of 1970. In this the object was to create a common marketing organisation with an intervention price system to be operated by 'recognised producers' organisations' in each member country. The basic concept was one similar to that of the CAP. There was to be an official guide price for each species of fish and a lower intervention price (a 'withdrawal' price) at which fish would be withdrawn from the market, a varying proportion of the intervention price being refunded to the producers' organisation by the Community. But there were no illusions that funds on the CAP scale would be available for these operations. The official guide price was to be (unlike CAP prices) realistic, being based on an average of actual market prices during the three preceding years; furthermore, the withdrawal price was to be significantly lower – anything up to 30 per cent lower – than the notional guide price. Producers' organisations would be able to reduce or supplement this official withdrawal price by up to 10 per cent but if they did so the burden of financing any supplement would be theirs, to be met from levies on their own (voluntary) membership. The bottomless purse of the FEOGA was conspicuous by its absence.

16.3 The Anglers' Dispute

There was never any likelihood that this policy framework, cobbled together in such obvious haste, would be instantly acceptable to the new members whose territorial waters were clearly its major target. Hence the treaties of accession signed in 1972 provided for temporary 'derogations' from the full corpus of Community law to allow for important details to be worked out before the fisheries policy came into full operation. In the case of the United Kingdom, for instance, one article provided that, principle of equal access or no, fishing within six miles of the British coast would be restricted to vessels which had traditionally operated within that limit and which operated from ports in that geographical area. Another article extended this restriction of access to a distance of 12 miles in specified areas of particular importance to Britain, especially off the coast of Scotland and north-east of England. But it was made clear that these were essentially temporary concessions, to apply only until the final details of a common fisheries policy were agreed or until 31 December 1982, whichever was the earlier. After that everything would be subject to agreement amongst the member countries as a whole. It was hardly surprising that when a similar proposition was put to the people of Norway the reaction was sharply negative.

In the years which followed the matter at the heart of the debates was that of the allocation of the Community Total Allowable Catch amongst the individual member countries. This was not merely a question of sharing out a single tonnage total amongst the interested parties; since species of fish vary greatly in their economic value, much turned on the quantities of particular species allocated to each country. Since the fecundity of different parts of the oceans varies equally, a great deal of importance was also attached to the allocation of TACs of different species in different geographical areas.

Given their different self-interests, the various member countries naturally argued for different bases for this critical allocation exercise. Since roughly two-thirds of the Community area in the Atlantic and North Sea had traditionally been its territorial waters, Britain argued that ownership should be the point of departure, claiming therefore that it should receive at least 45 per cent of the TAC. Other countries pointed out, however, that while some 60 per cent of the fish caught had indeed come from British territorial waters, the fish concerned (as mentioned earlier) had mostly originated elsewhere. While three-quarters of three-year-old cod had been caught in those waters, for example, they accounted for only some 14 per cent of the catch of one-year-old cod. How many fish came from 'British' waters was therefore a matter of fishing practice rather than one of immutable biological verity.

Britain and other countries also argued that the allocation should take account of the extent to which member countries had suffered through the extension of exclusive rights to a 200-mile radius and the consequent loss of traditional fishing grounds. Here Germany could argue that, while the British, French and Italians faced a prospective loss of around one-third of their traditional fishing grounds, the potential loss to German fisheries was nearly 70 per cent; Germany's claim to a correspondingly increased share of the TAC was therefore a strong one. An increase in the share of the TAC given to one country, however, necessarily implied a reduction in the share of some other countries. Not surprisingly, Denmark – which had traditionally fished almost entirely in the north-east Atlantic, and had therefore suffered relatively little from the extension of non-Community EEZs – then pointed out the illogicality of requiring sacrifices from a member country simply because it had always fished (patriotically, so to speak) in Community waters.

A third basis was argued by those countries, especially France and the Netherlands, which by long tradition had fished in the waters of other Community countries, particularly those of Britain and Denmark. To them the geographical distribution of quotas was at least as important as their overall tonnage. Denmark argued, in addition, that account should be taken of the fact that its fishing fleet, specialising as it did in 'industrial' fishing rather than supplies for direct human consumption, formed the basis for a large processing industry; any reduction in its share of the quota would therefore involve damage to its land-based economy of a degree much greater than that experienced in other member countries.

In the end, of course, the initial share-out of the Community TAC, shown in col. (7) of Table 16.1, was derived from a combination of all these considerations, the mixture being determined by the normal processes of political horse-trading rather than on any objective (even less any rational) basis. The agreement, arrived at in October 1982 (with the deadline of 31 December 1982 perilously close and thus exerting its own special influence), was in fact challenged by Denmark whose lack of consent, it argued, invalidated the whole transaction under the terms of the Luxembourg Compromise. In January 1983, however, after a nominal increase of 5 000 tonnes in its TAC allocation, the government of Denmark reluctantly indicated its acceptance of the deal and the Common Fisheries Policy came officially into existence.

Table 16.1
Fishing in the European Community, 1958–81

Country	Nominal fish catch (000 tonnes)					Agreed quotas 1982
	Europe 6		Europe 9		Europe 10	
	1959	1973	1973	1981	1981	000 tonnes
(1)	(2)	(3)	(4)	(5)	(6)	(7)
Belgium	62	53	53	49	49	25
France	577	814	814	778	778	162
Germany	728	478	478	331	331	186
Italy	175	401	401	450	450	—
Luxembourg	—	—	—	—	—	—
Netherlands	240	344	344	434	434	92
EC6	1782	2090	2090	2042	2042	465
Denmark			1465	1852	1852	305
Ireland			91	190	190	47
United Kingdom			1232	883	883	464
EC9			4878	4967	4967	1281
Greece					100	—
EC10	1782	2090	4878	4967	5067	1281

The agreement was to stand for 20 years with the possibility of a review after 10 years. It provided that fishing in Community waters was to be subject to the agreed allocation of TACs except that fishing in the area around the Orkney and Shetland Islands, of especial sensitivity to Britain, was to be subject to Community licences specifying the number of vessels from each member country which could operate in that area. In addition, the agreement provided for a three-year programme of financial aids to assist the modernisation of fishing fleets costing some ECU 323 million. National governments were free to adopt their own conservation measures in addition to those specified by the Commission but in doing so could not discriminate against fishermen from other member countries nor, of course, contravene any Treaty provisions – including the conservation rules laid down by the Commission.

16.4   The Future of the CFP

In a sense the Common Fisheries Policy benefited from having been pulled together in the light of the experience of the CAP and was therefore able to avoid some of the latter's manifest absurdities. The emphasis in it has been placed on the restriction of output rather than on anything comparable to the CAP's implicit invitation to Community farmers to indulge in an unlimited expansion of output with the promise of an open cheque to pay for it. Its price policy, infinitely more realistic than that of the CAP, has some relation to actual market prices in the recent past rather than to some notional producers' paradise. It has also been fortunate in that since its inception no major catastrophe comparable to the herring disaster of the 1970s has occurred, although a sharp decline in white fish stocks in 1988 came rather near it. Yet obvious problems lie ahead in the future.

The first of these is the reliance on production quotas, albeit designed to restrict rather than to expand output. Resting as it does on biological rather than economic criteria, the TAC system can lead to variations in production from year to year resulting in pressure on capacity (and hence high marginal costs) in some years and idle capacity in others. (The scientific estimates underlying the TAC concept are notoriously liable to error; the total haddock quota established for 1989 was no more than a half of that for 1988.) Quotas designed to maintain a steady capacity over a number of years would clearly make more economic sense. Equally, the distribution of the TAC allocation over time cannot remain unchanged in the face of changing technology and demand; resting as it does on political rather than objective criteria, however, changes in the distribution are likely to be a source of considerable friction.

In its first year of operation, the CRP distinguished itself with the remarkable achievement of fixing the national allocations of the 1983 TAC on 20 December of that year, a date which was a little late to be operationally useful. In later years, however, the Ministers have managed to agree both TACs and guide prices for each year by December of the preceding year, although a fair amount of acrimony has frequently distinguished the process. A major problem was of course the adjustment of the TAC distribution to take account of the third enlargement in 1986; the accession of Spain and Portugal increased the number of larger vessels in the Community's fleet (those over 500 gross registered tons) by well over 100 per cent, although this was offset to some degree by the fact that the average Spaniard eats twice as much fish as the average Community citizen. The problem was solved by providing for a ten-year transitional period during which mutual access to several fishing zones in which Spanish vessels have traditionally fished was agreed with a final review of the arrangements to be undertaken in 1995.

The problem of the enforcement of agreed measures relating to catches, net sizes and so on is clearly a very considerable one given the vast area over which, and the hostile environment in which, it has to be applied. The Community has appointed 13 inspectors who are entitled to descend on fishing vessels and check that their activities, recorded in a standard Community logbook, conform with the prevailing regulations. For the most part, however, the policy must rely on enforcement by national authorities – which are traditionally much more lenient towards their own nationals than towards fishermen from other countries.

Thirdly, the marketing element in the policy must necessarily be less ambitious than anything attempted for agriculture. Fish prices are notoriously volatile from day to day and the storage of surpluses is extremely expensive. Hence market prices typically vary widely in comparison with the official guide price. True, market prices are to some degree artificially supported by means of countervailing duties levied from time to time on competing imports allegedly entering at unduly low prices and, conversely, by export refunds on fish sold abroad at less than the withdrawal price. The extent of such intervention, however, in no way approaches the scale of the CAP. Unlike the latter, the CFP relates prices broadly to those determined by open market forces.

Given the very limited budget available to the CFP, things could hardly be otherwise. In the four years 1983–6 the total budgetary allocation for fishing, including that for various measures to improve the structure of the industry, averaged about ECU 83 million – about ECU 12.5 per tonne of fish landed in Community ports. A further limitation on its price-support policy is that part of it rests on the resources of voluntary producers' organisations relying on levies paid by its members. Fishermen are quite able to appreciate the fact that they can benefit from any such market support without being a member of (and hence contributing towards) the producers' organisation; the financial basis of this element in the marketing policy is therefore distinctly weak. But if the inability of the CFP to exert any significant influence on market prices is in one sense a weakness it is in another a strength – the follies of the CAP will be beyond its reach. By the same token, the miniscule budgetary resources available imply that the attempts to apply a long-term structural policy in the industry must necessarily be modest in the extreme, being largely confined to the mild encouragement of the retirement of obsolete vessels and the improvement of technology, marketing and fisheries research. Again given the precedent of the CAP, it may be as well that the modesty of its objectives are likely to match the scale of attainable results.

Yet, as remarked earlier, this is an area where a *common* policy can make a great deal of sense for all member countries because of the interdependence of the prosperity of the industry in all of them. In principle, the CFP's conservation policy is to some degree inconsistent with its attempts at a marketing (i.e. price-support) policy, since the aim of the former is to reduce, or at least contain, output while the effect of the latter would be to encourage it. If the market policy has had any effect, however, it has been to moderate to some degree the short-term instability of prices rather than to raise their absolute level, so that the inconsistency is more apparent than real. The knowledge that some effort is being made to enforce common conservation measures, on the other hand, is likely to encourage national governments to respect them. Nothing is so destructive of attempts to either enforce or obey rules of conservation than the belief that other parties are flagrantly disregarding them.

Finally, since the CFP came into existence the Community has collectively entered into mutually-advantageous agreements with virtually every major fishing country in the world. In a sector of more or less world dimensions, with intense competition and rivalry, the fact that the Community represents a third of total world fishing capacity gives it a bargaining strength of very considerable magnitude – certainly of far greater strength than that of any member country in isolation. That is a consideration on which even the Norwegians could do well to reflect.

Further Reading

European Commission, *The European Community's Fishery Policy* (Luxembourg, 1985).
Leigh, M., *European integration and the common fisheries policy* (London: Croom Helm, 1983).
Shackleton, M., 'Fishing for a policy: the common fisheries policy of the Community', in Wallace, H., (ed.), *Policy-making in the European Community*, 2nd edn (Chichester: John Wiley & Sons, 1977).
Wise, M., *The Common Fisheries Policy of the European Community* (London: Methuen, 1984).

Transport Policy 17

17.1 Why a Transport Policy?

Apart from agriculture (and fisheries) transport was the only domestic sector of the economy singled out by the Treaty of Rome, in Title IV of Part Two ('Bases of the Community'), as requiring a common policy. Furthermore, for many years the majority of Ministers attached especial importance to Article 84 of this Title. This stated baldly that the provisions of the Title should apply to transport by rail, road and inland waterway and that the Council should decide in due course if, and how, its provisions should be extended to sea and air transport. This implied, it was held, that other Treaty provisions, especially those concerning competition policy, did *not* apply to the particular field of transport. In this respect, as will be noted later, the Court of Justice ultimately held that the Ministers were in error.

This special treatment for one particular sector, accounting in 1958 for less than 5 per cent of the Community's total workforce, is less surprising than might seem at first sight. In the first place, transport costs appeared to be an obstacle to free trade within the Community of a kind more or less analogous to tariffs. This had certainly been true in the case of the ECSC, where the cost of transporting both the bulky inputs and outputs characteristic of coal and steel could seriously constrain trade between the member states.

This would have been true even if transport charges had merely reflected the natural and inescapable costs involved; measures to increase the efficiency of the sector would then have encouraged the growth of trade in the same way as the reduction of tariffs. In reality, however, it was well known that state intervention in this sector was very extensive; as a result, transport charges frequently discriminated between national and foreign users, the effect being to erect serious barriers to imports and to protect domestic producers against competition from abroad. Article 79 therefore required that, within two years of the entry of the Treaty into force, the Commission should propose, and the Council approve, measures to eliminate any discrimination in transport charges on the grounds of the country of origin or destination in traffic within the Community.

In compliance with this requirement, the Commission in April 1961 presented the Council with a Memorandum on the General Lines of a Common Transport Policy, this being known henceforth as the Schaus Memorandum in honour of the Commission's first transport commissioner, M Lambert Schaus. This laid stress on some of the special characteristics of the sector which had led to the extensive government intervention in its affairs. First, the 'natural monopoly' position enjoyed by railway systems by virtue of the exceedingly high overhead costs inherent in any rail system had necessarily led in almost all countries to some form of public regulation of their charges in order to prevent the exploitation of the consumers. With road traffic, on the other hand, some governments had introduced public regulation of charges for precisely the opposite reason – to prevent ruinous competition through unduly low charges. This might arise, it was argued, through the combination of, on the one hand, a fluctuating demand for road freight sevices as economies moved from boom to slump and, on the other, the inelasticity of supply inherent in an industry largely comprised of small, independent operators with highly specialised capital not easily switched to other uses when demand fell. The results could be cut-throat competition, in which prices were cut back to marginal cost; the resulting neglect of proper maintenance and replacement of equipment would then have serious consequences for safety and the environment. Hence the paradoxical situation in which public regulation of prices sought in some cases to prevent them from being too high and in others from being too low.

The second peculiarity of the sector to which the memorandum drew attention was that, unlike industry in general, most of its very considerable infrastructure requirements – the permanent way in the case of railways, roads, docks, airports and so on – are financed from the public purse. This implies an inevitable governmental involvement in the sector's operation; it also implies some difficult problems of calculating what the sector's true costs of operation are, especially when railway systems are usually required to meet the costs of maintaining their track whereas road traffic operators do not maintain the roads they use.

Thirdly, the transport sector impinges on other industries and other policy objectives to a degree seldom applicable elsewhere. Road or rail freight charges enter into the costs of other industries; systems of cross-subsidisation were therefore frequently used to give (concealed) assistance to heavy industries. Regional policy may dictate that transport facilities are extended to areas on grounds other than purely commercial ones. Social and environmental objectives are sometimes given a higher priority in transport measures than those of simple economic interest.

The complexity of these (frequently conflicting) considerations explains much of the disagreement and ineffectualness which distinguished the subsequent attempts to devise a common transport policy. The debate was to concentrate almost exclusively on road freight transport. This was understandable. With the exception of air transport – which was to achieve prominence only from the late 1970s onwards – passenger traffic is overwhelmingly concerned with the internal carriage of the citizens of the country concerned; its relevance to trade between member countries of the Community is therefore marginal. Rail freight services had of course been of considerable importance to the ECSC but most of the distortions which distinguished those services in the early 1950s had been ironed out by the ECSC by the end of that decade. In any event, the railways were rapidly being overtaken by the growth of road freight services for all but the heavy industries. In the 20 years 1963–83 the volume of freight carried by rail in the Six fell by 16 per cent; over the same period the stock of motor vehicles rose by about 240 per cent. As may be seen from Table 17.1, in 1981 nearly three times as much freight was being carried by road in the Community as by its railway systems; by 1986, road haulage accounted for about four times as much of the Community's freight tonnage as was carried by rail.

The Schaus Memorandum, and the Action Programme based on it and presented in 1962, laid down three basic objectives for a Common Transport Policy. First, and most obviously, the policy should seek to remove any obstacles to inter-Community trade created by transport facilities. Second, in order that transport should make a positive contribution to the growth of trade, as well as merely avoid negative effects on it, there should be created a single transport system throughout the Community. Thirdly, healthy competition should be stimulated throughout the sector, this to include traffic within each member country as well as that between members. The first of these created little real difficulty; as remarked above, much of the necessary work in this respect had already been done by the ECSC. The second and third objectives, however, were to prove elusive in the extreme.

17.2 The 1960s: the Uncommon Transport System

The Commission envisaged that a common transport system for the Community involved three major elements – complete freedom of establishment for operators in any member country to conduct their business freely in any other member country, the harmonisation of the technical requirements imposed on operators in different member countries and, finally, the formulation of a joint and common policy with regard to the industry's basic infrastructure requirement, the road network.

Freedom of establishment implied that freight carriers would be allowed to ply their trade anywhere within the Community; this would of course be subject to the proviso that, since all member governments applied restrictions to the total number of vehicles allowed to operate within their boundaries, there would need to be some comparable Community control over the size of the

Table 17.1
Transport in the European Community, 1981 (Units per head of population)

| Country | Freight Traffic | | | | | Passenger Traffic | | |
| | Rail | Road | Waterways | Sea | Air | Rail | Air | Buses |
(1)	(T.km) (2)	(T.km) (3)	(T.km) (4)	(T.) (5)	(kg) (6)	(No.) (7)	(No.) (8)	(No. per bn pop.) (9)
Belgium	762	1025	457	11.1	16.6	17.0	0.5	1.93
Denmark	313	1387	—	7.6	27.5	26.2	1.6	1.56
France	1176	1456	168	5.0	13.1	12.9	0.8	1.22
Germany	991	1537	696	2.2	12.6	18.0	0.8	1.15
Greece	72	874	—	5.6	7.2	1.0	0.9	1.85
Ireland	203	1250	—	4.6	16.0	4.4	1.0	0.87
Italy	301	1557†	5‡	4.5	3.9	7.0	0.3	1.10
Luxembourg	1639	820*	1782	—	196.7	32.8	1.6	2.73
Netherlands	232	1221	—	22.5	23.3	14.4	0.7	0.77
Portugal	112	n.a.	—	3.0	5.7	21.6	0.5	0.91
Spain	281	2527	—	3.6	8.0	4.7	0.9	1.14
United Kingdom	310	1681	—	4.6	11.0	12.8	0.8	1.37
EC 12	572	1615	258	5.1	11.0	12.1	0.7	1.22
United States	6527	3571	—	4.3	19.1	1.3	1.2	2.37
Japan	284	1217	—	n.a.	4.3	57.8	0.4	1.96

* 1982; † 1978; ‡ 1983

NOTE T = tonnes, T.km = tonne/kilometres, kg = kilogrammes.

sector. Movements of freight vehicles between member countries were (and remain) subject to quota agreements negotiated between governments on a bilateral basis – country A would allow enterprises from B to operate within its boundaries provided that B extended comparable facilities to enterprises from A. It was scarcely practicable to abolish this system overnight, but the Commission proposed that over the years these bilateral arrangements should be replaced by a Community quota, shared between member countries, under which the holder of a Community 'passport' would be entitled to ply for trade in any member country. In 1968, a regulation established such a Community quota, to be introduced for an experimental period of three years, of 1200 vehicles. (In the early 1970s there were nearly 5 million goods vehicles operating in the Six, although only around 40 per cent of their capacity was used for freight carried for hire and reward.)

Although the proposal was agreed in principle by the Council, in reality there was intense national resistance to the scheme. To allow carriers from other countries to operate within its borders on the basis of a Community, as opposed to a national, licence would mean that a national government had effectively lost its ability to impose restrictions on its own national carriers, other than those (if any) laid down by the Commission. Furthermore, the system would have given free entry to operators from other countries without any of the quid pro quo inherent in the bilateral-quota system. While the Community quota was nominally increased in subsequent years, therefore, member governments declined to make any real use of it. In 1988, twenty years after the introduction of the concept of a Community vehicle 'passport', the reality was that only 16 per cent of cross-border freight traffic, measured in tonne-kilometres, was covered by the Community permit. The remainder was still governed by the traditional system of quotas negotiated between individual governments on a bilateral basis.

The second element, the harmonisation of operating conditions amongst the member counties, ran into similar difficulties and made scarcely more progress. The Commission sought to ensure that taxes levied on vehicles, and their fuel, should reflect only the genuine costs imposed on society by those vehicles, and should not be used either for national revenue-raising purposes or to discriminate between different modes of transport. The cost imposed on society by the operation of heavy road vehicles, however, is far from being an unambiguous concept, especially if account is to be taken of the costs of providing the infrastructure – the road system – and not merely the wear-and-tear costs of day-to-day operation. Even if national governments had been willing to accept the implied restriction on their taxing powers, therefore – and they conspicuously were not – the problem of establishing an agreed basis for the calculation of social costs proved insoluble. The only point of substance agreed (in 1968) was that concerning the quantity of fuel which could be carried into each country in the tanks of road vehicles without being subjected to the fuel tax levied in the receiving country.

Somewhat more progress was made, although not without considerable argument, on two other matters relating to operating conditions. In 1969 the Council managed to reach agreement on a complex set of rules governing the maximum number of hours, daily and weekly, for which the driver of a vehicle was allowed to work, thus ensuring reasonably fair competition between operators in different countries. In the following year the Council was even able to agree on the method by which these rules were to be enforced – by the compulsory installation of the measuring instrument known as the tachograph in all commercial vehicles. This was to cause considerable internal difficulties for some member countries, not least the UK. Much heat was also generated, before agreement was reached in 1972, on the matter of the maximum weight to be permitted for road vehicles, the gains from economies of scale with such vehicles conflicting with their environmental impact; the Community agreed on a general maximum of 40 tonnes, but in 1981 the UK was allowed a lower limit of 32.5 tonnes to provide time for British bridges to receive the necessary strengthening.

The attempt to establish a common policy with regard to the Community road network proved an almost total failure. There was clearly much to be said for a Community-wide plan for a motorway network but the inescapable fact remained that the costs of road construction were necessarily a national responsibility; it was (and remains) obviously unlikely that national legislatures, having to find the revenues to finance projects, would then allow decisions about the disposal of those revenues to be left to officials and/or politicians outside their borders. Only very modest sums are provided in the Community budget for road-building projects involving two or more member countries – for example, a new Brenner tunnel through the Alps and approach roads to the Channel tunnel. In 1986 the total set aside in the budget for transport was ECU 76 bn, or 0.2 per cent of the total budget; this is not a sum likely to have a significant impact on total road expenditure in the Community.

17.3   The 1960s – the Pursuit of Competition

Given the background of virtually universal governmental regulation of prices in the market for transport, it is not surprising that the Commission's concept of 'healthy competition' in the Community did not envisage a complete absence of price control. Rather, it sought to create a system in which price regulation would have a basis which was common throughout the Community and which was derived from consistent and 'transparent' principles. There was in 1961 no suggestion of abolishing the general practice of enforcing a 'forked tariff' – that is to say, an officially-imposed range of permissible charges which ensured that, on the one hand, prices were below a level which could be construed as a monopolistic exploitation of the consumer but, on the other, they did not fall below the level necessary to ensure that all costs were covered in the medium run.

By the beginning of 1965 some progress had apparently been achieved in this direction. The Ministers agreed to phase in a system of compulsory rate brackets for freight traffic between one member country and another, whether by road or rail, and a system of voluntary or 'reference' brackets for freight transport within each member state. (By 'reference' brackets were meant ranges in which recommended minimum and maximum rates would be published but would not normally be made obligatory on carriers.) Unfortunately for the advocates of the system, the 'empty chair' policy of the French government intervened before this agreement could be translated into a Regulation.

When the Ministers resumed normal activities in 1966 it was clear that several had had second thoughts. The Dutch, traditionally international suppliers of transport services and thus exponents of much freer competition in the sector, disliked the essential principle of bureaucratic regulation; the Germans, on the other hand, long committed to the concept of transport as essentially a service existing only for the benefit of other policy objectives, thought the proposals too loose. The outcome was Regulation 1174 of July 1968 which might reasonably be described as neatly achieving the worst of both possible worlds. It created a system of rate brackets with a spread of 23 per cent between the minimum and maximum rates but these were to be entirely 'reference' brackets – statements which would indicate an official view of the range within which rates should be set but which would have no binding effect. In fact they did little more than formalise the range of tariffs which appeared to exist in reality. The Regulation was essentially a compromise between the exponents of open competition in the sector and those of close official control; like most compromises it satisfied neither party, lacked any real conviction and was in practice almost entirely ignored.

In its attempts to create both a harmonised structure for the transport sector and to regulate the day-to-day operation of the market, therefore, the Community had spent a decade in discussions which had almost no practical outcome. Two things had become very clear. First, the sector is one involving a large number of suppliers and consumers who, in the nature of the case, negotiated individual deals whose details varied widely from one case to the next. Transport is not a mass-produced, homogeneous commodity sold off the shelves of supermarkets at a single, constant price to all consumers; every transaction tends to be a special case, differing in detail from every other. Any attempt to enforce uniform terms or prices in the sector must therefore face enormous administrative problems of enforcement. Second, the national interests of the member countries differed sharply; some, especially the Dutch and Belgians were large-scale suppliers of transport facilities to other countries and therefore sought the most open market possible, whereas others saw their transport sectors as essentially servants of broader policy aims and thus wished to retain a high degree of internal control over it.

The question was not merely one of whether a common transport policy throughout the six member states was possible; more fundamentally it was whether such a policy was even desirable. It was with some considerable degree of understatement, therefore, that the Commission reported to the Parliament in 1971 that 'the common transport policy has not made striking progress in recent years'. The problem was one of overcoming in the member countries what the transport Commissioner referred to as 'the narrow vision of a policy designed as a compromise between their divergent interests'.

17.4   The 1970s – the New Pragmatism

This experience of a decade of virtual failure would in itself have encouraged a complete rethinking of ideas on the subject of a transport policy. The process was however further stimulated by the first enlargement of the Community in 1973. This resulted in a considerable shake-up in the personnel of the Commission, with the result that the transport directorate, DG VII, was headed by people less committed to the approach of the 1960s. More important, the three new member countries were different in character (in this context) from the original Six, being more concerned with international sea and air transport – both of which are governed by treaties and conferences of world-wide dimensions – and less with the traditional cross-frontier land routes of primary interest to the Six. Finally, the relative importance of the old, heavy industries whose bulk products were relatively amenable to rate-regulation was steadily declining; the importance of more sophisticated industries, whose products are far too varied to be easily classified, was correspondingly increasing.

A new Action Programme on Transport submitted by the Commission in 1975 therefore reflected a fundamental shift in attitude. The view might be taken, it observed, that in order to take account of features inherent to each member state Community regulations should do 'no more than lay down the general principles on which national regulations may be based'. To this end it suggested that a Community transport policy should seek to establish a balance between demand and supply in the sector *without* recourse to quotas or other quantitative restrictions, should progressively increase the rights of non-resident hauliers to conduct business in all member countries, and should encourage *the trade* to establish recommended tariffs on whatever basis it judged best.

This was all a very far cry from the highly interventionist approach of the 1960s. It amounts to little more than an application of the general rules of competition policy in the particular context of transport. The right of entry of non-resident hauliers would be no more than an application of the requirement of Article 52 that for all sectors, 'restrictions on the freedom of establishment of nationals of a Member State in the territory of another Member State shall be progressively abolished', such freedom to extend to 'the right to engage in and carry on non-wage-earning activities'. The agreement on the working hours of drivers, already referred to, is admittedly something which has no parallel in other sectors but is none the less within the spirit of general competition policy.

Since 1975, therefore, the Community can hardly be said to have sought, and certainly has not achieved, anything which could realistically be described as a distinctive transport policy. The Commission has devoted a great deal of effort to attempts to achieve uniformity in the taxation of road vehicles and their fuel in the different member countries in order to ensure fair competition both within and between them. This has been more than an attempt to merely establish the *same* level of taxation throughout the Community; a Directive of 1969 committed it to ensuring that the taxes levied or different types of vehicle should reflect their true costs in some sense. Its efforts have met with complete failure. As mentioned earlier, the proposal does not only threaten national powers to determine tax levels; it also poses problems of measurement which have so far proved insoluble.

The view that progress towards a Common Transport Policy had been virtually non-existent during the 1970s was clearly shared by the European Parliament. In January 1983, in an unusual fit of petulance, the Parliament resolved that the Council of Ministers should be arraigned before the Court of Justice for its failure to establish a Common Transport Policy as specifically required of it by the Treaty. In 1985 the Court upheld the allegation. The Council, it ruled, had undoubtedly infringed the Treaty by failing to ensure freedom to provide services in the sphere of international transport or to lay down the conditions under which non-resident carriers might provide transport services in a member state.

This rebuke was not entirely without effect. At the end of 1986 the Commission submitted a proposal to the Council that, as part of the programme for the completion of the single market by 1992 the Community quota of freight licences – at that time covering only 16 per cent of its cross-border journeys by road freight vehicles – should be increased by 40 per cent in each year between 1987 and 1991 and that all national bilateral quotas should be scrapped thereafter. This was accepted by the Council. It was also agreed that from 1992 the practice of *cabotage* should be permitted for both sea and road carriers - i.e. the collection and delivery of freight by carriers of one member country between destinations in another member country. Previously this had been illegal, with the result that in 1989 some 30 per cent of the Community's lorries were completely empty during their return journey home. The matter of 'fiscal harmonisation' in the context of transport, however, is one which is still 'under discussion'.

The outcome remains to be seen. But, even if quantitative and other obstacles to a free market in transport are wholly eliminated, it is doubtful whether the result could accurately be described as a 'common transport policy', any more than completely free trade in television sets would represent a common broadcasting policy. The Commission continues to proclaim the merits of joint action on the transport infrastructure of the Community, assisting and commending projects from the development of a high-speed rail system to the creation of an integrated road, rail and waterway network designed to bring a genuine single market into existence. But so long as the vast resources necessary for these developments have to be provided by national governments the Community's role can only be to exhort and encourage rather than to initiate and enforce. For all practical purposes the common 'policy' in transport amounts to no more – but equally no less – than the application to it of the prescriptions for full and free competition contained in Article 85 and the rights of establishment contained in Article 52.

As remarked earlier, it is inevitable that it should be so. The transport sector of any country is concerned predominantly with the carriage of internal traffic, freight and passenger, and no conceivable extension of international trade is likely to alter this situation. Domestic considerations are therefore bound to prevail in any special measures relating to transport adopted by national governments. It is not obvious that such considerations – concerned with population distribution, congestion in cities, the ecology of the countryside, the criminal law even – could ever be identical in all the member countries of the Community or could ever be given the same relative priority in all of them. To repeat; the issue is not only one of whether a common policy throughout the Community is administratively feasible but also one of the extent to which it is desirable. This issue – the balance of advantage between diversity and uniformity within the Community – is one which will surface many times in what still has to follow.

17.5   Freedom of the Skies

The ownership of a national airline appears to be regarded by most governments as being as essential for the assertion of national sovereignty as the entitlement to a seat at the United Nations. As a result, for many years air passenger traffic between the countries of Western Europe has been governed by a network of bilateral agreements between governments; these agreements are designed to ensure that air traffic between any two countries is carefully shared between their two national airlines to the exclusion of all others. Competition of the kind experienced in transatlantic air travel has been discouraged to the maximum extent possible.

The inevitable result has been that air fares between the member countries of the Community are notoriously high – on a seat-kilometre basis, about 60 per cent greater than on domestic flights in the United States. Admittedly this is due partly to the fact that the average route-length in the United States is almost twice that in Europe; since many of the costs of airline operation – ground handling, seat reservations and so on – are fixed whatever the route distance, this necessarily raises average costs in Europe. It is also true to say that the much larger volume of traffic in the United States permits the use of larger aircraft, with corresponding economies of scale; the operating cost per seat of the average European aircraft of 125 seats is around 10 per cent greater than that of the average American aircraft of about 163 seats. Even when allowance is made for these factors, however, there is no doubt but that the cartel arrangements operated by European governments have resulted in prices to the consumer which are anything up to 40 per cent greater than they need be.

The accession of Britain in 1973 brought to the Community a country which was a major international carrier catering for the transport of non-nationals to a much greater extent than the airlines of the remainder of the Community, with the exception of the Netherlands. In 1981 these two countries, the UK and the Netherlands, operated around 40 per cent of the Community's total fleet of commercial aircraft. In the late 1970s, therefore, they pursued a joint campaign to open up passenger air traffic within the Community to greater competition.

They were in fact the only countries to support two modest draft Directives on the matter presented by the Commission in 1980. One would have permitted free competition in traffic between secondary – i.e. regional – airports within countries by relatively small aircraft operating taxi-type services. The other proposed a general regime for air fares, requiring them to reflect operating costs, in which the Commission would act as arbitrator in the event of a potential operator being prevented by a government from offering fares below those currently charged by its national airline. Both Directives were rejected. The UK argued, with the enthusiastic support of the Commission, that Article 85 of the Treaty, which prohibits both price-fixing and market-sharing, should apply to the air transport business. The remainder of the Council took the view that Article 84, specifically including airways under the scope of an agreed common transport policy, overrode the provisions of Article 85.

This disagreement was unequivocally settled by the Court of Justice in April 1986 in the case of a French tourist agency, Nouvelles Frontières. This company had been offering tickets on Air France at less than the official regulated price and, as a result, had been threatened by Air France with a complete cut-off of its ticket supplies. The company argued that Article 85 applied to this industry and that the threats of Air France were a contravention of that article; the Court upheld both submissions. The Commission thereupon exultantly advised every member government that it was preparing a case against each of its national airlines for operating restrictive agreements in contravention of Article 85.

This naturally concentrated the minds of the Council. In December 1987 it reached agreement that bilateral fare-fixing between national airlines should be phased out and that such airlines would no longer be able to insist on keeping 50 per cent of the traffic on any given route; the guaranteed maximum share was to fall to 45 per cent immediately and to 40 per cent by 1990. Market access for new airlines on existing routes, or new services, is to be substantially eased and rules preventing airlines from operating *cabotage* – i.e. picking up traffic en route across other countries – were to be abolished. Furthermore, any airline could seek permissioin from the Commission to charge fares below those officially specified in the country concerned. Indeed, in April 1989 the Commission succeeded in obtaining a ruling from the Court that for air routes within the Community any agreement concerning fares between airlines is legal only if the Commission has expressly allowed it under the exemption provisions of Article 85.

All this falls somewhat short of the demands of the exponents of completely free competition, subject only to the imposition of safety requirements; it is also much more modest than the proposals originally advanced by the UK. Nevertheless it is clearly the first step on the road to that objective. It forms part of the long list of proposals for the creation of a single market in 1992, together with aspirations for a Community system for fares and market access rather than a network of national agreements and regulations. The evidence indicates that these changes are having the desired effect of reducing fares and improving services. If so it is a triumph not so much for Articles 74–84 of the Treaty, which call for a Common Transport policy, but rather for Article 85 which upholds the supremacy of market forces for all sectors of the economy.

Further Reading

Erdmenger, J., *The European Community Transport Policy* (Aldershot: Gower Press, 1983).
European Commission, *The European Community's Transport Policy*, 2nd edn (Luxembourg, 1984).
McGowan, F. and Trengrove, C., *European aviation: a common market?* (London: Institute for Fiscal Studies, 1986).
Whitelegg, J., *Transport policy in the EEC* (London: Routledge, 1988).

Energy Policy 18

18.1 The Energy Background

When the Treaty of Rome was being drafted in the late 1950s no energy problem was thought to exist; not surprisingly, therefore, the word 'energy' appears nowhere in the Treaty. Until the oil crisis of late 1973 no suggestion that a common policy was necessary for energy as a whole ever arose. That little progress has since been made towards an effective common policy for energy owes something to this lack of a juridical basis on which the Commission could rely to enforce one. More importantly, it also owes much to the fact that, as in the transport sector, the complexity of the sector necessarily makes uniformity amongst the member states both difficult and of doubtful applicability.

There are indeed many similarities between energy and transport. The sector is not really a single identifiable industry but several of a diverse nature. It includes the production of the primary sources of energy – coal, oil, natural gas and nuclear power; it also includes the secondary activities of electricity generation, oil refining and the distribution of gas and electricity. To all this can be added the relatively minor primary sources of energy such as hydroelectricity, wind, solar and tidal power. All these activities involve widely different types of organisations, ranging from state-owned enterprises to the multinational oil companies and a large number of private enterprises of varying size. Like transport again, the sector is the subject of many conflicting internal pressures; it is a key cost element for many unrelated industries, an important factor in the cost of living of individual consumers and, in recent years, a major battlefield for the defenders of the environment. Governments thus have a great deal more than simple commercial considerations to balance in their policy measures.

There are two additional factors, which the transport sector has been spared, making the formulation of any kind of Community policy in this area unusually difficult. First, the sector has been, and remains, subject to violent shocks originating from the outside world over which the Community has little or no

197

control. The massive increases in the world price of oil in 1973–4 and again in 1978–9 are obvious examples; so is the catastrophic explosion in the Soviet reactor at Chernobyl in 1986. Secondly, responsibility for the energy sector was inconveniently divided between the three initially separate components of the Community; the coal industry was the responsibility of the ECSC, nuclear power that of Euratom and the remaining activities were, residually, within the province of the EEC. What is more, the statutory bases of the three institutions made no provision for the formulation of a common policy as such; nor did the legal amalgamation of the three communities into one in 1967 entirely eliminate this rather fractured network of responsibility.

As remarked earlier, a serious attempt to create some co-ordinated common policy for the energy sector as a whole had to await the oil crisis of 1973. The nature of the problem faced by the Community, and its reactions to them, can nevertheless be understood only by surveying events prior to that year as well as afterwards. And the rather incoherent story is best explained by considering each of the three major energy sources – coal, oil and nuclear power – in turn.

18.2   The Rise and Fall of Coal

If the signatories of the Treaty of Paris in 1951 had been asked for their definition of the energy 'problem' they would have responded without hesitation by referring to the acute shortage of coal. At the end of the Second World War the output of the major producer amongst the Six, Germany, was less than 40 per cent of the 1938 level. In the Six as a whole it was less than 60 per cent of pre-war. The ECSC was therefore seen as a means by which coal production could be significantly expanded, within the framework of an industry which required modernisation. It was realised, however, that it also required a set of rules providing a single market in coal, a market freed of the traditional distortions created by national governments seeking to discriminate against foreign producers. The Community nevertheless appeared to have the enormous advantage of harmony amongst its members as to the essential policy objective – a sustained increase in output everywhere.

In pursuing this objective the ECSC could claim some success; by 1954 coal output in the Six was roughly double that of 1946. Ironically it was precisely at this point that the competitive position of European coal began to come under severe pressure. First, the improving balance-of-payments position of Western Europe was leading to relaxation in foreign-exchange controls and supplies of cheaper imported coal began to increase. Second, a vast increase was occurring in world production of oil, the impact of which on Europe was intensified by restrictions imposed by the United States on oil imports in order to encourage the expansion of its own domestic output. Third, the emergence of very much larger bulk carriers in the world shipping fleet sharply reduced the cost of imports of both oil and coal. In the decade 1956–65 the unit cost of Ruhr coal rose by more than 50 per cent in comparison with that of imported oil and by 100 per cent in comparison with that of coal imported from the United States.

The consequences of all this, combined with the first (mercifully brief) postwar recession of 1958–9, were predictable. Pithead stocks of coal, and with them unemployment in the older coal-mining areas of the Six, rose sharply. In May 1959 the ECSC High Authority sought to impose production quotas on domestic coal and quantitative restrictions on coal imports. The member governments failed to agree, revealing for the first time the conflicts of national interest which lay beneath the original harmony of objective. Belgium and the Netherlands, with important coal-producing areas, were naturally in favour of import restriction; France and Italy, on the other hand, with relatively small production in relation to their needs (Italy virtually none) were opposed to measures likely to raise the cost of their energy supplies. Germany, supplying roughly two-thirds of the Community's coal, was reluctant to accept production quotas imposed on its industry by this, or any other, supranational agency. The result was a failure to agree; individual governments resorted to such measures as they thought best – particularly, in the case of the main producers, restrictions on imports from third countries and state aids, of varying degrees of openness, for its domestic producers.

In the light of this unseemly disarray the High Authority sought to bring some order into chaos and in 1964 the ECSC Council agreed to implement a co-ordinated system of state aids for the coal industry. It was notable that there was no attempt to establish a policy comparable with that then emerging for agriculture, based on high prices and import restrictions. The substantial common interest present in agriculture was conspicuously absent in coal. France and Italy, heavily dependent on energy imports, fiercely resisted any restriction which would raise their costs. Subsidies, rather than high domestic prices, were already employed to protect the industry in all the producing countries, legally or otherwise, and to recognise this fact was more realistic than deploring it. Hence it was merely agreed that such subsidies would have to be justified by reducing unemployment, and should be aimed at raising productivity rather than keeping inefficient pits permanently in existence and, furthermore, they should not distort competition between member countries.

A proposal, two years later, that a guaranteed market (roughly comparable with the prevailing level of output) should be provided by the Community, rather along the lines of the CAP, failed to secure approval. Once again the conflict of national interests was clear; those countries heavily dependent on imported energy sources saw no reason why they should be expected to deny themselves cheap imports merely to protect high-cost production in other member countries. Furthermore, there was here no bottomless budget comparable with the FEOGA; the costs of unsold surpluses would have to be met from national budgets. The only measure agreed, therefore, was a very modest fund to enable Germany to subsidise its output of coking coal; German steel manufacturers could then use that output without being put at an 'unfair' disadvantage compared with their competitors elsewhere in the Community who enjoyed the advantage of cheaper imported supplies. This apart, the industry was left largely to national devices and its decline continued; by 1973 the output of the industry had fallen to less than two-thirds of the level of 1958.

The year 1973 brought two major developments in the Community's coal industry. First, British accession raised total Community output by around two-thirds. Second, the oil crisis at the end of that year led to the first formal Community Energy Policy. The details of this will be explored at more length in the following section; for the moment it is sufficient to note that the stabilisation of the Community's coal industry was intended to be an important part of it. A proposal that this end should be achieved by means of Community subsidies on the production and stockpiling of coal, and on its use in power stations, once again failed to secure agreement. As will be noted in the next section, the fact that the United Kingdom would have been by far the major beneficiary was largely responsible for its downfall. All that emerged in the event was an agreement that both the ECSC and the European Investment Bank should be encouraged to extend loans on reasonably favourable terms for the rationalisation and modernisation of the coal industry, a facility which the British industry has used to a considerably greater extent than any other member country. This scarcely amounts to a policy. Once again the future of the industry was left largely in the hands of consumers and national governments; as a result, by 1986 the output of the industry had fallen a further 20 per cent below that of 1973.

18.3 Oil in Troubled Waters

In 1950 the Six imported 22 million tonnes of petroleum products; by 1958 this figure had risen to 83 million tonnes, and oil was accounting for a quarter of their primary energy consumption. By 1973 oil imports had risen to 450 million tonnes and the Community was dependent on imports for 70 per cent of its energy consumption.

Before 1973 if this development had been regarded as a 'problem' it was largely, as has been seen, because of its consequential effects on the coal industry, although concern was certainly being felt in some quarters at the extent of the Community's dependence on imports for its energy requirements. The only policy measure which had been adopted in this context, however, had been an agreement in 1968 that member countries should maintain stocks of oil equivalent to 65 days consumption (later increased to 90 days) to prevent temporary shortfalls in supply from having adverse effects on import prices. An effort by the Commission in 1970 to persuade member governments to harmonise their excise duties on oil products failed ignominiously.

The outbreak of war between Israel and the Arab states in September 1973 was followed by the decision by the (mainly Arab) Organisation of Petroleum Exporting Countries (OPEC) to withhold oil supplies from countries which failed to condemn the Israeli cause; more to the point, OPEC proceeded to use its cartel power to raise the world price of Middle East oil dramatically. In October 1973 that price had been $3 a barrel; by January 1974 it was nearly $12 a barrel. This caused understandable alarm amongst the members of the Community. The Dutch, having expressed public support for Israel, were deprived of Middle Eastern oil and turned to their Community partners for support. Since such support carried the threat of an Arab embargo on their own oil supplies, the partners conspicuously declined to provide it, issuing instead a statement favouring the Arab side of the argument. Once again the political solidarity of the Community had proved to possess rather feeble foundations.

Much the same was true of the Community's presence at an International Energy Conference in Washington called by President Nixon in December 1974. This resulted in the creation of an International Energy Agency (IEA) to be operated under the auspices of the OECD. Its major policy aims were to secure agreement on a minimum price for oil so as to encourage the expansion of output by non-Middle-East producers, and on mandatory sharing of supplies between members should the supply to any one of them be significantly reduced. Once again the Community displayed something short of unity. The government of France considered the general stance of the conference unduly antagonistic towards the Arab states; unlike its partners in the Community, it declined to join the proposed Agency. (None the less it had the satisfaction of seeing the IEA's headquarters established in Paris, the location of the OECD.)

The Community itself obviously needed to formulate some kind of policy in the face of the new situation. At its meeting in December 1973 the European Council had instructed the Commission to draw up proposals for action in the energy field; shortly afterwards, in February 1974, the Council of Ministers even agreed to the ultimate measure signifying the existence of a crisis situation – it created a new committee. Aided by the addition of this new Energy Committee to the Community's armoury, by December 1974 the Commission was able to submit to the Council a detailed set of proposals under the title 'Community Energy Policy – aims for 1985' which the Ministers duly resolved to approve.

The document set out a framework of guidelines for national policies and for the producers and consumers of energy within the Community over the ensuing decade. Its basic aims were to increase the supply of alternatives to imported oil – i.e. coal, gas and nuclear power from domestic sources – to diversify the sources from which unavoidable imports of energy were derived, and to exploit alternative new sources of energy, from wind, waves and tides. By 1985, it was proposed, the imported element of the Community's energy supply should be cut from 63 per cent to 40 per cent. The contribution of oil to the total should be reduced from 61 per cent to 41 per cent; that of solid fuels, while rising in absolute total, should fall from 23 per cent to 17 per cent. A corresponding increase was envisaged in the contribution to be made by nuclear energy, from a mere 1.5 per cent of the total in 1973 to 16 per cent by 1985. In the meantime a programme of measures was recommended to slow down the growth in the demand for energy by its more rational and economic use. The aim was to achieve by 1985 a level of energy consumption which was 15 per cent below the forecast for 1985 contained in projections drawn up by the Commission at the beginning of 1973.

A policy implies rather more than a mere statement of desirable objectives: it requires some indication of the positive measures to be taken in order to attain them, and some indication of the manner in which it is proposed to obtain the resources necessary to implement those measures. The resolution of December 1974 was strong on the first element but almost totally silent on the others. In fact it represented little more than a summation of what individual member governments would have been forced to attempt in their own self-interest. When specific measures were suggested, little agreement was forthcoming.

In the course of 1975 efforts were made to formulate Community policy on energy for an impending international conference on economic co-operation between the developed and developing world. The United Kingdom, now at the beginning of its period as a major supplier of oil from the North Sea, insisted on being represented at the conference in its own right as an oil-producing country as well as sharing in the Community representation. This generated a good deal of ill-will, indicating (in the eyes of the remaining members) the dubious commitment of the British to the Community ideal and (in British eyes) the fundamental conflict of interest within it. A suggestion was advanced by the UK that the Community should guarantee a minimum supply price for oil so as to underwrite the risk which Britain would be taking in increasing its North Sea output in response (so it was argued) to the December 1974 resolution calling for increased indigenous energy supplies. The remaining member countries responded by seeking in return (not entirely unreasonably) a guarantee of supplies at a maximum price from Britain. When the latter was emphatically refused the whole proposal was abandoned. (A proposal for a minimum support price was in fact accepted later by the International Energy Agency, but the continued rise in world oil prices rapidly made the idea of little practical relevance.) In the general animosity resulting from these discussions the proposal for Community subsidies on coal production, referred to in the previous section, was also abandoned.

A similar failure to agree occurred two years later in connection with the growing problem of excess oil-refining capacity in the Community. Throughout the 1960s such capacity had been steadily increasing in response to the equally steady increase in the consumption of petroleum products. Between 1973 and 1977 the increase had continued, the delayed outcome of investment decisions made years earlier. Output of the end-products of the refineries, however, fell by

15 per cent over the same period as a combined result of recession, increased oil prices and the policy measures introduced to reduce energy consumption. Oil refining being a highly capital-intensive activity, operation at significantly less than full capacity causes a marked increase in unit costs and a serious threat to the viability of the industry.

In March 1977 the Commission therefore submitted proposals to the Council for a common approach to the problem. This would have involved financial assistance from Community sources for the closure of redundant refineries – especially the older plants with poor environmental characteristics – the banning of all state aids to refineries, and the cessation of all loans from the European Investment Bank for refinery expansion. This met with fierce resistance from the United Kingdom, whose crude oil production had now begun the meteoric rise which was to take North Sea production from below 400 000 tonnes in 1973 to well over 100 million tonnes in the early 1980s. British policy was that two-thirds of its crude oil should be refined in the United Kingdom; the proposed moratorium on new refinery capacity was thus totally unacceptable. Given the economies of scale (and, conversely, the diseconomies of excess capacity) oil-refining was logically a very suitable case for Community-wide policy; basic conflicts of national interest nevertheless made such a policy impossible.

Similar obstacles stood in the way of Commission efforts in the later 1970s and 1980s to tax away the monopoly profits being enjoyed by OPEC producers by means of a Community energy tax. National taxes on oil are undesirable, in its view, because they distort competition between high-energy industries as long as member countries have different levels of tax. A community-wide tax, on the other hand, would prevent this distortion; in addition it would act as an incentive to the efficient use of energy and simultaneously transfer monopoly profits from OPEC into the Community budget. For precisely this latter reason the Ministers would never agree; as is demonstrated in Chapter 20 below, of all the sovereign powers which national governments jealously protect, the power to tax its citizens is probably cherished above all others.

By 1985 the objectives of the December 1974 resolution had indeed been largely achieved. The import content of the Community's energy had indeed fallen to 41 per cent while the share of imported oil in its total energy consumption was only 30 per cent – back to the level of 1958. The contribution of Community *policy* to this happy outcome, however, can hardly be described as other than very marginal indeed. National governments pursued their own policies in their own ways. More to the point, the ineluctable power of market pressures had been shown. The protracted economic recession of the later 1970s and early 1980s had enforced an economy of usage which no amount of exhortation could have induced; the quadrupling of the price of oil in 1973–4, and the further doubling in 1978–9, however, had brought into operation the even more persuasive influence of price-elasticity of demand.

81.4 Nuclear Power

The 1957 Treaty establishing the European Atomic Energy Community, Euratom, had as its objective the joint development of nuclear energy for peaceful purposes by the six signatory powers. It envisaged that this aim would be achieved through the co-ordination of national programmes of research and development, through the finance of joint research carried out by a Community research centre and by the sharing of the results of this research work between the members. It also established a common Supply Agency with the right to purchase all nuclear fuels produced within the Community and the power to handle all agreements for the purchase of such fuels from countries outside it.

A final important element in the policy was to be the creation of 'joint undertakings' in the nuclear power station business whereby building consortia would embark on construction programmes in more than one country. In view of the enormous construction costs of nuclear power stations, and the economies of scale derivable from 'learning by doing' in such construction, this made a great deal of sense. The United Kigndom, a pioneer in this field, was discovering the hard way that constructing stations on a one-off basis, with new consortia being formed for each individual contract, was a sure and certain recipe for exceedingly expensive structures, each throwing up its own cost-escalating problems.

In the fifteen years following the Treaty positive action in pursuit of these aims was conspicuous by its absence. Early expectations concerning the speed with which nuclear power would become cheaper than that from conventional sources proved to be wildly optimistic as the result of a combination of unforeseen problems with the technology and the continuing abundance of cheap oil supplies throughout the 1960s. Even the expectation of acute shortages in the supply of uranium, and consequently high world prices for it, proved unfounded. In addition, within member countries public opinion (or at least a particularly articulate element of it) became distinctly hostile to the concept of nuclear power, partly through a real or imagined association between the civil and military applications of nuclear capability and partly through increasing concern about its potential environmental impact.

Even without these factors, however, there existed in this as in other energy fields fundamental differences of perceived national interest. France, which at that time lacked nuclear weapons, was interested in a nuclear programme for military as much as for civil purposes; it had been no coincidence that when Jean Monnet had sought to extend the ECSC experiment to other areas he had hit on nuclear energy, thus ensuring keen interest on the part of the French government. The remaining member countries, on the other hand, had little or no desire to join the military nuclear club and were primarily interested in the new form of (hopefully) cheap and abundant energy; they favoured concentration on the application of existing nuclear technology – if necessary purchased abroad – rather than on the pursuit of fundamental research in nuclear physics.

This uneasy balance of interests was highlighted by the frequent reluctance – refusal, even – of France to share some of the results of its research in this field (which was what Euratom was supposed to be about) on the grounds that to do so might compromise its national security. For more than a decade, in fact, the French were concentrating on the development of a technology based on natural uranium; by contrast, the other member countries preferred to follow the cheaper route of buying their technology from the United States, involving water-cooled reactors using enriched uranium.

It would be wrong to suggest that nothing whatever emerged during Euratom's first decade because of these underlying tensions. By 1970 the Community had spent around ECU 800 million on research at the Joint Research Centre referred to in Chapter 13, and about ECU 160 million on research contracts carried out within member countries. These totals were not trivial but they were certainly no more than marginal in comparison with national expenditures in the same field, most of which were deployed with only minimal reference to work proceeding elsewhere in the Community.

The oil crisis of 1973–4 to some extent breathed new life into what had become almost a moribund 'common' policy. The December 1974 Resolution called for the speeding up of the development of nuclear energy within the Community, the target being that it should account for 16 per cent of the Community's energy requirements by 1985, compared with less than 2 per cent in 1974. This implied a fourfold increase in the output of nuclear power from about 50 GWh to 200 GWh.

As may be seen from Table 18.1, this target was reached with remarkable accuracy; between 1973 and 1981 the Community's output of nuclear power was indeed quadrupled. Between 1981 and 1986 it was doubled yet again; one third of the Community's electricity is now derived from nuclear stations. To attribute this to the policy of the Community, however, rather than to that of individual national governments, would clearly be wrong. The result owed much, in fact, the French programme of nuclear expansion which alone accounted for 47 per cent of the total growth in output between 1973 and 1986; this was a response to its own perceptions of its national interest (i.e. its almost total lack of alternative energy sources internally) and not to any Community policy.

On the other hand, the Community is by no means a mere bystander in the fields of either the production or the development of nuclear power. In the decade ending in 1986 it had arranged loans amounting to around ECU 3900 million for investment in nuclear power, assisting in the finance of at least one nuclear station in each member country. Doubtless the stations concerned would have been built in any event, but the availability of finance from Community sources could have done no harm. Its activity in the research field has steadily grown, with substantial Community funding for major internation-

Table 18.1
Energy in the European Community, 1958–86

(1)	Units (2)	Europe 6 1958 (3)	Europe 6 1973 (4)	Europe 9 1973 (5)	Europe 9 1981 (6)	Europe 10 1981 (7)	Europe 10 1986 (8)	Europe 12 1986 (9)
1. Total primary production:								
(a) Coal		177	116	194	179	183	160	173
(b) Oil		7	11	11	98	99	144	146
(c) Natural gas	Million	6	88	112	125	125	124	125
(d) Other	tonnes	18	16	26	75	75	142	155
Total		208	231	343	477	481	570	599
2. Gross inland consumption	oil equivalent	308	668	914	899	914	959	1042
3. Net imports	Mn tonnes	92	469	609	433	445	423	480
of which, petroleum products		83	450	588	346	358	306	354
3 as % of 2		30.0	70.2	66.6	48.2	48.7	44.1	46.0
4. Electricity production	Thousand GWh*	228	685	973	1171	1193	1381	1523
of which, nuclear power		—	29	53	202	202	456	492

* GWh = 10⁶ kilowatt-hours.

al projects such as the Joint European Torus programme on the development of nuclear fusion referred to in Section 5 of Chapter 13, a network of national studies on reactor safety and, increasingly in recent years, the co-ordination of work on the disposal of radioactive waste. In 1983 the Council agreed on the allocation of ECU 4.2 billion for joint research programmes in the nuclear field over 1984–7. Although the non-emergence of an acute shortage in world supplies of nuclear fuels has limited the role played by the Community's Supply Agency, the Agency's ability to deploy the bargaining power of the Community collectively is still of advantage to the member countries. In the course of 1986 alone it negotiated 135 contracts with suppliers for uranium procurement or enrichment services, presumably a more effective arrangement than one in which twelve countries bargain separately – and therefore against one another. All this may indeed fall far short of a comprehensive policy in any real sense but it is something more than a negligible contribution.

18.5   The Prospect

In 1985 the Council of Ministers adopted a new resolution setting out the Community's energy policy objectives for 1995. In essence this reaffirmed the broad strategy of earlier resolutions – that is, on the one hand, to reduce dependence on imported supplies and, on the other, to increase the efficiency of energy utilisation – despite the fact that the astronomical increases in world oil prices during the 1970s had given way to equally dramatic falls. Oil should account for no more than about 40 per cent of the Community's energy consumption and the share of new and renewable fuels should be substantially increased.

Twenty years experience had demonstrated beyond doubt that the scope for a positive Community policy in the energy field must inevitably be limited. It could scarcely be otherwise; as may be seen from Table 18.2, the energy import-dependence amongst member countries in 1986 varied from 99 per cent for Luxembourg to − 17 per cent for the United Kingdom, and the variance of this dependence amongst the member countries was actually 50 per cent greater in 1986 than it had been in 1973. In reaffirming its long-term energy strategy, therefore, the Council of Ministers bowed to reality and recorded that all that the Commission could do was to continue 'checking' that national policies were in line with these objectives. This naturally skates over the delicate question of what exactly the Commission or Council could do if either was to discover that the policy of a national government was *not* 'in line' with Community objectives. The answer is, of course, not much.

But not necessarily nothing. It is now generally conceded that the disparity of interests and resources within the member states is such that any attempt to apply a strong, centrally co-ordinated Community policy would be futile. The

Table 18.2
Energy Import-dependence in the European Community

	1973				Net energy imports as % of gross inland consumption	
	Gross inland energy consumption	Primary energy production	Net energy imports			
			Total	Petroleum products		
	Million tonnes oil equivalent				1973	1986
(1)	(2)	(3)	(4)	(5)	(6)	(7)
Belgium	46.0	5.7	43.2	30.8	93.9	72.9
Denmark	19.6	0.1	20.4	18.5	104.1	74.5
France	173.4	32.9	146.1	128.8	84.3	56.0
Germany	261.3	118.0	147.5	144.9	56.4	54.6
Ireland	7.0	0.7	6.1	5.6	87.1	74.2
Italy	122.2	18.4	111.0	103.8	90.8	83.2
Luxembourg	4.6	—	4.6	1.7	100.0	99.4
Netherlands	60.4	56.7	16.6	40.2	27.5	17.5
United Kingdom	219.9	110.1	113.1	113.4	51.4	−16.8
Total, EC 9	914.3	342.6	608.5	587.6	66.6	42.3

Community cannot provide anything approaching the enormous sums of money devoted to the energy sector by national enterprises, nor can it create a community of interest where none exists. The Community's role in energy policy, in the words of evidence given by it to a House of Lords committee, is likely to be more important where it does not cost money. Although Community objectives cannot be legally enforced on national governments, the fact that the Commission is, so to speak, looking over governmental shoulders and enquiring as to what is being done in the context of those objectives may have a certain intangible effect.

The Commission is increasingly turning its attention to the question of the pricing of different types of energy in the member countries. It is known that there exist large and apparently unjustifiable differences in the prices paid by consumers in different countries, differences which (as in the case of transport) may well be attributable to the extensive governmental intervention in the sector. Such differences could substantially distort competition between energy-intensive industries within the Community and thus justify the Commission in deploying the weaponry of competition policy.

There are other areas in which joint action by the Community could clearly benefit individual member states. The possibility of exporting power from one country to another, either at times when peak demands do not coincide or continuously, indicates that some positive co-ordination of distribution networks could be of mutual advantage. The potential economies obtainable from joint construction programmes, although neglected so far, still exist. In all this the Council and Commission may have very limited power to decide or to finance; this is an area, however, in which the path of wisdom lies not in the pursuit of an unattainable uniformity of policy but rather in the identification of opportunities which national governments can then be encouraged to pursue for themselves.

Further Reading

House of Lords, Select Committee on the European Communities, *European Community Energy Strategy and Objectives*, Session 1983–84, 17th Report, HL208 (London: HMSO, 1984).

Lucas, N. D. J., *Energy and the European Communities* (London: Europa Publications, 1977).

Weyman-Jones, T., *Energy in Europe: Issues and Policies* (London: Methuen, 1986).

Social and
Environmental
Policy 19

19.1 The Social Foundations of the Treaty

The Treaty of Rome contained many, if rather vague and general, references to the social aspects of the customs union but more specific provision was made by the relatively brief Title III of Part Three (Articles 117 to 128) headed 'Social policy'. The title indicates, however, the very limited definition of social policy which was being adopted. It referred to the need for 'close co-operation between member States' in matters relating to employment, labour legislation, occupational training, accidents and diseases and social security. Two features will be immediately evident. First, the treaty envisaged 'close collaboration' rather than a common policy. Second, the specified matters exclude areas which would generally be regarded as major components of social policy – in particular, education, housing and health.

Both features derive from the basic philosophy of the treaty, which was essentially *laissez-faire* – with, of course, the obvious exception of its provisions for agriculture. Its object was fundamentally to secure the optimum allocation of resources and the maximum rate of economic growth through the operation of unimpeded market forces; by implication all other desirable social objectives (about which the views of the signatory states differed widely) could then be achieved nationally. The 'social policy' described in the Treaty was in essence the establishment of a single, efficient market for labour throughout the Community.

The creation of such a market implied action on two fronts. First, obstacles to the free movement of labour would need to be reduced as far as possible by the encouragement of mobility through national provisions for the retraining and

210

rehabilitation of unemployed (or, in the case of agriculture, under-employed) labour. Second, a common market in labour required the elimination of distortions in the market generated by 'artificial' variations in its cost among the member countries. For example, it was – and still is – believed that national differences in the distribution of social security contributions amongst employers, employees and government generate artificial distortions in the labour market. Such differences certainly do exist. In the early 1980s the proportion of total social security contributions borne by employers varied from 10 per cent in Denmark to nearly 60 per cent in France and Italy; conversely, the share carried by governments ranged from nearly 90 per cent in Denmark to less than 20 per cent in France.

Whether these differences generate corresponding distortions in relative labour costs is another matter; it could be argued that if high contributions are required from employers in some member countries these would be treated as part of the remuneration of labour and will then be offset by correspondingly lower money wage-rates. Whatever the truth of the matter, attempts to create a single social security system for the whole Community (in a sense a logical implication of a single labour market) quickly came to nothing. The old bogies invariably appeared. On the one hand, serious differences exist amongst the member countries on the matter of relative priorities for any such system; in 1983 the share of total 'social protection' expenditure going to old-age pensions ranged from less than 30 per cent in Denmark and the Netherlands to more than 40 per cent in the United Kingdom, while the share taken by family allowances varied from around 10 per cent in France and the United Kingdom to a little over 6 per cent in Italy. On the other hand, any common social security system would inevitably imply a transfer of income from relatively prosperous countries, with high incomes and low unemployment, to less fortunate countries with low incomes and high unemployment. Such transfers have proved feasible only when the net contributors in the transaction can identify some corresponding quid pro quo elsewhere. No such offset was ever discovered in this context.

The treaty did, however, contain one specific requirement in the social field, included at the insistence of France. Article 119 provided that in the course of the first of the treaty's three stages each member state should establish, and subsequently maintain, the principle of equal remuneration for equal work as between men and women. The target of the end of the first stage – i.e. December 1961 – proved hopelessly unrealistic. It was in fact 1976 before the principle was (broadly) established throughout the Community; whether this laudable outcome would have been achieved, or achieved as rapidly, without the obligation imposed by the Treaty must remain a matter of speculation. But at least it was achieved.

This rather specific objective apart, the treaty laid down broad aims rather than specific measures. The translation of these aims into positive action was left to the operation of the European Social Fund created by Articles 123–125 of the treaty.

19.2 The European Social Fund

The European Social Fund (ESF) was charged with the task of improving employment opportunities within the Community through the promotion of employment facilities and the geographical and occupational mobility of workers. The total of its resources was not specified, this delicate matter being left to the Council of Ministers. Article 200(2) of the treaty, however, specified how the sum, once determined, was to be raised from each member state. Germany and France were to contribute 32 per cent each; Italy, on the other hand, was required to provide only 20 per cent, compared with the 28 per cent it was required to find (like France and Germany) of the general Community budget. It was clearly intended that the main beneficiary of the whole ESF concept would in fact be Italy.

The terms of reference laid down for the ESF made clear that its aims were modest. It was permitted to meet 50 per cent of the expenditure by any member government on schemes of occupational retraining or resettlement, or on grants to workers to maintain their wage-levels during periods in which their employers were converting to new types of production. (The latter, though, only after they had been back in full employment for six months.) The modesty of the aims of the ESF was matched by the modesty of the resources allocated to it; as may be seen from Table 19.1, during the 1960s its annual budget averaged ECU 166 million – hardly an extravagant sum to spread over a total workforce of around 75 million people. (By comparison, over this period the ECSC was spending an annual average of around ECU 62 million on redeployment aid to the coal and steel industry alone.)

While the Fund doubtless contributed to many worthy schemes it was obviously not an instrument of a major Community policy. It could assist only schemes submitted to it by national governments; the implication is therefore that any projects it financed would almost certainly have gone ahead in any event. What was more, its terms of reference ensured that most of its resources necessarily went to those countries which had the most extensive and generous provisions for retraining and resettlement. In fact, over the period 1960–71 payments to Germany accounted for 44 per cent of the total, compared with the 36 per cent which went to Italy – the intended main beneficiary. The fund may have been useful: it was manifestly not a policy.

The Council of Ministers apparently took the same view. In 1971 the ESF was changed in three fundamental respects, the changes coming into operation from 1972. In the first place, the fund was absorbed into the general budget and thus ceased to be financed by a separate scale of contributions. Secondly, the resources allocated to it were substantially increased, from an annual average of ECU 166 million in 1961–71 to one of ECU 819 million over 1972–7. Thirdly, its expenditure was to be divided equally between two sections. One section was to be devoted to grants towards the retraining and resettlement of particular

Table 19.1
The European Social Fund, 1960–88 (ECU million at 1986 prices)

	Vocational training	Resettlement			Total
Phase 1, *1961–71*					
Total	1 769	53			1 822
Annual average	161	5			166

	Young people	Regions		Other	Total
Phase 2, *1972–83*					
(a) 1972–7					
Total	644	2 730		1 537	4 911
Annual average	108	455		256	819
(b) 1978–83					
Total	3 948	3 720		2 190	9 858
Annual average	658	620		365	1 643

	People under 25 years of age		People aged 25 years and older		Other	Total
	Less-favoured regions	Other	Less-favoured regions	Other		
Phase 3, *1984–8*						
Total	4 177	5 503	1 310	1 479	411	12 880
Annual average	835	1 101	262	296	82	2 576

categories of workers specified by the Council; initially these were workers in agriculture or textiles who had been especially affected by the integration process, but handicapped people and young persons were subsequently added to the list. The other section was to be allocated to schemes aimed at the 'correction of unsatisfactory employment situations' – i.e. projects in backward or depressed regions. The division reflects a dilemma which has faced the Community's social policy throughout its existence – whether aid should be directed, on the one hand, to groups of individuals, irrespective of their location or, on the other hand, to the poorest member-countries of the Community.

A distinct shift of emphasis occurred at the end of 1978. Between 1970 and 1978 a marked increase had occurred in the level of unemployment in the Community; over those eight years the number of people unemployed had risen by more than 180 per cent, from 2.1 to 6 million. Amongst young people, however – defined as those under 25 years of age – the increase had been proportionately much greater, at nearly 400 per cent. The Council therefore authorised a new form of aid from the ESF to assist not merely retraining but also job-creation schemes aimed at young workers. The dramatic change may be seen from Table 19.1 – assistance aimed at young people increased sharply not merely in absolute amount but also as a proportion of total expenditure, from 13 per cent in 1972–7 to 40 per cent in 1978–83.

Another revision occurred in 1983. Because claims for eligible schemes had consistently exceeded the resources available, the total resources available to the ESF were further increased – by about 40 per cent. The perennial conflict over the claims of countries with high unemployment and those with low average incomes was resolved by the decision that at least 40 per cent of the ESF funds should go to the poorer regions of the Community, the rest being directed to the unemployed wherever they were to be found. In addition, it was resolved that 75 per cent of the latter should be allocated to unemployed people of under 25 years of age, especially those under the age of 18. As may be seen from Table 19.1, in 1984–6 these objectives were achieved; the result was that the fund's resources were directed almost exclusively to the relatively poor countries of the Community, the five richest (Belgium, Denmark, Germany, Luxembourg and the Netherlands) together collecting less than 10 per cent of the total.

19.3 Seeking a Policy

Admirable though the work of the ESF may have been, it was at best a source of encouragement and (perhaps) co-ordination rather than an instrument of policy; the initiative for the programmes to which it contributed aid lay unquestionably with individual national governments. In 1972 the Council had called for vigorous action in the social field and, in particular, for some systematic attempt to secure full and better employment, improved conditions of work and greater participation by workers (and employers) in the life of the Community. Ever willing, the Commission prepared a 'Social Action Programme' which it placed before the Council in January 1974; this received concept approval and the Commission was instructed to formulate specific proposals to implement it.

In truth, the Social Action Programme was a list of some 35 proposals of a disparate nature and involving for the most part action by national governments rather than by the Community collectively. To achieve fuller employment, action was proposed to co-ordinate national employment services and a common vocational training policy. To improve living and working conditions, consultation and co-operation were called for on social protection policies and on measures concerned with health and safety at work. The progressive involvement of both workers and managers in the decision-making process of the Community was called for. In all these areas Directorate-General V of the Commission continues to encourage governments to move in what it considers the right direction. But it would be difficult to describe these activities as a coherent Community policy.

The essentially passive nature of the Commission's activity is due partly to the fact that 1974 was arguably the worst possible moment to seek to establish any positive policy in this field. The level of unemployment, which had stood at 2.5 per cent in 1973, had doubled by 1977; by 1983 it had doubled again. Every member government therefore had its own unemployment problem without needing to concern itself with the problem elsewhere; the contribution made by the ESF or other agencies in the Community could only be miniscule in comparison with national expenditures in the areas concerned. There remain also the deep differences in national philosophies to which reference has already been made. These are clearly illustrated by the failure to secure agreement in two important areas of social policy of interest to the Community – the treatment of migrant labour and the formalisation of worker-participation in industry.

Articles 48–51 of the Treaty contained provisions relating to 'migrant' labour, including the proposition that such workers should be given the same social security benefits as those given to citizens of the country in which they were working. It is clear what the Treaty meant by the term 'migrant' labour – i.e. citizens of one member country employed in another member country. This is not what the term came to mean in reality. By 1983 there were some 6 million 'migrant' workers in the Community, but of these three-quarters, 4.5 million, had come from countries outside the Community altogether. During the expansionary years of the 1960s and early 1970s the influx had been welcome; the migrants typically took on the dirty, unskilled, unpleasant lower-paid jobs which indigenous workers preferred to avoid. With the recession of the mid-1970s, and the sharp rise in general unemployment, however, the economic and social tensions generated by the growth of foreign ghettos in the decaying inner cities began to be a source of serious concern.

It seemed an obvious area for Community rather than national action. If there is to be free movement of labour throughout the Community, measures governing immigration would logically need to be the same in all member countries. Admission to, and rights of residence in, any one member country should theoretically give comparable rights in every other. Attempts to establish such a common policy, however, failed utterly. Some governments (Germany and the United Kingdom) were conspicuously unenthusiastic over the proposition that control over the entry of drug-pedlars or potential terrorists into their countries could be safely left in the hands of the police forces of others. Many countries, for historical and other reasons, give preferential rights of citizenship to immigrants from certain countries and it is not obvious to other member countries that they should necessarily be required to do the same. Immigrants from the (East) German Democratic Republic, for example, are automatically granted citizenship of the Federal Republic of (West) Germany; residents of Norway and Sweden may become naturalised citizens of Denmark after only two years' residence compared with the seven years required for other nationalities; France gives nationality automatically to children born in France, including those of the two million or so of its residents of North African origin. On the other hand, none of the existing member countries was willing to concede immediate and automatic rights of entry to emigrants from Spain and Portugal after the accession of those countries to the Community.

Similar conflicts of national interest have long blocked agreement on the matter of the rights of workers to share in the control of enterprises employing them, despite the proclamation in the Social Action Programme of 1974 that priority should be given to 'the progressive involvement of workers or their representatives in the life of undertakings in the Community'. The ill-fated draft Fifth Directive of 1972 sought to harmonise the structure of public limited liability companies in line with the European Company statute first proposed in 1970, under which companies could be registered under European rather than national law. It provided that every enterprise with more than 1000 employees should have a Supervisory Board overseeing the Board of Managers responsible for its day-to-day running; between one-third and one-half of the members of this Supervisory Board would be employees elected from amongst themselves, unless the workers negotiated some alternative system (e.g. a works council) which gave them comparable rights. This provision was insisted upon by Germany; its domestic law contained such a requirement and the German government was anxious to ensure that companies could not escape that requirement by incorporating themselves under a Community law having no such provision. It followed logically that all other national governments would need to modify *their* domestic company law to include such provisions; unless they did so, their own companies would be reluctant to use a Eurocompany mechanism which *did* impose the requirement. Another draft Directive in 1983 (the 'Vredling directive') sought to impose substantial requirements on large companies to disclose commercial information to their employees. It also required compulsory prior consultation with employees on corporate decisions which could be held to affect their livelihood.

These proposals met (and continue to meet) resistance from many quarters. Employers organisations in virtually all member states – not surprisingly – are hostile to such proposals and make their views known to their respective governments. Governments themselves are divided on the issue; many dislike in principle the idea of having a dual system of corporate law, one national and one European, while others (in particular, the United Kingdom) do not regard such matters as falling within the Community's proper sphere of competence. Even trade unions vary in their attitude. Some (like the Trades Union Congress in Britain) oppose the idea of worker-directors being elected by employees rather than being appointed by and from trade union officialdom; others, in Italy especially, are fundamentally opposed to the capitalist system and thus to anything which smacked of participation in it.

As a result, by the late 1980s the Commission had been driven to lower its sights considerably; it declared its intention as being to achieve worker participation by 'a more flexible system better adapted to national circumstances'. In a draft Company Statute, submitted to the Council in July 1989, under which a company could operate in any member country, provision was made for worker representation in any one of three ways. The first was the German system of a supervisory board with worker representation; the second was the French system of totally separate workers' councils; the third was any other system agreed by the workforce concerned through collective bargaining – although this did not permit a decision that there should be no worker representation at all. In any event it was provided that the workers in any enterprise would have the right to receive adequate information and to be consulted on important decisions. The attraction offered by the draft statute was that any company incorporated under its provisions would have the right to write off losses incurred in one member country against profits made in another for tax purposes. Misgivings still remained, particular on the part of the British government, but it seems likely that the draft statute will become law in or soon after 1990.

This is unlikely to be the only area of social policy in which the misgivings of one or two member countries will be over-ridden. One of the stated five priority objectives of the Single European Act had been to 'strengthen the economic and social cohesion' of the Community in the face of the proposed movement to a single market and, from 1988 onwards, to a genuine monetary union. At its summit meeting of December 1988, therefore, the Council of Ministers directed the Commission to prepare draft proposals for a Community charter of fundamental social rights, a task in which the Commission sought the assistance of the Economic and Social Committee. Such a draft Social Charter was laid before the Council in October 1989 and from this is likely to follow an action programme calling for national laws based on the Charter. Given the misgivings of some member governments, the Commission is unlikely to make the mistake of seeking to make its proposals a matter of compulsion but it is clear that it will be seeking to create Community-wide regulations governing such sensitive matters as maximum working hours, minimum wages, the rights of part-time workers and equal rights of men and women. These are matters which will certainly bring to the centre of discussion the crucial issue of the proper limits, if any, to the competence of the Community in what have traditionally been regarded as matters for purely national determination.

19.4 Enter the Environment

If the treaty provisions relating to social policy were relatively few and restricted, those relating to environmental issues are scarcely visible.

True, its preamble refers to the objective of 'the constant improvement of the living and working conditions' of the population but it would require a rather strained interpretation of this phrase to read into it what has come to be called environmental policy. In the late 1950s the absence of concern with such issues was not surprising. It is only in the context of relative affluence that societies feel able to indulge in the luxury of concern over the quality of living, as opposed to the quantity of the output of its economic system.

By the beginning of the 1970s, after two decades of more rapid and sustained economic growth than ever known previously, the problem of the possible conflict between economic growth and the preservation of the environment had become too obvious to be ignored. Too many of the expanding industries were disposing of their waste products in their surrounding soil, rivers and atmosphere with remarkably little regard for the consequential impact on the human and animal life of society as a whole. The increasing urbanisation of Europe, as some 6 million people left the agricultural workforce, had been allowed to generate sprawling housing and congested towns; the growth of an immigrant workforce, as noted earlier, had led to social stresses in the decaying city centres. Even in the countryside the CAP's open-ended invitation to unlimited production was leading to the disappearance of hedgerows and marshes, to soil impregnated with nitrogenous fertilisers and pesticides and even to farm buildings as reminiscent, and as repellent, as factories – often befitting the type of activity conducted inside them.

Inspired by a United Nations conference on the environment held in Stockholm earlier in the year, the European Council meeting in Paris in October 1972 resolved that the Community should formulate a common policy to tackle these environmental problems. The lack of any specific juridical foundation for any such policy has already been noted. To some degree, however, it was possible to call in aid the provisions of competition policy. National measures to reduce or prevent pollution invariably impose additional costs on producers: there is seldom a cheaper way of disposing of industrial effluent than pouring it into the nearest river or canal, or of dealing with atmospheric pollution than by cheerfully leaving its victims to endure it. If national regulations governing such matters are more stringent in one member country than in another, therefore, the production costs of some producers will be artificially raised in comparison with those of producers elsewhere, thus distorting competition. Conversely,

measures adopted by member countries, nominally for environmental
frequently have the effect (coincidentally, of course) of hindering impor
other member countries with differing standards and requirements; once again
competition within the Community is distorted.

This was hardly a sufficient basis, however, for a policy which sought to
create and raise environmental standards rather than to merely prevent
distortions arising from variations in standards between member states. The
Council therefore fell back on a very general provision which the founding
fathers had prudently inserted into the sixth and final part of the Treaty –
Article 235. This provides that if (a) any action appears necessary to achieve one
of the aims of the Community, but if (b) no specific provision has been made in
the Treaty for the requisite powers, then (c) the Council shall enact the
appropriate provisions acting by means of a unanimous vote. This remarkably
flexible provision was quite sufficient to form the basis for an environmental
policy – as, indeed, it would be for practically any other policy.

The Council therefore resolved that since prevention is better than cure,
measures should be drawn up to prevent pollution at source; that the environmental effects of other Community policies – agriculture, transport, energy etc.
– should be taken into account when any decisions were being taken on them;
and that both collective and national research projects should be encouraged to
discover better methods of protecting and preserving the environment. The
Council, in other words, saw a common environmental policy as essentially
comprising the pursuit of co-ordination and harmonisation in the development
of national policies. The Commission was duly charged with the task of
translating these general principles into a programme of specific actions.

19.5 The Environmental Action Programmes

The First Action Programme, covering the four years 1974–7, was presented to
the Council and adopted by it in November 1973. Its proposals fell into three
broad categories: first, those aimed at the reduction or prevention of pollution;
second, general measures to improve the environment and general quality of life
in the Community; third, proposals to establish joint Community action in
international organisations dealing with environmental matters. Since that
time, each programme has been successively extended; the Fourth Action
Programme, covering the six years 1987–92, was approved by the Council in
December 1986.

Over this period the Commission has drawn up, and the Council has
approved, well over a hundred pieces of legislation – regulations, directives or
decisions – bearing on environmental matters. The bulk of these have been
concerned with measures to reduce or prevent pollution. That the Community
has attempted and achieved most in this area is understandable; it is the context

in which a common policy, as opposed to a mere co-ordination of national policies, makes most sense. The Community is a group of countries which border upon one another, or are at least in geographical proximity, and the pollution of the atmosphere or of rivers and seas is no respecter of state frontiers. Efforts by one country in isolation may therefore benefit others or, conversely, be rendered useless by different actions (or a lack of them) by another member country. A set of common Community standards also reduces the danger that the competitive position of an industry in one member country can be compromised if its government enforces anti-pollution standards which are more demanding, and therefore more costly, than those required elsewhere.

Over the years, therefore, the Community has slowly accumulated a set of agreed standards and requirements. To combat water pollution, these include definitions of minimum quality requirements in fresh and sea waters, depending on the purposes for which they are being used, and regulations to prevent water pollution through the disposal of toxic materials. Air pollution is dealt with through a large number of directives defining compulsory air quality standards in terms of the maximum volumes of sulphur dioxide, lead and nitrogen dioxide which may be discharged into, or be present in, the atmosphere. Others limit the sulphur content of fuels and the lead content of petrol; a directive issued in 1985 is aimed at the general introduction of lead-free petrol throughout the Community by October 1989; another provided that all new cars sold within the Community should be required to meet defined emission standards by October 1988. Even noise pollution is dealt with; directives and decisions define the maximum noise levels permitted in different types of equipment, from subsonic aircraft to lawnmowers.

In other aspects of environmental policy, where the interaction of national policies is less evident, the work of the Commission has necessarily consisted of attempts to encourage and co-ordinate national programmes rather than the initiation of positive action. Given the very limited resources at its disposal, it could hardly be otherwise; it was estimated that in 1983 the total expenditure by the Community on environmental matters (0.05 per cent of its total budget) was below that of the German government alone. It does indeed conduct its own research into environmental matters at the Joint Research Centre in Ipra, and a substantial part of the energy research budget is concerned with nuclear safety and waste disposal. Its main function in the research area, however, is to make modest contributions to research programmes and pilot schemes involving environmental management undertaken by national governments, and thus, hopefully, encourage co-operation and co-ordination in them. This apart, the essence of the common environmental policy, apart from the establishment and enforcement of pollution standards, must be an insistence on the recognition of, and due allowance for, the environmental aspects of decisions in other policy areas such as agriculture and transport, something which has indeed been visible from the early 1980s onwards. It would therefore be better to speak of the social and environmental *dimensions* of Community policies rather than a single, freestanding common policy under either heading.

Social and environmental issues in the Community therefore have much in common. The scarcity of the common resources available – for which the enormity of agricultural spending has much to answer – must necessarily reduce the Community's direct role to marginal dimensions. Where cross-frontier interaction is prominent, as in the case of pollution or the working hours of international freight drivers, the case for common action at a Community level is clear and the Commission's authority must therefore be high. In most instances, however, the national dimension usually dominates over the international; as a result, different perceptions of national interest militate against any high degree of uniformity throughout the Community.

Both social and environmental issues were embodied in the Single European Act of 1986 and are thus included in the corpus of central policies to which the member states are formally committed. It is significant, however, that the agreement to move to majority voting was specifically *not* extended to the delicate matter of the right of individuals to cross the border of another member state nor to legislation concerning the rights of employees. Wider national considerations were deemed to be involved and, in the face of these, Community interests took the inevitable second place. It is likely to remain so over much of the subject-matter of this chapter. Given the very different histories and traditions of the member countries, indeed, it is far from obvious that a single, uniform approach – for example, to the general aim of improved worker-participation in industry – is desirable, even if it were possible.

Further Reading

Collins, D., *The Operation of the European Social Fund* (London: Croom Helm, 1986).

European Commission, *The Social Policy of the European Community*, 3rd edn (Luxembourg, 1983).

European Commission, *The European Community and the Environment*, 3rd edn (Luxembourg, 1987).

Johnson, S. P., *The Pollution Control Policy of the European Communities*, 2nd edn (London: Graham & Trotman, 1983).

Park, C. C. (ed.), *Environmental Policies: an International Review* (London: Croom Helm, 1986).

Shanks, M., *European Social Policy: Today and Tomorrow* (Oxford: Pergamon Press, 1977).

Taylor, D. *et al.*, 'EC environmental policy and the control of water pollution', *Journal of Common Market Studies*, Vol. xxiv, No. 3, 1986.

Tax Harmonisation 20

20.1 The Role of Taxes

The fiscal policy of any government is concerned with the level and structure of its revenues and expenditures. The domestic role of fiscal policy is a complex one. In the first place it influences the allocation of resources amongst different ends: obviously it determines the share of those resources absorbed by the public and private sectors respectively, but it will also influence their allocation amongst different products within each sector, taxes (and their negative counterpart, subsidies) making some products relatively more expensive to consumers than others. Secondly, it influences the distribution of income amongst different groups of individuals or different regions within a country. Thirdly, Keynesian economists argue that the balance between government revenues and expenditures, and the manner in which the difference is financed, can exert a considerable degree of influence on the overall level of aggregate demand in the economy and thus on the levels of output, employment and prices. They therefore attribute a crucial macro-economic role to fiscal policy; by contrast, economists in the monetarist tradition would deny that it has any such role.

These are the domestic aspects of fiscal policy, and therefore of the taxes which play a key role in such policy. There are two respects, however, in which the level of taxes within any member country of the European Community can have important consequences for the Community as a whole. On the one hand, domestic taxes can have an effect on international trade in a manner largely (but not wholly) analogous to that of tariffs – which are, after all, only one particular form of taxes. Secondly, since the Community has to operate a general budget with the aid of revenues paid over from member states, the taxation policy of a member country could have, in certain circumstances, financial consequences for the Community as a whole. This budgetary aspect of taxation is left over for discussion in the following chapter.

At the outset of the Community the level and structure of taxation systems differed widely amongst its member countries. All had some form of direct taxation of personal or corporate incomes; the relative importance attached to such taxation, and the efficiency of its enforcement, were naturally greater in some countries than in others. Equally, all relied extensively on taxes on expenditure – the so-called 'indirect' taxes – but the form of these taxes also differed sharply within the Community. Three broad categories of indirect tax systems could be distinguished, although the permutations and combinations of them approached infinity. First, countries such as Germany and the Netherlands relied primarily on a turnover tax under which a standard rate of tax was levied on more or less all commercial transactions whenever and wherever they occurred. On the other hand, France operated a value-added taxation system. Under this a standard rate of tax was also levied at every point of sale, but the crucial difference between it and the turnover tax was that a productive enterprise was permitted to claim a refund of any tax paid on its own purchases. This effectively restricted the incidence of the tax to the *value added* by the enterprise itself in the course of its operations, rather than being applied to the gross sales value of every transaction. Finally, the United Kingdom operated a Purchase Tax system under which a relatively high rate of tax was applied to a restricted range of (allegedly) luxury goods, but only at the point of final sale. All countries in addition relied heavily for revenue on a small number of excise duties levied on the traditional revenue-raisers, alcohol, tobacco and petroleum products.

Virtually the only taxes which did not present formidable difficulties of principle, therefore, were the import duties inherent in the Common External Tariff. These were by definition to be the same for any product in every member country once the transitional period had been completed. Further, they necessarily became part of the Community's budget revenue, not that of individual member countries because the point of final sale of the products concerned could be anywhere within the Community, whatever their country of entry. As will be seen, this certainly gave rise to questions of equity in the Community budget but at least a common policy for the taxes themselves was automatically achieved. For all other taxes, however, and especially those levied on expenditure rather than incomes, the wide variations in national practice seemed inherently incompatible with the creation of a single market encompassing the Community as a whole.

20.2 The Road to the VAT

Part Three of the Treaty of Rome was concerned with the policies to be adopted by the Community and the second chapter in this was devoted to fiscal provisions. In particular, Article 99 provided that the Commission should consider how the varying laws within member states concerning turnover taxes, excise duties and other forms of indirect taxation could be harmonised in the interest of the Common Market. It went on to add – inevitably but ominously – that the Council would act on the Commission's proposals by means of a unanimous vote. This requirement was to result in an argument which took 15 years to be finally resolved.

With commendable expedition, the Commission set up an expert committee of 16 academic authorities in such matters, the chairman being Professor Fritz Neumark of Frankfurt University. The report of this committee, inevitably known as the Neumark Report, was presented in 1962 and was to form the basis for the policy subsequently pursued. The Committee took the view that, given the relative immobility of labour, variations in personal income taxes within the Community were unlikely to have any significant effect on the allocation of resources and therefore on the Common Market. Such taxes, it concluded, could therefore sensibly be left in the hands of national governments. Direct taxes on companies, however, could scarcely be assumed to be totally neutral so far as location was concerned; corporate head offices are in fact notoriously mobile in the face of pecuniary inducements and penalties. As will be seen later in this chapter, corporation taxes were to prove a very delicate and difficult area of operation. Even so, they seemed to the Committee to be a matter of relatively small importance at this stage.

Expenditure taxes, however, were another matter altogether. In the view of the Committee, they had a direct influence on product prices and thus on resource allocation; in effect they were a kind of tariff and therefore, like the common external tariff itself, needed to be harmonised across the member countries. As already noted, the analogy between expenditure taxes and a tariff is not entirely exact. Tariffs within the Community could be made neutral by the simple expedient of setting them all at zero. The complete abolition of all expenditure taxes, however, was scarcely feasible, and the fact that the tax on any particular product is the same in all member countries by no means implies that its effect on resource allocation is therefore neutralised. The extent to which a tax can be passed on to the purchaser rather than absorbed into the costs of the producer depends critically on the relative elasticities of the demand for and supply of that product. (The proof of this proposition may be found in the appendix to Chapter 9.) Since these elasticities inevitably differ in the different member countries, a single rate of tax by no means implies that all producers and consumers are affected equally. Nevertheless the committee concluded that if a common market was to exist, all members of the Community needed to adopt a single type of expenditure tax, using a common definition of the basis on which the tax was to be calculated and, ideally, levying the same rate of tax on any given product.

The turnover tax was the commonest form then in use and in many respects is the easiest to administer. Nevertheless the Committee expressed a preference for the Value Added Tax for two main reasons. First, expenditure taxes are invariably levied by the government of the country in which they are sold. If tax rates differ between countries (as they obviously do) it is standard practice for any such tax paid on goods which are subsequently exported to be refunded by the revenue authorities at the time of exportation. If this were not done the goods concerned would effectively be taxed twice – once in the country of manufacture and then again in the country of sale – so making their export uncompetitive. It is therefore important that the amount of tax which has been levied on goods prior to their export should be known accurately; to refund too little tax would put the exporter at an unfair disadvantage, while to refund too much would be a form of export subsidy, a practice to which competing producers in the receiving country would naturally take strong objection.

Since a turnover tax, by definition, is levied at every stage of production, the business of calculating how much tax has been levied on the final product is extremely complicated. The simple example of Table 20.1 will illustrate this. In column (2) it is assumed that three firms are involved in different stages of the product concerned. Firm A, supplying the basic materials, pays the standard turnover tax of 0.855 per cent of the value of its sales to Firm B. The latter processes the materials further and then sells the semi-finished product to Firm C, once again paying a tax of 0.855 per cent on the transaction. Firm C then completes the production process, selling it after payment of the tax at a final price of 3000. The total tax paid is thus 500.

Now suppose that exactly the same productive processes are carried out but that Firms B and C have amalgamated into one. The outcome is shown in column (3). The sale by B to C is now eliminated because the semi-finished products are simply transferred from one section of a single firm to another. The outcome is that although the product is finally sold at the same price as before, 3000, the total tax paid has fallen from 500 to 322. In order to establish how much tax has been paid, in other words, a record of every single transaction leading up to the final product would need to be presented and scrutinised – a very formidable administrative burden indeed.

Columns (4) and (5) of Table 20.1 demonstrate how this problem is avoided by a Value Added Tax system. Here a tax of 20 per cent is levied on every transaction but the crucial difference is that each firm is able to claim a refund of any VAT paid on its purchases from other firms. Effectively, therefore, the tax is only paid in reality at the very last stage of the sale of the final product. (The tax also has the advantage of being, in principle, self-policing; in order to reclaim tax each purchaser will insist on documentary evidence of the tax paid on inputs into the production process.) In column (4), in which B and C operate as separate firms the final selling price is 3000 and the total tax paid is 500, as in column (2). If B and C now amalgamate, as in column (5), the amount of tax payable is unaffected because the total value added in the whole production chain is unchanged by the merger. To calculate the tax refund due on exports, therefore, is a very simple matter. It is the difference between the final price of the product and that price divided by (in this example where VAT is 20 per cent) 1.20.

Table 20.1
Turnover Tax vs. Value Added Tax

	Turnover tax of 0.855%		Value-added tax of 20%	
	B & C Separate firms	B & C Integrated firm	B & C Separate firms	B & C Integrated firm
(1)	(2)	(3)	(4)	(5)
Firm A:				
Value added	1 000	1 000	1 000	1 000
Tax paid	86	86	200	200
Selling price	1 086	1 086	1 200	1 200
Firm B:				
Bought from A	1 086	1 086	1 200	1 200
Less tax refund	—	—	− 200	− 200
Value added	1 000	1 000	1 000	1 000
	2 086		2 000	
Tax paid	178		400	
Sold to C	2 264		2 400	
Firm C:				
Bought from B	2 264		2 400	
Less tax refund	—		− 400	
Value added	500	500	500	500
	2 764	2 586	2 500	2 500
Excess profit	—	178	—	—
Tax paid	236	236	500	500
Final price	3 000	3 000	3 000	3 000
Total tax paid	500	322	500	500

This simple example illustrates the second defect which the Neumark Committee identified in the turnover tax. In column (3) of Table 20.1 the amalgamation of the two firms B and C raised their joint profits by 178, on the assumption that the final price of the product remained at 3000. This additional profit was, of course, equal to the government's loss of tax revenue. In other words, a turnover tax provides a strong incentive to firms to amalgamate, whether that be justified on grounds of economic efficiency or not, with a corresponding increase in the degree of monopoly existing in the system. It also tends to discourage imports, since firms will obtain a tax advantage in producing their own components rather than importing them, even if this results in a productive process which is technically less efficient. As column (5) demonstrates, a VAT system provides no financial incentive to such artificial distortions of the productive process.

Despite marked reluctance on the part of the Netherlands and Italy, therefore, in 1967 the principle that the Community should adopt VAT as its standard form of expenditure tax was finally accepted.

Agreement on a principle, however, is one thing: agreement on its detailed application is quite another. Few member countries applied expenditure taxes to every single transaction; agreement had therefore to be reached on the scope of the tax base – that is, on which goods and services were to be subject to the tax and which were not. It was 15 years before the famous Sixth Directive covering these structural matters was finally agreed. Broadly, the common VAT base in all member countries includes all types of consumer expenditure (but not capital goods) with the important exceptions of financial and legal services (for which tax assessment is in practice very difficult) and 'merit goods' such as health and education. Exports are exempt but the tax is levied on all imports of qualifying products. There is also broad agreement concerning the rules governing the exemption of certain categories of producer, particularly small-scale traders for whom the administrative costs – to both the tax authorities and the taxpayers – of applying VAT would be excessively high in relation to the revenues involved.

The issue of the *rate* of VAT to be levied was one which defied agreement. In the view of the Neumark Committee the ideal was undoubtedly a single uniform rate for any specific category of product throughout the Community. With such a common rate, VAT could be collected in the country in which the goods originated. Rebates on exports and the collection of VAT on imports would be unnecessary, since all products would carry the same rate of tax wherever sold in the Community. The need for frontier controls would disappear; a genuine single market would exist in the sense that a product would carry precisely the same indirect tax regardless of the member country in which it was finally sold.

As Table 20.2 shows, the Community is very far from this happy ideal. In 1988, with the exception of Denmark, every member country was operating more than one rate of VAT, distinguishing between categories of expenditure which it deemed to be of greater or lesser importance in social welfare. The low rates varied from zero on food, fuel and children's clothing in the United Kingdom (i.e. no VAT is levied on the sale of these products – accounting for around 30 per cent of consumers' expenditure – but VAT payments on inputs to their production are refunded) to 10 per cent in Ireland. The high rates varied from 25 per cent in Belgium to 38 per cent in Italy. Given this, it is somewhat unrealistic to speak of a single market for any given product. Furthermore, the need to ensure that VAT refunds and liabilities are accurately calculated and duly paid results in formidable documentation requirements as goods pass

Table 20.2
VAT Rates in the European Community, January 1988 (%)

(1)	Reduced rates (2)	Standard rates (3)	Higher rates (4)
Belgium	1, 6, 17	19	25, 33
Denmark	—	22	—
France	2.1, 4, 5.5, 7	18.6	33.3
Germany	7	14	—
Greece	3, 6	18	36
Ireland	2.2, 10	25	—
Italy	2, 9	18	38
Luxembourg	3, 6	12	—
Netherlands	6	20	—
Portugal	8	16	30
Spain	6	12	33
United Kingdom	0	15	—
Proposed EC rate	4 to 9	14 to 20	—

SOURCE   Based on data given in *IMF Survey*, 14 November 1988, p. 358.

through border controls. In 1986 it was reported that a driver carrying a load from the United Kingdom to Italy – i.e. from one part of the theoretical single market to another – could require as many as 47 different documents in order to thread his way across the various frontiers.

The Single European Act of 1986 inevitably called for serious action on this front in order to achieve a genuine single market by 1992. So long as VAT rates differed between the member countries, the abolition of customs barriers – and therefore of national frontiers themselves – would seem to be impossible. Prominent amongst the Commission's shopping list of proposals for 1992 was therefore one calling for much greater uniformity in tax rates. Evidence from the United States indicates that differences of less than 5 per cent in indirect taxes in contiguous states have no significant impact on trade flows. Hence the Commission proposed in 1987 that by 1992 the existing array of VAT rates in the Community should be replaced by a system in which each country would have one 'standard' rate and one reduced rate applicable to 'items of basic necessity', each of these rates to lie within a range of about 5 percentage points. The rates proposed by the Commission are shown in Table 20.2. Any revenue losses arising from the abolition of the VAT levy on imports, it suggested, could be prevented by a system under which VAT payments could be based on documentation relating to initial sales rather than the crossing of national borders. Thus the VAT which would previously have been levied at the frontier on imports would instead be paid over by the government of the exporting country; similarly, VAT which would previously have been refunded to exporters would be handed over instead to the government of the importing country. The mechanism assumed a degree of honesty amongst member governments which some regarded as slightly unrealistic.

In the event, stubborn opposition from finance ministers in Brussels at the end of 1988 forced the Commission to concede defeat. To accommodate the British government's electoral commitment to retaining a zero VAT rate on food and children's clothing, in May 1989 the Commission proposed that the lower-rate band of 4–9 per cent should be adjusted to one of 0 to 9 per cent. To meet the objections of high-rate countries such as Denmark, the Commission suggested that the standard-rate proposal should be changed to one in which there would be a minimum of 15 per cent but no ceiling. Even this very attenuated version of harmonisation could not be agreed by the Ministers. There is clearly something to be said for setting a *minimum* VAT rate on specified, tradeable products in order to prevent competitive (and therefore counter-productive) rate-cutting by member states. It is not obvious, however, why the *maximum* tax rates should not be left to national choice – and the forces of international competition.

20.3 The Excise Men

For revenue purposes governments have traditionally relied heavily on excise duties on a small range of products which are generally regarded as being luxury products – 'sumptuary' goods was the old term. They are also products distinguished by a very low price-elasticity of demand, a prime qualification for ensuring that high tax rates on a product do not have the counter-productive effect (from the tax revenue point of view) of sharply diminishing the quantity of it which consumers are willing to purchase. Pre-eminent amongst these revenue favourites are alcohol, tobacco and petroleum in all their different manifestations, and a Directive approved by the Council in 1972 ruled that attempts to harmonise excise duties in the Community would in fact be confined to these three.

Although the primary purpose of such taxes is to raise revenue, rather than to influence resource allocation, the fact is that they vary greatly both in amount and in structure in different member countries, and these differences do indeed lead to distortions in competition. Considering alcohol first, in all member countries the objective of raising revenue is combined with the secondary objective of protecting domestic producers against competition from foreign suppliers. Thus the tax tends to bear more heavily on some forms of alcohol than on others. In the United Kingdom, for example, the excise duty on wine (which it does not produce) was roughly five times, in relation to alcoholic content, that on beer (which it does) until a ruling by the Court in 1984 forced it to commence some reduction of this differential. In Denmark a careful manipulation of specific duties, related to alcoholic content, and *ad valorem* duties, related to selling price, had the happy effect of favouring Denmark's domestic product, acquavit, at the expense of imported products. In France, excise duties bear much more heavily on whisky (which it does not produce) than on cognac (which it certainly does).

Such variations clearly had the effect of distorting competition between member countries, whether the primary object of the taxes was to raise revenue or not. In 1981 the Commission submitted a compromise proposal to the Council under which, first, all excise duties on alcoholic beverages in the Community would be standardised at a single level related to alcoholic content and, second, common rules would be established concerning the application of VAT to such products. The Council failed to agree. As may be seen from Table 20.3, wide differences of treatment continue. In the great wine producing countries of France, Italy and Spain the duty on wine remains at or close to zero, while in the northern countries of Denmark, Ireland and the United Kingdom it remains at between three and four times the Community average. The tax levied on beer is less than half the Community average in seven countries and more than double it in two.

The story with regard to tobacco has been very similar. The problem here is not so much the overall level of taxation on tobacco products – which tends to be around 70 per cent of retail price in all member countries – but rather its structure. In some countries, such as Denmark, Ireland and Britain, primary reliance is placed on a relatively heavy specific duty related to tobacco content; in others, such as France and Italy, more emphasis is laid on an *ad valorem* tax related to the price of the finished product. These differences are not entirely insignificant in the matter of resource allocation. A reliance on an *ad valorem* tax implies that the tax burden is heavier on more expensive (presumably higher quality, and usually imported) products than on the relatively low-quality products of the domestic industries. Again, a substantial variation in the relative importance of specific and *ad valorem* taxes implies that inflation will have differential effects on final products. Suppose that the cost structures of a given product in two countries, A and B, are as follows:

	A	B
1. Production costs, materials etc.	30	30
2. Specific excise duty	20	50
3. *Ad valorem* tax on 1 + 2	50	20
4. Final price	100	100

The total tax raised is the same in both countries, but A is operating a 100 per

Table 20.3
Excise Duties in the European Community, 1987 (EC Average = 100)

| Country | Wine | Beer | Petrol | Heating gas oil | Cigarettes | | Tobacco | Arithmetic average |
| | | | | | Specific | Ad valorem | | |
(1)	(2)	(3)	(4)	(5)	(6)	(7)	(8)	(9)
Belgium	57	44	77	0	10	125	67	54
Denmark	271	120	139	381	395	74	128*	215
France	5	13	109	85	5	134	118	67
Germany	34	31	75	13	138	83	82*	65
Greece	0	44	103	176	5	113	115*	79
Ireland	481	360	106	77	251	64	127	209
Italy	0	76	164	287	10	130	129	114
Luxembourg	22	22	61	0	10	121	69	44
Netherlands	57	89	100	71	133	68	102	89
Portugal	0	31	104	37	10	123	47	50
Spain	0	13	75	61	5	98	56	44
United Kingdom	266	218	80	39	221	64	123*	144
Coefficient of variation	110	88	33	102	98	28	26	40
Proposed EC rate	29	76	100	81	100	100	100	

*Arithmetic average of range.

SOURCE Based on Bos, M. and Nelson, H. 'Indirect taxation and the internal market', *Journal of Common Market Studies*, Vol. XXVII, No. 1, September 1988.

cent *ad valorem* rate and B a 25 per cent rate. If production costs now rise from 30 to 50 in each country, the final price of the product will be raised from 100 to 140 in country A but only from 100 to 125 in B.

In 1972 the Council was able to agree on a phased harmonisation of the structure of tobacco taxation. In the first stage, the specific element was to be within a range of 5 to 75 per cent of the total; a further directive in 1977 required this range to be reduced to 5–55 per cent by the end of 1981. Because agreement could not be reached on the next step, this second stage was extended for a further year. It has remained extended ever since.

So far as petroleum products are concerned the problem is somewhat less serious in the sense that the variation of tax rates between member countries is smaller than with the other excise duties. Even so it remains significant; as Table 20.3 reveals, in 1987 the duty levied on petrol varied from 40 per cent below the EEC average in Luxembourg to 60 per cent above it in Italy. Since (unlike the products previously discussed) petroleum derivatives are an important element in production costs, this variation must necessarily distort comparative costs of production. As was noted in Chapter 18, however, successive attempts by the Commission to establish a uniform EEC energy tax have met with stubborn resistance.

As part of its campaign for the creation of a Single European market in 1992, in 1987 the Commission submitted proposals for the harmonisation of these major excise duties as well as for VAT rates. (The proposals are shown in Table 20.3; essentially the Commission was proposing harmonisation at the arithmetic average of the existing rates.) But, as with the VAT proposals, the concept of a single Community rate of excise duty was flatly rejected at a meeting of finance ministers in December 1988. How successful the Commission will be in persuading the Council to accept closer harmonisation in the future must also remain to be seen; on the evidence of its experience so far it would seem unwise for the Commission to be particularly optimistic.

20.4   Direct Taxation

It has already been noted that the Neumark Committee regarded personal income tax as broadly neutral with regard to resource allocation between member states, on the ground that international labour mobility is unlikely to be high enough for its geographical distribution to be significantly affected by variations in the incidence of income tax between the member countries. As already noted, however, in principle the taxation of companies might be a different matter. Companies may – indeed, obviously do – determine the location of their head offices, and sometimes their operations, in the light of, amongst other things, different tax treatment in different countries. There has never been any serious suggestion, however, that the rate of corporation tax should be standardised throughout the Community. One reason for this is that the Treaty provides no authority for any such proposal; its references to taxation are confined entirely to indirect taxes. Another reason is itself the cause of this omission from the declared ambitions of the Treaty – the fact that there is no prospect whatever in the foreseeable future of member governments surrendering their powers of direct taxation to any supranational institution.

The structure and basis of corporate taxation nevertheless raise issues of legitimate Community concern. On the one hand, it is desirable that differences in tax systems should not artificially impede cross-boundary operations by Community enterprises. On the other hand, tax regimes should not be such as to distort the Community capital market by discriminating between profits earned by enterprises – or returns received by individual investors – in different parts of what is supposed to be a single market.

The problem is that the structure of the corporate tax system varies considerably in the different member countries, and has indeed varied through time within individual countries. Some countries, such as the United Kingdom, favour a single corporation tax (with relatively minor concessions to small companies) which is completely separate and distinct from personal income tax. Others, such as Germany, favour a split-rate system under which the rate of tax applied to profits which are distributed to shareholders differs from that applied to profits which are ploughed back into the business. Others again, like France, adopt the 'imputation' system under which corporation tax paid by a company can be offset by its shareholders against their personal income tax.

The upshot of all this is that the net rate of return on an investment can vary significantly across the Community because of the location, for tax purposes, of the investment (or the investor) rather than as the result of strictly economic considerations, thus distorting what should be a single capital market. In an attempt to reduce such distortions, in 1975 the Commission submitted a draft Directive seeking to harmonise the basis of corporation tax throughout the Community along the lines of the imputation system; this would have had the result of making the net return on an investment substantially unaffected by its location within the Community. Predictably, the draft promptly disappeared into the labyrinth of Community disagreement and was soon regarded as a lost cause even by the Commission itself.

A similar proposal was advanced by the Commission in February 1989 for a standard withholding tax of 15 per cent on income paid to non-residents of each member country on bonds, bank deposits and other savings accounts. This, it was hoped, would encourage the removal of exchange controls on capital movements by countries, such as France, which persist in retaining them for tax enforcement purposes, thus preventing the creation of a single, free market in capital throughout the Community. Predictably, the two major international financial centres in the Community – Britain and Luxembourg – expressed immediate and unqualified opposition.

Practical achievements in the field of corporate taxation have therefore been limited to useful but marginal measures seeking to reduce some of the more obvious, and more unnecessary, obstacles to a unified market which are created by corporate taxation – agreed procedures for handling the tax consequences of cross-border mergers between companies, common arrangements for the tax treatment of parent companies and their subsidiaries, more or less standard definitions of what constitutes taxable profits (and tax-allowable losses) and so on. It is a far cry from any notion of a common corporation tax policy.

20.5   A Suitable Case for Harmonisation?

After 30 years, the only substantial achievement which the Community can claim in this very important field of taxation is the adoption of an agreed form of general sales tax in the VAT. Even under this heading, however, considerable variation still exists in the tax level in different member countries, leaving the ideal of a complete abolition of national frontiers as distant as ever. In other aspects of the tax system agreement has been conspicuous by its absence to a greater degree than in most of the other policy areas to which the Community has turned its attention.

It would be easy to attribute this unimpressive record to the undoubted hostility on the part of national governments towards any reduction of their sovereign powers. Yet it must be proper to consider an alternative explanation – that it is due to the inherently limited scope for common policies in this area. As remarked at the outset, taxation is a complex and multi-purpose component of all national economic armouries. In some respects the logic of a common market does indeed point to uniformity amongst its members: in so far as differences in rates of indirect taxation lead to artificial differences of product prices and to complex border formalities, they must be inconsistent with the concept of a genuine single market. Again, in so far as the tax system is used as the basis of national contributions to the Community budget, uniformity of structure is in principle desirable – although, as the following chapter will show, such uniformity by no means guarantees equity in the distribution of the budgetary burden.

Even so, the internal role of taxation in national economies must necessarily dominate over its international consequences. Taxes play a major role in influencing important components of the social welfare function of every member country, whatever its political and social philosophy – the division of the national income between private and public uses, between current expenditure and provision for the future, between the consumption of goods which are regarded as socially desirable and those which are not, between one income or social class and another. The delicate task of maximising that social welfare function is the primary responsibility of government; the adoption of identical types and levels of tax in every member country would be compatible with that responsibility only if social welfare functions were also identical in all those countries – a manifest impossibility.

In principle the solution of a problem which implies fiscal uniformity for some (Community) purposes but fiscal diversity for other (national) purposes would be solved by allocating some taxes exclusively to the former and reserving the remainder for the latter. If the Community were being constructed on, so to speak, a greenfield site such a solution would be feasible. But it is not; the only taxes exclusively reserved for Community purposes are those levied on imports – totalling in 1986 about 0.25 per cent of the Community's GDP. For the rest, any Community power over taxes has to wrested from the hands of twelve diverse, old-established sovereign states whose social and economic priorities conflict sharply not merely with those in other states but continuously within themselves.

If the Commission's 1987 proposals on indirect taxes had been accepted, for example, the government of Denmark would have lost nearly 5 per cent of its total tax revenues, Luxembourg's considerable income from tourists attracted by the lowest tax rates in Europe would have been threatened, and the Italian government would have faced the considerable wrath of vast battalions of wine-growers whose product would be taxed for the first time. These are not consequences to be contemplated lightly by any democratic politician. Are they justified? If uniformity is an aim in itself, then the goal of fiscal uniformity must continue to be laboriously pursued. If, on the other hand, the aim is the maximisation of social welfare it is not obvious that such uniformity, even if feasible – which, in the light of experience, must be very questionable – would necessarily be desirable.

Further Reading

Bos, M. and Nelson, H., 'Indirect taxation and the internal market', *Journal of Common Market Studies*, Vol. xxvii, No. 1, September 1988.

Guien, P. and Bonnet, C., 'Completion of the internal market and indirect taxation', *Journal of Common Market Studies*, Vol. xxv, No. 3, March 1987.

Puchala, D., 'Worm cans and worth taxes: fiscal harmonisation and the European policy process', in Wallace, H., *et al.*, *Policy Making in the European Community*, 2nd edn (Chichester: John Wiley & Sons, 1983).

Robson, P., *The Economics of International Integration*, 2nd edn (London: Allen & Unwin, 1984).

Part IV
Macroeconomic policies

The Community Budget 21

21.1 The Budget Procedure

For reasons explained earlier, it is inherent in any customs union that some central budgetary system must exist. A common external tariff implies that import duties collected in any member country must be treated as revenues of the union as a whole and some mechanism must therefore exist for collecting and disposing of those revenues. This apart, provision had to be made in the case of the Community for the costs of central administration – the Commission, Parliament, Court and so on – and for those of any common policies requiring expenditures at a Community level.

Part Five, Title II of the Treaty of Rome therefore made detailed provisions for the preparation and administration of a Community budget; in the light of subsequent events the provisions proved to be extraordinarily ingenuous in several major respects. The first article provided that the budget should be in balance as to revenues and expenditures – one of the few Treaty provisions which have remained substantially intact.

It would be wrong to conclude from this, however, that the Community undertakes no borrowing and lending activities. At the time of the Treaty of Rome the ECSC (then a separate organisation) had and exercised powers to borrow funds on the open market in order to re-lend the funds concerned to finance investment projects in member countries, and these powers remained after the amalgamation of the Communities in 1967. By end-1986 total lending by the ECSC had in fact amounted to nearly ECU 12 bn. Second, under the Euratom Treaty loans amounting by end-1986 to some ECU 2.4 bn had been made to member countries, mainly in connection with the construction of nuclear power stations. Thirdly, in 1975 the Community itself took powers to indulge in borrowing to assist member countries with balance-of-payments problems (especially those arising from the oil crisis of the previous year); these were supplemented in 1978 by a so-called 'New Community Instrument' – more generally known as the Ortoli facility in honour of its inventor – by which funds could be lent to member countries to finance investments designed to assist their 'economic convergence' in the Community. Finally, the European Investment Bank (EIB) was created by Articles 129–130 of the Treaty in order to contribute to the 'balanced and smooth development of the Common Market' on a non-profit-making (i.e. non-loss-making) basis; by the end of 1986 the EIB had borrowed on the open capital market, and re-lent, somewhat over ECU 50 bn.

None of these lending operations, however, breach the principle of a balanced budget for ordinary Community activities. They all relate essentially to capital transactions rather than day-to-day expenditures, and all assume that the transactions will be self-financing in the sense that the loans will be serviced and ultimately repaid. Even so, in practice the Community can never achieve precise equality between its revenues and expenditures in any one year and the Treaty therefore permitted balances to be carried over at the end of each year, although only until the end of the following year. In fact, during 1971–86 the annual surpluses or deficits in the Community's general budget have averaged less than 2 per cent of total expenditure, although there have been occasions – in 1985, for example – when resort has been necessary to the elegant concept of 'non-repayable advances' from member governments in order to balance the books for the year.

The Treaty provided that initially the revenues for the budget would be contributed by member governments on a scale broadly related to their capacity to pay. Article 201, however, charged the Commission with the task of studying the ways in which these financial contributions would be replaced in due course by 'other resources of the Community itself'. The long saga which followed as a result of this innocent-sounding direction will be discussed in a later section of this chapter. On the expenditure side, the Treaty laid down a fairly detailed procedure. By 30 September in each year the Commission was required to assemble estimates of expenditures by the various institutions during the following calendar year and to submit its draft expenditure budget to the Council of Ministers. Within the following month, and acting on a qualified majority, the Council was to approve the draft budget (which would not necessarily be identical with that submitted by the Commission, of course) and send it to the Parliament. The Parliament in turn was given a month in which to consider the draft budget and to pass its comments back to the Council. The Council, again acting on a qualified majority, would then determine the final budget.

It will be observed that this procedure, commencing not later than 30 September, could leave the final stage as late as December, which was cutting things rather fine for a budget which was due to come into operation on 1 January. Provision was therefore made to cover the possibility that agreement might not be reached in time; if a final budget was not agreed by the beginning of the year concerned, the Commission was to act on the basis that spending in each month must be limited to one-twelfth of the total budget for the previous year.

In two respects the budget so determined is different in form from those typical of national governments. In the first place, because several different currencies are involved in both expenditures and revenues it has always been necessary for the Commission to translate all the budgetary items into a single common unit. Thus from the outset the budget has been constructed in terms of a special Community accounting unit. Until 1977 the unit employed (the Unit of Account, UA) was defined as being the equivalent of 0.8887 grams of fine gold – the official gold content of the US dollar until 1972. Between 1978 and 1980 the budget was drawn up in European Units of Account, EUA, a weighted average of all the Community currencies. Since 1980 the budget has been drawn up in European Currency Units (ECUs), a currency unit discussed at some length in Chapter 23. Since the market rates of exchange between the currencies of the member countries and this common unit vary from day to day the Commission has to draw up its forecasts for the following year on an assumed rate of exchange – that prevailing on 1 February of the year in which the estimates are being prepared. As a result there are always complicated adjustments to be made subsequently to national receipts and payments as the actual exchange rates prevailing at the time when transactions occur differ from this assumed rate.

The second peculiarity of the Community budget is that it is actually drawn up on two bases – one provides appropriations for *payments* in the course of the year while the other provides appropriations for *commitments* entered into in that year. This duality also was to give a great deal of trouble. If the budget makes commitments for future years (for example, approving expenditure proposals for the European Social Fund which do not actually take place until subsequent years) an accumulation of such inherited commitments may pose a threat that the appropriations for *payment* in that year will be insufficient to meet total expenditure requirements.

Provision was of course made for the proper use of budgetary funds; as noted in Chapter 4, a committee of auditors (subsequently known as the Court of Auditors) was to be comprised of persons 'of indisputable independence' to scrutinise the accounts at the end of each financial year.

It has to be noted that the budgetary procedure outlined here differed from that common in national governments in two fundamental respects. First, the Parliament had virtually no effective role. The Council of Ministers was required to 'discuss' any amendments suggested by the Parliament; as was noted in an earlier chapter, however, the Council, having considered the representations made by the Parliament, was not required to pay the slightest attention to them in finalising the budget. For twelve years the final budget was always virtually identical with the Council's first draft; the Council was the sole budgetary authority.

Secondly, the budget thus being processed was exclusively concerned with expenditures and left entirely open the question of the raising of revenues to finance them. Neither the Parliament nor the Commission had any powers whatever in regard to revenue. In practice, once the expenditure total had been determined the contributions required from member governments was automatically determined. This separation of decisions concerning expenditure from those concerning their finance was to prove a source of continuous and acrimonious debate.

21.2   Parliamentary Budgetary Powers

The virtually complete absence of Parliamentary powers in the budgetary process was scarcely tenable once the prospect of a directly-elected Parliament was approaching and also after the decision in 1969 (discussed later in this chapter) to move to a system of Community 'own resources' rather than one of fixed national contributions. Hence the Luxembourg Treaty of April 1970, embodying this latter decision, provided for the creation of real, if initially marginal, Parliamentary powers; for the first time the Parliament was formally declared to be part of the Community's Budgetary authority. For an interim period, 1971–4, the powers given to the Parliament were vestigial. Any modifications it proposed, provided they did not involve an increase in total expenditure, would stand unless rejected by a qualified majority of the Council of Ministers. Any such modifications which did involve an increase in total expenditure, on the other hand, would automatically be lost unless positively approved by a qualified majority of the Council.

For the 1975 budget onwards, however, the increase in parliamentary powers was a little more substantial. Total expenditures were henceforth to be divided into 'compulsory' and 'non-compulsory' categories, the former being defined as expenditures which arose directly from Treaty obligations. This naturally provided scope for considerable argument as to the category appropriate for any particular expenditure and a Conciliation Committee was subsequently created to sort out such disagreements at the very outset of the budgetary process. The basic principle of the existence of third-party rights, however, has now been generally established: if a third party has a right to payment by the Community, whether by virtue of the treaties or secondary legislation derived from them, then the expenditure must be treated as 'compulsory'.

The Parliament was empowered to amend non-compulsory expenditures and, if it thought proper – which it usually does – to increase the total of such expenditures by up to one-half of the maximum rate of increase specified by the Council for total non-compulsory expenditure in that fiscal year. (This matter is explained in the next section.) If such amendments were not acceptable to the Council they could be referred back to the Parliament for a second reading, but the Parliament could then merely confirm them. On such items of expenditure then, and within the prescribed limits, the Parliament was to have the last word.

This was regarded at first as a very minor concession: in 1974, the year before the new system came into operation, the Commission estimated that only 13.9 per cent of the budgetary expenditure in that year could be classified as 'non-compulsory'; the scope for Parliamentary intervention therefore seemed very small. The subsequent growth of the 'structural' funds – the Social and Regional funds – plus demonstrations of Parliamentary determination in the definitional process have made quite a difference: in the 1987 budget some 26 per cent of the appropriations were deemed to be concerned with 'non-compulsory' items.

A further boost to Parliamentary power in the process was provided by the Budgetary Powers Treaty signed in Brussels in 1975, which from 1977 onwards transferred the authority for declaring that a budget had been finally approved from the President of the Council of Ministers to the President of the Parliament; Parliament thus acquired the power to reject the entire Budget outright at its second reading and to demand that the entire budgetary process be recommenced. This it was hardly expected to do, since the Parliament was usually seeking to increase Community expenditure on 'non-compulsory' items rather than to prevent them altogether.

Somewhat to the consternation of the Council of Ministers, however, the first directly-elected Parliament in 1979 promptly proceeded to flex its muscles by rejecting the budget proposed for 1980. It has in fact used the same power on several occasions since for its considerable nuisance value, usually forcing the Council to make small but significant concessions in order to avoid the inconvenience of requiring the Community to rely on the one-twelfth rule for a protracted period. As a result a conciliation procedure has been built into the budgetary process; the Council customarily discusses the budget's proposals with a Parliamentary delegation before its first and second readings and often on a third occasion before the Parliamentary second reading is completed. Even so there have been occasions when the President of the Parliament has declared that a budget has been approved when members of the Council have declared equally firmly that it has not, a disagreement requiring the intervention of the Court of Justice for its resolution.

The substantive effectiveness of the Parliament in the arcane budgetary processes of the Community – as opposed to its formal legal powers – is a matter on which opinions differ. The Parliament's powers are certainly not trivial. But one inescapable fact of reality must remain: history demonstrates that power ultimately resides not with those empowered to spend public funds but with those who have the right to extract them from the taxpayer. That is a right which the European Parliament is unlikely to possess for a very long time to come.

21.3 The Control of Expenditure

The pattern of the Community's budgetary expenditures since its inception may be seen from Table 21.1. For the first decade little real problem existed. Total expenditure was very modest in relation to the total national income of the member states – less than 0.1 per cent of community GDP, in fact. Moreover, it was reasonably spread, with roughly a quarter going to each of the four major expenditure headings. The introduction of the CAP guaranteed price system in 1967–8 transformed the situation. Not only did total expenditure rise dramatically; the great bulk of budgetary expenditure was being absorbed by the CAP, so severely constraining the development of other policies.

The agreement in 1969 to move to a system of 'own resources' and therefore to grant budgetary powers to the Parliament required some mechanism for ensuring that the enthusiasm of elected politicians for spending public funds was contained within some limit. The Luxembourg Treaty of 1970 therefore provided that there should be some formal limit to annual increases in the non-compulsory expenditures over which Parliament was to be given real, if limited, power. From 1975 onwards the Commission was to calculate the maximum rate of increase permitted in these non-compulsory expenditures in any one year. For any budgetary year N this was defined to be the arithmetic average of (a) the rate of increase in real Community GNP in year $N-2$, (b) the increase in the national budgetary expenditures of member governments in year $N-2$, and (c) the change in the general price level (measured by the GNP price deflator) in year $N-2$. In practice this means an average of the change in the current value of GNP and of the change in national budgets. Thus, if in 1990 national budgetary expenditures had risen 12 per cent and the Community GNP (in current prices) had risen 6 per cent, the limit for non-compulsory expenditures in 1992 would be 109 per cent of the corresponding expenditures in 1991. Over the decade 1975–84 the average maximum rate of increase, so calculated, was 13.6 per cent.

By Community standards this seemed a relatively simple and foolproof method of retaining control over at least part of Community expenditure. In practice Community procedures are never simple. In the first place, the effective rate of increase in non-compulsory expenditures could easily (and legally) exceed this theoretical maximum. If the maximum rate of increase for a given year were defined as, say, 8 per cent and the Council proposed a budget in which non-compulsory expenditures were raised by 6 per cent, the Parliament could then exercise its right to further increase such expenditures by one-half of the maximum rate, i.e. 4 per cent; the final budget could therefore show an increase of 10 per cent in non-compulsory expenditures. Even more potent was an escape clause written into the Luxembourg Treaty whereby some other rate of increase could be agreed between Council and Parliament 'where the activities of the Communities so require'. Needless to say, since 1975 it has been the rule, rather than the exception, for this escape clause to be invoked.

Table 21.1
The General Budget of the European Community, 1958–88 (Appropriations for Payments: Annual Averages – ECU m at 1986 Prices)

(1)	EEC 6 1958–67 (2)	EEC 6 1968–70 (3)	EEC 6 1971–2 (4)	EEC 9 1973–6 (5)	EEC 9 1977–80 (6)	EEC 10 1981–5 (7)	EEC 12 1986–8 (8)
Expenditure							
1. Administration	215	465	595	966	1 280	1 342	1 698
2. Agriculture	238	9 066	8 216	12 138	17 876	19 179	24 836
3. Fishing	—	—	—	—	17	72	213
4. Regional policy	—	—	—	227	998	2 664	2 708
5. Social policy	39	126	269	470	888	1 527	2 639
6. Research & energy	303	297	269	244	381	1 012	915
7. Developing countries	284	553	679	517	635	1 128	1 014
8. Reimbursements etc.*	—	—	581	995	1 534	1 324	2 792
Total expenditure	1 079	10 505	10 608	15 557	23 608	28 248	36 815
Revenue							
9. Agricultural levies	—	—	2 335	1 512	3 228	1 595	1 330
10. Sugar levies	—	—	551	273	723	1 033	1 228
11. Customs duties	—	—	2 918	8 348	8 904	8 789	8 456
12. Value-added tax	—	—	—	—	4 953	15 283	22 588
13. GNP-based own resources	—	—	—	—	—	—	1 870
14. Financial contributions	1 079	10 505	4 210	6 356	5 193	251	202
15. Miscellaneous†	—	—	186	453	456	1 900	367
Total revenue	1 079	10 505	10 201	16 943	23 457	28 850	36 041
16. Deficit	—	—	407	−1 386	152	−602	774
Total	1 079	10 505	10 608	15 557	23 608	28 248	36 815

*Mainly reimbursement of tax-collection costs but also includes refunds to the UK and other items.
†Balances carried over from earlier years but also other revenue sources such as staff taxation.

SOURCE For 1958–79, based on D. Strasser, *The Finances of Europe* (Brussels: European Perspectives Press, 1981), Annexes 9–11; for 1980 onwards, based on data given in *Eurostat Review*, various.

By the early 1980s, with the limit to its budgetary revenues rapidly being approached, the Community faced the reality that if matters were left as they were the continuous rise in agricultural spending would not merely prevent the development of other policies but would positively squeeze out what progress had been made in them. The essential weakness in the system was only too obvious. The bulk of the Community's resources were being pre-empted by annual decisions concerning the guaranteed prices for agricultural products over the ensuing year, decisions taken by meetings of agricultural ministers who bore no responsibility for finding the resources to implement them. (In 1988 the Italian Finance Minister, Guilio Andreotti, was heard to lament: 'I sit here talking all day about soya beans and I don't even know what the wretched things look like.') Control over expenditure was further eroded by the habit of escaping revenue limits in any one year by voting extra appropriations for commitments rather than payments in the current year, thus accumulating inescapable liabilities for some future year. During the six years 1980–85 the total voted for commitments exceeded the total voted for payments by 11.6 per cent.

An attempt to come to terms with this problem occurred at the Fontainebleau summit of 1984 where it was agreed, in particular, that net agricultural spending should not grow more rapidly than the total of the Community's own resources. Expenditure on non-compulsory items was not to increase in any year by more than the permitted maximum rate of increase in total expenditure for that year. Good intentions, however, are no guarantee of results. As may be seen from Table 21.1, in 1986 net agricultural spending (item 2 minus items 9 and 10) amounted to 65.7 per cent of other own resources (items 11 to 14), compared with 63.1 per cent in 1981–5.

A further attempt to enforce control over total budgetary expenditure was therefore made at the Brussels summit in February 1988. It was agreed that, in future, the total appropriated for payments on all items other than the European Development Fund (discussed in Chapter 25) should not exceed 1.2 per cent of the Community's GNP in the preceding year while appropriations for commitments should not exceed 1.3 per cent of Community GNP. (By a happy coincidence, increases proposed by the Parliament in its first reading of the 1988 budget brought total budgetary expenditure to exactly 1.3 per cent of the Community's GNP.) This would in fact permit a significant increase in the Community's total budget, thus allowing for the agreed doubling in expenditure on the 'structural' funds – the Regional and Social funds and the guidance section of the FEOGA – over the period 1988–93. Within this total, however, the permissible annual rate of increase in expenditure by the guarantee section of the FEOGA was to be constrained to 74 per cent of the growth of Community GDP. If these latest decisions prove effective, and assuming a rate of increase in Community GDP of 2.5 per cent per annum, the result would be that by 1991 the total Community budget will have increased by over 50 per cent in comparison with 1986 but the share of it taken by the agricultural price support system will have fallen to a little less than 50 per cent.

The world can only await events – inevitably with some scepticism – but it has to be recorded that there have been some early indications of success. In the agreed version of the 1989 budget, total expenditure was planned to be only 2.4 per cent higher than in 1988, compared with increases (in 1987) in the Community's GNP of 2.8 per cent in real terms and 5.6 per cent in money terms. Even more remarkable (thanks to the favourable developments in the world food situation referred to in Chapter 15), the share of agricultural spending in the total was reduced to less than 60 per cent. Long experience reveals only too clearly that in Community affairs one swallow emphatically does not make a summer: but at least the bird appeared to be flying in the right direction.

21.4 Collecting the Revenues

As was noted earlier, the Treaty envisaged that in its initial stages the Community's expenditures would be financed by means of national contributions calculated on a scale corresponding roughly to the capacity of each member country to pay. In reality the contribution scales were somewhat more complicated than might appear. In the first place, a separate scale of contributions was provided for the European Social Fund. Secondly, the Euratom Treaty provided for a slightly different scale of contributions in which, as with the Social Fund, the relative burden laid on Italy was much lower than in the general budget. Thirdly, in the early years of the FEOGA national contributions were partly modified according to the net imports of each member state from non-member countries. Finally, the scales of contributions to the European Development Fund (see Chapter 25) were also modified so as to reduce the proportionate contribution by Italy. In its initial stages, therefore, the Community operated on revenue contributions determined largely by political considerations.

The Treaty had envisaged that this system of financing should be replaced by a system of 'own resources' when the Common External Tariff had been finally established. This was easier said than done; initial proposals by the Commission in 1966 had been partly responsible for the famous 'empty chair' policy by France. By the end of 1969, however, the Council of Ministers had agreed that a system of 'own resources' – the direct transfer of specified tax revenues from national governments to the Community – should be brought into effect with effect from 1 January 1971. This agreement was embodied in the Treaty of Luxembourg signed on 21 April 1970.

The switch could scarcely be done overnight. Hence it was agreed that in 1971 all levies on agricultural imports from outside the Community, together with 50 per cent of any customs duties on other imports – less 10 per cent to cover national collection costs – would become Community property. (Because the ECSC is financed by a levy on the production of coal and steel, prior to 1989 import duties on such products were excluded from this arrangement, a fact of continuing irritation to the Commission.) The proportion of customs duties accruing to the Community was then to rise year by year, reaching 100 per cent by 1975. It was also agreed that from 1 January 1974 a levy on all national expenditure falling within the common VAT base would be payable to the Community, up to a limit of 1 per cent of such expenditure. In the event that the VAT base in any country had not been fully harmonised with the rest of the Community, or if indeed a country had not yet introduced VAT at all, during the period 1974–7 the contribution of any country would be related to its share in the Community GDP. (These arrangements were applied to Greece, Portugal and Spain during their transitional years of membership of the Community.) By 1978, however, the Community was expected to be operating wholly on an own-resources basis. As matters turned out, this objective was not achieved until the budget of 1980.

The pattern of revenue receipts in the Community budget may be seen from Table 21.1. The amounts derived from agricultural levies have varied markedly. In the early to mid-1970s they fell markedly as world food prices rose and only low levels of protection were required to keep the prices of imported products at or above the guaranteed domestic levels; for some products, indeed, levies were required on Community exports to prevent massive outflows to world markets and an unacceptably high domestic price level. Later in the 1970s, however, a combination of poor Community harvests and a fall in the world price level of foodstuffs caused an equally sharp increase in levies. Similar factors operated over this period on the revenue from sugar levies, although the sustained increase in Community output has generated a consistently upward trend since the early 1970s.

Since the second enlargement of the Community in 1973 the average level of receipts from customs duties (in real terms) has remained extraordinarily stable; given the rise of some 66 per cent in the volume of extra-EEC imports during that period, this is at first sight rather surprising. The growth in the value of imports from the rest of the world has been offset, however, by the abolition of tariffs on imports from the new member states and by various trading arrangements discussed in Chapters 25 and 26. These include tariff concessions on imports from a large number of countries with which the Community has association agreements, or other preferential trading arrangements, and world-wide tariff reductions negotiated under the General Agreement on Tariffs and Trade (GATT).

The overall effect of all these factors has been that the 'traditional' resources – agricultural and sugar levies and customs duties – remained virtually unchanged in real terms between 1973–6 and 1986, over which period real budgetary expenditure by the Community more than doubled. The burden of the increased expenditure was therefore thrust almost entirely on the one dynamic component of the Community's revenue base, the VAT contribution.

The 1970 Treaty had limited the contributions of member countries to 1 per cent of the (theoretically) uniform VAT base. By 1983 the take-up necessary to balance the budget had reached 0.998 per cent; the end was obviously near. After a great deal of argument, it was agreed at the Fontainebleau summit of 1984 that (subject to the limit then established on agricultural spending) this limit should be raised to 1.4 per cent with effect from 1 January 1986. The possibility of a further increase to 1.6 per cent in 1988 was accepted, but any such increase was to be subject to the unanimous agreement of the Council of Ministers. Needless to say, the full 1.4 per cent VAT contribution was called on, and swallowed up, by the 1986 budget.

The suggestion that the VAT limit should be raised to the 1.6 per cent level was firmly resisted by some of the member countries, most especially the United Kingdom. Although the VAT contribution was supposed to reflect 'Member states' economic capacities', experience had shown that its relationship to capacity to pay is erratic, to say the least. Because capital goods, exports and 'merit goods' such as health and education are excluded from the VAT base, differences in the relative importance of these types of expenditure generate differences in VAT liability which have little bearing on genuine ability to pay. What is more, the reliability of the statistics on expenditures coming within the theoretical VAT base varies markedly from one country to another; in Italy, in particular, the evasion of reporting such transactions to the authorities is believed to amount to at least 40 per cent of the total.

At the Brussels Summit of 1988, therefore, the decision went against a further increase in the VAT take-up rate. Indeed, it was agreed that if the notional VAT base in any country exceeded 55 per cent of its GNP, the VAT levy should apply only to 55 per cent of GNP. A new kind of own resource was therefore agreed upon to finance any expenditure not covered by the conventional own-resources. This was to be an 'additional contribution' based on the total GNP at market prices of each member country. The Council of Ministers resolved, however, that the total raised from 'own-resources' of all kinds should have an overall limit, rising from 1.15 per cent of Community GNP in 1988 to 1.2 per cent in 1992.

To an extent, then – and presumably to an increasing extent as the years go by – the Community has added a kind of income tax to its sources of revenue. Since the central government of every Federation in history has come to rely primarily on taxes on income, rather than on taxes on expenditure, this is a logical step. It introduces a more explicit element of equity into the distribution of the burden of Community expenditure. It also opens up, unfortunately, the possibility of considerable argument over the accuracy and consistency of the statistical services of the member states. Since it creates a more or less open-ended source of finance, it also adds increased importance to the effective control of Community expenditures.

21.5　The British Problem

Had the benefits of the Community's steadily rising expenditure been spread more or less evenly over the member countries, and had all national governments carried a more or less equal share of the corresponding tax burden, the financial burdens of the Community might have been borne with more equanimity. Neither of these conditions, unfortunately, has been satisfied; on both counts the system appeared to be operating with manifest unfairness with regard to the United Kingdom.

Given that anything up to three-quarters of the Community's total budgetary expenditure has been devoted to agricultural support over the years, it was inevitable that the United Kingdom, with its very small agricultural sector, would receive correspondingly little benefit. Over 1980–84, in fact, of the four largest countries three (France, Germany and Italy) each received an average of a little over 21 per cent of CAP spending while the United Kingdom received an average of 11 per cent. Conversely, the tendency of the United Kingdom to import a relatively high proportion of both food and manufactures from non-EEC sources meant that it carried a relatively large burden of the 'traditional' own resources of agricultural and sugar levies and customs duties. During 1980–84 the same three large countries, France, Germany and Italy, each contributed an average of 18.1 per cent of these traditional own-resources while the United Kingdom paid an average of 24.9 per cent. Finally, the United Kingdom tended to devote a relatively low proportion of its national expenditure to VAT-exempt categories such as investment and exports. All this had been foreseen in the British White Papers of 1970 and 1971, a fact which some member countries (especially France) were quick to emphasise; the British, it was politely pointed out, knew the rules of the club when they sought membership and therefore had no valid grounds for complaint. Whatever its merits, the argument failed to impress the British government. At the Dublin Summit of March 1975 it sought some redress of what it alleged to be a manifest injustice, and it was agreed by the Council of Ministers that a 'corrective mechanism' to reduce the financial burden on the UK should be introduced. The resulting formula was to apply for an experimental period of seven years beginning in 1976. By design or otherwise the mechanism so devised was of such stupendous complexity, and specified so many conditions which had to be satisfied before it could activated, that it never came into operation.

It has to be conceded that the problems of calculating the precise contributions paid to, and amounts received from, the Community budget are very formidable. Import duties are recorded at the port of entry, whereas they may ultimately be paid by consumers in a totally different country; conversely, export refunds on farm products sold overseas would be recorded as being paid in the country from which they were exported, whereas the ultimate recipients, the producers, could well live elsewhere. (It will be appreciated that the

Netherlands accounts for less than 5 per cent of the Community's population but its ports, principally Rotterdam, handle more than 20 per cent of its seaborne freight.) The VAT expenditure recorded in one country may originate with residents of another; exports and imports each account for around 97 per cent of the national income of Luxembourg. Brussels being the main residence of the Community's multinational secretariat, the bulk of its administrative expenditure is necessarily recorded as being received there. National allocations of Community receipts and expenditures are therefore liable to be somewhat misleading.

That being said, the estimates of net contributions to the Community budget shown in Table 21.2 – that is, payments into the Community exchequer less receipts from expenditure headings allocable to individual member countries – are reliable enough as indicators of broad orders of magnitude. (With, certainly, the exception of Luxembourg, a country so small and with such a special position in the Community that its per capita statistics are wildly erratic.) The estimates in column (3) indicate that, had some corrective mechanism not been applied in the two years 1980 and 1981 – the first years after the end of the

Table 21.2
Net EC Budgetary Contributions, 1976–86 (Annual Averages: ECU per head at 1986 prices)

| Country | 1976–9 | 1980–81 | | 1982–6 | Per capita GDP 1976–86 EC = 100 |
| | | Before financial adjustment | After financial adjustment | | |
(1)	(2)	(3)	(4)	(5)	(6)
Belgium	22.9	34.3	50.4	44.1	97.5
Denmark	− 122.3	− 94.1	− 82.8	− 74.6	107.4
France	10.3	− 14.7	− 5.5	8.4	106.3
Germany	37.0	38.5	51.0	58.4	108.0
Greece	—	—	—	− 119.7	55.8
Ireland	− 229.3	− 282.5	− 275.7	− 304.1	61.0
Italy	− 2.6	− 18.9	− 13.2	− 18.5	94.2
Luxembourg	− 4.9	38.8	51.4	121.3	112.1
Netherlands	− 15.2	− 36.8	− 21.9	− 21.2	103.6
United Kingdom	14.6	65.0	28.7	27.7	96.5
Total	8.2	9.2	9.2	7.6	100

SOURCE Based on data in *Eurostat Review*, various.

transitional phase of UK membership – the net budgetary contribution of the United Kingdom would have amounted to nearly ECU 65 per head, or seven times the Community average.

The distribution of the net burden of Community expenditure was especially bizarre when compared with the relative income levels of the member countries. In 1980–81, Denmark, with one of the highest levels of income in the Community, would have been a net beneficiary on a scale exceeded in per capita terms only by Ireland, with the lowest level of income. (It was not surprising that around this time a Danish member of the European Parliament was heard to declare: 'Scandinavia is the mistress whom we love: the Community is the rich wife who keeps us.')

Not without reluctance, the Ministers agreed in 1980 that some correction had to be made. For the two years 1980 and 1981 a refund of about two-thirds of the UK net contribution was decided on, the cost being divided amongst the other member countries. The change so effected may be seen by comparing columns (3) and (4) of Table 21.2. By 1981 some more systematic solution to the financing problem was to be devised. In fact this proved very much easier said than done; it was not until the Fontainebleau summit of 1984 that it emerged in exchange for the UK's agreement (which was essential) to the increase in the VAT ceiling from 1 per cent to 1.4 per cent. The correction mechanism then created was to apply to 'any member state sustaining a budgetary burden which is excessive in relation to its relative prosperity'.

The settlement was characteristically complex. For the year 1984 the United Kingdom was to receive a simple refund of ECU 1 bn. For 1985 onwards it was to receive a rebate equal to two-thirds of the difference between its share of allocable expenditure and its share of VAT contributions at the going rate. The complex mechanism is perhaps best understood with the aid of the simple numerical example shown in Table 21.3. Suppose that total VAT payments due in the year concerned amount to ECU 30 bn, of which the UK would normally contribute 20 per cent, or ECU 6000 m. Suppose also that the UK share in allocable expenditure was only ECU 5100 m. Then of the difference between these two figures, i.e. ECU 900 m, two-thirds, or ECU 600 m, would be refunded in the following year as a deduction from VAT payments due from Britain.

The revenue deficiency thus created would be filled by proportionately higher VAT payments by the other members. (The object of this cumbersome procedure was to avoid making the rebate an expenditure item and thus bringing it into the category of non-compulsory expenditure subject to the approval – or more precisely, the disapproval – of the Parliament.) As may be seen from Table 21.2, however, easily the biggest net contributor to the budget is Germany, and the government of Germany naturally showed some distaste at the prospect of being called on to make an even larger contribution in order to bring relief to the British. It was therefore agreed that Germany would be required to pay only two-thirds of its 'normal' share of the rebate. Thus in the

Table 21.3
The Fontainebleau Mechanism

	UK	Germany	Rest	Total
(1) National VAT bases, (ECU bn)	600	900	1 500	3 000
(2) Share of VAT base (%)	20.0	30.0	50.0	
(3) VAT contributions at 1% (ECU m)	6 000	9 000	15 000	30 000
(4) Actual expenditure shares	5 100	9 000	15 900	30 000
(5) UK rebate (2/3rds of (3) − (4))	600			
(6) UK adjusted payment	5 400			
(7) Share of (5) according to (2)		225	375	600
(8) After German adjustment		150	450	600
9) Final payments of VAT	5 400	9 150	15 450	30 000
(10) As % of VAT base	0.900	1.017	1.030	1.000

NOTE   Assumed total expenditure planned = ECU 40 bn; assumed 'other' own resources =
ECU 10 bn; hence assumed expenditure to be financed by VAT = ECU 30 bn

example of Table 21.3, the German contribution to the cost of the UK rebate, based on its share of the total non-UK VAT base, would have been ECU 225 m; this would be reduced by one-third to ECU 150 m with a corresponding increase in the contributions required from the remaining member countries. As will be seen from line (10) of Table 21.3, the final result would be the application of three different VAT rates in the year concerned, rather than one. (The highest of these would be the operative one so far as any VAT-rate ceiling is concerned.)

This complicated arrangement was not affected by the introduction of the new GNP-related contribution in 1988; the rebate system now applies to the total of VAT and GDP-related payments rather than VAT alone. It can be said to have ameliorated the UK problem rather than to have disposed of it. To some extent, no more could be expected. In the first place, there is no treaty provision for equality in the net contributions made by member states to the Community budget; indeed, such a concept could be said to be incompatible with a Community attitude, as opposed to the seeking of mere national self-interest. (According to the French, the very concept of a *juste retour* from the budget is very definitely *non-communautaire*.) Secondly, the fact that the bulk of Community expenditure has so far been concentrated on one particular sector, and its revenues drawn from a very limited number of sources, inevitably implies that net benefits will be unevenly spread. It is precisely because of the multiplicity of both expenditures and taxes in national systems of public finance that national governments are able to achieve a high degree of equity in the imposition of tax burdens on their citizens, if indeed they seek to achieve that particular policy aim.

If the aim of reducing the proportionate importance of agricultural spending is achieved in future years, and if the GNP-related contributions increase in relative importance, the ill-will and argument generated by budgetary matters in the early 1980s need not recur. The damage done by it to Community affairs was certainly totally disproportionate to the amounts involved. An American observer of the 1984 Summit remarked, with some justice, that the Council of Ministers was spending interminable hours arguing over 'an amount which is less than the loss made by the New York subway every day'. The great federations of the United States and nineteenth-century Germany took some-thing of the order of 100 years before finalising their systems of federal 'own-resources'; that the Community may take at least a half of that time in achieving the same goal would not seem unreasonable.

Further Reading

European Commission, *The European Community's Budget*, 4th edn (Luxembourg: Commission of the European Communities, 1986).

European Commission, *Community Public Finance: the European budget after the 1988 reform* (Luxembourg: Commission of the European Communities, 1989).

Strasser, D., *The Finances of Europe*, revised edn (Luxembourg: European Perspectives, 1981).

Wallace, H., *Budgetary Politics: the Finances of the European Communities* (London: Allen & Unwin, 1980).

Wallace, H., 'Distributional politics: dividing up the Community cake', in Wallace, H. (ed.), *Policy-making in the European Community*, 2nd edn (Chichester: John Wiley & Sons, 1983).

European Monetary Union – the Theory

22

22.1 The Nature of Monetary Union

In any Keynesian-type view of the economic system the budget, in a national economy, has a major macroeconomic role as well as having microeconomic functions in allocating resources between sectors or between groups of people. By this is meant that the level and net balance of budgetary receipts and expenditures can exert a significant pressure on the level of output, employment and prices in the economy as a whole, as distinct from the relative levels in particular sectors of it. The Treaty of Rome envisaged no such macroeconomic role for the Community budget; its very small size in relation to the national incomes of the member states has in any case ruled out such a possibility.

The importance of macroeconomic considerations was forcibly drawn to the attention of the Six in 1969, however, when movements in the foreign exchange rates of two major member countries appeared to throw the Common Agricultural Policy into disarray, a matter which was discussed in Chapter 15. Such exchange-rate movements may have many causes, but prominent amongst them has always been a misalignment in the rates of inflation within the different trading partners, as was indeed being experienced in 1969. Although the treaty made no reference to a common monetary policy, or monetary union, therefore, the Six were forced to address their minds to such a policy as a necessary condition for the success of any other common policy. This chapter is concerned with the general principles involved in a monetary union; the succeeding chapter will examine the actual course of events in this context during the 1970s and 1980s.

A monetary union between two or more independent countries requires the participating countries to commit themselves to the maintenance of two essential conditions so far as their monetary systems are concerned. First, each must undertake to maintain complete convertibility between its own currency and that of the partner country. (For the sake of simplicity the matter will be discussed in terms of a union between only two countries; the principles are the same, of course, if there are more than two.) In other words, the residents of each country must be free to convert their currency into that of the partner country without restriction. Such a situation is indeed implicit in any customs union so far as current trade transactions are concerned; there could scarcely be free trade between the partners if the currency of each was not freely available to residents of the other. Convertibility here, however, extends to capital transaction as well as current – to the purchase and sale of physical and financial assets as well as to that of current goods and services.

The second essential requirement is that the rate of exchange at which the currency of one partner can be converted into that of the other must be permanently fixed within no more than the very narrow limits of fluctuation unavoidable in the ebb and flow of day-to-day transactions. The exchange rates of the partner currencies may vary significantly against those of the rest of the world but cannot vary against one another.

These aims are most easily, clearly and unambiguously achieved by the adoption by the partner countries of a single currency, as with the States within the United States of America or within England, Wales and Northern Ireland. But this need not necessarily be the case; the partner countries may retain physically distinct currencies (as with the English and Scottish pounds) so long as they are freely interchangeable at a fixed rate. Whichever course is adopted, two very far-reaching implications are involved.

First, a central, common control must be established over the total money supply in the partner countries. The price of a currency (i.e. its rate of exchange) is subject to the same laws of demand and supply as any other commodity. If, all other things being equal, the supply of apples increases in comparison with the supply of pears, apples and pears can no longer exchange for one another at the previous price; similarly, if the number of French francs in existence increases in comparison with the number of German deutschemarks, the state of demand for each currency remaining constant, a fixed rate of exchange between them cannot long be maintained. If each country has a central bank responsible for controlling its own money supply, therefore, those central banks must be absorbed into one or (as in the case of the Federal Reserve Banks of the United States) must co-ordinate their activities with effectively the same result. Some power of independent action is also removed from governments. In isolation a national government may choose to finance a budget deficit by borrowing from its central bank (thereby adding to the total stock of money in the system) rather than from the general public. In a full monetary union, with central control of the money supply, this possibility ceases to exist; national budget deficits, if they exist, can be financed only by borrowing money which already exists in the hands of the general public, not by the creation of new money.

The second implication is that the exchange rates of the currencies of the partner countries with the currencies of the rest of the world must be managed jointly; put alternatively, their reserves of foreign exchange must be operated as a single pool, and by a single body, rather than separately. Suppose, for example, that the agreed fixed exchange rate between the partners is Frs 4.00 = DM 1.00 and that DM 1 is currently exchanging at $0.80. Then the Fr/$ exchange rate must be $0.20 and cannot be allowed to depart significantly from it, either because of a weakness in the French balance of payments with regard to the United States or through deliberate action by the French central bank to engineer a different rate. Suppose the franc were to fall on the Paris bourse to, say, Fr 1 = $0.18, the deutschemark remaining at $0.80. A shrewd observer in Paris could now borrow Frs 10 m from his bank, convert the Frs 10 m into DM 2.5 m at the official (fixed) rate, sell the DM 2.5 m for $2 m in Frankfurt and then convert the $2 m back into francs in Paris at the market rate of Fr 1 = $0.18, ending up with Frs 11.1 m. After repaying the bank loan he would be left with a comfortable profit from a transaction which might well have taken no more than a few seconds.

Obviously the ensuing rush to sell francs for deutschemarks and to sell deutschemarks for dollars could only have one or other of two consequences. Either the price of the francs would fall in relation to that of the deutschemark, or the deutschemark would fall against the dollar. The former could not be permitted in a monetary union. The latter would mean that the German exchange rate was being dictated by the French balance of payments, a state of affairs scarcely acceptable to the German government. Once a country enters a monetary union, therefore, its power of independent determination of its exchange rate with *any* other currency is effectively lost.

Monetary union thus implies for its members the loss of national sovereignty with regard to two crucial weapons in the armoury of economic policy – control over its domestic money supply and the ability to vary its foreign exchange rate. These are considerable sacrifices; what advantages could be secured through entry into a monetary union by way of compensation?

22.2   The Gains from Monetary Union

The circumstances surrounding the surge of interest in the subject of monetary union within the Community at the end of the 1960s illustrate its primary attraction for a customs union. The movements in the exchange rates of the franc and the deutschemark rate appeared to call into question the feasibility of a genuine single market in any situation in which exchange rates could vary. So long as the possibility of such variation exists it is simply not true to say that there is no distinction between the domestic market of one partner in a customs union and those of the other partners, which is what a common market is supposed to mean.

Suppose that a British car manufacturer is contemplating the expansion of sales in Germany of a model which market research establishes can be sold there at a price of DM 60 000. The current exchange rate is £1 = DM 3, and the manufacturing and sales costs of each car are put at £15 000 or DM 45 000. The estimated gross profit is therefore DM 15 000, or £5000, which represents a rate of return on capital employed of, say, 10 per cent. The company proceeds on this basis but by the time the deliveries occur the exchange rate has moved to £1 = DM 3.5. The manufacturing and sales costs are now the equivalent of DM 52 500 and the profit margin has fallen to DM 7500 or about £2140. The rate of return on capital, expected to be 10 per cent, turns out in fact to be only about 4.3 per cent. The venture into a partner country's market has proved to carry risks which would be absent in a similar development within the domestic market. Over a short period the losses may be avoided by buying forward-exchange cover in the commercial foreign-exchange market, although this necessarily raises costs and reduces profit; this is simply not feasible, however, over the entire lifetime of a long-run investment.

The potential gains of a customs union from increased specialisation and economies of scale are therefore unlikely to be fully exploited in product markets as long as these exchange fluctuations can occur. Investment in a partner country will involve risks over and above those inherent in domestic investment. Furthermore, if restrictions exist, or may be introduced, on the freedom to convert one currency into another, a single market in capital will manifestly not exist either.

There are two other less obvious but none the less important advantages claimed for a monetary union. First, if full convertibility at a fixed exchange rate exists between member countries, no foreign exchange reserves need be held to cover balance-of-payments deficits with partner countries. Just as a bank operating several branches within a single country can use surplus deposits in one branch to finance additional lending by another, so in a monetary union any country can use its own currency to settle debts with any other partner. The only *foreign* exchange reserves needed, therefore, will be those of the central monetary authority regulating exchange rates with the rest of the world. As with a branch banking system, economies of scale arise because the reserves needed to cover the group as a whole will be smaller than the sum of those needed if each country operates individually.

The second point follows from this. The internal rate of growth of an economy is frequently compromised by the emergence of balance-of-payments problems with the outside world. But no balance-of-payments problem can arise if the trading partners are using what is in effect the same currency, any more than they can arise between one region and another in the same country.

The domestic growth rates of the members of a monetary union will therefore be subjected to less restraint from balance-of-payments problems.

These are considerable advantages, albeit scarcely quantifiable. As always in economic matters, however, there is a trade-off; in return for these advantages each country has lost its power to control its domestic money supply and to vary its rate of exchange. Before discussing the implications of this loss of economic sovereignty a small digression will be necessary.

22.3   Two Views on Unemployment

For the sake of simplicity a whole spectrum of perceptions of the manner in which an economy works will here be polarised into two limiting cases called, respectively, the Keynesian and the monetarist views. In reality there is of course an infinite gradation between these two extremes, some tending towards one limit and some towards the other. The difference between them is not in fact one of principle but rather a pragmatic one involving time – views as to, first, how rapidly an economy can be expected to react to any given stimulus and, secondly, how far into the future it is appropriate for policy to be targeted. The relevant issue here is that of how these two perceptions would explain the relationship between unemployment and inflation in any country.

Consider first the Keynesian view illustrated in Figure 22.1(a). The right-hand quadrant contains the famous Phillips curve which asserts, in essence, that there is a more or less predictable relationship between the level of unemployment, measured on the horizontal axis, and the ensuing rate of wage inflation, measured on the vertical axis. The reasoning is fairly simple; the higher the level of unemployment the more reluctant is organised labour to press for higher wages, the long unemployment queue being an effective deterrent. In the right-hand quadrant the line WI (wage-inflation) traces out the consequences of a given rate of wage inflation for the general rate of inflation as higher costs are passed on to consumers in the form of higher prices. It will be noticed that this WI line does not commence at the origin; this is because the annual growth in labour productivity is assumed to permit some increase in money wages without a corresponding increase in unit costs. (If productivity grows by 5 per cent a year, money wages can grow at 5 per cent a year without any effect on prices.)

Suppose that unemployment is initially at the level U_0; at this level the rate of increase in money wages being demanded by labour amounts to W_0, the rate of growth of productivity, so that inflation is zero. The government seeks to reduce unemployment to U_1; through an appropriate fiscal or monetary policy it raises the level of spending in the economy, thus increasing the demand for labour. Unemployment falls but the increased demand for labour enables trade unions to force the rate of increase of money wages to W_1; inflation rises correspondingly to P_1. The story is vastly over-simplified but the principle is clear.

FIGURE 22.1
Unemployment and Inflation

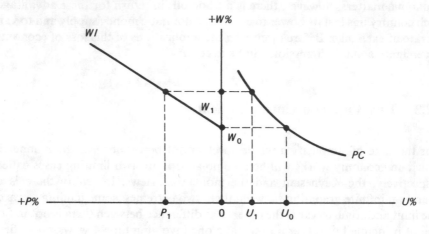

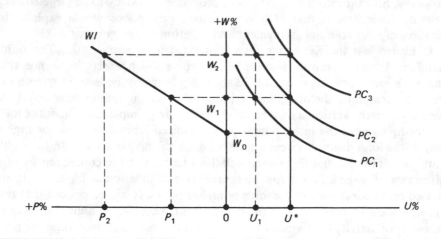

Government can choose that combination of unemployment and inflation (neither of which is desirable) which maximises social welfare. Some will regard unemployment as a much greater evil than inflation and will therefore go for a low-unemployment high-inflation mix; others will choose the opposite mix.

The view being labelled here as monetarist reaches a different conclusion; it is illustrated in Figure 22.1(b). Again commencing with unemployment at a level U^*, the rate of increase of money wages is equal to that of productivity and inflation is zero. Once more the government reduces unemployment to U_1 and inflation rises to P_1. At this point, however, the stories diverge. The Phillips curve PC_1 which traces out these consequences was the relationship existing *when inflation was zero*; the rate of increase W_1 in money wages would therefore be expected to be the same thing as a rate of increase W_1 in *real* wages – wages in terms of their ability to buy goods and services. When inflation rises to P_1, however, workers realise that they were mistaken; in terms of purchasing power the wage increase was only W_0, as before. Those misled by these expectations – the newly employed $U_1 U^*$ – will therefore withdraw from the labour market. With the previous rate of increase in the real wage, W_0, they had chosen unemployment rather than work; since the new rate of increase, W_1, is exactly the same in real terms, logically they will still prefer unemployment. The original curve PC_1, based on a perceived inflation rate of zero, will now be replaced by PC_2 based on a perceived inflation rate P_1 and the unemployment situation will revert to its original level.

If the government attempts to restore the initial fall in unemployment by further increases in aggregate demand – through fiscal or monetary policy – the process will be as self-defeating as it was before. Working now on PC_2, unemployment will be reduced again to U_1 only at the cost of an even higher rate of increase in money wages, W_2, and a corresponding acceleration in the rate of inflation to P_2. But as soon as this is seen to have prevented any increase in the rate of change of real wages the same reaction will occur; a new curve PC_3 becomes applicable and unemployment reverts back to U^*.

The implication is clear. Any movement of unemployment away from U^* must be transient. Workers, being rational, look to the rate of increase in real wages and are not fooled by mere movements in money wages. But in this neoclassical, competitive world real wages must equal the real product of labour and can therefore increase only at the same rate as productivity is increasing. Hence any rise in money wages above this level must express itself in inflation, which then brings real wages back to where they started. The level of unemployment prevailing at this pre-ordained rate of increase in real wages is therefore the only one feasible; it is the 'natural' (or, portentously, the non-accelerating-inflation rate of unemployment, NAIRU). No tinkering with aggregate demand by governments can alter this fact. (Although microeconomic policies, such as improved retraining and resettlement schemes, might.) The extreme exponents of this view would even deny that the *temporary* fall in unemployment postulated here could occur. Workers, they would argue, being rational persons will be able to *foresee* the inevitable inflationary consequences of the attempt and will therefore not be fooled even by the initial rise in money wages.

The contrast between the two perceptions has been drawn in deliberately stark and over-simplified terms. In practice few monetarists would deny that some temporary fall in unemployment could be induced by increased aggregate demand before the confidence-trick effect of inflation is exposed. But most would argue that the time-lag will be short, especially when the experience of inflation has become a familiar one; hence the fall in unemployment will be both small and short-lived and before long the natural rate is inexorably restored.

Few Keynesians, on the other hand, would suggest that the effects of inflation will *never* feed back into the labour market in the manner suggested by the monetarists. Most would argue, however, that in a world in which prices are administered (i.e. fixed for periods of time by producers or unions rather than instantaneously responding to demand) a considerable period of time may elapse before a change in money wages is fully reflected in prices. Equally, if many workers have commitments, such as mortgages or consumer debt, fixed in money terms rather than in real terms, an equal increase in the general price level and in money wages may not imply an unchanged real income. A fall in unemployment secured by increased aggregate demand may therefore persist for a long time – for as far ahead, in other words, as it is practicable for any policy to be projected. The 'long run' in which the monetarist mechanism will eventually work itself out may be so long that at its end the whole situation will have been transformed anyway. (Hence the classic Keynesian slogan: in the long run we are all dead.)

The essence of the disagreement therefore comes back to time. If the monetarist perception of the economy is nearer the truth, any trade-off between inflation and employment is so brief as to be worthless. If the Keynesian perception is closer to reality, the trade-off may be long-lasting and substantial. It is also a question of time in that views will differ as to the balance to be struck between gains and losses in the short run (however that may be defined) and those envisaged in the long run – in which some, but conceivably not all – will be dead.

22.4   The Costs of Monetary Union

It is now possible to consider the question of the possible burdens imposed on a country by entry into a monetary union, again using the two limiting cases for purposes of exposition. It is assumed that goods and services flow freely between the two member countries, A and B, but at this stage it is assumed that there is no mobility of capital and labour between them. Initially they are fully independent countries but then decide to form a single monetary union.

The Keynesian view is examined in Figure 22.2(a) and (b). Figure 22.2(a) illustrates the Keynesian conception of how a country, A, by the use of appropriate policy instruments, can attain what it perceives to be the optimum combination of inflation and unemployment and simultaneously maintain equilibrium on its balance of payments. The internal choice is shown in the top two quadrants; initially the level of unemployment is U_0, giving a rate of inflation of P_0. The problem of external equilibrium is shown in the bottom left-hand quadrant. The rate of inflation in the trading partner, B, is P^*; if A is to

FIGURE 22.2(a)
Balance-of-payments Equilibrium: the Keynesian View

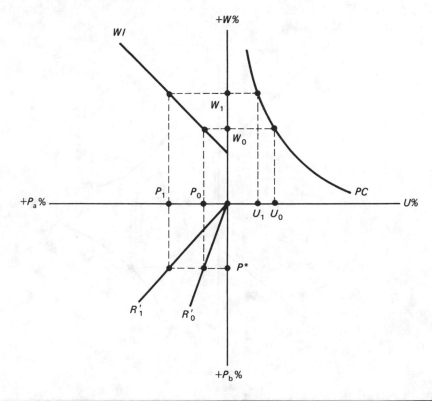

remain in balance-of-payments equilibrium, therefore, the external prices of its exports must change at the same rate. This it achieves by an appropriate adjustment, R_0', in its foreign exchange rate. Suppose now that A wishes to reduce its unemployment to U_1; using fiscal measures to raise aggregate demand, unemployment is reduced and, as a result, inflation is raised to P_1. To prevent a loss of competitiveness in its exports, country A reduces its rate of exchange, so that a rise of P_1 per cent in domestic prices becomes one of only P^* in terms of its prices to B. Country A is thus using one policy instrument, fiscal policy, to achieve internal equilibrium and another, the rate of exchange, to achieve external equilibrium.

Let A and B now form a monetary union, as shown in Figure 22.2(b). The internal position in B initially is shown in the bottom half of the diagram: B has chosen a combination in which its rate of unemployment, U_{0b}, is higher than in A but its rate of inflation, P_{0b}, is lower. Since the exchange rate of their

FIGURE 22.2(b)
Monetary Union: the Keynesian View

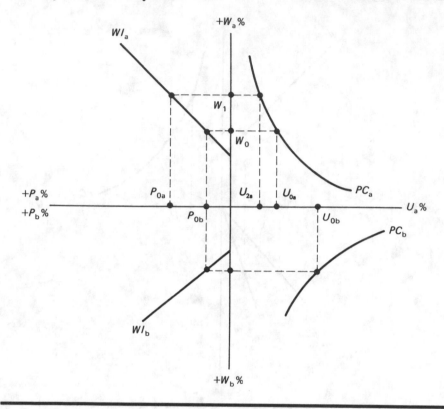

currencies with one another is now by definition fixed, the inflation rates in the two countries can no longer differ. Country B therefore insists that A's inflation rate be reduced to P_{0b}; the consequence is that A has to move to the earlier and higher level of unemployment, U_{0a}, which it had considered less desirable than the lower rate of inflation it has now accepted. The cost of monetary union to A is therefore the welfare loss associated with this suboptimal combination of unemployment and inflation.

In this simple case all the burden is thrown on A, with B suffering no change in its internal position. In practice a compromise might be reached in which B accepts a somewhat higher rate of inflation (and hence a lower rate of unemployment) in order to meet A halfway. This means that the loss is shared rather than eliminated; both countries end up with a combination of inflation and unemployment different from that they would have chosen, so that economic welfare is reduced in both.

FIGURE 22.2(c)
Monetary Union: the Monetarist View

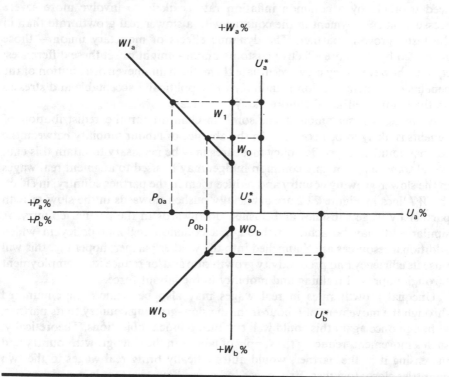

The monetarist position is shown in Figure 22.2(c). Here there is by definition no trade-off between inflation and unemployment; the natural rate is fixed at U^*_a in country A and U^*_b in country B. Forcing the inflation rate down in country A therefore imposes no real loss on A: its unemployment is unaffected. The only sacrifice (if it can be called such) imposed on both A and B is the loss of the power to determine their own inflation rates independently; since the inflation rate is a purely monetary phenomenon, however, having no bearing on real income and output, it has no welfare significance at all. In real terms, monetary union is costless.

22.5 Factor Mobility

Whatever view is taken of the consequences of entry into a monetary union, it is singularly unlikely its effects will be felt equally by each of the partner countries.

Productivity growth would be identical in each country only by a miraculous coincidence, so that a common rate of inflation would almost inevitably imply an unequal rate of growth in real incomes in the two countries. Similarly, the need to abide by a common inflation rate is likely to involve more severe pressure on employment in the country with a slower real growth rate than in the faster-growing partner. The dynamic effects of monetary union – those generated by the more effective customs union – might offset these differences; equally, however, they may accentuate them. Such an uneven distribution of the benefits of monetary union is unlikely to be politically acceptable and stresses on the union itself are therefore likely to increase.

As in a customs union, then, some mechanism for the redistribution of benefits is likely to be necessary. In the absence of labour mobility between the partner countries, specific policy measures may be necessary to attain this end. Fiscal transfers through a common budget may be used to augment real wages in the slower-growing country and reduce them in the partner country; in effect, the *WI* lines in Figure 22.2 are artificially pushed upwards in the slow-growth partner by wage subsidies and pushed downwards in the partner country. A similar end may be achieved through a common regional policy in which additional resources are channelled into the weaker partner; hopefully, this will raise its efficiency and productivity growth rate and/or reduce its unemployment through improved training and mobility in the labour force.

Unequal growth rates in real wages may also be reduced or eliminated through the movement of labour from the slow-growing country to its partner, although once again this could well run into political objections. Theoretically, such a movement, reducing the supply of labour in the slow-growth country and increasing it in the partner, would automatically bring real wages in the two countries closer together. Experience indicates, however, that in practice such a movement could increase rather than reduce income differentials; labour mobility tends to be highest amongst the young and skilled, so that the exporting country may be weakened rather than strengthened by the process.

Much the same is true if mobility of capital exists between the partners. Again in theory the slow-growing country will suffer a loss of resources as its imports from the partner exceed its exports. The corresponding relative decline in its money stock (the two countries, after all, share a single money supply) will then lead to a rise in its interest rates in comparison with those in the partner country. In theory, capital will then flow from the partner country in response to the interest rate differential, raising productivity in the recipient country and reducing the productivity differential. Once again experience suggests that in practice capital movements may accentuate an initial disequilibrium rather than reduce it; capital may flow to the stronger, high-profit partner and away from the weaker, low-profit partner.

As usual, the matter of timing is of the essence. In the theoretical long run of the neoclassical world, factor mobility will ultimately eliminate all differences in real wage-rates and profits throughout the monetary union. In the real world of imperfect factor markets and labour immobility this long run may be a very long time coming; the losses suffered by the weaker partner in the meantime may not be politically tolerable.

22.6 The Implications for Policy

It will be clear from all this that the specification of the conditions required for a successful monetary union will depend entirely on perceptions of how the economies in question are likely to operate in reality. Few would accept in real life either of the theoretical limiting cases – the 'pure' Keynesian scenario in which monetary union implies very long-term losses more than offsetting the rather dubious gains, or the 'pure' monetarist scenario in which it involves no losses whatever.

If it is considered that, nevertheless, the Keynesian perception of imperfect markets, administered prices and limited factor mobility is reasonably close to reality, the implications are clear. A monetary union should not be embarked upon until the macroeconomic characteristics of the prospective partners are broadly similar; this implies more or less equal rates of inflation and real economic growth and something approaching equilibrium in their balance-of-payments situations. In the absence of these requirements, the adjustment losses imposed on the weaker partners are likely to be severe – and to persist for a significant period of time. It also implies that even given these conditions an essential element in the monetary union will be the provision of substantial resources from a central source; these will be required to finance the inevitable transitory balance-of-payments deficits, eliminating the need for severe deflationary policies in the weaker partners, and for the necessary measures of regional policy over what may very well prove to be a protracted period.

Those inclining to the monetarist perception of the economic system would take a quite different view. Since the costs of monetary union, in their view, are small (if they exist at all) and purely transitory, there is no need to wait for a high degree of convergence amongst the partner countries; on the contrary, the monetary union is itself the mechanism by which such convergence will automatically be secured. The sequence is thus reversed: harmonisation of economic policies is not a necessary precondition for monetary union but an inescapable consequence of it. Hence any provision for assistance to partner countries with balance-of-payments or regional problems can be quite temporary and of modest scale.

On one thing, however, all parties would agree: if a monetary union is to have any prospect of success a total and permanent commitment to it must be evident on the part of all the participating countries. As long as even a suspicion exists in the outside world that the theoretically permanent link between the exchange rates of the partner countries might be sacrificed if the solution of internal difficulties in one or more of them should so require, the thing will not survive. At the first sign of trouble, speculation against the weaker currencies will inevitably ensure that the allegedly permanent fixed rate becomes unfixed. As Keynes remarked of the gold standard, monetary union is a jealous God.

Further Reading

Coffey, P., *Europe and Money* (London: Macmillan, 1977).
Denton, G., *Economic and Monetary Union in Europe* (London: Croom Helm, 1975).
Robson, P., *The Economics of International Integration*, 2nd. edn. (London: Allen & Unwin, 1984).
Sumner, M. T. and Zis, G., *European Monetary Union* (London: Macmillan, 1982).
Tsoukalis, L., *The Politics and Economics of European Monetary Integration* (London: Allen & Unwin, 1977).

The European
Monetary System

23

23.1 Monetary Union is Born

The adjustment of the foreign exchange rates of the Community's two major members in 1969 had a traumatic effect on the Community. Initially it generated the belief that the Common Agricultural Policy, its alleged corner-stone, had been fundamentally compromised; in fact, the subsequent invention of the tortuous system of Monetary Compensatory Amounts was to prove that this fear was not entirely justified. More generally, however, it very definitely undermined the implicit assumption that the exchange-rate stability enjoyed by the Community since its formation would continue indefinitely. The potential gains from integration in the areas of production and trade based on a large single market were clearly being jeopardised by this instability in the monetary sector.

In March 1970 the Council of Ministers established a high level group to prepare plans for a full economic and monetary union, rather than a mere customs union, amongst the Six. It comprised the Presidents of all the main economic committees and the members of the Committee of Central Bank governors; the chairman was M Pierre Werner, then Prime Minister and Minister of Finance of Luxembourg and inevitably it was with his name that the results of its deliberations were labelled. The group worked with inordinate speed; its report was in the hands of the Council by October 1970.

The Committee naturally set out the two approaches to the establishment of a monetary union discussed in the previous chapter, although in somewhat different terms. It did not appear to think worthy of discussion the proposition that monetary union might not be feasible at all. Convergence between the economies of the member states was assumed to be within the control of their governments, whether through the fiscal policies typical of the Keynesian approach or through the establishment of a common money supply, as asserted by the monetarists. No attention was given to the possibility that the divergences between member countries could be due to deep-seated structural characteristics of the different economies which were partially, if not totally, beyond the control of political institutions and devices.

The issue was therefore not whether but how. Should the Six go immediately for irrevocably fixed exchange rates in the conviction that, as the monetarists asserted, this in itself would rapidly induce convergence within the member states? Or should they aim first at establishing greater convergence of economic policies as a prerequisite of monetary union, as the Keynesian approach suggested? After the fashion of committees, the Werner group recommended a compromise between the two. It proposed that the Community should proceed towards a full monetary union between 1971 and 1980 but that the process should be split into two phases. The first phase, a concession to the Keynesian view, was to be devoted to the promotion of greater economic convergence rather than the creation of a full union; the second, or monetarist phase, was to see the establishment of a monetary union in its full rigour.

In phase 1, intended to extend over 1971–3 the central banks of the member countries were to operate in foreign exchange markets so as to maintain the exchange rates of member currencies within narrower limits than those laid down at the time by the International Monetary Fund (IMF) – i.e. a range of ±0.75 per cent of the official parity. (Subsequently, in December 1971, this IMF band was widened to ±2.25 per cent.) To this end, a European Exchange Stabilisation Fund was to be created with contributions from each member country, this fund to provide short-term loans to central banks to assist in the finance of such operations. In this phase governments were also to participate in prior consultation with each other before formulating any changes in their domestic fiscal and monetary policies.

In the second phase there would be no question of merely limiting fluctuations in relative exchange rates; the member countries were to establish 'the total and irreversible convertibility of their currencies, the elimination of margins of fluctuation in exchange rates, the irrevocable fixing of parity ratios and the total liberalisation of movements of capital.' The Stabilisation Fund would be converted into a European Reserve Fund holding a single common pool of all the foreign exchange reserves of the member countries. The consultative procedure of phase 1 would be replaced by the creation of a 'Centre of Decision' – in effect a European Economic Ministry – and a 'Community system for the central banks' – a Community equivalent of the Federal Reserve System of the United States. Together these new institutions would assume responsibility for the fiscal and monetary policies of all member countries.

The importance of the fact that these changes should be seen to be permanent and irreversible was heavily emphasised by the Werner committee. As a result it recommended that an intergovernmental conference should be held before the end of phase 1 in order to embody the full proposals in the Treaty of Rome itself; once the process was embarked upon, in other words, there was to be no turning back.

In March 1971 the Council of Ministers accepted the broad principles of the Werner Report, resolving that as a first step towards its objectives the exchange rates of member currencies should be maintained within ±0.6 per cent of each other from 15 June 1971 onwards. It also agreed on the creation of a mutual credit facility totalling the equivalent of ECU 7.5 bn to assist central banks in meeting this obligation. But in crucial respects the Council's acceptance of the proposals was severely qualified. The supranational concept of a single 'Centre of Decision' operating common fiscal and monetary policies was too much for the French in particular to swallow; the precise relationship between national governments and this proposed Centre, they argued, should be left for further discussion and should certainly not be prejudged. Nor were the French happy at the proposal that a commitment to monetary union should be formally embodied in the treaty. This not unnaturally provoked the Germans into declaring that, if an irrevocable commitment was not forthcoming from all member governments, they on their side could not commit themselves to financing the proposed European Reserve Fund for more than five years if no agreement was reached on the progression to phase 2 of the operation. It was not an entirely auspicious beginning for the great adventure.

23.2 The Short and Brutish Life of the Snake

The launch date of June 1971 could hardly have been less happily chosen. In May 1971 a long-gathering cloud burst over the United States dollar. Large speculative movements of short-term funds seeking to benefit from the expected collapse of the dollar exchange rate caused havoc in the foreign exchange markets, leading to their total closure for two weeks in Germany, Belgium and the Netherlands and to the resort to drastic exchange controls in France. Throughout the remainder of 1971 the dollar crisis continued, making any definition of absolute values of equilibrium exchange rates, let alone their relative values, virtually impossible. An international monetary conference in Washington, at the Smithsonian Institution, in December 1971 agreed on measures to deal with the crisis – notably a reduction in the official exchange rate of the dollar and the widening of the bands within which official IMF exchange rates were permitted to vary, from ±0.75 per cent to ±2.25 per cent. Roughly a year behind schedule, on 24 April 1972, the Community's agreed exchange-rate arrangements came into force. The exchange rate of each member currency was to be kept within a band which was precisely one-half of that required by membership of the IMF – i.e. ±1.125 per cent compared with the new IMF range of ±2.25 per cent. (Hence the system was almost universally referred to as 'the snake', referring to the narrower band of permissible fluctuations within the 'tunnel' of the wider IMF band.) A European Monetary Co-operation Fund (usually known by its French acronym FECOM) was established by the central banks to arrange and assist in the market intervention necessary to keep market rates within these limits. In anticipation of their impending membership, the United Kingdom, Denmark and Ireland joined in the arrangements.

The venture was short-lived. The speculative fever in international money markets, temporarily assuaged so far as the dollar was concerned by the Smithsonian devaluation, switched in mid-1972 to the pound sterling; as a result, the United Kingdom was forced to abandon efforts to maintain a fixed parity and left the pound to find its own value in the markets. Within six weeks of entry into the snake, therefore, the pound made its exit from the arrangements, taking with it the Irish punt. Six months later, in January 1973, the Italian government abandoned its attempts to keep the lira within the required limits *vis-à-vis* the other Snake currencies, especially the deutschemark, and also withdrew. A year later, in January 1974, the French government followed suit; the franc rejoined the system in July 1975 but the restoration was short-lived and in March 1976 the franc departed again, this time permanently. In less than four years, therefore, three of the four major Community currencies had dropped out; the Snake had been reduced to an arrangement whereby the smaller countries bordering on Germany – the three Benelux countries and Denmark – maintained relative stability between their currencies and the deutschemark. (Since Germany absorbed around 40 per cent of their exports, this was hardly surprising.) By common consent the great experiment had been an abysmal failure.

Two features of this period are beyond dispute. First, the international monetary pressures of 1971–3 were not mere temporary aberrations; they revealed the final collapse of the postwar Bretton Woods system of exchange rates based on parities fixed at a world level. The attempt to establish exchange-rate stability in Europe had been launched at precisely that moment when the foundations of the entire world exchange-rate system were crumbling. Second, the monetary crisis was immediately followed, in 1973–4, by the oil crisis with its dramatic effects on inflation and on the balance-of-payments situation of the industrialised world. It was not merely that the average rate of inflation in the Community in 1974–5 was double that of 1973. The differential effects of the oil crisis sharply increased the gap between Community inflation rates; in the four major Community countries, the lowest and highest inflation rates in 1973 had been separated by less than 7 per cent, but the gap had grown to 13 per cent in 1974 and to 18 per cent in 1975. Exchange-rate stability between countries in general implies similar rates of inflation between them; under these circumstances such stability was an impossibility.

Inevitably the arguments and recrimination over the causes of the failure persisted. The Keynesian commentators claimed that their essential point had been confirmed. A monetary union had been attempted before a reasonable degree of convergence had been achieved amongst the economies of the participating countries; it had therefore failed, just as they had predicted. The monetarists, on the other hand, pointed out that the experiment had been launched without *their* essential prerequisite: a total and irreversible commitment to it. Monetary union had not been tried and found wanting; it had not been seriously tried at all. But all agreed that the Snake was dead. A study group on the state of play regarding economic and monetary union in the Community, headed by M Robert Marjolin, reported sadly in 1975 that the Community was, if anything, further away from monetary union than it had been in 1969. There was only one thing to do about the proposed phase 2 of the Werner plan, due to commence on 1 January 1974: forget it.

23.3 Mr Jenkins's Phoenix

Within three years, at summit meetings in Copenhagen and Bremen, monetary union was back at the top of the Community's agenda. The credit for this remarkable turnaround in attitude is conventionally given to the Commission's President between 1977 and 1980, Mr Roy (now Lord) Jenkins. To the surprise of many – not least the majority of his fellow-Commissioners – Mr Jenkins took the opportunity of the first Jean Monnet Memorial lecture at the University of Florence in October 1977 to relaunch the apparently sunken ship of monetary union. (Given Mr Jenkins's very considerable political experience, however, it seems unlikely that he would have raised so fundamental an issue without some prior knowledge of its likely welcome in influential quarters.) Most of the arguments advanced were familiar; in particular it was asserted once again that the full benefits of a common market could not conceivably be attained in a context of exchange-rate instability and uncertainty. If the European Community was to regain the momentum it had so clearly lost since the early 1970s, a major initiative in the monetary field was the obvious candidate.

To these largely familiar arguments were added two considerations on which the Werner report had had little to say. First, it had now become obvious that the Bretton Woods system of exchange rates fixed at world level – in practical terms, the use of the dollar as the basis of the system – had gone for ever. Given the disparities in world economic development it was unlikely that anything similar – that is to say, a universal system using any single currency as its base – could replace it. A world of completely free and fluctuating exchange rates, on the other hand, had been shown to be inimical to world trade and steady economic growth. But exchange-rate stability within a small number of reasonably homogeneous regions – i.e. areas within which countries traded predominantly with the other countries inside the same region – was perfectly feasible and the Community could clearly constitute such a region. To European governments and central banks which had seen the domestic value of their foreign exchange reserves held in dollars decline by about 20 per cent within a decade, the point was a persuasive one.

Secondly, the twin giant evils of the mid-1970s, inflation and unemployment, could both be conquered by monetary union. Floating exchange rates were inherently inflationary since money wages invariably rise in response to devaluations but never fall when currencies appreciate; a joint control over the money supply would therefore give the Community not only a common rate of inflation but a lower one. The removal of balance-of-payments considerations between member countries, on the other hand, would allow the Community to embark on a common rate of economic expansion and thus generate the aggregate demand needed to reduce unemployment. The argument appealed neatly to both the monetarist and the Keynesian schools of thought.

This (apparently surprising) resurrection of the idea of monetary union was seized upon with some enthusiasm by the German Chancellor, Helmut Schmidt, at the Copenhagen summit six months later and again at the first summit of the German Presidency at Bremen in July 1978. As a result, agreement was reached to proceed to the formulation of plans, not for the resumption of grandiose proposals for full economic and monetary union but for a more cautious 'Zone of monetary stability' within the Community.

That Germany should have embraced the idea was not entirely surprising. The periodic weakness of the dollar (and the pound) as major reserve currencies had elevated the deutschemark into the primary safe haven into which funds were liable to be transferred by the banking systems of the world whenever doubts arose concerning the ability of other currencies to retain their current values. Such a development was very far from being welcome to Germany. If these speculative flows of capital were allowed to push up the exchange rate of the deutschemark the competitiveness of German exports would be damaged; if, on the other hand, the effects on the exchange rate were neutralised by an offsetting expansion in the supply of deutschemarks (i.e. an increase in the German money supply) the domestic inflationary consequences would be even less acceptable. Fixed links with other currencies – in effect the creation of a single European currency – would reduce this relative (and unwelcome) attractiveness of the German currency for foreign exchange speculators, or at least spread the burden over the currencies of some other member countries.

Strong support for a proposal from the German government does not make its acceptance inevitable but it gives it a very good start. By the end of the German Presidency in 1978 the Council of Ministers had adopted a resolution on 'the establishment of the European Monetary System and related matters'. As with the Werner plan, two phases were envisaged, the first to begin on 13 March 1979, and the second two years later. The snake, or something rather like it, was back in business.

23.4   The Framework of the System

The European Monetary System (EMS) had four components and in two of them there were features which made it a snake of a different species. The first element was the creation of a new unit in which the relative values of the member currencies were expressed, in contrast to the previous arrangement in which currency values were expressed in terms of each other. This was the European Currency Unit, known by its acronym, the ECU. (The French were none the less quick to point out that the *Ecu* was also the name of a coin struck by the Emperor Charles V in the sixteenth century for circulation in an empire whose geography bore a considerable resemblance to the Community.) The ECU is an accounting device rather than a tangible monetary unit – although the government of Belgium did mark the 30th anniversary of the Treaty of Rome by striking ECU coins in both gold and silver as a memorial of the occasion.

The initial content of the ECU in March 1979 is shown in col. (3) of Table 23.1. When the units of each national currency component were converted into (say) US dollars at the prevailing market exchange rates, the total value of the

Table 23.1
The Composition of the ECU, 1979–89

Country	Currency	Percentage weighting in the ECU		
		March 1979	September 1984	September 1989
(1)	(2)	(3)	(4)	(5)
Belgium	Franc	9.2	8.2	7.6
Denmark	Krone	3.1	2.7	2.5
France	Franc	19.8	19.0	19.0
Germany	Deutschemark	33.0	32.0	30.1
Greece	Drachma	—	1.3	0.8
Ireland	Punt	1.2	1.2	1.1
Italy	Lira	9.5	10.2	10.1
Luxembourg	Franc	0.4	0.3	0.3
Netherlands	Guilder	10.5	10.1	9.4
Portugal	Escudo	—	—	0.8
Spain	Peseta	—	—	5.3
United Kingdom	Pound	13.3	15.0	13.0
Total		100	100	100

currency basket was about $1.43. The quantities of each currency included in the basket were broadly related to the importance of the country concerned in Community trade. Thus it contained DM 0.828, which at prevailing exchange rates represented 33 per cent of the total value of the unit; the French franc accounted for 20 per cent of the total, the pound sterling for 13 per cent and so on. Provision was made for a revision of these relative weights (by agreement) every five years. Such a revision occurred in September 1984 when the opportunity was taken to add the Greek drachma to the currency list and in September 1989 when the escudo and peseta were added; the consequential changes may be seen in cols. (4) and (5) of Table 23.1.

The original intention was that this new currency unit should be used exclusively by the central banks of the member countries in the course of intervention operations in the foreign exchange market designed to keep the exchange rates of currencies within the prescribed limits. Whenever central banks borrow from one another, in order to support their currencies in the foreign exchange markets, they incur the risk that when the time for repayment of the loan arrives the prevailing exchange rates may involve them in significant loss. The use of the ECU for intervention purposes in effect spreads these exchange risks over all member countries and thus reduces the burden on individual central banks. Suppose the German central bank credits DM 1 m to the French central bank to assist it in preventing a further fall in the franc at a time when the market exchange rate is DM 1 = Frs 3; it thus acquires a claim of Frs 3 m on the central bank of France. If by the time of repayment of this credit the current exchange rate has fallen to DM 1 = Frs 3.3, the German central bank will end up with only DM 0.91 m, thereby incurring a loss of 10 per cent. If the loan had been in ECUs, however, the loss would have been reduced to 2 per cent, since the 10 per cent devaluation (of the franc) would relate to a currency accounting for only 20 per cent of the ECU.

In fact the use of the ECU has been somewhat wider than this. In 1981 it was adopted as the official accounting unit of the whole Community, displacing the European Unit of Account previously used for budgetary purposes. In addition, as will be seen, it has been used to a modest degree in private transactions. Banks and other enterprises involved in international borrowing and lending have seen the advantage of having loans denominated in a composite currency; they involve less risk from exchange-rate fluctuations than those expressed in any one currency in isolation.

The second element of the EMS is its exchange-rate mechanism – the method by which the variation in the relative values of member currencies is confined within narrow limits. Unlike the Snake, in which the target exchange rate for each currency was defined in terms of each other participating currency, in the EMS a 'central' rate for each currency is defined by agreement in the Council of Ministers in terms of the ECU rather than any other single currency. Thus in 1979 the central rate for the deutschemark was defined to be DM 2.49 = ECU 1, that for the French franc was Frs 5.86 = ECU 1, that for the pound sterling was

£0.65 = 1 ECU, and so on. The central bank of each country participating in the mechanism (which does not include the United Kingdom) is then obliged to intervene in foreign exchange markets to ensure that the current market exchange rate for its currency does not vary by more than 2.25 per cent on either side of this central rate; in the case of Ireland and Italy, allegedly as a transitional measure, this permissible margin was increased to 6 per cent on either side, a concession of which the Irish authorities chose not to avail themselves.

It will be noted that this arrangement differs in two substantial respects from the old Snake arrangements. In the first place, the permitted margins of variation are much wider – ±2.25 per cent compared with ±1.125 per cent. Secondly, the margin is related to the ECU as a whole, rather than to individual currencies. This much reduces the danger, pre-eminent in the Snake, of one currency – the deutschemark – forcing action on the rest because of its rise in relation to all other member currencies. The mechanism in fact included a so-called 'divergence indicator' under which the central banks operating the main currencies were expected to take remedial action if their currency moved beyond 1 per cent of its central rate. The thinking here was that any appreciation of the deutschemark, accounting for a third of the value of the ECU, would in itself increase the value of the ECU as a whole and thus force lesser currencies towards the lower limit of the permitted margin. It was proper, therefore, that some responsibility for restoring equilibrium should be accepted by the appreciating currency and not rest solely with the currencies being forced by it into an effective depreciation.

It was realised that the central rates agreed at the outset could not conceivably be fixed for ever. It was therefore provided that from time to time realignments of the central rates could be agreed by the Council of Ministers. Obviously, if the arrangement was to establish a 'zone of monetary stability' such realignments would need to be infrequent. In addition it was hoped that the range of permitted variation, large by the standards of the Snake, 'should be gradually reduced as soon as economic conditions permit'.

The third element in the EMS was a formidable collection of credit facilities aimed at assisting member countries to comply with their obligations under the exchange-rate mechanism. It was agreed to establish a network of mutual overdraft facilities between the central banks of the participating countries to finance day-to-day intervention operations in the market. A scheme for short-term monetary support was established to provide credits for up to three months (later six months) to finance temporary balance-of-payments deficits which might otherwise exert undue pressure on exchange rates. A total equivalent to ECU 30 bn was made available for such loans on a quota basis, the funds to be contributed, also on a quota basis, by other member countries. Finally, a total equivalent to ECU 25 bn was to be contributed to a fund for medium-term financial assistance – loans for up to five years to assist countries with relatively long-term balance-of-payments problems.

The final element in the EMS was to be the creation in phase 2 of a European Monetary Fund. During phase 1 the old FECOM established for the Snake in 1972 was to continue to administer market intervention and the short-term monetary support arrangements. To this end each central bank agreed to deposit with the FECOM 20 per cent of its foreign exchange reserves in exchange for ECUs – such deposits to be returned and re-lent every three months so as to leave their true ownership in no doubt. In phase 2, however, the FECOM would be replaced with the European Monetary Fund which would not only borrow reserves from national central banks to conduct its operations but would be able to create ECUs of its own with which to do so. This ability to create its own ECU debts, to be treated by national central banks as part of their international reserves, would mark a profound change in its status: it would become in effect a Community central bank in its own right.

Whatever else might be said about the EMS at its inception in March 1979, it could hardly be described as lacking weaponry. The possession of weapons does not, however, guarantee the attainment of targets.

23.5   The EMS in Action

The objectives of the first phase of the EMS were three in number: to achieve a high degree of stability in the relative exchange rates of the participating currencies, to encourage greater convergence in the economic policies of the member countries and to establish the ECU as a new form of international currency. In phase 2, originally planned to begin in 1981, the objective was to be the far more fundamental one of full economic and monetary union.

If success in the stabilisation of relative exchange rates is defined to mean a complete absence of changes in such rates, the EMS cannot be judged a success. In the decade following its inception there were in fact no fewer than 12 realignments of one or more central rates. As may be seen from Table 23.2, the cumulative effect of these was fairly considerable. The central rate of the strongest currency, the deutschemark, had appreciated by 18 per cent over those ten years while that of the weakest, the lira, had depreciated by 29 per cent; the relative exchange rates of these two major currencies had therefore changed by nearly 50 per cent.

To consider the EMS rates in isolation, however, is misleading. In a sense the system was as unlucky as the Snake in being initiated shortly before a marked increase in world oil prices and in the midst of inflationary pressures arising from it. A more realistic test of success in the stabilising role of the EMS would therefore consist of a comparison between the degree of instability exhibited by the EMS currencies over this period and that experienced by currencies outside the system. This is attempted in line 1 of Table 23.3. where a standard measure of instability in a variable over time (the coefficient of variation) is used to

Table 23.2
Central ECU Rates, 1979–89

Country	Currency	Central rates: Units per ECU		
		March 1979	September 1989	1979 % of 1989
Belgium	Franc	39.46	42.46	93
Denmark	Krone	7.09	7.85	90
France	Franc	5.80	6.90	84
Germany	Deutschemark	2.51	2.06	122
Greece	Drachma*	—	178.1	—
Ireland	Punt	0.66	0.77	86
Italy	Lira	1148	1484	77
Luxembourg	Franc	39.46	42.46	93
Netherlands	Guilder	2.72	2.32	117
Portugal	Escudo*	—	173.8	—
Spain	Peseta	—	129.8	—
United Kingdom	Pound*	0.66	0.67	99

* Rate implied by other central rates and contemporary market exchange rates.

compare the experience of the EMS currencies with that of non-EMS currencies before and after the establishment of the system. This indicates a considerable degree of success; the instability of the EMS currencies after the establishment of the EMS was only a half as great as before, whereas the instability in non-EMS currencies was virtually unchanged. (Since it remains outside the exchange-rate mechanism the pound sterling is treated here as a non-EMS currency.) The trap of *post hoc ergo propter hoc* must be carefully avoided, but at least it can be said that the evidence is consistent with the proposition that the creation of the EMS was followed by a markedly greater degree of stability in the participating currencies than that achieved by currencies outside it.

The record under the heading of policy convergence is distinctly less impressive. The important consideration here of course is not the absolute magnitude of various indicators of economic performance but their relative variation within the EMS group – hence the coefficient of variation is a reasonable measure. Lines 2 to 6 of Table 23.3. show the evidence for five major macroeconomic variables. In all but one of them, the degree of dispersion within the EMS group was actually higher during the period after March 1979 than before it. It cannot be concluded that the EMS actually *caused* greater divergence in the economic behaviour of the member countries but it certainly has to be said that it did not appear to reduce it. True, the degree of dispersion

Table 23.3
The Performance of the EMS, 1979–84 (Coefficients of variation for major economic variables)

Economic variable	1974–8			1979–84		
	EMS countries	Non-EMS countries	(2) as % of (3)	EMS countries	Non-EMS countries	(5) as % of (6)
(1)	(2)	(3)	(4)	(5)	(6)	(7)
1. Exchange rates	22.6	37.9	60	10.7	36.8	29
2. Inflation rates	35.5	58.2	61	43.8	86.7	51
3. Growth of (narrow) money supply	27.5	54.2	51	50.0	113.6	44
4. Growth of total domestic credit	24.5	48.6	50	29.9	69.5	43
5. Budget deficit % of GDP	88.0	50.0	176	60.3	48.8	124
6. Unit labour costs	40.0	44.6	90	74.0	76.9	96
Overall average	39.8	48.9	81	44.8	72.1	65

SOURCES Line 1 is based on data given in J. van Ypersele and J. C. Koeune, *The European Monetary System* (Luxembourg: Commission of the European Communities, 1985), Table IV–1, p. 74. The pre-EMS data relate to 1976–8 and the non-EMS currencies concerned are the dollar, yen, pound sterling and Swiss franc. Lines 2–6 are based on data given in *The Economist*, 4 July 1987, p. 22. Post-EMS data for inflation and unit labour costs relate to 1979–85.

experienced in the non-EMS countries increased even more between 1974–8 and 1979–84 but the difference between the two groups is not particularly great. In any event, by 1981, when phase 2 of the EMS was due to begin, the disparities within the member countries were too large for movement to full monetary union to be contemplated; in that year, for example, the consumer price index increased by 6.3 per cent in Germany but by 13.4 per cent in France and 17.8 per cent in Italy. The most dedicated monetarist would have misgivings concerning monetary union when differences of this magnitude exist. In 1983 the Community quietly resolved to adjourn the commencement of phase 2 indefinitely.

The record under the third heading – the establishment of the ECU as an international currency and a new form of international reserves – has also proved rather disappointing. Over the period 1979–85, total purchases and sales of foreign exchange by the EMS central banks totalled the considerable sum of ECU 390 bn, but two-thirds of these transactions were conducted through the medium of US dollars; less than one-third involved the use of ECUs. Before

1987 very little use was in fact made of the complex network of credit facilities set up for the EMS; over the period 1979–85 usage of the very short-term facility of the FECOM amounted in total to only about ECU 31 bn while the medium-term lending facility was used on only three occasions. To some extent this was due to the fact that usage of the FECOM facilities was originally permitted only when a currency had reached its lower limit; most central banks prefer to act before this critical point is reached and therefore have to finance their market operations from their own resources. The situation is likely to be improved in the future by an agreement in 1987 that FECOM resources can be called upon for 'intra-marginal' intervention – i.e. that undertaken before a currency has reached an extreme point of its permitted limits – and that repayments may be made in ECUs for the whole amount of the borrowing rather than for only 50 per cent as hitherto.

By contrast, the use of the ECU by the private sector, which had scarcely been intended in the first instance, has shown some considerable progress. In December 1983, assets denominated in ECUs held by European commercial banks totalled the equivalent of only around ECU 16 bn; four years later, at the end of 1987, this total had grown to nearly ECU 80 bn. Furthermore, this growth in the private use of the ECU is likely to accelerate in the future as the result of a belated agreement by the German government in 1987 to legalise the holding by German banks of assets denominated in ECUs. The government of Belgium may have been a little quixotic in creating an ECU coin in 1987, but the gradual extension of the private use of the ECU may do much to offset the apparent reluctance of central banks to use ECUs rather than more conventional currencies as a form of international reserve.

23.6 Alors, Delors: Towards Monetary Union?

The launch of the EMS had been surrounded with a good deal of scepticism on the part of many observers whose memories of the ill-fated Snake were still fresh. Ten years later that scepticism had not proved well-founded. In the first place, the EMS had survived a decade without a single member country defaulting, a marked contrast with the Snake. Secondly, while its achievements in the realm of exchange-rate stability had perhaps fallen short of what some would have regarded as complete success, they had nevertheless been significant; the exchange rates of the EMS currencies had become markedly more stable in relation to one another than had those of currencies outside the EMS. True, the ECU had not become a dominant form of international reserve for the Community's central banks, as the founding fathers had hoped, but it had definitely established itself as sufficiently credible an entity to commend itself to increasing private use. Finally, almost all governments within the Community had come to accept the facts that, with all its imperfections, the EMS was a workable monetary system and that there was no better alternative foreseeable. None believed, as many did in the early 1970s, that there could be some form of a revived Bretton Woods system (or any other world system) to fall back on in the event of the collapse of the EMS.

Yet, to the advocates of a progressive integration of the Community economies, at the end of that decade the defects of the EMS were equally clear. The most obvious was the inclusion of four member-country currencies (most especially the pound sterling) in the ECU unit but their absence from the exchange-rate mechanism arrangements. It clearly made little sense for EMS countries to seek stability in terms of a unit which was partly composed of currencies whose market values were left free to oscillate without limit in terms of the other components.

The refusal of the United Kingdom in particular to participate in the exchange-rate mechanism – i.e. to maintain its currency within narrow limits of the other EMS currencies – has been defended by British governments at different times with different arguments, arguments which have in fact been inconsistent with one another. In reality the basic reason was always the British reluctance to concede sovereignty in this admittedly important area of economic policy. Hence the phrase 'when the time is right', repeatedly used by the British Prime Minister to indicate when the pound sterling would join the exchange-rate mechanism, was universally construed as meaning 'never'. The economic foundations of this position, however, are perceived by most to be exceedingly flimsy; in the world of reality, as contrasted with that of theory, the degree of sovereignty possessed by a government (any individual government) in the matter of foreign exchange rates in strictly limited. Hence the stance was essentially a political one; and only political considerations were likely to change it.

The second major weakness of the system (sometimes called in aid, rather unconvincingly, of the United Kingdom position) was that while it defines the position of any member currency with regard to all other member currencies, it has no provision for a common policy for the EMS currencies collectively *vis-à-vis* the rest of the world, and especially the US dollar. This clearly does not make much sense. As was shown in the preceding chapter, if two currencies are fixed in relation to one another, the value of either in terms of any third currency must be such as to be consistent with that relationship. But without a mutually-agreed policy on the matter, each member country will have to regard its dollar exchange rate as something of an unknown, the outcome of obscure forces emanating from the activities of central banks beyond its borders. This is clearly unsatisfactory, most of all for countries whose trade with the United States is especially important. The rate of exchange between the US dollar and the ECU (and therefore its own currency) may not be a matter of great moment for the Netherlands, which sells less than 5 per cent of its exports to the United States; it is a rather different matter for the United Kingdom, which sells nearly 15 per cent of its exports in that market. The scope for national conflict is obvious; so therefore is the need for some single central authority to determine and maintain the rate of exchange between the ECU (and thus all its component currencies) and the other major currencies of the world.

·Even leaving aside these technical defects, however, the enthusiasts for greater economic and political integration within the Community also perceived the transformation of the EMS into a genuine monetary union to be, as Mr Jenkins had argued, the major initiative which could restore real impetus to the process of integration. The drafters of the Single European Act therefore sought to have the creation of a monetary union embodied in the Treaty as a specific commitment, and one, furthermore, to be achieved by 1992. In this they were only partly successful. The Act did indeed cause economic and monetary union to be written into the Treaty as a formal objective to which all members of the Community are committed. It also imposes on them an obligation to co-operate in order to ensure the convergence of their domestic policies with a view to that end. But their opponents (the government of the United Kingdom being conspicuous amongst them) also insisted on a provision that any further institutional change in the monetary field – such as those implicit in the proposals for phase 2 of the EMS – would require a formal amendment of the Treaty, something which requires unanimity. The reluctant integrationists probably believed that this provision would make further progress towards monetary union more rather than less difficult.

If so, they had seriously underestimated the determination of the President of the Commission, M Jacques Delors, who in 1988 had persuaded the Council of Ministers (despite obvious misgivings on the part of Mrs Thatcher) to give him the task of 'studying and proposing concrete stages leading towards economic and monetary union'. A Committee under his chairmanship, comprised mainly of governors of the central banks of the Community (including that of the Bank of England), not only completed this formidable task by April 1989 but did so in a report which was unanimous. In many ways it echoed the Werner Report of 1970, treating the case for monetary union as being largely self-evident and recommending that the Community should proceed towards such a union in three stages. As in the Werner report, however, it was emphasised that the path to monetary union was a single, continuous one: embarking on stage 1 was effectively a decision to embark on stages 2 and 3.

The first stage (the only one for which a specific date was suggested) would commence on 1 July 1990 but its length was left undefined. During this stage the four Community currencies still outside the EMS exchange-rate mechanism (those of Greece, Portugal, Spain and the United Kingdom) would become full participants in it. (The Spaniards proceeded to surprise everyone by promptly putting the peseta into the mechanism, with a 6 per cent margin on either side of its central rate, in June 1989.) The first stage would also involve the dismantling of any exchange controls restricting the conversion of any member currency into any other, greater co-ordination 'within existing frameworks' of the fiscal and monetary policies of member governments, stronger regional policy, the completion of the single internal market and the creation of an integrated financial area within the Community.

The Committee envisaged stage 2 as a transitional period during which the EMS would take on some of the trappings of a genuine monetary union. The permitted range of fluctuation around central rates would be reduced below its current value (generally ±2.5 per cent) and realignments of the central rates themselves, while remaining permissible, would become measures of last resort only. More controversially, during this stage the existing central banks of member countries would be amalgamated into a single European System of Central Banks (ESCB) broadly comparable with the Federal Reserve System of the United States. As in the Federal Reserve System, the policy of the ESCB would be formulated by a council composed predominantly of central bankers nominated by national governments; members of the council, however, would possess security of tenure and would be wholly independent of their national governments. This institutional development would obviously call for appropriate amendments to the Treaty of Rome. The Committee anticipated that in the meantime the role of the Community's existing Committee of Central Bank Governors would be strengthened; it would be consulted in advance on the shaping of national monetary policies – i.e. decisions concerning domestic monetary targets. Even more controversially, during this second stage the Council of Ministers (acting on a majority vote) would also lay down limits to the size of the budget deficits permitted for national governments and prescribe the methods by which such deficits could be financed.

In the third and final stage no fluctuations whatever would be permitted in the relative exchange rates of member currencies; the ECU would become the Community's common currency and replace national currencies. The ESCB would hold all the Community's foreign exchange reserves and become the sole authority for monetary policy within it. To maintain that authority, the Community would acquire powers to not merely limit the size of national budget deficits but also to impose budgetary *policies* on individual member governments if this was considered necessary in order to maintain monetary stability within the Community.

These proposals obviously implied profound political changes. If implemented, national governments would not merely surrender the right to vary their own exchange rates; they would be transferring to central Community institutions all power over monetary policy and most of their power to determine budgetary policy. The Delors committee was proposing a version of monetary union which led inescapably to a federal European government presiding over national governments with little more effective economic power than the county councils of the United Kingdom. Not surprisingly it was from that country that the strongest and most explicit opposition came when the proposals were laid before the Madrid summit in June 1989, although this is not to say that serious misgivings were not felt in other, less articulate quarters.

The outcome of the summit in Madrid in June 1989 and a meeting of Finance

Ministers in Brussels in the following month was inevitably a compromise. It was agreed that stage 1 of the Delors process should commence on 1 July 1990; even the United Kingdom was forced to go along with this, rather than run the very real risk of being left on one side, powerless to influence future developments. The British stance of 'when the time is right' with regard to the entry of sterling into the EMS exchange-rate mechanism was therefore softened into the proviso that two conditions in particular must be satisfied – first, that the British inflation rate must be at or below the Community average and, second, that the exchange controls applied by France and Italy in particular should have been abolished. At its Strasbourg meeting in December 1989, the Council also resolved that by the end of 1990 preparatory work should have been completed for discussions concerning the various possible forms which stages 2 and 3 could take and for an intergovernmental conference which would then be called to draft the necessary amendments to the Treaty of Rome.

In brief, the Delors Committee had succeeded in shifting the debate away from the question of whether monetary union should be attempted and on to the questions of the form which it should take and the sort of timing which should be attempted. The Committee itself had opted firmly for an extreme monetarist version in which monetary union necessarily leads to a single currency, a single central bank and (for all practical purposes) a single government. There is, however, a respectable intellectual case for an alternative, Keynesian-type view that monetary union involves costs as well as benefits, and that the retention of some flexibility – in the form of margins of permitted fluctuation and/or occasional revaluations of central rates – may well be prudent. Monetary systems resting on rigid, inflexible rules – as did the old international gold-standard system – are liable to snap under the stress of changes in the economic environment rather than to bend in adjustment to them and thus survive. It is also a fact that the constituent states of monetary unions such as the United States or Canada retain a considerable degree of fiscal autonomy, so that the highly centralised federalism of the Delors version is unnecessary even if it were – which some would question – inherently desirable.

The shape of European monetary union thus remains to be seen. In all probability it will emerge, as does most Community policy, as a compromise between, on the one hand, the enthusiasts satisfied with nothing less than a full-blown United States of Europe and, on the other, the pragmatists profoundly suspicious of any changes in excess of the minimum strictly necessary for the attainment of a specified and limited end. It is true that at the end of the day any changes to the Treaty of Rome require unanimous consent, giving the United Kingdom the theoretical power to indefinitely postpone stage 2 of the process. The power of the veto, however, like the ultimate deterrent of nuclear capability, is effective only so long as it is threatened but not activated; as President Mitterrand stated with brutal clarity in July 1989, if the United Kingdom attempted to bar progress on a path along which the overwhelming majority is determined to proceed, then it will simply be left behind as the rest of the Community proceeds under an agreement separate and distinct from the Treaty itself. The Community is never wise to attempt to ride roughshod over legitimate objections from even its smallest member; individual member governments, on the other hand, would be equally wise to avoid pushing their veto power beyond the limits of Community patience. The classic advice given to those who 'can't beat them' is both well-known and well-founded.

Further Reading

Coffey, P., *Europe and Money* (London: Macmillan, 1977).

Denton, G., *Economic and Monetary Union in Europe* (London: Croom Helm, 1975).

European Commission, *The ECU*, 2nd edn (Luxembourg, 1987).

Levich, R. M. and Sommariva, T., *The ECU market: current developments and future prospects* (Lexington, Mass.: D. C. Heath and Co., 1987).

Ludlow, P., *The Making of the European Monetary System* (London: Butterworth, 1982).

Padoa-Schioppa, T., *Money, Economic Policy and Europe* (Luxembourg: Commission of the European Communities, 1985).

Sumner, M. T. and Zis, G., *European Monetary Union* (London: Macmillan, 1982).

Tsoukalis, L., *The Politics and Economics of European Monetary Integration* (London: Allen & Unwin, 1977).

Ypersele, J. van, *The European Monetary System* (Luxembourg: Commission of the European Communities, 1985).

Regional Policy 24

24.1 The Role of the Regions

That prosperity is unevenly distributed between countries and within them is a fact of life. Climate, mineral resources, ease of communication, fertility of soil, the productivity of working populations: fair or otherwise, certain geographic regions are better endowed with these things than others. As a result, at any time some countries, or regions within them, will be growing more rapidly than the rest; some may even be experiencing growth while populations elsewhere are experiencing economic decline.

A government committed to an extreme form of *laissez-faire* might regard such inequalities as not merely inevitable but an inherent feature of the growth process itself. It might therefore be content to leave them to the free play of market forces, with some sections of its population experiencing high and growing incomes – and thus perhaps congestion and environmental deterioration – while others undergo decline and decay and the depopulation of their land. Such governments are rare; most would be conscious of the political and social stresses set up within a society by gross disparities of this kind. The majority therefore establish some mechanism for cushioning the impact of differential growth rates in different regions of a country or for reducing the magnitude of those differentials. Traditionally, then, the term 'regional policy' has been used to describe policy measures adopted by governments in order to influence the geographical distribution of income and output within their boundaries.

It would not be entirely accurate to say that prior to the early 1970s the Community as such showed no interest in regional policy in this sense. It is a fact, however, that the noticeable increase at that time in the interest shown in the idea of monetary union brought a totally new dimension to the expression 'regional policy'. Those considering the issue from a Keynesian point of view believed the trade-off between inflation and unemployment to be the heart of the matter, implying considerable burdens on weaker economies forced by the stronger to reduce their rates of inflation. Such a trade-off has a strong regional element; levels of aggregate demand high enough to generate something approaching full employment in weak regions would produce excessive pressures, and therefore inflation, in more prosperous regions. Reductions in aggregate demand in an attempt to reduce inflation would have the reverse effect; relatively mild consequences would follow for buoyant regions but an intolerable deflationary burden might be placed on declining regions. A reduction in regional inequality would therefore give an improved wage-rate/unemployment trade-off for the country as a whole and thus reduce the losses imposed by entry into a monetary union. Monetary union, in other words, would make regional policy more important.

Unfortunately, it would also make regional policy more difficult for individual national governments. A fixed rate of exchange, together with a complete absence of tariffs and other obstacles to trade, in effect makes one single market out of what was previously a number of separate markets. The implication is that the local multiplier effect of expenditure in any one region – say, a public works programme aimed primarily at reducing local unemployment – is likely to be reduced; an increasing proportion of the incomes so generated will be spent on imports from the rest of the expanded market and less will be spent on local output. A regional multiplier is necessarily smaller than that for the country of which it is a part; monetary union effectively makes member countries into regions of a single larger whole, so that demand in one country is more likely to diffuse itself over others. Hence monetary union makes conventional regional policy measures less effective.

The implication was clear. In a monetary union each national government would be forced to give priority to securing the equilibrium rate of inflation for the country as a whole; the regional dimension would necessarily be relegated to second place. In the long run national and regional policies may well supplement each other; in the short run, however, they would inevitably conflict. On the other hand, the likely emergence of greater regional inequalities would make some form of regional policy essential to the success of a monetary union. Hence the union collectively – in this case, the Community – would need to supplement national policies with regard to regions, now more constricted in their effect, with a regional policy of its own.

The emergence of the objective of monetary union, then, had given a new meaning to regional policy. The regions in question now would be parts not of national entities but of the union as a whole; indeed, they might well need to relate to the entire area of individual member states. This was indeed the logic of the theoretical analysis of monetary union in Chapter 22; if differences in the growth of real income in the member states are to be kept within acceptable limits, some common policy measures are likely to be necessary to contain them, or at least compensate for them.

24.2 The Early Days of Regional Policy

Since the Treaty of Rome made no reference to monetary union it logically made no provision for a common regional policy. Such references as it contained to regional matters dealt with national reactions to the regional impact of other common policies. Thus Article 39 dealing with the common agricultural policy provided that due account should be taken of 'natural disparities between the various agricultural regions'. Article 75, dealing with transport, noted that member states could make special provision if common measures 'seriously affect the standard of living and the level of employment in certain regions'. Article 92, dealing with state aids to industry (which were in general frowned upon), provided for exemptions for 'aids intended to promote the economic development of regions where the standard of living is abnormally low or where there exists serious unemployment'.

Most of the regional measures adopted by the Community during the 1960s were in fact aimed primarily at preventing the abuse of this latter provision by national governments attempting the concealed protection of domestic industries under the guise of regional policy. In other words, they were an element of the Community's competition policy rather than a conscious attempt to formulate a common regional policy. Most of the discussions in the regional area were concerned with attempts to standardise three aspects of national policies with regard to regions in order to limit the extent of concealed protection – which regions should be permitted to qualify for such special aid, what forms that aid might legitimately take, and how much aid should be permissible.

Initially there was a tendency for national governments to work in terms of whatever regional structure they had acquired over the years. Their definition of the relative poverty or backwardness of a region was therefore determined by a historical structure which had little economic validity. In Germany, for example, Hamburg and Bremen were defined as separate regions simply because in the distant past they had once been city-states and therefore had separate constitutions; Belgium, with a population of less than 10 million, divided itself into 43 regions (of which 41 were claimed to merit aid) while France and Italy, with populations in excess of 50 million, worked mostly in terms of only 20 or 21 regions. Worst of all, poverty or backwardness was defined in terms of other regions within the same country, so that a 'poor' German region such as Schleswig-Holstein actually had a higher per capita income than the 'richest' region of Italy. It was not until 1975 that agreement was reached on a standard list of some 86 Community regions (known as the Nomenclature of Territorial Units for Statistics, thus yielding the pleasant French acronym of NUTS); in this list, Ireland and Luxembourg are each treated as single regions.

Much argument continued over the criteria by which these regions were or were not to be classified as qualifying for special aid. In 1973 the *Report on the*

Regional Problems of the Enlarged Community (the Thomson report, of which more later), proposed four criteria – per capita income below the Community average, more than 20 per cent of the population engaged in agriculture or a declining industry, unemployment persistently 20 per cent above the national average and a high rate of emigration. These were generally agreed to be appropriate criteria, but there was no rule governing the relative weighting to be given to each of the four; as a result, a region continued to be defined as 'poor' whenever the government concerned found it convenient to describe it as such.

Governments adopt a wide variety of measures in the name of regional policy – tax reliefs, subsidies, low-interest or interest-free loans, investment grants and so on. From the outset the Commission sought to establish principles for such aid which were consistent (or at least minimally inconsistent) with its general competition philosophy. These were that regional aids should be calculable with reasonable certainty – and that they should be aimed at raising productivity rather than merely seeking to ensure the survival of the inefficient. Again, these excellent principles secured general agreement, but their application in particular instances inevitably gave rise to much argument. The result was usually (but by no means invariably) that national governments ended up doing whatever they had intended to do in the first place.

The third issue concerned the amounts of aid which national governments might legitimately give to projects in regions which, rightly or otherwise, had been classified as deserving of assistance. As with the other two issues, the tendency was for governments to be allowed to continue whatever they had done previously unless this was demonstrably in flagrant contravention of the basic principle of free competition. Nevertheless, agreement on some kind of standardisation was assisted by the awareness of member governments that competitive bidding against one another to attract external investment into their regions would do none of them any good. An element of self-interest therefore encouraged the resolution by the Council of Ministers in 1971 that from 1973 onwards such state aid should not exceed 20 per cent of the value of an investment in so-called 'central' – i.e. prosperous – regions but could amount to 30 per cent in less prosperous regions. (For Ireland, the south of Italy and Greenland even this limit could be exceeded.) Since few if any national governments exceeded these limits in practice everyone was more or less happy. In this, as in the other respects, what was passing for regional policy was in reality no more than a very broad standardisation of national practices combined with an attempt to eliminate the most flagrant abuses of them.

Even so, it would be wrong to conclude that no element whatever of positive regional policy was evident during the first decade of the Community's existence. The Treaty had established the European Investment Bank whose purpose was to contribute to the 'balanced and smooth development of the Common Market'. It was not specifically a regional agency but the first of the fields of interest specified for it in the Treaty was that of 'projects for developing less developed regions'. Equally it was not intended to be, and has not become, an aid agency in the sense that it is a means whereby regions receive subsidised loans at the taxpayers' expense. The EIB exists to make long-term loans with the aid of resources derived overwhelmingly from its own borrowings in the open international capital market and is charged with operating on a non-loss-making as well as a non-profit-making basis. Its high credit standing, however, enables it to borrow and re-lend at rates significantly lower than those which would be faced by the authorities of depressed regions if they were borrowing on their own account.

By the end of 1973 the Bank had lent out the equivalent of ECU 12.7 bn, 85 per cent of which had been used within the Community; by end-1986 this total had grown to more than ECU 53 bn, with nearly 90 per cent of this being lent within the Community. Loans for regional projects have consistently amounted to more than 50 per cent of the EIB's total, and the redistributive nature of its work is reflected in the disproportionate share of its lending which is directed towards Italy and the United Kingdom; the annual share of EIB disbursements taken by these two countries has consistently been around two-thirds of the total.

The European Social Fund, equally, was not intended to have a primarily regional function but none the less the nature of its activities during the 1960s was such that its resources tended to be channelled disproportionately towards the poorer regions. As was noted in Chapter 19, however, the regional dimension of its activity was not made explicit until 1972. All in all it remains true to say, therefore, that despite the activities of these more positive agencies of the Community the main thrust of regional measures during the 1960s was the avoidance of abuses rather than the creation of policies. The rather motley collection of qualifications and derogations which had accumulated by the end of that decade could hardly be said to have added up to an integrated and coherent regional policy.

24.3 Regional Policy Emerges

It has been suggested above that it was the emergence of the objective of monetary union in the early 1970s which was the main cause of the growth of interest in a Community, as opposed to national, regional policy. Lord Thomson, the Commissioner with special responsibility for regional matters – admittedly hardly a totally disinterested witness – declared in his 1973 report that monetary union within Europe was 'inconceivable' without a strong Community regional policy. Nevertheless there were other factors working to enhance the importance attached to regional measures. Prominent among these was the obvious need to make belated provision for some redistributive mechanism within the Community budget in view of the impending accession of the United Kingdom. If it could do nothing else, a Community regional policy could at least transfer resources from some member countries to others in a reasonably systematic manner.

A further feature of the early 1970s made a more positive approach to regional policy both more important and more difficult. The decade of the 1960s had been one of phenomenal growth in the economies of all the member countries in the Community and in such circumstances regional disparities of income tend to fall – both because of the spillover effects of economic expansion on depressed regions and because affluence enables governments to pour more resources into them. In Table 24.1 are shown two related measures of inequality in regional incomes – the Thiel index of income disparities and the simpler coefficient of variation. They allow a distinction to be made between the two separate causes of such disparities within the Community – those which arise because of differences between member countries in *national* levels of incomes and those which arise because of regional differences *within* member countries. The gap between the income of a poor region in country A and a rich region in country B may narrow, in other words, either because average income in country A is rising more rapidly than in country B or because poor regions in A are gaining relatively to rich regions in country A.

The estimates in Table 24.1 suggest that regional disparities within the

Table 24.1
Regional Variances in the European Community, 1950–82 (Per capita incomes, 1970 = 100)

Year	Between countries		Within countries		Total regional variance	
	Thiel index	Coefficient of variation	Thiel index	Coefficient of variation	Thiel index	Coefficient of variation
(1)	(2)	(3)	(4)	(5)	(6)	(7)
1950	503	225	146	127	252	176
1960	298	174	128	119	178	147
1970	100	100	100	100	100	100
1976	80	91	102	102	95	97
1982*	75	89	92	109	87	99

* Excludes Greece.

SOURCE   *1950–60*: Calculated from data in W. Molle *et al.*, *Regional Disparity and Economic Development in the European Community*, Farnborough: Saxon House, 1980; GDP figures are $US at contemporary exchange rates. *1970–82*: Calculated from data in *Yearbook of Regional Statistics* (Luxembourg: Commission of the European Communities, 1981 and 1985). GDP figures are in ECUs at purchasing power parities.

Community declined dramatically between 1960 and 1970 – by 78 per cent on the Theil index and by 47 per cent as measured by a simple coefficient of variation. Both indicate, however, that this was overwhelmingly due to a decline in differences in national average incomes rather than from reduced inequality within countries. (The Theil index suggests that about 80 per cent of Community regional differences in 1960 were due to differences in national incomes rather than inequalities within countries.) The major cause at work was that the poorer countries had grown more rapidly than the richer ones. In 1958 Luxembourg had been the richest of the Six (in terms of income per head) and Italy the poorest; over 1958–72, however, the annual growth rate of real income per head had been 4.6 per cent in Italy compared with 3.0 per cent in Luxembourg.

From 1973 onwards the overall growth rate in the Community fell dramatically and unemployment rose sharply; the main engine of regional equality slowed down and, as Table 24.1 reveals, the dramatic progress of the 1960s came to an end. (According to some commentators, including the Commission itself, regional inequality actually increased sharply in the middle 1970s; as is explained below, however, this conclusion was based on national income estimates of a misleading nature.)

In the eyes of many, this development increased the urgency attached to regional policy within the Community. It was unrealistic to suppose that further progress could be made towards economic and monetary integration while governments were being confronted with pockets of quite acute distress within their own countries. As the Commission remarked in a 1977 report, the strengthening of Community (regional) policy was 'not only desirable; it is now one of the conditions of continuing European integration'. Unfortunately the worsening of the overall economic situation also made effective regional policy more difficult. Measures aimed at attracting new developments to poorer regions have little effect if the flow of new developments available has dried up; equally, resources to improve regional infrastructures are more difficult to find in the context of an economy growing slowly, or not at all, than in a situation of relative affluence.

24.4   The European Regional Development Fund

At the Paris summit of 1972 the European Council had resolved to create a new agency – the European Regional Development Fund (ERDF) which, it was stated, was 'needed to correct the structural and regional imbalances which might affect the realisation of economic and monetary union'. In the following year the new Regional Commissioner, Lord Thomson, presented the Council with a report, *Proposals for a Community Regional Policy*, the bulk of which was subsequently approved by the Council and formed the first basis of a Community regional policy. (Naturally it became known as the Thomson Report.)

The ERDF was to be the primary instrument of this new policy; it was to channel Community resources into regional development projects by means of investment grants and loans at subsidised interest rates. Initially, investment grants could amount to 20 per cent of the capital costs of a project or 50 per cent of the aid being given to it by the national government concerned. ERDF funds could also be passed to the European Investment Bank to enable it to provide loans for such projects at 3 per cent less than the normal (i.e. market-determined) rate. It will be observed, however, that all this fell a good deal short of a genuine Community policy. The resources of the ERDF could be used only to contribute towards the cost of projects submitted by national governments. Its role was therefore a passive one, the initiative in regional development remaining with national governments.

Inevitably there was considerable argument over the amounts which member governments were to be required to contribute to the coffers of the ERDF. At one extreme, the German government sought a small fund (the equivalent of ECU 2.7 bn at 1986 prices) and a narrow definition of qualifying regions; at the other, the main prospective beneficiaries, Britain and Italy, wanted a large fund (about ECU 8 bn) with quotas allocated on a national basis rather than on some restrictive Community definition of need. In the result the sum agreed for the first three years, 1975–7, was a compromise amounting to about ECU 3.5 bn. The concept of national quotas was also agreed – they are shown in col. (2) of Table 24.2; the result was to ensure that Britain and Italy between them were guaranteed more than two-thirds of the total.

This system of national allocations was a fundamental departure from the original proposals of the Thomson report. It demonstrated beyond doubt that, whatever its original intention, the ERDF was being used primarily as a redistributive agency; by allocating funds on a national basis, rather than according to regional needs as perceived on a Community basis, the essentially passive nature of the fund was re-emphasised. Projects were determined by national governments; the ERDF was simply a means by which those governments would be partly reimbursed for expenditures which they would have undertaken in any event.

As the first phase of ERDF operations approached its close, the Commission expressed its unhappiness over these features in a memorandum *Guidelines for Community Regional Policy* in 1977. In it the Commission proposed, first, that the criteria by which regions should be appraised should be defined in terms of the appropriate level of policy action rather than in terms of their weakness or strength. Four categories were proposed. The first would be areas requiring long-term aid to remedy a lack of basic infrastructure and the second those requiring medium-term assistance to replace industries now in decline. For both of these, it was argued, remedial action could and should be taken by national governments rather than by the Community collectively. The third category,

Table 24.2
Quotas in the European Regional Development Fund (% of Total)

Country	1975–7	1978–80	1981–4	1985		1986 onwards	
				Min.	Max.	Min.	Max.
(1)	(2)	(3)	(4)	(5)	(6)	(7)	(8)
Belgium	1.49	1.39	1.11	0.90	1.20	0.61	0.82
Denmark	1.29	1.20	1.06	0.51	0.67	0.34	0.46
France	14.87	16.86	13.64	11.05	14.74	7.48	9.96
Germany	6.34	6.00	4.65	3.76	4.81	2.55	3.40
Greece	—	—	13.00	12.35	15.74	8.36	10.64
Ireland	6.46	6.46	5.94	5.64	6.83	3.82	4.61
Italy	40.00	39.39	35.49	31.94	42.59	21.62	28.79
Luxembourg	0.10	0.09	0.07	0.06	0.08	0.04	0.06
Netherlands	1.69	1.58	1.24	1.00	1.34	0.68	0.91
Portugal	—	—	—	—	—	10.66	14.20
Spain	—	—	—	—	—	17.97	23.93
United Kingdom	27.76	27.03	23.80	21.42	28.56	14.50	19.31
Total	100	100	100	88.63	116.56	88.63	117.09

however, would comprise areas which were being adversely affected by Community policies and the fourth those which could be called 'frontier' regions – divided by national boundaries and requiring integrated action by two or more governments. For these regions, the Commission argued, Community rather than national action was required.

Hence the resources of the ERDF, the Commission argued, should be divided into two sections: one, allocated on national quotas, to be used for the first two categories, and the other, to be allocated on Community criteria without reference to nationality, for the third and fourth categories. While no precise figure was put on this 'non-quota' element, it was clearly intended to be a substantial fraction of the total; at a later stage the Commission indicated that it had around 20 per cent in mind. Further, it was proposed that grants under this non-quota element should require approval by only a qualified majority of the Council, rather than its unanimous approval.

It was clear that the Commission was struggling to remove the ERDF from its essentially national basis and move it, at least partly, to a Community basis. Perhaps for that reason the proposals received a severe mauling in the Council; when approval was finally given, the non-quota section of the ERDF was limited to a mere 5 per cent of the total and it was specified that every project financed from this section would require the unanimous approval of the Council.

The Council did agree, however, to another of the Commission's proposals – that increased attention should be given to regional measures (including the regional dimension of other policy measures) at both national and Community level. A systematic monitoring of developments at a regional level was therefore approved and the Commission was instructed to submit periodic reports on the state of the regions. It was also agreed that the criteria for 'regional imbalance' justifying support from the ERDF should be simplified and clarified.

24.5 Reappraisal and Reform

In its first periodic report on the state of the regions in 1980, the Commission expressed some disappointment at the progress of the Community's regional policy despite the changes agreed in 1977. In the first place, it expressed the view that regional differences within the Community appeared to be increasing rather than narrowing. It is true that, when per capita incomes are converted into ECUs using current exchange rates, average per capita income in the Community's poorest region (Calabria in Italy) in 1970 had been 26 per cent of that in its richest region (the Ile de France) whereas by 1978 it had fallen to 21 per cent. The use of current exchange rates to effect the conversion into ECUs, however, undoubtedly distorts the comparison; when the conversion is based on the Commission's estimates of the relative purchasing powers of the various currencies, the deterioration over these years is seen to have been much more modest – from 30 per cent in 1970 to 28 per cent in 1978.

The evidence of Table 24.1, in fact, suggests that the degree of regional inequality within the Community as a whole continued to decline during the 1970s, although at a much more modest pace than in previous decades and entirely because of smaller income differences between member countries rather than within them. But if the Commission had perhaps been unduly pessimistic in claiming a positive worsening of the regional position since the commencement of the ERDF it was certainly justified in claiming that the situation had not improved significantly.

Part of the explanation for this rather unimpressive performance, in the view of the Commission, was that far too much of the ERDF resources was being applied to individual projects in member countries – new roads, bridges, harbours and so on – while too little was being used for integrated development programmes generating employment which would continue after the construction stage had been completed. (Over 1975–85 as a whole, in fact, 97 per cent of the assistance granted by the ERDF went to individual projects, more than 80 per cent of these being classified as 'infrastructure'.) What is more, such projects inevitably raised the old problem of additionality – the suspicion, to put it no higher, that ERDF grants were being obtained for expenditures which would have occurred anyway, so that ERDF funds were being reduced to nothing more than gratuitous contributions to national budgets.

The Commission also noted disapprovingly that, while the allocation of ERDF resources had been heavily weighted in favour of the relatively poor countries, a substantial share was nevertheless still going to countries which could well afford to finance their own regional programmes. The evidence shown in Table 24.3 tends to confirm this; over 1975–84 the six countries with above-average per capita incomes absorbed 23 per cent of the Fund's total outlays. The Commission therefore proposed that the ERDF quotas for Belgium, France, Germany and the Netherlands should be abolished altogether.

Finally, the Commission noted that the take-up rate of the miniscule non-quota section of the ERDF had been very low. In most of the years since the introduction of the non-quota section, in fact, part of the funds allocated to it had to be transferred into the quota section for want of applicants. The

Table 24.3
Grants from the ERDF, 1975–88 (Annual averages – Appropriations)

Member state	% of total grants			ECUs per head at 1986 prices		
(1)	1975–80 (2)	1981–5 (3)	1986–8 (4)	1975–80 (5)	1981–5 (6)	1986–8 (7)
Belgium	1.5	0.8	0.9	11.0	7.7	2.7
Denmark	1.1	1.0	0.3	19.5	19.8	2.1
France	17.8	13.0	9.8	25.0	23.9	5.5
Germany	8.0	3.3	2.8	9.5	3.3	1.4
Greece	—	13.8	9.3	—	141.6	29.1
Ireland	6.6	6.0	4.3	151.8	176.1	38.6
Italy	37.2	37.0	24.0	49.7	65.2	13.1
Luxembourg	0.1	0.1	0.1	17.9	25.6	6.0
Netherlands	2.0	1.1	0.6	10.8	7.4	1.4
Portugal	—	—	11.3	—	—	34.0
Spain	—	—	18.9	—	—	15.3
United Kingdom	25.5	24.0	17.7	33.7	42.3	9.7
Total*	100.0	100.0	100.0	27.7	31.2	9.7

* Excluding very small grants which are not allocable to individual member countries.

SOURCE General Reports of the activities of the European Communities, various. The per capita totals are based on the populations existing in the first year of each period, while the conversion to 1986 prices is based on the average GDP deflator for the period as a whole.

Commission had no doubt about the reason for this: in allotting the non-quota element a Community, rather than a national, dimension was applied in deciding whether a particular project was or was not worthwhile. National governments found this submission to Commission questioning and judgement unacceptable, and therefore avoided exposure to it. The remedy proposed by the Commission was the introduction of a progressive increase in the relative size of the non-quota section, beginning with an increase to at least 20 per cent of the total; this would force member governments to choose between their pride and their pockets.

The Commission would scarcely have expected its proposals for revising the ground-rules of the ERDF to be greeted with unqualified enthusiasm, and it was not disappointed. Any proposed change in the distribution of Community funds is destined to receive rough handling in the Council of Ministers and is lucky to survive at all, let alone to emerge unscathed. The Council took three years to consider the proposals and its 'new' regional policy, embodied in Regulation 1787 of 1984, embodied a rather pale reflection of the Commission proposals.

In the first place, the 1984 revisions restated the ultimate objectives of Community regional policy in simpler and more general terms. The objective was now declared to be the restructuring of the areas in the Community most affected by industrial decline and the 'structural adjustment' of regions experiencing delayed development. This fell short of the Commission's suggestion that the richer countries should be altogether excluded from the scope of the ERDF but did at least imply that genuine relative poverty, measured against a Community scale, had to be established before a region could lay claim to ERDF funds.

The Council did approve what had in fact been a long-standing Commission practice – the replacement of detailed and complex qualification criteria by a simple, if crude, 'poverty index'. For any region this consists of the arithmetic mean of (a) its relative per capita income and (b) its relative level of unemployment, both measured against the Community average. An index of less than 75 per cent would qualify for assistance. In practice the Commission tended to simplify the index even further by concentrating on relative per capita income; this was formalised by the Council of Ministers in 1988 and embodied in the rule that a region qualified for assistance if its per capita GDP during the preceding three years fell below 76 per cent of the Community average.

The measure is scarcely a sophisticated one and is sensitive to both the methodology and the accuracy of estimates of regional income. Its simplicity, however, could reduce the scope for special pleading inherent in the more complex criteria of earlier days. On the other hand, the Council decision of 1988 left something of a special-pleading door open by adding Ireland and the French overseas *departements* to the list of qualifying 'regions' without reference to the GDP measure; even worse, it ruled that other regions narrowly failing to qualify under the GDP rule could be added to the list 'for particular reasons'.

Secondly, the Council went some way towards meeting the Commission's view that more emphasis needed to be placed in Community policy on development programmes which generate permanent employment and less on one-off projects. It was agreed that from 1985 onwards, and within three years, at least 20 per cent of ERDF assistance should go to integrated development programmes (compared with a mere 1.6 per cent in 1984). Further, it was agreed that the maximum ERDF contribution should be raised from 30 per cent to 50 per cent for projects, and to 70 per cent for development programmes. This attempt to switch emphasis seems to be succeeding; appropriations for programmes amounted to only 7 per cent of the total in 1985 but to 22 per cent by 1988.

Finally, although the Council found the proposals for a drastic reduction in the quota element of the ERDF too much to swallow, it agreed to a modest movement in the suggested direction. From 1985 the simple distinction between the quota and non-quota elements was abolished and replaced by a minimum/maximum range for each country. The difference between the minimum and maximum share is to be available for grants to support proposals appraised against Community (i.e. Commission) criteria rather than those of the applicant governments. About 11 per cent of the ERDF total available each year would therefore be put up for tender, so to speak, amongst member governments but be subject to Community rather than national appraisal.

The proposed ranges are shown in cols (5) and (6) of Table 24.2. (The revisions for 1986 onwards resulting from the admission of Portugal and Spain are shown in cols (7) and (8).) It will be observed that the new quotas were rather cleverly calculated so that, with the single exception of Denmark, all member countries were theoretically able to obtain a larger share of the total than under the previous regime. The outcome for 1986–8 indicates the degree to which individual countries availed themselves of this opportunity to obtain more than their minimum share. Belgium, Italy and Ireland obtained 90 per cent or more of the maximum available, while France, Germany and the Netherlands made almost no use of the facility. Whether this reflects the relative urgency of regional problems in the countries concerned or, by contrast, their relative disinclination to be subject to Commission scrutiny and questioning, must remain a matter of speculation.

The Single European Act and the commitment to a single market by 1992 added yet another round of debate to the regional question. The Single European Act called for greater 'economic and social cohesion' in the Community, but the poorer member countries bordering the Mediterranean feared that left to themselves the competitive forces unleashed by the movement to a single market would widen, rather than diminish, the differences of wealth and prosperity between member countries. Hence in February 1988 the Council of

Ministers resolved that in the five years 1989 to 1993 the resources placed at the disposal of the 'structural' funds – the Social Fund as well as the Regional Fund – should be doubled in real terms, so that by 1993 they would be absorbing a quarter of the total Community budget.

In February 1989 a parallel adjustment was made to the policy to be adopted in the use of the Fund's resources. Largely because of the reduction in population migration within the Community since the early 1970s, it was held, economic convergence within it had halted; by 1985 regional differences in unemployment rates were more than twice as great as in 1975. Hence regional aid was to be concentrated more than ever on the less-developed regions – most of Southern Europe and Ireland and areas of industrial decline featured by long-term unemployment. Special regional programmes are to be pursued to meet specific problems – programmes for the overseas territories adversely affected by the Single Market (Poseidon) and for areas affected by the restructuring of the steel industry (Resider) or the shipbuilding industry (Renaval). The role of the private sector and local or regional authorities is to be increased while that of direct central governments is to diminish. Above all, the principle of additionality was reiterated – funds from the Regional Fund must be in addition to expenditures by national governments, not substitutes for them. As ever, the government of the United Kingdom demurred, arguing that ERDF resources could properly replace domestic expenditures provided that equivalent sums were spent on additional projects in the same regions. The debate continues.

24.6   The Prospects for Regional Policy

The arguments in favour of a Community policy for the regions of Europe have remained much the same over the 20 years or so since the case was first seriously discussed. On the one hand, regional disparities within the Community of Nine may have diminished slightly over that period – the evidence is something less than overwhelming – but the accessions of Greece, Portugal and Spain, on the other hand, have extended the Community to include countries whose average per capita income is little, if any, higher than that of the poorest regions of Italy. The advocates of closer integration within the Community argue that the case for monetary union is as persuasive as ever; yet monetary union is unlikely to be achievable without an effective regional policy.

In truth, the Community remains as far removed from a genuinely *common* regional policy as it was in 1970. The ERDF exists and is, doubtless, of value; over 1981–8 its average annual appropriation in the Community budget was three times the average for 1977–80 in real terms, and in 1988 the Council resolved that its resources should be doubled again by 1993. But, as Michael Shanks has remarked in this context, a Fund is not a policy. The resources of the ERDF are almost trivial in comparison with those deployed on regional affairs by national governments. (It has been estimated that in 1982 national governments allocated funds to regional development – *excluding* expenditure on infrastructure – which totalled more than five times the entire ERDF budget for that year.) And of the resources which the ERDF does dispense, nearly 90 per cent are in any event absorbed in national quotas which are little more than contributions to general domestic budgets. Regional policy in the Community remains effectively little more than a collection of national policies dedicated to the pursuit of national ends.

It has to be recorded that the Community itself is scarcely beyond reproach in its handling of regional matters. The delays, bureaucratic procedures and vulnerability to the unremitting pursuit of national self-interest, for which Brussels has become renowned, has not left DG XVI, the Commission's regional policy arm, unscathed. Applications for ERDF funds have been known to spend years seeking approval; only recently has any real attempt been made to co-ordinate the activities of the ERDF with other funds having regional impact; other policies of the Community itself, most obviously the CAP, can and do have regional implications far outweighing anything within the scope of the ERDF.

This very limited progress towards a common policy indicates the need to assign a more modest role for Community action in this field than some of the more sweeping statements of the early 1970s in this context might have indicated. That there is scope for Community action in the regional field must be beyond dispute, but that is a far cry from uniformity of both means and ends throughout the length and breadth of the 12 member countries. The social welfare rankings attached to those ends and means are unlikely to be identical throughout the Community; if a trade-off exists between regional inequality and the overall national rate of growth, as can be argued, the optimum choice could scarcely be the same for all. When common policies are as slow to emerge as seems to have been the case with the regions of Europe the explanation may lie in a multitude of conflicting ends as much as in the congenital reluctance of national governments to will the means.

Further Reading

European Commission, *The European Community and its Regions* (Luxembourg, 1985).

Keating, M. and Jones, B., *Regions in the European Community* (Oxford: Clarendon Press, 1985).

Molle, W. and Cappellini, R , *Regional Impact of Community Policies in Europe* (Aldershot: Avebury Press, 1988).

Molle, W. *et al.*, *Regional Disparity and Economic Development in the European Community* (Farnborough: Saxon House, 1980).

Pinder, D., *Regional Economic Development and Policy* (London: Allen & Unwin, 1983).

Vanhove, N. and Klaasen, L. H., *Regional Policy: a European Approach*, 2nd edn (Aldershot: Gower Publishing Co., 1987).

Yuill, D. (ed.), *Regional Policy in the European Community* (London: Croom Helm, 1980).

Commercial Policy – Friends and Neighbours 25

25.1 From Rome to Yaoundé

At the time of its inception there was a good deal of nervousness in the world at large that the Community would build itself into an inward-looking fortress, increasingly isolating itself from the outside world. Formally, this was never a well-founded fear. In the first place, Article 237 of the Treaty provided that any like-minded European state could apply for membership and, as has been seen, in fact the Community has been enlarged on three occasions since 1958. Secondly, Part 4 of the Treaty (Articles 131 to 136) provided that 'non-European countries and territories which have special relations' with the member countries could be brought into association with the Community. Thirdly, Article 238 provided that a similar special association, embodying reciprocal rights and obligations, could be created between the Community and any other third country or group of countries. Finally, Articles 110–116 provided for the formulation by the Community of a common commercial policy which would contribute, hopefully, to 'the harmonious development of world trade'. All this was scarcely indicative of an inherently isolationist and protectionist stance.

The three enlargements of the Community have been discussed in Chapter 3, while the Community's common commercial policy towards the world in general will be discussed in Chapter 26. In this chapter the Community's relationships with its associated territories and close neighbours will be summarised. That special provision should be made in the treaty for the countries which were, or had been until recently, colonies of the member states was inevitable, espdially for France. French overseas territories were treated as part

303

of France itself, so that trade discrimination against them in the shape of the common external tariff would have been unthinkable. Even if it had been politically feasible, there were very good economic reasons why such discrimination was unacceptable. A major part of the return on French investments in these territories took the form of exports to France; to apply the common external tariff to them would in effect be imposing a tax on French profits. On the other hand, French exports enjoyed preferential treatment in these territories and the logic of a customs union dictated that such preferences could scarcely be extended to one member of the Community and not to the others. This raised the spectre of the extension of preferential treatment to the exports of other member countries – Germany, in particular – which had borne none of the burden of development assistance to these territories; such a development, obviously, could only be to the considerable disadvantage of French exporters.

The Treaty of Rome therefore provided that for the first five years of its operation any reductions in the tariffs on trade between the member countries would be extended to trade with these associated territories – 26 dependencies or trustee territories, of which 22 were French possessions in Africa. These territories, in turn, were to extend Most Favoured Nation treatment to imports from all the Community countries; in effect, all the member countries were to receive the same preferential treatment as the metropolitan countries concerned. In addition, an Annex to the Treaty provided for the creation of a Development Fund (EDF) to finance investment projects in the associated territories; over the five years 1958–62 this was to provide funds amounting to the equivalent of ECU 3.6 bn. Two-thirds of this total was contributed in equal shares by France and Germany, but about 90 per cent of the disbursements occurred in French dependent territories.

The Treaty provided that by the end of the first five years of its operation the Council would determine what further provisions should be made for the associated territories in the light of the experience of those five years. The outcome of protracted negotiations during 1961–2 was the Yaoundé convention of July 1963 which takes its name from the capital of Cameroon in which it was signed. This agreement came into operation in July 1964 and ran for five years; its successor, Yaoundé 2, was signed in 1969 and ran until 1975.

By 1963, most of the overseas territories associated with the Community at the time of its creation had moved from the status of colonies to that of independent states. The first Yaoundé convention therefore created a formal institutional framework for the participating countries. The group was now labelled AASM – Associated African States and Madagascar – and set up for itself a Council of Ministers and a permanent secretariat. Under Yaoundé 1 there were 18 such member countries, the total rising to 19 for Yaoundé 2 with the accession of Mauritius. Provision was made, however, for other African countries to be 'associated' with the arrangements and by 1969 Nigeria, Kenya, Tanzania and Uganda had all negotiated associated status.

Essentially the conventions extended the provisions of the initial five years; exports of manufactured goods from the AASM countries enjoyed preferential (usually duty-free) access to the Community, with a much lesser degree of preference for exports of agricultural products. In granting these preferences it was necessary for the Community to apply a set of rules determining the real origin of prospective imports in order to ensure that the goods concerned were indeed the product of the country to which the preferential arrangements applied, rather than goods originating elsewhere and being shipped via that country merely to obtain preferential treatment. In general the Community operates a change-of-tariff-heading system. This means that to qualify as domestic output the product concerned must have a tariff classification different from that of any imported components it contains. The application of the rule is in fact much more complicated than this may suggest, with separate lists setting out products for which (a) satisfying this test is not sufficient in itself and (b) satisfying this test is not required if other conditions are met.

In return for this preferential treatment of their industrial exports to the Community the AASM countries were required to give comparable preference to Community exports; since few of the AASM countries had any significant industrial base this requirement did not in fact present any great difficulty. The flow of aid via the EDF was maintained; under Yaoundé 1 the total made available for the whole period was around ECU 4.0 bn, while under Yaoundé 2 it fell to around ECU 3.4 bn.

The creation of these preferential trading arrangements between the Community and a limited number of African countries inevitably caused some ill-feeling in the countries excluded from them. The favourable treatment of Community exports to the AASM countries necessarily implied discrimination against exports to the AASM from non-Community countries, not least the United States; conversely, the preference given to AASM exports by the Community necessarily implied a corresponding discrimination against comparable exports from other developing countries. In fact the evidence does not suggest that these preferences had much practical effect. During the period of Yaoundé 1 there is some indication that they may have given the AASM countries an advantage; their exports of manufactures to the Community rose from 35.4 per cent of the total for the developing world in 1963 to 38.4 per cent in 1968. During Yaoundé 2, on the other hand, the situation was reversed; by 1973 the share of the AASM countries in manufactured exports to the Community from the developing world fell back to 33.6 per cent. As the following chapter records, the 1960s was a decade of world-wide tariff reductions, so that the relative importance of tariff preferences granted in 1963 had been much reduced by the end of the decade.

25.2   Lomé 1 to Lomé 4

As the life-span of Yaoundé 2 moved to its close it was obvious that substantial modifications were needed to it. As has just been noted, the practical value of its benefits to the participating countries seemed more modest than had originally been expected. More important, the impending accession of the United Kingdom to the Community brought into the reckoning a vast array of overseas Commonwealth territories with which Britain had long enjoyed preferential trading arrangements similar to those which had so exercised the French government in 1957. The questions raised by these territories were in one sense trickier than those raised by the AASM countries; in many of them the process of industrialisation, while still at a relatively early stage, was nevertheless sufficiently advanced to raise serious problems of trade conflict. The French government, in addition, was not anxious to see the preferential system of the Yaoundé agreements extended over too wide an area; it argued, not unreasonably, that every extension of the geographical scope of the arrangements necessarily reduced the value of the comparative preference given to the existing associated territories. As a result the United Kingdom secured the inclusion of its associated African territories in the Community's preferential arrangements but failed to achieve their extension to the great Commonwealth countries of Asia – India, Pakistan, Malaysia, Singapore and Hong Kong – just as, earlier, the government of the Netherlands had failed in its attempts to have Indonesia included in the list.

The outcome was a series of agreements, or Conventions, which broadly speaking extended the Yaoundé arrangements in terms of both time and scope. The first Convention was signed in Lomé, the capital of Togo, in February 1975 and covered the period 1975–80. It was succeeded by Lomé 2, running from 1981 to 1985, and this in turn was succeeded by Lomé 3, which ran from 1986 to 1990. Lomé 1 covered 46 countries, predominantly in Africa but now including smaller territories in the Caribbean and the Pacific. Hence the label AASM was replaced by that of the African, Caribbean and Pacific States, ACP. Membership had risen to 59 by the time of the signing of Lomé 2 and to 66 by the time of Lomé 3 in May 1986. It is fair to say that virtually the only characteristic which these countries have in common, apart from historical links with one or other Community country, is that of extreme poverty.

Although each of the three Lomé Conventions differs from the others in points of detail, their essential characteristics are the same. In the first place, they provide that virtually all exports of manufactured products from the ACP countries are allowed to enter the Community free of tariff or quota restrictions. In contrast with the Yaoundé agreements, no corresponding reciprocal concession is required on the part of the ACP countries. This sounds like a considerable concession on the part of the Community but it has to be recorded that, first, manufactured goods account for only a small proportion of the ACP countries' total exports and, second, that their major export products attract a zero, or at most a very low, tariff in any event. It also has to be noted that the Community's rather complex rules of origin apply to ACP manufactured exports to the Community in order to ensure that the bulk of their value does in fact originate in the exporting country itself; this does not make exporting to the Community an entirely painless process.

Second, special provision is made in the Conventions for agricultural exports of the ACP countries which compete with products covered by the Common Agricultural Policy. Something considerably less than free trade is permitted for such products, needless to say. In general, the CAP levies imposed on such imports as are permitted are smaller than those imposed on imports from non-ACP countries. More important, special arrangements are made for imports of sugar and beef. For sugar in particular, an annual quota of 1.4 m tonnes is distributed amongst ACP producers; these imports are then guaranteed the same price as that paid to domestic beet growers under the CAP. As is noted in the next chapter, however, the value of this concession to the ACP countries is somewhat qualified by the impact of the CAP on the price for sugar obtainable by those countries in other markets.

Thirdly, the first Lomé Convention introduced a system known as STABEX whereby a shortfall in the revenues derived by the ACP countries from exports to the Community of their major export products, in excess of a specified size – in general, any shortfall greater than 2 per cent of the average level of earnings over the preceding four years – is made good by grants or (nominally) interest-free loans. In Lomé 2 this was supplemented by a parallel arrangement for mineral products known as SYSMIN. At the time this was regarded as something of a breakthrough in the business of aid for the developing world, protecting the poorer countries, as it seemed to do, against the curse of instability in their foreign exchange receipts.

The effectiveness of the schemes in practice seems to have been dubious. If prices are generally rising, as they mostly have been since 1975, export receipts can fall in real terms without the absolute fall in monetary terms required to qualify for assistance. Secondly, a decline in export receipts from a product which accounts for a large proportion of exports may be too small to qualify, whereas a larger decline in receipts from a minor export product may qualify. Thirdly, the system inherently discourages the ACP countries from diversifying their exports in terms of either destination or degree of processing. Finally, the rules and regulations under which the schemes are operated are notoriously complicated: of the 70 applications for assistance under STABEX in 1988 no less than 27 were rejected as failing to qualify.

The volume of resources made available from the EDF has steadily risen in monetary but not in real terms. Under Lomé 1 the total was equivalent to ECU 8.0 bn at 1986 prices, under Lomé 2 to ECU 6.7 bn and under Lomé 3 to ECU 7.4 bn. Over that period, unfortunately, the total population of the ACP countries rose by nearly 40 per cent to 430 million. The allocation in Lomé 3 therefore accounts for an annual average of ECU 3.4 per head of population – not the sort of sum likely to stimulate a development explosion. Nor is the effectiveness of the EDF increased by the fact that remittances from it are made by national governments, not by the Commission centrally; as a result pressure is inevitably brought to bear on recipient countries to ensure that the funds involved are used for contracts with enterprises domiciled in the donor country. It is perhaps not entirely surprising to find that nearly 30 per cent of EDF aid has been used for contracts with French firms but less than 20 per cent has been spent on contracts with firms located within the ACP countries themselves.

As with the Yaoundé agreements – and for much the same reasons – the evidence does not suggest that the trade preferences extended to the ACP countries have been particularly effective. As will be seen from Table 25.1, the Community had absorbed over 70 per cent of the total exports from the ACP countries to the industrialised world in 1963 and this share had fallen to 62 per cent by 1970; by 1979, however, the share had fallen even further to only just 50 per cent – and this during a period in which the developing countries as a whole were increasing their share of the Community's total imports. Similarly, the share of the EEC in the total imports of the ACP countries had fallen from 65 per cent to 53 per cent between 1963 and 1970; by 1979, however, it had

Table 25.1
ACP Trade with the EC 9, 1963–79 (% of ACP Trade with the Whole Industrialised World)*

	ACP exports			ACP imports		
	1963	1970	1979	1963	1970	1979
Food and beverages	73.7	62.4	70.0	54.8	52.2	56.8
Basic materials	65.1	61.7	60.8	32.6	35.1	41.3
Processed materials	80.8	67.5	61.3	67.0	61.2	61.1
Fuels	60.1	57.4	37.5	63.3	60.2	89.2
Machinery	100.0	68.8	54.3	66.9	55.9	68.5
Transport equipment	58.8	40.0	47.4	64.2	43.8	51.5
Consumer goods	35.7	21.4	59.0	70.9	65.4	70.4
Other	19.1	15.7	61.4	66.7	28.5	71.2
Total	70.6	62.4	50.4	64.8	53.2	62.2

* The data for the ACP countries refer to the 53 countries (apart from the Community) covered by the Lomé agreements in 1979. By 'the whole industrialised world' is meant the European Community, the United States, Japan, Australia, Canada, New Zealand and the Union of South Africa.

SOURCE   Statistical Office of the European Communities, *EC–World Trade: a Statistical Analysis, 1963–1979* (Luxembourg, 1981), Table F.

recovered to 62 per cent. The rather disturbing implication is that the Lomé arrangements probably benefited exports from the Community more than those from the ACP countries themselves. This may not be wholly surprising: the truth of the matter is that the problems of most of the African countries south of the Sahara – a low level of technology and a relentlessly increasing population – are too deep-rooted to be solved by means of the quite limited tariff concessions provided by the Lomé agreements.

Even the aid component of the agreements appears to have brought limited satisfaction. The ACP countries, on their side, complain that the amounts available have failed to keep pace with the combined effects of inflation and their steadily-expanding geographical scope. Several Community countries, on the other hand, have expressed misgivings concerning the uses to which EDF funds have been put; too much, it has been suggested, has been devoted to grandiose prestige projects and too little to the correction of the underlying poor technology, low productivity and inadequate food production which are at the root of the problem of poverty in Africa. The Community can reasonably claim that the Yaoundé and Lomé agreements demonstrate its eagerness to grapple with the problems of the developing world, but not even its most sanguine supporter would suggest that they have significantly reduced the magnitude of those problems.

25.3 The European Free Trade Association

It was noted in Chapter 2 that the formation of the EEC in 1958 led to a defensive reaction on the part of seven countries in Western Europe which for one reason or another were unable to join in the venture – Austria, Denmark, Norway, Portugal, Sweden, Switzerland and the United Kingdom. Fearing that the elimination of tariffs within the Community would damage their exports to it, these countries formed EFTA; by this it was hoped, free-trade treatment for their industrial exports would provide an offsetting preference within the EFTA market. The removal of internal tariffs within EFTA proceeded more or less in line with the dismantling of tariffs within the EEC during the 1960s. With the subsequent association of Finland and Iceland, EFTA thus became a significant preferential trading bloc in manufactured products. By the mid-1960s, trade between the EFTA countries had risen (according to the estimates of its own secretariat) to 40 per cent more than would have been expected in the absence of special trading arrangements, and by common consent the greater part of this increase represented a diversion of trade from the EEC Six resulting from the preferential tariff treatment accorded to imports from the members of each trading group.

In the early 1970s the impending accession of Denmark and the United Kingdom (and initially of Norway as well) to the European Community obviously created a formidable problem for the remaining EFTA members. The 'defecting' countries, Denmark and the United Kingdom, which had hitherto extended preferential access to the exports of EFTA countries, accounted for some 60 per cent of total EFTA trade; for these countries to be transformed into markets which positively discriminated against EFTA through the Community's common external tariff was a depressing prospect.

Fortunately it was obvious to all concerned that it was in the common interest to avoid this fragmentation of the European market. Denmark and the United Kingdom were naturally reluctant to see important traditional markets damaged by the reversal of preferences. Similarly, the Six themselves could see advantage in the EFTA arrangements for industrial free trade; the EFTA countries accounted for only 10 per cent of the Community's imports of manufactures – and thus presented relatively little threat to its industry – while the Community accounted for nearly 60 per cent of EFTA imports of manufactures.

During 1970–71, therefore, a series of agreements was concluded between the Community on the one hand and each of the seven remaining EFTA countries on the other. (Negotiation with each EFTA country individually was necessary in order to preserve the political independence and neutrality which in many cases was the fundamental reason for standing apart from Community membership.) In five cases these agreements became operative on 1 January 1973 and followed the timetable of Danish and British integration into the EEC, thus avoiding the creation of new preferences; Norway's decision to withdraw from Community membership delayed the commencement of its Treaty of Association until July 1973, while that with Finland commenced on 1 January 1974.

By the end of 1977 trade in almost all industrial products between the Community and the EFTA countries had been placed on a duty-free basis. A small number of 'sensitive' products – mainly those related to timber and aluminium in which the comparative advantage of the Scandinavian countries presented some local difficulties within the Community – remained subject to tariff or quota limitation, but even the last of these exceptions (newsprint) had disappeared by 1984.

The main difficulty in the implementation of these agreements arose from the insistence of the Community that the rules of origin applied in the Yaoundé and Lomé agreements should also apply to trade with EFTA. These rules are in fact more complex and cumbersome (intentionally so) than those which the EFTA countries had been applying. Under EFTA rules a product could be treated as domestic if *either* at least a half of its value had originated in the country concerned *or* if a specified production process, inherent in the nature of the product concerned, had been carried out in that country. The Community's rules of origin, it has to be said, are basically designed to restrict the grant of domestic-origin status, whereas the EFTA rules were designed to facilitate it.

Despite this problem the effect of the network of agreements with EFTA has undoubtedly been to encourage a substantial expansion of trade between the two trading blocs – much of it admittedly a reversal of the trade diversion generated by the initial creation of the two blocs in the early 1960s. There were some fears in the rest of the world, especially in the United States, that the arrangements would lead to a diversion of trade from the outside world, as the preferential treatment now being extended to imports from each partner bloc generated an 'unnatural' displacement of imports from the rest of the world. The evidence of Table 25.2 indicates, however, that little such 'excess' trade diversion could have occurred. The Community's share of EFTA exports to the industrialised world had declined noticeably between 1963 and 1970 from about 68 per cent of the total to around 62 per cent as a result of the trade-diverting effects of the customs union. Between 1970 and 1979 the Community's share in the total was restored to almost precisely its 1963 value. An exactly parallel decline occurred in the Community's share of EFTA imports from the industrialised world between 1963 and 1970, and an exactly parallel reversal occurred between 1970 and 1979. Hence it seems reasonable to conclude that any net trade diversion effect is likely to have been considerably smaller in magnitude than the trade creation generated by the formation of a free-trade

Table 25.2
EFTA Trade with the EC 9, 1963–79 (% of EFTA Trade with the Whole Industrialised World)*

	EFTA exports			EFTA imports		
	1963	1970	1979	1963	1970	1979
Food and beverages	75.0	61.7	53.5	59.1	63.9	63.3
Basic materials	79.1	76.5	77.5	43.9	40.2	77.5
Processed materials	74.0	68.7	70.6	74.3	68.2	70.6
Fuels	63.2	54.6	73.7	92.2	89.2	85.5
Machinery	61.7	57.8	60.0	74.5	72.2	71.1
Transport equipment	33.2	40.8	54.7	76.9	65.8	70.3
Consumer goods	60.1	47.1	58.0	77.3	68.4	71.4
Other	42.5	68.1	94.1	76.0	61.4	76.2
Total	67.7	61.7	67.6	73.1	67.8	72.1

* The data for the EFTA countries refer to Austria, Finland, Iceland, Norway, Sweden, Switzerland and Yugoslavia. By 'the whole industrialised world' is meant the European Community, the United States, Japan, Australia, Canada, New Zealand and the Union of South Africa.

SOURCE Statistical Office of the European Communities, *EC–World Trade: a Statistical Analysis, 1963–1979* (Luxembourg, 1981), Table F.

area in manufactured goods extending over 19 countries with a total population more than 50 per cent greater than that of the United States.

25.4 Mediterranean Neighbours

The countries bordering on the Mediterranean in North Africa and the Middle East are inevitably of especial importance and concern to the Community. They constitute important markets for its exports; more importantly, the Community is for them an export market of considerable significance, so that they would be particularly vulnerable to any trade diversion effects of the customs union. Three of these countries – Morocco, Tunisia and Algeria – had been French colonies or protectorates until shortly before the signing of the Treaty of Rome; as a result, they enjoyed preferential trading arrangements with France which could scarcely be repudiated overnight. All of them collectively are crucially important to the political balance of the Middle East; the Community would have no wish to see instability of relations within and between these countries made the excuse for a trial of strength between the United States and the Soviet Union.

A protocol to the Treaty of Rome provided that existing customs arrangements by particular member countries for some of these ex-colonial territories (e.g. Morocco and Tunisia) should remain unchanged, but for the most part it was necessary for the Community to negotiate separate agreements with each country, defining the particular trading arrangements which would exist between that country and the Community collectively. In the course of the 1960s, therefore, a series of such agreements was signed. Some, like those with Greece and Turkey in 1962–3, were Association Agreements under Article 238 envisaging the ultimate membership of the countries concerned. Others were no more than trade agreements under Article 113, providing for widely varying degrees of preference and reciprocity. The result of this *ad hoc* approach to the problem was a bewildering collection of arrangements having little if anything in common, a sure recipe for discontent and friction: each participating country inevitably discovered in other agreements at least one respect in which other countries had been treated more favourably than itself. The impending accession of Britain and Denmark, and hence the need to extend the coverage of this motley collection of arrangements, inspired the Council of Ministers in 1972 to charge the Commission with the task of bringing some coherence into the Community's policy with regard to the Mediterranean countries as a whole.

This the Commission sought to do in September 1972, proposing the renegotiation of all these agreements and their replacement with a standard form applicable to all. The Commission indicated that this task could be completed within a year, which proved to be wildly optimistic; it was the end of 1978 before the task had been substantially completed. Revised agreements were signed in 1975 with Israel, in 1976 with Malta and the three Maghreb countries (Algeria, Morocco and Tunisia), in 1977 with the four Mashreq countries (Egypt, Jordan, Lebanon and Syria) and in 1978 with Cyprus. (The terms 'Maghreb' and 'Mashreq' are Arabic expressions meaning, basically, West and East.) A trade agreement was also signed with Yugoslavia in 1980 and a Treaty of Association with Turkey was also renegotiated during that year.

The detailed provisions of these agreements naturally still varies to take account of the individual characteristics of the countries concerned. In essence, however, they are the same. They provide, first, for tariff-free entry into the Community of virtually all manufactured goods originating in the countries concerned, with quotas or ceilings being imposed on certain particularly sensitive products – especially textiles. The treatment of agricultural exports, as might be expected, is less liberal, given the need to protect the interests of farmers in the Mediterranean areas of France, Greece and Italy – and, subsequently, of those in Portugal and Spain. Where Community production is relatively small, fairly substantial reductions of tariffs or variable levies are conceded; where the threat to domestic producers is significant, however, the concessions are modest and imports may be permitted only in off-season and to a limited degree.

The degree of reciprocity required in the Mediterranean countries varies considerably. Initially it was envisaged that fully reciprocal treatment – i.e. duty-free access for Community exports – would be the ultimate aim but this has proved in practice to be unattainable except in the case of Israel. Apart from its inherent lack of realism, the suggestion that the Community should enjoy preferential access to these markets generated considerable hostility from other potential competitors, especially the United States. In international trade, unfortunately, a preference in favour of X is almost invariably the obverse of a discrimination against Y.

Almost all the agreements provide for some degree of technical co-operation and technical aid, the latter taking the form of a mixture of loans (frequently through the EIB at subsidised interest rates) and outright grants. The sums concerned are not large; over the first ten years of the agreements with the Mashreq and Maghreb countries and Israel the total available amounted to the equivalent of ECU 2.8 bn.

It seems most unlikely that the tariff preferences in themselves have had any substantial impact on the development of trade between the Community and the Mediterranean countries. As Table 25.3 shows, the Community's share in the total exports of the Maghreb/Mashreq countries to the industrialised world, having remained relatively stable during the 1960s, fell very sharply indeed during the 1970s. Since the exports concerned are substantially agricultural – and in many instances compete directly with Community producers – this is hardly surprising. There is some evidence that manufactured exports to the Community, particularly those of manufactured consumer goods like textile products, have benefited from their preferential treatment; given the existence of

Table 25.3
Maghreb/Mashreq Trade with the EC 9, 1963–79 (% of Maghreb/Mashreq Trade with the Whole Industrialised World)*

	Maghreb/Mashreq exports			Maghreb/Mashreq imports		
	1963	1970	1979	1963	1970	1979
Food and beverages	94.5	91.5	85.9	43.1	46.6	49.9
Basic materials	73.5	64.9	58.6	37.1	36.0	29.1
Processed materials	80.0	75.8	78.9	79.4	72.8	65.3
Fuels	97.7	88.0	45.9	87.3	86.4	83.4
Machinery	100.0	100.0	97.0	76.2	79.7	72.6
Transport equipment	100.0	100.0	98.4	79.6	74.8	73.5
Consumer goods	66.7	76.9	94.2	78.8	73.6	69.6
Other	66.7	30.0	79.9	66.7	36.7	37.5
Total	89.7	83.0	52.6	70.3	68.7	65.4

*The Maghreb/Mashreq countries comprise Algeria, Morocco, Tunisia, Egypt, Jordan, Lebanon and Syria. By 'the whole industrialised world' is meant the European Community, the United States, Japan, Australia, Canada, New Zealand and the Union of South Africa.

SOURCE   Statistical Office of the European Communities, *EC–World Trade: a Statistical Analysis, 1963–1979* (Luxembourg, 1981), Table F.

the wider arrangements for textiles discussed in the following chapter, however, any gains so secured by Mediterranean producers are likely to have been secured at the expense of those in other developing countries outside the Community's preferential arrangements. The Community's share of Maghreb/ Mashreq imports from the industrialised world, on the other hand, seems to have remained remarkably unaffected by all these special trading arrangements. If the network of trade agreements throughout the Mediterranean has achieved any significant gain, in other words, it is likely to have been – as it was intended it should be – political and diplomatic rather than economic.

25.5   Conclusion

A map indicating the growth of the Community's special relationships with countries having close geographical or political links with it would undoubtedly appear impressive. So far as tariffs are concerned, the Community has created a vast free trade area in manufactured goods, an area extending over the whole of

Western Europe, over much of its surrounding borders and over the greater part of Africa. That is no mean achievement; it certainly calls into question any allegation that the Community has set out to create an introverted, fortress economy in splendid isolation from its neighbours.

Tariffs, unfortunately, are by no means the only, nor even the most important, barriers to trade; nor are manufactured goods the only constituent of it. As tariffs on manufactures have diminished in importance the attitudes of member governments to non-tariff barriers and to agricultural trade have become of correspondingly greater significance. As the following chapter will show, the record of the Community in these respects is hardly impressive.

Further Reading

Hine, R. C., *The Political Economy of European Trade* (Brighton: Wheatsheaf Books, 1985).

Sjostedt, G., *The External Role of the European Community* (Farnborough: Saxon House, 1977).

Twitchett, C. A., *A Framework for the Developing World: the EEC and the ACP* (London: Allen & Unwin, 1981).

Commercial Policy – The World at Large 26

26.1 The Common Commercial Policy

When Articles 110–116 of the Treaty provided for a 'uniform commercial policy' to govern the Community's relationships with the rest of the world they were doing no more than acknowledge the inevitable. In joining a customs union each member state necessarily sacrifices its right to establish or amend tariffs on imports from non-member countries; a joint policy applicable to all member countries is inescapable. Article 110 indicated that the Community should adopt a commercial policy which would be conducive 'to the harmonious development of world trade' but the extent to which it has achieved this admirable objective is open to some debate. Certainly by its sheer size the Community must exert considerable influence on the world economy; in 1986, even excluding intra-Community trade, it accounted for 21 per cent of world exports – a share equal to that of the United States and Japan combined.

The major mechanism for the conduct of negotiations concerning international trade since the end of the Second World War has been the General Agreement on Tariffs and Trade (GATT), a permanent organisation created in 1947 with 23 member countries and its own headquarters and secretariat. It now boasts 92 member countries in what must be called (for lack of a better label) the non-Communist world; in 1986 it embarked on the eighth round of bilateral negotiations held amongst its members since 1947. The basic philosophy of the GATT is that country A and country B should engage in strictly bilateral talks concerning their tariffs on trade with each other; mutual reductions are then more likely to be agreed precisely because A can secure from B specific concessions on tariffs on its exports which will compensate it for parallel

316

concessions on tariffs on imports from B. The essential GATT rule is then that any concessions offered to one GATT member must automatically be extended to every other GATT member; bilateral deals are thus effectively transformed into multilateral agreements. These tariff bargaining rounds are inevitably very protracted affairs; the eighth round, which officially opened in Punta del Este in September 1986 ('the Uruguay round'), is not expected to conclude before 1993 at the earliest.

The fifth round of negotiations in the GATT was generally referred to as the 'Dillon round' in acknowledgement of the fact that it was substantially initiated by the US Secretary of State, James Dillon. This occurred during 1960–62, but the preliminary negotiations leading up to it were under way at the time of the formation of the EEC in 1958; as a result, the Six participated mainly as individual countries rather than as a single bloc. The broad target of that round was a general reduction of about 10 per cent in tariff levels throughout the industrialised world, and this reduction was built into the Common External Tariff from the outset; the common tariff was set at 90 per cent of the average of the previous separate tariffs. This did something to calm the fears felt by the outside world – and especially by the United States – that the Community was going to turn itself into a protectionist trade bloc.

In the succeeding GATT round, the Kennedy Round held during 1964–8, the Community, rather than its individual member countries, participated as a single bargaining unit. It proved to be somewhat less accommodating than had been hoped from the US point of view, a fact not unconnected with the ascendancy of President de Gaulle in Community affairs at that time. The broad target of a further cut of around a third in the overall level of tariffs was in general achieved but in two major respects the Community adopted what to the eyes of the rest of the Western industrialised world appeared to be an unhelpful stance. First, it refused totally to allow agriculture to be brought into the negotiations; the Common Agricultural Policy was commencing and the Community had no intention of allowing the frankly protectionist character of the CAP to be compromised by the possibility of free international trade in agricultural products. This was a considerable setback for countries like the United States, Canada and Australia to whom exports of temperate food products are of enormous importance. Secondly, while adopting a liberal attitude to trade in manufactures in general, the Community insisted on 'special provisions' – i.e. quota or other restrictions – for so-called 'sensitive' products such as textiles and chemicals. In other words, there was more than a suggestion in the general stance of the Community that it was in favour of free trade – except when its domestic producers might be adversely affected thereby.

The same considerations dominated the seventh, or Tokyo, round of GATT negotiations during 1975–8 in which the United States initially sought the total elimination of industrial tariffs within a period of perhaps five years. This proved to be more than the Community was prepared to concede, but a compromise was arrived at whereby tariffs would be reduced by a further 30–40 per cent over 10 years. This perhaps sounds more impressive than it was; as a result of the continuous series of tariff reductions over the postwar period, by the late 1970s tariffs in the industrialised world were very low and even a reduction of a third was unlikely to amount to a change of more than one or two percentage points for most products.

The relationship between the Community and the rest of the industrialised world, and especially the United States, deteriorated sharply for different reasons. First, the disruption to world trade in agriculture caused, in American eyes, by the Common Agricultural Policy had now reached an intolerable degree; nevertheless the Community refused to allow agriculture to be brought to the negotiating table along with manufactures. Second, while tariffs were being steadily reduced they were also becoming largely irrelevant as instruments of protection; during the 1970s non-tariff barriers of all kinds had clearly become the greatest threat to world trade, but the GATT made little systematic provision for them. Seven years of negotiation made virtually no progress in either field and the Tokyo round, according to the more pessimistic observers, proved to be almost entirely unproductive. A decade later, when the Uruguay round opened in the GATT, the major issues in world trade, and therefore in the Community's commercial policy, remained the same; it is on its attitude to these that the Community will be judged as the negotiations proceed.

26.2   Trade Issues for the Rich World

The major source of conflict between the Community and the rest of the world remains agriculture, which has traditionally been kept largely outside the scope of GATT. The United States is inevitably the major complainant, since one third of its exports to the Community consists of agricultural products, but Australia, Argentina and Canada also believe themselves to have been injured by the Common Agricultural Policy. The complaint is not merely that the Community's variable levies deny them access to a major market but that by disposing of farm surpluses through dumping at subsidised prices the Community has unfairly deprived its competitors of traditional markets and has destabilised world trade in food products. Other measures adopted by the Community – such as the ban on meat imports from the United States in 1989 because of their allegedly harmful hormone content – have also been regarded as symptomatic of the unfair protectionism inherent in the CAP.

It is not easy to resist the force of these arguments, but the Community does its best to do so. It is fair to say that Europe is by no means the only offender when it comes to the matter of agricultural protection; the United States government spends roughly the same amount on its farmers annually as does the Community (although its farmers are typically much wealthier than the European average) while Japanese consumers are forced by their government to pay roughly three times the world price for their rice for the greater glory of their farmers. It so happens that the methods of protection adopted by these other governments do not include export subsidies on the European scale but their ultimate objective is the same: to protect the domestic farmer at the expense of farmers in the rest of the world. The solution advocated by the Community has therefore always been much the same – some kind of international agreement on the prices of major products rather than restrictions on domestic policy measures. Unfortunately, faced with the reality that any successful version of the former necessarily implies some degree of the latter, the Community has always proved unwilling to translate this generality of principle into details of application.

Nor is the Community the only offender in the matter of the non-tariff barriers to international trade which have spread dramatically since the early 1970s and which have largely, if not wholly, offset the progress which has been made in the reduction of tariffs. It has been estimated that by the mid-1980s at least 40 per cent of the trade of the industrialised world was covered by restrictions other than tariffs, particularly by the so-called 'voluntary export restraints' (VERs) under which an exporting country is induced (usually by the implicit or explicit threat of an alternative of openly punitive measures) to limit 'voluntarily' the volume of its sales in the country concerned. Such measures have been particularly favoured by some Community member countries as a defensive reaction to the progressive removal of barriers to internal trade.

For technical reasons connected with Japan's late entry into GATT, a general EC–Japan agreement under its auspices has not so far proved possible. Hence restrictions on Japanese imports continue to be applied by individual member countries rather than by the Community collectively. In France and Italy, for example, the application of 'voluntary' export agreements with respect to Japanese cars in the early 1980s reduced the share of such cars in their domestic markets to virtually nil – compared with a share of 32 per cent in Denmark, which operated no such agreement. In its present state the GATT is powerless to take action against such restraints of trade; unlike attempts to increase tariffs, there is nothing illegal about them.

Knowledge of the propensity of member countries to indulge in such devices has increased the nervousness of the outside world concerning the possible impact of the movement to a single European market after 1992. If each Community country has to eliminate all restrictions on imports from other member countries, there is an obvious risk, to put it no higher, that the Community as a whole will be driven to the position of the lowest common denominator in so far as its policy towards the rest of the world is concerned. If there are to be no restrictions whatever on the transfer of new cars from Denmark to France, for example, it will be futile for the French to seek to hold down Japanese car imports unless they can prevail on the Danes to do the same thing. Indeed, the process can be taken further. Because the output of Japanese-owned assembly plants in one member country can enter another member country freely if they are treated as the product of the former, attempts have been made to raise the 'local content' requirement to whatever level is necessary to have them defined as external imports. Conversely, preferential treatment currently given by the United Kingdom to encourage imports of lamb from New Zealand and bananas from the Caribbean involve some corresponding control over imports of these products from other sources via other Community countries; it is not easy to see how the preference can be maintained if the single market becomes a reality.

The effects of international market-sharing arrangements are difficult to measure but they clearly contravene the basic GATT principle of non-discrimination. All the progress made in the reduction of nominal trade barriers will come to nothing unless the rules of GATT can be extended to deal with them. Without a much more liberal approach from the Community than it has displayed in the recent past this will be impossible.

26.3 Preferences for the Poor

Arguments on the international trade scene have by no means been confined to the richer countries of the world since the Second World War. The poorer countries of the world have consistently complained that the GATT, with its fundamental commitment to the principle of non-discrimination in world trade, was essentially designed to advance the interests of the relatively rich countries. Given the enormous gap in technology and resource endowment between the industrialised and the developing world, the apparently liberal concept of non-discrimination would condemn the latter to a permanent existence as hewers of wood and drawers of water. The developing world, it is argued, needs positive discrimination in its favour rather than non-discrimination.

This philosophy was fiercely advanced at the United Nations Conference on Trade and Development (UNCTAD) in 1964, from which emerged a permanent UNCTAD organisation dedicated to the cause of the developing world, with its own programme and philosophy. Rather than pursuing the principle of non-discriminatory tariffs, it was argued, the richer countries needed to adopt a policy whereby their tariffs positively discriminated in favour of the manufactured exports of developing countries; otherwise those exports would never have any prospect of breaking into the markets of the industrialised world. This demand was directed with particular intensity by the Latin American and Asian countries to the European Community; the Yaoundé Agreements were granting tariff discrimination in favour of the Community's associated territories in Africa and were therefore positively discriminating against the poorer countries not covered by those agreements.

Precisely for this reason, the demand was not received initially with much sympathy by the Community. To extend the scope of preferential treatment is effectively to reduce its significance for those already in receipt of it. Nor was the attitude of the United States particularly favourable. Preferential tariff treatment, it was argued, merely led to artificial trade diversion from more efficient to less efficient sources and thus wasted resources. In any case, it was also argued – somewhat inconsistently – tariff levels were now becoming so low that any preferential treatment would be too small to exert any significant effect.

Given the undoubted fact that the Community's average external tariff is now very low (and still falling) this latter point merits a little more attention. It is certainly true to say that if the nominal rate of tariff on a product is only 10 per cent, say, then the maximum preference which can be given – i.e. the application of a zero tariff on exports from the favoured source – is itself only 10 per cent, which is perhaps unlikely to make very much difference to the competitive position of the prospective exporter. The *effective* rate of a tariff, however, may be quite different from its *nominal* rate. Suppose that in the domestic market each unit of a product requires raw material inputs costing 60 and value added (labour and capital costs) amounting to 40; the domestic product can therefore sell profitably at 100. If a prospective exporter also has raw material costs of 60 but faces a tariff barrier of 10 per cent, his labour and capital costs will have to be held down to 30 (even neglecting transport costs) if he is to compete: his final selling price will then be $60 + 30$ plus a 10 per cent tariff of $9 = 99$. The nominal tariff of 10 per cent amounts to an effective protective tariff of 25 per cent in terms of value added. If developing countries rely for their exports on products in which raw material costs comprise a large proportion of the total, therefore – as is the case with textile and clothing products, for example – an apparently low tariff wall may represent a considerably greater barrier than appears at first sight.

Despite their misgivings the industrialised countries were prevailed upon to adopt a Generalised System of Preferences (GSP) under which, broadly speaking, duty-free treatment was extended to specified annual volumes (quotas) of manufactured or semi-manufactured exports from what were defined to be developing countries. (The decision as to whether a country should or should not be defined as 'developing' was a delicate one; even national pride usually subsides, however, when commercial advantage is forthcoming.) The products to be given this favourable treatment were specified separately for each pair of countries, so that the GSP is a collection of a large number of separate agreements with individual developing countries. (The Community's GSP now runs to some 128 countries and 22 dependent territories, although about a half of these operate under the more favourable terms given to them by the Lomé or Mediterranean agreements.) The concessions do not in general apply to textile products (see the following section) but do apply to some non-sensitive agricultural products. They are non-reciprocal: no corresponding concession is expected from the developing country concerned. As a result they are not strictly negotiable and in theory (occasionally in practice) can be arbitrarily withdrawn at any time.

The Community's GSP arrangements were the first to be introduced and came into operation in 1971. In some ways its GSP arrangements were more liberal and flexible than those introduced by other countries, notably the United States; there was a distinctly political character to the qualifications for eligibility for the latter. Even so, the system appears to be rather more liberal in principle than it is in practice, and unhappily has become increasingly protectionist with the passage of time. The products included under the heading 'non-sensitive' – which means products for which the quota restrictions are seldom if ever applied in reality – have tended to be those in which the competitiveness of the developing world has been weakest; products in which domestic industries would face serious potential competition have been included under the heading of 'sensitive' products for which quotas have been held down and fairly rigorously enforced. Similarly, it is notable that the allocation of quotas has tended to favour the poorest and least competitive countries and has militated against the exports of the newly-industrialising countries – Brazil, Singapore, Hong Kong and South Korea – which are increasingly capable of competing effectively not only in the traditional exports of textiles and clothing but in more upmarket product areas such as steel and electronics.

Furthermore, since the revision of the original quota arrangements from 1981 onwards the protectionist overtones of their administration have become more explicit; the annual review of quotas has tended to restrict them within the estimated growth of internal demand, which means frequently that they have been held constant or raised only marginally. In 1986, indeed, South Korea and Hong Kong were excluded altogether from the quota allocation for 11 sensitive products while their quotas for four other products were cut by 50 per cent.

In the light of all this – and of the administrative complexities inherent in the whole system – it is hardly surprising that it has proved impossible to detect in the evidence any indication whatever that the GSP has had any significant impact on the export of manufactured goods to the Community; in fact, total imports by the Community from the developing world fell from 13.2 per cent of its external trade in 1970 to 12.7 per cent in 1980. Much the same conclusion must hold as for the effects of the Lomé Conventions. Where tariff concessions have been given they have necessarily been small in magnitude; on those products for which the concessions would be likely to have most effect, the ability of the developing countries to exploit them has been carefully limited through the application of quota restrictions. The Community cannot be held to have conducted itself with a degree of liberalism noticeably smaller than that exhibited by other parts of the industrialised world; equally, however, it can hardly be described as having provided a shining example.

26.4 Preferences for Products

Because the export revenues of the developing world are derived predominantly from the sale of primary products, the advocates of aid for the Third World have always argued strongly for the operation of international commodity agreements. Like the CAP, it is suggested, in the short run these could eliminate damaging instability in prices, and therefore in export earnings, and in the long run they could raise the average world price of the products concerned. A very large number of such agreements do in fact exist and the Community partici- pates in almost all of them. The reality is, however, that hardly any have had anything other than the most transient effect. As with the CAP itself, the aim of eliminating short-term instability has inevitably become confused with the quite different aim of the maintenance of producers' incomes in the long term. When it has been sought to support world prices through restrictions on production, sooner or later (and usually sooner) ranks have been broken by producers seeking to take advantage of a relatively high price by raising output. On the few occasions on which prices have been held up successfully, the effect has been to stimulate the development of synthetic substitutes or alternative sources, irreversible processes which have an effect on long-term price precisely opposite to that sought. In the cases of two types of commodities of particular interest to the developing world, however, the Community has played a significant role over a considerable period of time.

The first of these is textile products. These, the classic labour-intensive exports of developing countries in the earliest stage of industrialisation, can and do compete directly with domestic producers in the richer countries. Indeed, in the late 1950s the growth of such exports led to retaliation by the industrialised countries through an increasing resort to quantitative restrictions on imports. Through the good offices of GATT in 1962, however, a 'Long-term arrange- ment on the cotton textile trade' was established; under this the industrialised countries agreed to remove their quantitative restrictions provided that the developing countries undertook to apply 'voluntary' restrictions on their textile exports.

In 1973 this rather odd arrangement was extended to wool and synthetic fibres and renamed the Multifibre Arrangement (MFA), covering some 30 major importers and exporters of textile products. Like the later GSP, it was really a structural framework for a series of bilateral agreements; these provide for duty-free access to the markets of the industrialised countries, subject to annual quota limits laid down for each product and each country. The Community has reached agreements with 25 exporting countries, covering some 120 product categories, under these arrangements.

Under the first MFA, running from 1974, it was envisaged that the annual import quotas would be increased by 6 per cent a year, the rate of growth in the years preceding the agreement. The economic recession which began in that year, however, soon inspired a pronounced protectionist emphasis in the arrangement. By 1978 the Community was insisting that it should have the right to introduce 'reasonable departures' from the agreed quotas to take account of unexpected difficulties being experienced by domestic producers, and in the renegotiations of the arrangements in 1977, 1981 and 1986 the average growth rate of the quotas was steadily reduced from the 6 per cent of 1974–7 to about 1.2 per cent in 1978–85 and less than 1 per cent in the mid-1980s.

The second commodity deserving of comment in this context is sugar, a product of crucial importance to several of the poorest developing countries. At the instigation of UNCTAD an International Sugar Agreement was signed in 1968; the Community was invited to become a party to this but declined to do so. The reason was fairly clear. The first permanent regulations for the inclusion of beet sugar in the CAP were coming into effect that year; membership of the international agreement, however, implied a commitment to restrict the production and export of sugar whenever necessary to maintain its world price, a commitment which would obviously be incompatible with the open-ended price guarantees of the CAP. By contrast, however, the United Kingdom, the world's largest importer of sugar, operated a Commonwealth Sugar Agreement as part of these international arrangements; this gave a guaranteed market of 1.7 million tonnes to Commonwealth suppliers, including an allocation of over 0.3 million tonnes for Australia.

The accession of the United Kingdom to the Community in 1973 inevitably raised the issue of the future of these market guarantees to Commonwealth producers. The solution was the absorption of the UK commitment into the first Lomé Convention, with the exception of the quota for Australia; the sugar producers concerned were thereby guaranteed a substantial market for their sugar at something well above world market price. Yet the guarantee covers only approximately 60 per cent of the output of the producers concerned, and it is by no means obvious that the generous provisions of the Lomé conventions are sufficient to offset the other effects of the CAP on the world sugar market. In 1974, immediately after the UK accession, Community imports of sugar exceeded its exports by 1.04 million tonnes; by 1982, imports fell below exports by some 4.2 million tonnes. These net exports were necessarily dumped on world markets at well below the cost of production, and the impact on world prices was inevitably dramatic; in 1985 Community sugar, bought from its farmers at the equivalent of $400 a tonne, was being sold on world markets at around $50 a tonne. Excellent news for those poor countries which were net importers of sugar, but quite the reverse for those who produced it.

The contribution of the Community to the cause of the developing world must thus remain a doubtful quantity. The evidence presented in Table 26.1 indicates that the creation of the Community has indeed led to a formidable shift in the relative pattern of the international trade of its members. Between 1958 and 1985, the share of the total accounted for by intra-Community trade rose sharply, from 35 per cent to 52 per cent, with a corresponding decline in the

Table 26.1
The Community's Trade with the World, 1958–85 (Merchandise Imports + Merchandise Exports – ECU bn at 1986 prices)

Trade with	EC 10			% of total	
	1958	1973	1985	1958	1985
(1) Rest of EC	165	636	901	34.6	52.0
(2a) EFTA Countries	54	127	181	11.3	10.4
(2b) Mediterranean Basin*	40	87	130	8.3	7.5
(2c) ACP Countries[†]	30	37	46	6.3	2.7
(2) Total, EC and EC-related	289	887	1258	60.5	72.6
(3a) United States	46	96	154	9.6	8.9
(3b) Japan	3	20	39	0.6	2.3
(3c) Other Industrial[‡]	53	81	104	11.0	6.0
(3) Total, non-EC Industrial	101	197	297	21.2	17.2
(4) Non-market economies	19	49	71	4.0	4.1
(5) Rest of world	68	69	106	14.3	6.1
Total	476	1202	1732	100	100

* Mainly Spain, Israel and the Mahgreb/Mashreq countries.
[†] 63 member countries in 1985.
[‡] Other Western Europe, Australia, Canada, New Zealand and Union of South Africa.

SOURCE   Statistical Office of the European Communities, *External Trade: Statistical Yearbook 1986*, Series A, (Luxembourg: 1986), Table 5.

importance of trade with the outside world. Evidence discussed earlier suggested that in the first decade of its existence the Community, through the trade-creating effect of its high rate of growth, almost certainly benefited the developing world by the provision of expanding markets. As will be noted from Table 26.1, however, of the increase of 17 percentage points in the intra-Community share of total trade over 1958–85 as a whole, about a half occurred at the expense of the 'rest of the world', which is for all practical purposes the developing world having no special relationship with the Community. The share of the non-related industrialised countries, on the other hand, fell by only about 4 percentage points.

The special trade preferences which the Community has extended to its own associated territories certainly do not appear to have offset this general trade-diversion effect, and such effect as they may have had probably operated largely at the expense of less-favoured parts of the developing world. The overall impression left is that the perceived requirements of the domestic economy have led the Community towards a generally protectionist stance in which the interests of the developing world have tended to be relegated to a secondary position. It is only fair to add that the Community has not been conspicuously less liberal in its trading policies than the industrialised world in general. Nevertheless the results fall somewhat short of the aim, expressed in the preamble to the Treaty, 'to confirm the solidarity which binds Europe and overseas countries and ... to ensure the development of their prosperity in accordance with the principles of the Charter of the United Nations'.

26.5   Summary

In its broad stance with regard to the outside world the Community could conceivably have inclined towards one of two extremes. On the one hand, it might have set out to discourage trade with non-member countries to the maximum degree feasible, turning in on itself as an introverted and largely self-contained entity. On the other hand, having embraced the virtues of completely free trade within its own boundaries it might logically have sought to abolish all obstacles to trade with the rest of the world as well. The first would have been catastrophic for the growth of the world economy after 1958; the second would have perhaps tended to blur the uniqueness of the Community – indeed, its logical conclusion would have been a single world-wide free-trade area which would have compromised the ultimate political objectives of the Community itself.

Some intermediary position was inevitable but the general conclusion of most observers is that the outcome has been characterised by a rather stronger tendency towards protectionism, certainly from the early 1970s onwards, than could have been desired from the point of view of the world economy as a whole. To some degree this has been due to certain characteristics inherent in the Community itself. In the first place, all major decisions have to be taken by the Council of Ministers acting, usually, under the rule of unanimity. Inevitably this has tended to result in policies based on the lowest common denominator; a change threatening the interests of any single member country has usually been ruled out, even though it might well be broadly beneficial for the Community as a whole. The extension of majority voting by the Single European Act, and the movement towards a single market after 1992, should theoretically much improve matters in this respect, but the effects in practice remain to be seen. As was noted earlier, many fears exist in the outside world that the completion of the single market will tend to make the Community more, rather than less, restrictive in its attitudes to trade with non-member countries.

Such suspicions are not entirely groundless. So far as goods are concerned, the Community is certainly deeply committed to the GATT principle of non-discrimination but the insistence of some member countries on the retention of quantitative restrictions on some sensitive imports is likely to result in the transfer of such restrictions to Community rather than national level. In 1989, for example, the Commission was contemplating changing its 'local content' rules in such a way that photocopiers made by Japanese-owned plants in the United States would be defined as Japanese rather than American exports, thus becoming subject to a 20 per cent anti-dumping duty when consigned to a Community country. So far as services are concerned, the Commissioner for External Relations (M de Clerq) rather let the cat out of the bag in 1988 when he stated publicly that he saw no reason why the benefits of an internal liberalisation should be extended unilaterally to third countries which did not give reciprocal access. If a country did not allow, say, Spanish banks to set up offices in its capital, then its banks should not be allowed to set up office *anywhere* in the Community. The world, once again, must await events.

Secondly, the process whereby negotiations are carried out between the Community and the rest of the world is inevitably time-consuming and complicated. The work must necessarily be carried out by the Commission but responsibility for final decisions must rest with the Council of Ministers. Since the latter tends to be somewhat suspicious of the former, outside negotiators frequently discover that the Commission is working within closely-defined guidelines and has constantly to refer back to its political masters before being able to respond to any new turn the discussions may take. On top of this, many matters of trade administration (for example, quotas) remain in the hands of national governments, rather than the Commission, so that non-member countries find themselves having to negotiate with two sets of people at the same time.

Finally, Council policies being themselves the outcome of a complex and frequently protracted process of compromise and mutual wheeling-and-dealing, a Community negotiating position is usually a delicately-balanced one in which an adjustment on one matter may undermine a network of a whole series of compromises on other, not obviously related matters. A reluctance to threaten the whole complicated balancing-act therefore tends to show itself in an apparently inflexible negotiating position in which the other parties seem to be given only the option of taking it or leaving it. Even in a trade environment more expansive and relaxed than that enjoyed by the world since 1973 this would have imposed severe restraints on the ability of the Community to pursue a liberal and flexible commercial policy. Perhaps it is surprising not that its policy in the 1980s has been marked by incipient protectionism but, rather, that it has not been totally overwhelmed by it.

Further Reading

Farrands, C., 'External relations: textile politics and the multi-fibre arrangement', in Wallace, H. (ed.), *Policy-making in the European Community*, 2nd edn (Chichester: John Wiley & Son, 1983).

Federal Trust, *The European Community and the Developing Countries* (London: Federal Trust, 1988).

Mendes, L. B. M. and Kohl, J., *European Trade Policies and the Developing World* (London: Croom Helm, 1988).

Stevens, C., *The EEC and the Third World: a Survey* (London: Hodder & Stoughton, 1984).

Part V
Conclusion

1992 and All That 27

27.1 Retrospect

Commenting in 1982 on the 25th anniversary of the signing of the Treaty of
Rome, the weekly journal *The Economist* remarked that 'A 25-year-old in a
coma is a pitiful sight'. In the same year, a study by five international political
scientists, all enthusiasts for the European ideal, was predicting that if nothing
were done Europe was facing the disintegration of its most important achievement since the Second World War. National administrations, they warned, were
obstructing and delaying every stage in the Community's decision-making
process; the Commission was suffering the ills which afflict all bureaucracies,
building its own fiefdoms and baffling the outside world with a jargon of an
obscurity which the languages of other countries had taken centuries to achieve;
for the ordinary people of Europe the Community had become a distant and
soul-less organisation.

The pessimism was perhaps exaggerated. Thirty years after its creation the
Community remained intact and, indeed, had widened its membership rather
than reduced it. True, it had become an organisation constantly consumed by
argument and dissent, but this was surely a vast improvement on those other
battlefields over which the European nations had traditionally settled their
differences. Positive policy achievements were far from negligible. The complete
removal of internal tariffs, and the movement to a common external tariff, had
been achieved well before the target dates specified in the Treaty; this was hardly
unconnected, in turn, with the fact that over the 25 years following 1960 the
volume of exports generated by the members of the Community had increased
at an annual rate averaging 6.3 per cent compared with one averaging only 5.3
per cent for the world as a whole.

Internally, also, many of the objectives of the Treaty had clearly been
achieved. The CAP, whatever its merits or lack of them, had become an
operating reality; a common fisheries policy had been created; a common

331

commercial policy had evolved, even if it had proved to be somewhat less liberal than many would have wished. The Community was still far from being a full monetary union but the European Monetary System, at least a first step in that direction, had become an established reality. Political co-operation between the member states in their day-to-day foreign affairs, something scarcely mentioned in the treaty, had become a matter of routine. Differences certainly persisted between the member states on almost every conceivable issue, but the crucial fact was that a permanent mechanism had been created by means of which those differences could be, and were being, resolved. As the President of the European Parliament remarked in 1982, '25 years is not long in a process which involves changing the map of Europe'. It is a very brief span, in fact, compared with the period of time which had elapsed before the other great federations of the world had achieved anything approaching their final shape.

Yet the declaiming of this record, creditable although it was, could not conceal the fact that in many vital respects the Community of the mid-1980s was still far removed from the economic and political union which had been the vision of so many of the founding fathers. The dismantling of internal tariff barriers, admirable though it had been, seemed to have been largely, if not wholly, offset by the proliferation of non-tariff trade barriers on a massive scale, so that while the Community could be described as a customs union it was far from being a genuine common market. Several positive policy goals had indeed been achieved (although the Common Agricultural Policy was not universally regarded as a howling economic success) but it was significant that with one or two exceptions – notably the EMS – all of these policies had been largely constructed in the 1960s; since the early 1970s the Community seemed to have come to rest on a rather dismal plateau.

Some were ready to attribute this to the expansion of the Community's membership from the original, relatively homogeneous, Six to the much more disparate Nine in 1973 and the prospect of yet further dilution into an even more disparate Twelve. In the view of many observers this expansion threatened the credibility of the Community as a natural economic unit. Any German government, it was said, would inevitably be more concerned with its relationships with Austria, a non-member, than with those with Portugal; the second and third enlargements had greatly increased the relative size of the Mediterranean populations, whose interests clashed rather than coincided with those of Northern Europe; Greece appeared to have more interest in relationships with the Soviet Union and Eastern Europe than in NATO and the Atlantic.

This dispersion of interests underlined the growing lack of credibility of the Council of Ministers, a body in which the pursuit of national interests usually appeared to take precedence over any concept of common Community interest. Its potential as a decision-making body seemed increasingly suspect; the Commission reported in 1984 that there were nearly 640 items awaiting a decision by the Council, more than 110 of which had been outstanding for more than six years. To the world at large the Council appeared to be irrelevant as well as ineffective; its energies seemed to be absorbed by unending wrangles over fish quotas and budget contributions rather than by the real economic problems of unemployment, inflation and growth.

Nor had the other institutions of the Community managed to win the interest or regard of the population at large. The Parliament, almost bereft of any effective power, appeared monumentally irrelevant and useless; membership of it was valued only in so far as it might assist the path to a national legislature. In June 1989 fewer than 60 per cent of the population could bother to vote in elections for it – despite the fact that in one member country, Belgium, such voting is compulsory. (To no one's surprise, the turnout in Britain, at 37 per cent, was the lowest in the whole Community.) The fact that prior to 1987 the average attendance of members at its plenary sessions barely exceeded 40 per cent was indicative of its own perception of itself. The Commission, for its part, had acquired a reputation for delay and elephantine procedures far exceeding that of national bureaucracies; a steady accretion of evidence of corruption as well as incompetence in the administration of Community funds did little to enhance its popular prestige.

In reality it is likely that the major braking force operating on the Community from the mid-1970s onwards was not the dilution and disparity of its membership, nor the ineffectiveness of its institutions, but rather the pronounced decline in Europe's rate of economic expansion following upon the oil crisis of 1973–4. Compared with the pressures exerted by increasing unemployment and high inflation within member states, Community considerations were necessarily relegated to a position of low priority. Even so, by the mid-1980s there was a widespread feeling in Europe that the Community had reached a crisis situation in which an unsatisfactory status quo could not be allowed to persist indefinitely into the future. The Community, it was said, was like a bicycle: it could move forwards or, conceivably, backwards, but any attempt to remain stationary inevitably invited complete collapse. So it was that the arrival of new brooms in both the Parliament and the Commission in 1984 led to a combined campaign for advance in the shape of two documents to which frequent reference has been made earlier. On the one hand, in what was to become the Single European Act, the Parliament sought to breathe new life into the Community's vision of itself and to remedy the arthritic tendencies of its political processes. On the other hand, and more or less simultaneously, the Commission launched an attack on the prevailing economic inertia in the form of a report, 'Completing the Common Market', placed before the Council in June 1985.

27.2 Creating the Single Market

At the end of 1984, shortly before taking up office, the incoming President of the Commission, M Jacques Delors, toured the Community capitals seeking the reactions of Ministers to a list of four major initiatives which could break the apparent impasse in the progress of the Community and form the theme of the Commission's work over its (hopefully) two terms of office between 1985 and 1992. Not surprisingly, most support was forthcoming for the proposal that the Community should concentrate on the creation of a genuine single market in goods and services; this seemed an essentially practical proposition, more or less devoid of doctrinal overtones to which objection could be taken by at least one member government. At its Brussels meeting in March 1985 the European Council formally embraced this proposal and instructed the Commission to draw up detailed proposals, with a timetable, for its implementation. Three months later, at its June meeting in Milan, the Council was duly presented with the Commission's White Paper 'Completing the Common Market'; this listed some 300 separate measures which, the Commission argued, needed to be adopted to ensure that a genuinely single market would exist throughout the Community by the end of 1992.

Strictly speaking, there was nothing in this document which was not implicit in the original Treaty. The Treaty of Rome, after all, had defined the objectives of the Community so as to include the elimination of not only customs duties on trade between the member countries but also of 'all other measures with equivalent effect'; it embraced not only merchandise trade but also the 'free movement of persons, services and capital'. Yet non-tariff barriers persisted in almost all sectors of the Community, making it necessary for this long list of positive measures to be embodied in the laws of the member states in order to eliminate those barriers. The European Council did not merely accept these proposals; twelve months later, in the Single European Act, the achievement of a single internal market in the Community by 1992 was embodied as a formal objective of the Treaty, the single market being defined as 'an area without internal frontiers in which the free movement of goods, persons, services and capital is ensured'. The width of this definition is noteworthy; it did not imply a reduction or minimisation of the obstacles to movement across national boundaries, but called instead for their complete abolition.

In an accompanying study, the Commission emphasised three distinct categories of non-tariff trade barriers whose abolition would raise economic welfare within the Community collectively by the equivalent of between 4 and 5 per cent of its total GDP within eight years. The first of these were the physical obstacles to trade created by customs controls and formalities. These, it estimated, currently added about 2 per cent to the cost of all cross-frontier consignments (about ECU 11 bn in all); the administration of these controls also involved governments in the expenditure of a further ECU 1 bn of taxpayers' money. Cross-border traffic in the Community as a whole involved the operation of more than 70 different customs-clearance documents. The Commission was able to make early progress in this respect by securing the approval in 1986 of Directives under which a Single Administrative Document became applicable to all intra-Community trade from January 1988. Five of the original Six went a good deal further, in fact; by the Schengen Agreement of 1985 it was resolved that all frontier formalities between France, Germany and the Benelux countries were to be abolished by January 1990.

The bulk of frontier formalities, however, are caused by the second category of non-tariff obstacle – the fiscal barriers resulting from the application of widely differing rates of indirect taxes (VAT and excise duties) in the member states. These necessitate customs documentation on exports to support claims for the repayment of taxes paid on them in the exporting country; conversely, the governments of importing countries inevitably require documentation to ensure that imported products pay taxes equal to those levied on the corresponding domestic product. Hence the proposals discussed in Chapter 20 to harmonise such taxes within a narrow range; given the adoption of these, the Commission argued, all indirect taxes could be levied in the country of origin, so eliminating the need for both border controls and the frontiers themselves.

As noted earlier, the proposal that there should be complete equality in rates of indirect taxation provoked fierce and continuing opposition from the national capitals but by mid-1989 agreement was close on a much more pragmatic set of proposals – that the standard VAT rate should have a common floor of 15 per cent (but no specified ceiling) and that there should be a lower band of 0–9 per cent on socially sensitive items. The idea of a full alignment of excise duties had been virtually abandoned, but the Commission argued that their enforcement could be ensured by internal policing (e.g. through local tax stamps) without requiring border controls.

The main enemy of the genuine single market in the view of the Commission, however, was the third category of obstacles to trade – technical barriers against imports. These could take the form of national regulations imposed (nominally, at least) in the interests of safety, health, environmental or consumer protection and so on. Alternatively, they could be embodied in differing national product standards and certification procedures, or in the procurement policies adopted by national or regional governmental agencies, or in exchange controls and other administrative devices which had the effect – whatever their nominal intention – of making it difficult for a product of country A to be sold in country B on equal terms with the local product.

The Commission attached considerable importance to the wastage arising as the result of the fragmentation of the Community market in the procurement of goods and services by central and local government agencies, which were estimated in 1989 to amount to no less than 15 per cent of Community GDP. Since 1971 official purchasing agencies had been required by Community rules to put large construction contracts (those over ECU 1 m) out to open tender in all member countries; in 1977 this requirement was extended to purchases in excess of ECU 200 000. In practice, whatever the letter of the law had been, only about 2 per cent of such purchasing had found its way to firms in other member countries. There were several possible explanations of this but the main one, in the Commission's view, was the exemption from this rule granted to purchases in the fields of energy, telecommunications, transport and water. Originally this exemption had been based on the grounds that such areas (which amount to about a half of total public procurement contracts) were 'strategically important' to the countries concerned.

Whatever the merits of this argument, the result was that member governments were in effect creating suppliers geared to their own national market and operating well below the levels necessary to achieve potential economies of scale. Within the Community there were 15 manufacturers of industrial boilers, operating at 20 per cent of capacity, when four would be sufficient; there were 16 manufacturers of locomotives when three or four could meet the market with a reduction of 13 per cent in average costs, and so on. Altogether, the Commission estimated that the excess costs imposed by restrictions on the tendering for public contracts amounted to some ECU 86 bn. By the end of 1989, however, the Commission could claim only very limited progress as the result of sustained national opposition to its attempts to monitor (and if necessary suspend) public contracts which it believed had been awarded in a non-Community manner. Its only success, in fact, was a 'compliance' directive enabling it to request a government to investigate any contract which the Commission suspected had been unfairly awarded.

Another area in which the Commission foresaw immense potential gains from the removal of regulatory barriers at national level was that of financial services. Banks and insurance companies naturally had the right of establishment in all member countries under Article 52 of the Treaty but, since each national government has its own (highly complex) laws governing the operation of banking, any institution seeking to operate across the Community as a whole would need to incorporate its offices under twelve different sets of law, a virtual impossibility. As a result, the Community's market in financial services is a particularly fractured one, with too many institutions operating on too small a scale. The Commission found that the interest-differential between money-market rates and bank consumer loans was exactly three times greater in Germany than in Belgium, whereas the differential between money-market rates and house mortgages in Britain was less than 40 per cent of that in Spain.

Two major requirements were identified by the Commission before the gains from the creation of a single financial market, put at the equivalent of 1.5 per cent of GDP, could be achieved. First, the creation of a single Community 'passport' for financial institutions which would allow a firm incorporated in one member country to operate in any other. This in turn clearly implies some measure of harmonisation of the national rules and regulations governing operating conditions – for example, minimum capital requirements – specified in the various member countries for such institutions. Secondly, a single financial market necessarily involves the removal of national restrictions on international transfers of capital and on the purchase or sale by residents of assets denominated in other currencies; in 1986 France and Italy were still operating such exchange controls. The enthusiasts for a Delors-type monetary union, of course, go further and argue that a single financial market implies a single European currency to which all member currencies are rigidly tied – if, indeed, national currencies remain in existence at all.

By mid-1989 the Commission could claim some considerable success in the sphere of financial services. All member governments had agreed to dismantle their exchange controls by July 1990, or shortly thereafter in the cases of Ireland, Portugal and Spain. A banking directive had been approved which permits Community banks to operate in any member country, provided only that they conform to the 'prudential' operating regulations specified by their home country; agreement had also been reached on the observance of minimum capital requirements and solvency ratios recommended by the Bank for International Settlements in Basle.

The removal of all types of technical barriers to trade are expected to bring direct benefit to consumers through their effect in reducing the cost of cross-border operations. The Commission estimated that the greatest gains of all, however, amounting to more than a half of the total, would come from what it called the 'supply-side' effects of the removal of non-tariff barriers to trade in goods and services generally – the resulting economies of scale made possible by the larger market and the impact on operational efficiency of the increased competition which would ensue from it. Here the major thrust of the Commission's attack involved a fundamental change in tactics.

In previous years the solution to the problem of varying national standards and specifications had been sought mainly in attempts to lay down detailed technical standards, product by product, for the Community as a whole. Inevitably this had led to sterile arguments of infinite duration over the definition of Eurobeer or Eurosausages or the maximum noise level permitted for lawnmowers. Now it proposed to rely much more heavily on the far more flexible concept of 'mutual recognition' – the rule embodied in the *Cassis de Dijon* case that a product legally on sale in one member country may be excluded from sale by the government of another only if the latter can adduce positive and specific proof that the product is dangerous or otherwise harmful. This was in fact embodied in the Single European Act in the statement that the Council of Ministers 'may decide that provisions in force in a member state must be recognised as being equivalent to those applied by another'. It is on this simple principle, indeed, that the 'passport' for cross-border operation by financial institutions was able to rest.

There is no doubting the energy with which the Commission has pursued its campaign to, so to speak, enact its 1985 White Paper. The initial list of 300 proposals submitted by the Commission to the 1985 Milan Summit was quickly reduced to 279 draft Directives to be laid before the Council of Ministers. By the mid-term point, four years later at end-1989, just over 98 per cent of these had been embodied in directives put before the Council and the Council had managed to adopt about 60 per cent of them. Progress had been most rapid in the sphere of technical standards, thanks to the application of the *Cassis de*

Dijon principle. The programme had clearly fallen behind schedule, however, in some key areas – principally those governing fiscal approximation, the free movement across national borders of people, plants and animals, and the attempt to give the single market a 'social dimension' in the shape of a Community Social Charter.

This is scarcely surprising. It was suggested at an earlier stage that a high degree of harmonisation of taxes, which is implicit in the aim of 'an area *without* internal frontiers', involves the sacrifice of a basic component of national sovereignty; it also assumes a similarity of welfare-priorities amongst the member countries which is neither probable nor self-evidently desirable. True, the Commission was able to devise a system of tax payments which would allow tax revenues to be reclaimed on exports and levied on imports without the necessity of border formalities. It must be said, however, that the system assumed a degree of both accuracy and frankness in the network of official revenue agencies which some considered distinctly altruistic.

Even if taxes did not exist, however, the fact remains that frontier controls are often required for other reasons. The attitudes of national governments in the Community to such matters as animal and plant diseases, firearms or drugs, for example, differ widely; an absence of frontiers implies, however, that each member country is content to accept without question the controls (or lack of them) applied by any of its fellow-members – in effect, the application of the *Cassis de Dijon* principle again. As was mentioned in Chapter 19, for example, almost all member countries make the right of entry or to citizenship easier for nationals of some foreign countries than for others. They do this for what seem to be good and proper reasons. To other member countries, however, it may be far from self-evident that the people concerned should then automatically enjoy unrestricted entry to every other Community country. Similarly, it may be difficult to enforce measures to prevent the spread of rabies in one member country if no control whatever exists over entry into it of animals from countries which attempt little or no such control.

When the exact details of their administration are being worked out, similar considerations may arise with other aspects of the process of eliminating frontiers: the apparently simple and wholly admirable concept of the single market can begin to look a good deal less than simple. That an insurance company should be free to operate in every member country of the Community seems reasonable enough until it is discovered that in country X stringent precautions are taken to protect citizens from operators investing in unsuitable assets whereas in country Y citizens are deemed to be perfectly capable of judging these things for themselves and are left to act accordingly. Free competition could then appear to mean that firms domiciled in Y will have an unfair advantage over those in X; it could also mean that citizens are not given the degree of protection which their own government believes necessary. Again, abolition of exchange controls seems eminently desirable until difficulties begin to arise in the detection and prevention of crime or tax evasion.

Similar difficulties arise with the exhortation of the Single European Act that the single market emerging at the end of 1992 should have a 'social dimension', and with the attempts, especially by the French, to embody this objective in a Social Charter imposing various obligations on member governments – to establish a maximum working week and a minimum working age, for example, to define a 'fair' wage, or to specify the rights of workers to vocational training, collective bargaining and so. Adoption of the *Cassis de Dijon* principle would imply an obligation on all member governments to respect the right of all other member governments to make up their own minds in these highly contentious areas in which opinions as to the extent of legitimate state intervention can and do differ widely. Unfortunately this would leave open the possibility of an unfair competitive advantage for firms in A, whose government prefers to leave these things to the free play of market forces, compared with those in B, whose government imposes extensive (and expensive) social obligations on its entrepreneurs.

Considerations such as these are not fatal to the cause of frontier abolition, of course, but they go a long way towards explaining the continuance of national borders more than 30 years after the signing of a Treaty in which they have no logical place. They explain also the lack of realism in any notion that there is some sort of magic in the formula *Quatre-Vingt-Douze* – the idea that suddenly, on 31 December 1992, an unbroken and undifferentiated market will exist across the length and breadth of the Community. The potential gains obtainable from the creation of a genuine single market in the Community as a whole are undoubtedly very large – certainly for member countries which are both well endowed with the high-technology industries in which they will rise and be willing to respond to the challenge. But the transformation will not be evenly spread and certainly will not be sudden. An Italian observer probably had it about right: 1992 will surely come about, he said – but probably not until 1998.

27.3 Creating the Single Government

The political equivalent of the economic concept of the single market was the embodiment in the Single European Act of a redefinition of both the Community's ultimate aims and its decision-making process. As was explained in Chapter 12, the Act represented something of a triumph for the enthusiasts for political union who had begun to lament the inertia which appeared to have overcome the integration process. Indeed, it is regarded by some as a fundamental change in the Community scene, heralding an inevitable and irreversible movement towards the creation of a federal government in Europe. In the first place, the Act significantly widened the formal aims of the Community – the creation of a single market by 1992 being merely one of the additional objectives – to which the member governments were committed. Secondly, it conveyed additional powers to the Parliament, giving it the right of a second reading on a wide range of proposals and extending its right to consultation on others. It also laid down stringent requirements which must be satisfied before the Council of Ministers can override its views. It thus endowed the Parliament with at least powers of delay in the areas concerned. Thirdly, over a substantial range of subjects it formally required the Council of Ministers to proceed by qualified majority voting rather than being constrained by the stultifying requirement of unanimity.

Opinions differ on the likely practical consequences of these changes in the Community's legal framework. In 1988 the President of the Commission, M Jacques Delors, publicly made the somewhat rash prediction that, as a result of these changes, within ten years 80 per cent of the economic and social legislation governing member countries would be formulated at Community rather than national level. Members of the Parliament, echoing this conviction that the right of national veto has now disappeared for three-quarters of all new legislation, declare that national sovereignty has become a myth for members of the Community in most areas outside fiscal and monetary law. The embodiment in the Act of a formal commitment to the abolition – abolition, it must be repeated, not reduction – of frontiers within the Community, they argue, implies the disappearance of the reality of national sovereignty as well as that of the symbolism of border control posts.

All this is almost certainly a considerable exaggeration of the likely conse-quences of the Single European Act. It is true that objectives such as political co-operation, monetary union and regional and environmental policy were formally included among the aims of the Treaty; it is far from obvious, however, that this fact will in itself much increase the Community's role in these matters in practice. The arrangements specified for co-operation in foreign policy matters, for example, are largely those which existed before the Act and whose procedures are in any case separate from, and independent of, the normal machinery of Community decision-making. Again, the provisions relating to monetary union require formal Treaty changes – and thus unanimity amongst the member states – for further institutional developments, such as the creation of a Community Central Bank; they thus rendered such developments *within* the *existing framework* less rather than more likely. It is also significant that the protagonists of further integration failed in their attempts to have other subject areas – energy and education, for example – added to the Treaty list, with the result that future Community developments in these areas are unlikely to be easy.

As was suggested in Chapter 5, the extension of the powers of the European Parliament resulting from the Act is likely to be relatively marginal. Parliament has been given the right of veto over new membership or treaties of association but it is unlikely that the number of occasions on which it could, or would wish to, exercise this power will be large. On other matters, it is not immediately obvious why it should prove able to persuade the Council to change its mind through its second reading if it could not do so through its first. (In the first full year during which these extended powers operated, 1988, the Council of Ministers accepted about 40 per cent of the amendments suggested by the Parliament in the course of first readings but less than 20 per cent of those suggested at second readings.) And additional power to delay Council decisions is of relatively little value to a Parliament whose major complaint is typically that the Council is itself delaying too long.

The requirement that unanimity may be required in the Council to reject a Parliamentary/Commission proposal certainly opens up a real possibility of an effective alliance between a Parliamentary majority and a Council minority. Nevertheless, the inescapable fact remains: a legislature without taxing power is one with little real leverage in any other area of policy. It can, and does, exert its will in matters not involving budgetary expenditure – for example, in defining standards for motor-car exhaust emissions. But when resources are required, as they usually are, the old rule remains: power lies ultimately with he who holds the money-bags.

The formal requirement that over a wide policy-area the Council should use majority voting was certainly the major achievement of the Act. It has ensured that decisions are now reached in circumstances in which stalemate would almost certainly have prevailed previously. In 1988, for example, both Greece and Portugal were outvoted on a directive permitting cross-frontier competition which their domestic insurers would have much preferred to be spared. Similarly, even the Germans found themselves outvoted over a directive requiring owners of more than 10 per cent of the shares of a company to disclose that ownership, an openness of approach which did not at all commend itself to German banks acting as proxies for clients who preferred anonymity. Prior to 1987 it took the Council an average of at least two years to approve directives laid before it by the Commission; since then the average has fallen to less than one year.

But, again, there are clear limits to the extent to which this loosening in the decision-making procedure of the Council will accelerate the process of integration. On the one hand, while the commitment to majority voting was accepted for matters relating to the internal market of the Community, it was specifically not accepted for other areas of great importance, in particular fiscal and monetary matters, the movement of individuals across national borders and the rights and interests of employed persons. On the other hand, even in areas to which majority voting applies, some would argue that the Luxembourg compromise was unaffected by the Act; while governments may endure the experience of being outvoted on issues of relatively minor importance, it may prove to be a different matter when the national stakes are high. Whatever the President of the Commission may assert, the Prime Minister of Great Britain for one was quite clear that the ultimate right to a national veto was unaffected by the Act; in this, as in other contexts, the heads of other governments may differ from her only in their lesser enthusiasm for expressing themselves loudly and clearly. But, as remarked earlier, the ultimate deterrent of the veto, like that of the bomb, is liable to damage its user more than its target.

The combination of the Commission's prescription for the single market and the parliamentarians' modest gains in the Single European Act will no doubt encourage the closer integration of the economies of Western Europe in the last decade of the twentieth century. In itself, however, it can scarcely be held to determine the fundamental character which the Community will have acquired by the end of that decade. The debate over the true destiny of the Community is still open. On the one side stand the maximalists, to whom the political unification of Europe is the ultimate goal and for whom any movement towards that goal is desirable in itself. On the other stand the minimalists, or more accurately the pragmatists, for whom further integration is a means rather than an end, to be pursued if the resulting gains are clearly positive but to be rejected if the costs imposed by it, whether economic or political, are adjudged too great.

27.4   The Europe of Unity

The founding fathers used the opening words of the Treaty of Rome to make abundantly clear that its – and their – primary intention was 'to establish the foundations of an ever closer union among the European peoples'. There is, of course, only one ultimate outcome of any political relationship in Europe which becomes 'ever closer', and that is the creation of a single United States of Europe. To the maximalists, then, the creation of a single market and the advances of the Single European Act are merely stepping-stones along that path. Further economic and political integration is not something to be pursued if and when it appears to be advantageous; it is an end in itself, and, furthermore, an end of the highest importance. The continued existence of national boundaries and allegiances, on the other hand, is nothing other than a perpetuation of the possibility of war in Europe.

The next developments to be attained within the Community in the near future would be fairly obvious to proponents of this view. On the economic front it is important that the disparity in the levels of indirect taxes within the Community should be drastically reduced as a matter of urgency; only then is it likely that frontier formalities will become redundant (in their view other ways of protecting health and security can easily be found) and the Community become a genuinely open, single market. Of even greater importance is the early movement towards genuine monetary union as set out in the Delors report. This of course implies the replacement of national central banks by a single Community central banking system and the adoption of a single currency throughout the Community. Equally it involves the transfer of powers over monetary and fiscal policy from national to Community level. Only when the members of the Community dispense with frontiers and use a single currency, as do the states of the United States of America, can anything approaching a genuine United States of Europe be said to have come into existence.

At the political level all this would imply much more far-reaching changes than those embodied in the Single European Act. Experience shows that developments as significant and wide-ranging as these will never occur so long as they require unanimity amongst twelve disparate member countries. Movement to the adoption of majority voting for virtually *all* decisions is therefore clearly necessary. If the Luxembourg Compromise is to be retained at all it can only be in the context of a specific and highly restrictive definition of the circumstances under which it could be invoked. In any event a substantial transfer of sovereignty from national to Community level must be involved. Under such circumstances it would not be possible for the Council of Ministers to remain the mere collection of national spokesmen it has been hitherto; when the powers being exercised by it are no longer merely those derived from national parliaments then the Council would necessarily have to become directly answerable to the European Parliament.

The maximalists are hardly so unrealistic as to suppose that the acceptance of such fundamental changes in the political framework of the Community by all its existing members is conceivable in the near future. The alternative to inertia, in their view, may therefore be to allow those countries which are willing to proceed further along the integration path to do so without being held back by the less venturesome members. Precisely that path was recommended by President Mitterrand in the event of continued British resistance to the Delors plan for monetary union. Use of the UK power of veto to prevent progress via amendment of the Treaty of Rome would be negated by resort to a new Treaty signed separately by the remaining member states.

The idea is far from new. It was embodied in the conception of a *directoire*, an idea at one time espoused by President de Gaulle – an inner membership of countries prepared to proceed rapidly towards increasing economic and political union (almost certainly the original Six) and an outer membership of countries associating themselves in a looser manner with some but not all Community policies. A similar idea was that of the *Europe à la carte* proposed by Ralph Dahrendorf in the 1979 Jean Monnet lecture: an arrangement by which each member country could elect to adopt some of the Community's common policies but not others, so that the membership of the Community would in a sense vary according to the policy area concerned.

27.5 The Europe of Diversity

The minimalists take a more pragmatic view. The expansion of the Community from the original Six to the present Twelve, they would argue, has been a gain in the sense that it now embraces almost the whole of Western Europe rather than a small section of it. This gain in geographical scope must necessarily involve some sacrifice in depth. The notion of a continuous and rapid progression towards complete unification may have been a realistic one for the six original members of 1958 – although the experience of the Gaullist era which followed must cast considerable doubt on even that proposition. The notion is hardly realistic, however, in the context of the much more diverse and disparate Community of 1990. To persist in seeking the inherently unattainable would therefore be counterproductive, bringing into question even what has already been achieved. A more realistic approach would be to seek agreement on measures which can be shown to be mutually advantageous and to pursue them only to the extent necessary to secure those advantages. Uniformity should be sought only where it is genuinely necessary and beneficial rather than as an end in itself.

This concept of a Europe marked by diversity between its co-operating members was defended by Mrs Thatcher in an address at the College of Europe in Bruges in 1988, arguing on grounds of principle rather than on those of expediency. The strengthening of a liberal society in Europe, she argued, requires the preservation of diverse traditions, languages and parliaments rather than the creation of a centralised and bureaucratic conglomerate in Brussels, even more remote from the ordinary citizen than are existing national capitals already. Willing and active co-operation between sovereign states, the argument runs, is not merely one possible form of the European community – it is the only one likely to succeed. To attempt to fit member countries into some form of identikit European personality, imposed by more and more detailed regulation from some bureaucratic centre, would be nothing short of folly.

The philosophy is hardly new; it was inherent in the other (more characteristic) Gaullist advocacy of *l'Europe des patries* in the 1960s. By all means let unnecessary obstacles to trade be removed and programmes of mutual benefit be pursued, but to seek to impose uniformity of taxation, or worker representation, or monetary/fiscal policies on widely differing member countries is quite unnecessary to those ends. Indeed, given the inevitable variations in the social welfare functions of the different member countries the imposition of uniformity of policy must necessarily reduce overall economic welfare rather than increase it. Hence the robust wisdom of the principle of 'subsidiarity' – the proposition that policies are most effective when administered at the lowest possible level of government at which the desired aims can be achieved.

This, after all, is the essential philosophy of the principle of 'mutual recognition' derived from the Cassis de Dijon case. As the Commission itself found, it was scarcely profitable to pursue the (probably) unattainable aim of establishing uniform standards for everything, from jam content to corkscrew specifications, or the times of year during which crows and magpies might be shot in Britain. In general it was more sensible, and certainly more effective, to concentrate on the removal of obstacles to trade and then let the operation of market forces do the rest. If levels of indirect taxes differ excessively between member countries, after all, the flows of imports and exports induced as a result are likely to provide their own correction. If one form of worker representation is more effective than another, why should there be any need for Regulations and Directives to force employers to adopt it? In other words, the pragmatists argue, the single market will do all that is necessary for the future development of the Community. Whenever it is advantageous, uniformity of practice will evolve naturally from the free play of market forces. But would it necessarily be a tragedy if it did not? If diversity persists within the Community, will it not do so precisely because of the differences in national cultures, traditions and priorities which constitute the Europe of reality rather than the notional Europe of political theorists?

There are plenty of precedents in the Community's history to indicate that it is capable of flexible solutions whenever strict uniformity is unnecessary or undesirable. The ERDF quotas are biased specifically to take account of differing national characteristics; Western Germany is permitted to ignore the common external tariff in its trade with Eastern Germany; member countries are permitted to subsidise butter supplied to schools but are not required to do so; Britain is allowed a derogation from the 1980 Directive on the metrification of weights and measures in deference to the deep attachment of its citizens to milk and beer delivered in pints rather than litres; the Italian currency was permitted to vary by up to 6 per cent on either side of its central EMS rate while other currencies were required to remain within 2% of their central rates. And so on. Such variations, if not in positive conflict with the aims of the Treaty, could scarcely be regarded as threats to the foundations of the Community.

27.6 Europe 2000

Along which of these two apparently divergent roads the Community will progress during the final decade of the twentieth century remains to be seen. If past experience is any guide, it will probably oscillate somewhat uneasily between them; periodic calls for new initiatives will originate from the dedicated advocates of political union but their translation into action will be modified and moderated by the demands of political reality. Indeed, it is vital that the Community should not commit itself too heavily to either path.

Total victory for the first school of thought would inevitably lead to the creation of, effectively, two groups of first and second class members; this, in turn, could lead all too easily to the emergence of one super-state over-shadowing a group of increasingly nervous and suspicious small neighbours – precisely the reverse of the 'ever closer union' with which the founding fathers sought to eliminate the tensions and rivalries of Europe's unhappy history. Total victory for the second school of thought, on the other hand, could involve regressing in practice to little more than a fairly loose system of international co-operation based on the foundation of historic national sovereignties and dwelling uneasily under the perpetual shadow of imminent disintegration. The acceptance of this as the only attainable end would amount in fact to the abandonment of the hope of anything approaching a United States of Europe for many generations to come.

An outcome midway between the two, derived from compromise and concessions on both sides, may have little intellectual appeal to either maximalists or minimalists; compromises are seldom glamorous or exciting in any context. But such solutions are clearly conceivable in any policy area, even if they achieve less than some would have wished and attempt more than others think necessary. The alternative – an outcome involving the disappearance of the Community, or any likely development of it – would surely be regarded as catastrophic by the governments of even those member countries, such as the United Kingdom, which were and remain most sceptical of the more ambitious plans for political integration in Europe. Despite the apparently unending pursuit and conflict of perceived national interests, the seemingly inevitable triumphs of short-term political manoeuvre over long-term social vision, and the ineffably delaying and constricting activities of placemen, bureaucracies, office-seekers and officialdom, the thing survives. It moves on occasion with excruciating slowness: but it moves. All too often it is used as an arena in which the politicians indulge their art for the benefit of the audience at home, but at least it can be viewed, as *The Economist* remarked on its 25th birthday, 'as a better place for commercial and political battles to be fought out than on those earlier battlefields in Europe, studded with millions of crosses of the dead'.

There is always a tendency in these things to expect too much too soon. The creation of the great federations of modern history, from the United States of America to Australia, were matters which occupied centuries rather than decades, despite the advantage enjoyed by their architects in starting with open fields and new societies. It is no more than realistic to expect a more distant horizon for the countries of Europe whose roots go centuries deep into a tempestuous, bitter and frequently tragic history. It is surely proper that the final word should be left with the man having the strongest claim to be honoured as the prime mover of it all – Jean Monnet, speaking two years before the Treaty was signed:

> The building of Europe is a great transformation which will take a very long time. . . . Nothing would be more dangerous than to regard difficulties as failures.

Further Reading

Burgess, M., *Federalism and European Union, 1972–1987* (London: Routledge, 1989).
Butler, M., *Europe: More than a Continent* (London: Heinemann, 1986).

Cecchini, P., *The European Challenge 1992: the Benefits of a Single Market* (Aldershot: Gower Press, 1988).

Dankert, P. (ed.), *Towards tomorrow* (London: Cassell, 1989).

Emerson, M. *et al.*, *The Economics of 1992* (Oxford: University Press, 1988).

Her Majesty's Stationery Office, *The Single Market: the Facts*, 3rd edn (London, 1989).

Institute of Economic Affairs, *Whose Europe? Competing visions for 1992* (London: Institute of Economic Affairs, 1989).

Lodge, J. (ed.), *The European Community and the Challenge of the Future* (London: Pinter, 1989).

Pelkmans, J. and Winters, L. A., *Europe's Domestic Market* (London: Routledge, 1988).

Royal Institute of International Affairs, *The European Community: Progress or Decline?* (London: Heinemann, 1983).

Taylor, P., *The Limits of European Integration* (London: Croom Helm, 1986).

Tugendhat, C., *Making Sense of Europe* (London: Viking Penguin Books, 1986).

Wallace, H., *Europe: the Challenge of Diversity* (London: Routledge & Kegan Paul, 1985).

Wallace, W., 'Less than a federation, more than a regime', in Wallace, H. (ed.), *Policy-making in the European Community*, 2nd edn (Chichester: John Wiley & Sons, 1983).

Wistrich, E., *After 1992: the United States of Europe* (London: Routledge, 1989).

Statistical Appendix

The compilation of statistical series over a period of years for a single country is a hazardous enough undertaking. Official statisticians have an admirable, but none the less disconcerting, habit of constantly revising both their methodology and their sources which makes a consistent series over time a matter of statistical engineering rather than mere calculation. To attempt the same task for the European Community is to encounter such problems on a multiplied scale. The member countries adopt different definitions and have data sources of varying reliability; they use different currencies; in addition, the membership of the Community has varied through time.

For 1970 onwards many of these difficulties can be left in the hands of the Community's Statistical Office, since their annual *Eurostat Review* presents data for the member countries both individually and collectively in an admirably consistent fashion. In general, the user's only problem is to deal with the fact that periodic revisions often lead to different figures being shown at different times for any given time period. In what follows the basic principle adopted was a simple one: the data for any year are those given by the most recent publication, and where these differ from those given in previous years the earlier series have been adjusted to make them compatible. The consistency and comparability of the series over time, in other words, have been taken to be the primary objectives.

For years prior to 1970 the data are less conveniently assembled and less comprehensive. Apart from *Eurostat Review* recourse was had to the Community's own *The Common Market, Ten Years On: Selected Figures*, published in Luxembourg in 1968 and to the useful, but frequently incomplete, annual *Statistical Yearbooks*. These have had to be supplemented by various statistical publications of the OECD and United Nations. The result is something of a statistical mongrel but provides, it is hoped, a set of reasonably consistent estimates for the major economic variables over virtually the lifetime of the Community.

The European Community, 1958–88 – 1: the People

Year	Total population (m)	Civilian labour force					Real value added per person employed 1973 = 100		
		Total (m)	Percentage distribution						
			Agriculture	Industry	Services	Unemployment	Agriculture	Industry	Total
(1)	(2)	(3)	(4)	(5)	(6)	(7)	(8)	(9)	(10)
EC 6									
1958	168.67	74.14	21.9	40.2	34.5	3.4	51.0	52.5	48.1
1959	170.24	73.85	21.6	40.4	35.1	2.9	49.6	55.5	50.7
1960	171.71	73.67	20.5	41.5	35.9	2.1	52.7	59.0	54.7
1961	173.34	73.85	20.2	41.8	36.4	1.6	53.9	62.1	57.7
1962	175.44	73.85	18.9	43.1	36.5	1.5	59.2	63.2	60.9
1963	177.61	74.00	17.6	43.2	37.8	1.4	63.7	64.9	63.3
1964	179.63	74.36	16.2	43.2	39.2	1.4	69.2	69.0	66.8
1965	181.60	74.52	16.2	43.6	38.5	1.7	69.3	71.2	69.8
1966	183.32	74.40	15.5	43.2	39.5	1.8	72.6	74.7	73.1
1967	184.74	74.18	15.0	42.5	40.2	2.3	72.0	77.3	75.8
1968	185.86	73.95	14.3	42.6	40.9	2.2	75.0	80.5	80.5
1969	186.98	74.77	13.5	43.8	40.9	1.8	78.3	81.2	85.2
1970	188.10	76.02	12.0	42.6	43.5	1.9	85.0	85.4	88.8
1971	189.77	76.34	12.1	42.0	43.6	2.3	85.1	88.9	91.5
1972	191.17	76.39	11.4	41.3	44.8	2.5	88.3	94.3	95.2
1973	192.54	76.97	10.8	41.1	45.6	2.5	100.0	100.0	100.0

EC 9

1973	256.63	105.72	9.0	40.9	47.6	2.5	100.0	100.0	100.0
1974	257.78	106.12	8.6	40.5	48.0	2.9	103.6	101.1	101.8
1975	258.41	106.43	8.3	38.9	48.4	4.4	105.7	96.3	101.8
1976	258.80	107.60	7.9	37.9	49.3	4.9	103.9	102.5	106.2
1977	259.08	108.32	7.6	37.1	50.3	5.0	116.1	104.2	108.4
1978	259.58	109.01	7.4	37.0	50.3	5.3	122.1	106.1	111.3
1979	260.23	110.19	7.1	36.7	50.9	5.3	123.6	109.5	114.0
1980	261.08	111.38	6.9	36.0	51.3	5.8	117.1	109.7	114.8
1981	261.78	112.13	6.5	34.4	51.4	7.7	120.0	106.7	116.5

EC 10

1981	271.51	115.81	7.3	34.3	51.0	7.4	112.0	118.2	114.8
1982	272.02	116.33	6.9	32.9	51.2	9.0	125.6	122.9	117.1
1983	272.42	116.86	6.8	31.7	51.4	10.1	121.7	127.8	119.7
1984	272.80	117.91	6.6	30.8	52.1	10.5	127.5	133.1	122.2
1985	273.25	118.98	6.4	30.1	52.7	10.8	122.0	138.2	124.5
1986	273.90	119.68	6.2	29.7	53.3	10.8	124.4	127.9	126.9

EC 12

1986	322.77	137.91	7.3	29.4	51.7	11.6	114.3	128.2	126.4
1987	323.70	139.20							
1988	324.53								

The European Community, 1958–88 – 2: Income and Output

Year	Gross Domestic Product*					Index of production 1973=100		Sectoral distribution % of total GDP		
	ECU bn at current prices	Volume index 1973=100	ECU: 1986 prices		Annual growth rate (%)	Agriculture	Industry	Agriculture	Industry	Services
			Total (bn)	Per head						
(11)	(12)	(13)	(14)	(15)	(16)	(17)	(18)	(19)	(20)	(21)
EC 6										
1958	153.9	46.3	1059.3	6225	2.69	66.6	40.4	10.1	46.9	43.0
1959	163.0	48.6	1112.1	6474	4.99	69.5	42.8	9.2	47.2	43.6
1960	183.9	52.4	1196.9	6920	7.63	72.7	47.7	8.6	47.8	43.6
1961	204.6	55.4	1266.7	7248	5.83	74.0	50.9	8.2	48.0	43.8
1962	220.6	58.4	1336.2	7549	5.49	77.6	53.8	8.0	47.8	44.2
1963	248.7	60.9	1392.0	7775	4.18	78.0	56.6	7.7	47.3	44.9
1964	274.9	64.5	1475.4	8143	6.00	81.2	60.6	7.3	47.7	45.0
1965	298.2	67.6	1544.9	8442	4.71	81.9	63.1	7.0	47.5	45.4
1966	321.2	70.6	1614.7	8734	4.51	82.8	66.3	6.7	47.2	46.1
1967	340.1	73.1	1670.2	8974	3.44	90.0	67.5	6.2	46.3	47.3
1968	370.5	77.3	1767.6	9432	5.83	92.3	73.2	5.8	45.5	48.7
1969	413.8	82.8	1892.9	10042	7.09	91.5	81.1	5.4	44.6	50.0
1970	466.7	87.7	2004.2	10574	5.88	94.7	86.2	5.0	43.8	51.2
1971	520.4	90.7	2074.7	10839	3.52	97.9	87.9	4.9	43.6	51.5
1972	579.6	94.5	2161.2	11210	4.17	94.9	93.1	4.6	43.7	51.7
1973	663.0	100.0	2286.4	11778	5.79	100.0	100.0	4.7	43.9	51.4

EC 9

1973	871.5	100.0	2999.7	11695	5.85	100.0	100.0	4.2	43.0	52.8
1974	998.1	101.8	3053.7	11853	1.80	100.9	100.6	4.1	42.7	53.2
1975	1132.3	100.5	3014.7	11673	−1.28	98.5	93.9	4.1	41.2	54.7
1976	1312.3	105.4	3161.7	12223	4.88	98.1	100.8	3.7	41.8	54.5
1977	1478.4	108.2	3245.7	12535	2.66	101.6	103.2	3.9	41.4	54.7
1978	1683.4	111.5	3344.7	12973	3.05	106.7	105.6	3.9	40.9	55.3
1979	1932.8	115.4	3461.6	13298	3.50	110.8	110.8	3.7	40.8	55.5
1930	2211.6	116.8	3503.6	13427	1.21	113.1	110.2	3.4	40.4	56.2
1931	2459.3	117.0	3509.6	13414	0.17	112.5	107.7	3.3	39.2	57.5

EC 10

1931	2508.8	117.2	3582.3	13194	0.20	113.0	107.7	3.5	39.1	57.4
1932	2787.6	118.1	3606.8	13259	0.77	119.1	106.1	3.7	38.9	57.4
1983	3071.0	119.8	3658.7	13430	1.44	118.7	107.1	3.5	38.6	57.9
1984	3353.3	122.8	3753.5	13759	2.50	122.4	110.1	3.5	38.4	58.1
1985	3644.1	125.8	3845.2	14072	2.44	121.7	113.8	3.2	38.4	58.4
1986	3943.0	129.0	3943.0	14396	2.54	123.8	116.0	3.1	34.4	62.5

EC 12

1986	4395.4	129.1	4395.4	13618	2.62	121.8	116.6	3.4	34.6	62.0
1987	4703.8	132.7	4519.6	13962	2.83		119.0			
1988	5082.3	137.7	4691.0	14455	3.79		124.1			

*At purchasing-power-parity valuation.

The European Community, 1958–88 – 3: Trade and Finance

Year	Merchandise trade				Annual average rate of exchange (Units per ECU)		Prices 1973=100			Domestic inflation rate % per annum
	Volume of trade 1973=100		Intra-EEC as % of total				GDP deflator	Agricultural prices	Import prices	
	Imports	Exports	Imports	Exports	Dollar	Pound				
(22)	(23)	(24)	(25)	(26)	(27)	(28)	(29)	(30)	(31)	(32)
EC 6										
1958	28.3	27.3	29.6	30.1	1.10	0.39	50.5	59.5	80.5	6.0
1959	29.6	29.9	33.3	32.4	1.06	0.38	50.9	59.3	76.6	2.9
1960	34.5	33.6	34.3	34.5	1.06	0.38	53.4	59.1	77.4	4.8
1961	35.7	34.8	36.4	36.8	1.07	0.38	56.1	61.4	77.4	5.1
1962	38.8	36.1	37.5	39.7	1.08	0.38	57.4	64.4	76.6	2.2
1963	40.5	36.6	38.9	42.4	1.07	0.38	62.1	67.6	76.6	8.2
1964	43.2	39.7	40.2	43.2	1.07	0.38	64.7	69.5	78.2	4.3
1965	45.5	43.2	41.7	43.5	1.07	0.38	67.1	72.8	78.9	3.6
1966	49.0	47.0	42.7	44.1	1.07	0.38	69.1	72.8	79.7	3.1
1967	50.9	50.5	43.9	43.7	1.07	0.39	70.7	70.5	78.9	2.4
1968	57.9	58.5	45.9	45.0	1.06	0.44	72.8	71.0	78.2	2.9
1969	68.7	66.6	48.1	48.2	1.06	0.44	75.9	75.7	80.5	4.3
1970	76.8	73.5	48.4	48.9	1.02	0.43	80.9	77.7	84.3	6.5
1971	81.8	79.1	50.0	49.3	1.05	0.43	87.1	77.7	88.1	7.7
1972	89.5	88.3	51.5	49.7	1.12	0.45	93.2	87.2	87.6	6.9
1973	100.0	100.0	50.3	49.0	1.23	0.50	100.0	100.0	100.0	7.3

EC 9

Year										
1973	100.0	100.0	51.7	52.7	1.23	0.50	100.0	100.0	100.0	8.2
1974	99.1	107.1	46.9	50.6	1.19	0.51	112.5	105.2	142.6	12.5
1975	93.5	101.0	48.3	49.4	1.24	0.56	129.3	118.2	147.1	14.9
1976	106.5	111.1	48.3	51.7	1.12	0.62	142.9	138.4	163.2	10.5
1977	108.4	118.2	49.5	50.6	1.14	0.65	156.8	149.2	176.5	9.7
1978	115.9	124.2	50.8	51.7	1.27	0.66	173.2	154.8	184.4	10.5
1979	126.2	132.3	50.9	53.6	1.37	0.65	192.2	165.4	204.7	10.9
1980	127.0	133.6	48.1	54.3	1.39	0.60	217.3	178.6	240.8	13.1
1981	120.7	137.6	47.6	51.5	1.12	0.55	241.2	200.1	279.6	11.0

EC 10

Year										
1981	120.1	136.7	47.7	51.4	1.12	0.55	241.1	200.1	286.0	11.0
1982	122.0	138.2	48.8	52.4	0.98	0.56	266.0	223.3	301.2	10.4
1983	125.7	142.1	50.4	53.0	0.89	0.59	288.9	238.5	308.3	8.6
1984	134.6	153.3	50.1	52.6	0.79	0.59	307.5	249.0	332.9	6.4
1985	141.3	160.9	51.7	53.1	0.76	0.59	326.2	257.0	342.6	6.1
1986	149.3	165.2	53.9	53.9	0.98	0.67	344.2	261.1	297.7	5.5

EC 12

Year										
1986	148.7	167.1	58.0	57.6	0.98	0.67	344.2	266.1	297.7	5.5
1987	158.7	171.3	59.0	59.1	1.15	0.70	358.2	261.9	291.2	4.1
1988	172.4	181.0	58.3	60.0	1.18	0.66	372.9		294.3	4.1

Author Index

356

Subject Index